The Digital Musician

The Digital Musician is an introductory textbook for creative music technology and electronic music courses. It is written for 'digital musicians' who may come from any musical background. It examines creative practice, cultural awareness, artistic identity and musical skills through the prism of recent technological innovations. The overall focus is on creative and aesthetic issues, rather than technical matters. Each chapter of the second edition contains creative projects, information boxes for technical matters, discussion questions and recommended listening lists. The companion website includes additional projects and repertoire, the complete set of interviews with the case studies, playlists of examples, illustrations, learning tools, the author's blog and other resources.

Features:

*   Creative projects throughout the book
*   Annotated listening lists for each chapter, with accompanying playlists on the companion website
*   Further reading and discussion questions at the end of each chapter
*   Case studies of actual digital musicians with contributed projects

Andrew Hugill is Director of the Institute of Creative Technologies at De Montfort University, Leicester, UK, where he founded the Music Technology programme.

The Digital Musician

SECOND EDITION

Andrew Hugill
De Montfort University, UK

Routledge
Taylor & Francis Group

NEW YORK AND LONDON

Second edition published 2012
by Routledge
711 Third Avenue, New York, NY 10017

Simultaneously published in the UK
by Routledge
2 Park Square, Milton Park, Abingdon, Oxon OX14 4RN

Routledge is an imprint of the Taylor & Francis Group, an informa business

© 2012 Taylor & Francis

First edition published by Routledge 2008

Library of Congress Cataloging-in-Publication Data
Hugill, Andrew.
  The digital musician / Andrew Hugill. – Second edition.
  pages cm
  Includes bibliographical references.
  1. Music—Philosophy and aesthetics. 2. Electronic music—History and criticism.
  3. Computer music—History and criticism. I. Title.
  ML3876.H84 2012
  786.7—dc23
  2011052513

ISBN: 978-0-415-80659-6 (hbk)
ISBN: 978-0-415-80660-2 (pbk)
ISBN: 978-0-203-11179-6 (ebk)

Typeset in Bembo and Helvetica Neue
by Swales & Willis Ltd, Exeter, Devon

Printed and bound in the United States of America
by Edwards Brothers, Inc.

This book is dedicated to my students, past, present and future, with grateful thanks for all they have taught me.

TABLES

Preface

In *The Digital Musician*, the word 'musician' is extended to cover all those working creatively with sound. Resistance to this extension is fairly strong from both the traditional musicians (who play 'notes' on 'instruments') and from the sonic artists (who may want to lose the connotations of 'music'). However, I take the view that music is the name given to the organization of sound (and silence) and that both groups have a great deal in common, whether they accept it or not. I therefore do not shrink from applying some useful 'musical' ideas to the field of music technology, nor from cheerfully ignoring those aspects of music which are irrelevant when working with the new technologies.

This book is written for a new kind of 'digital' musician, and examines issues of cultural awareness, artistic identity and musical skills, through the prism of recent technological innovations. The book has come about because of a seismic shift in 'music' and particularly music education over the past couple of decades. Many universities now offer programmes in 'music technology', a subject which was once the exclusive domain of engineers, organologists and acousticians. What has greatly accelerated the change is, of course, the advent of the personal computer and, hence, the ready availability of sophisticated audio manipulation and music production tools. The phrase 'music technology', then, is code for creative music production, often using digital technologies.

Most of the existing books on music technology (and there are many) concentrate on the *technology*. There are good reasons for this: it can be complicated and difficult; most students want to know *how* to do things; aesthetic issues are hard to discuss; the world is changing fast; and so on. A smaller number of books focus on the musical or artistic aspects of sonic manipulation, exploring this or that approach to electronic, electro-acoustic or computer music, sonic art, sound-art and sound design.

The Digital Musician, on the other hand, is about the musician. It is the result of more than ten years of research and is a synthesis of ideas that are influential in music and relevant to the digital age. These ideas are integrated with a discussion of the technology and its implications for the musician. Technical issues are outlined where appropriate and bibliographic references supplied for further study; however, this book does not provide a 'how-to-make-computer-music' reference manual, of which there are many good examples already in existence. Instead, it concentrates on questions raised for the individual musician by all this potential to make music: What music? What is there to 'say'? Why create music? What about existing music – how to approach that? Which music to approach? How do we know what is good?

The answers to these questions involve developing a personal aesthetic, an awareness of the context for the work, specific musical and technical abilities and an individual identity. 'Digital musicians' must find a distinctive musical 'voice'. They may build on what has gone before, or they may sidestep existing work. Either way, they become a new kind of musician: one who originates *and* performs, who creates *and* produces, and who harnesses the potential of technology in new and exciting ways.

This human focus created two problems in writing the book. The first was: how much technical information to include? Given that it is well explained elsewhere, an initial decision might have been: none at all. However, to omit technical discussion entirely would have led to a lack of clarity about the precise nature of the subject. I therefore set out to provide a map of the territory that today's musician inhabits. The scale of the map may be large, but the landscape must be clearly indicated. The overlapping fields of science, technology, music and ideas are significant features on the map. They are consequently described in sufficient detail to be recognizable as such.

This led on to a second problem: to what level of detail? More or less all the chapter headings, and sub-headings, could become a book in their own right. In fact, books do exist on most of the topics, as the recommended reading lists will show. The digital musician is expected to cover an enormous range and diversity of knowledge and plainly cannot become an expert in *all* these areas. *The Digital Musician* therefore covers only *one* subject in sufficient detail: the digital musician. All the chapters and sub-chapters are doorways into areas for further activity, research or study. It is probable that the readers will eventually want to specialize in one or more of the larger areas, and the given projects and recommended reading and listening lists should support that.

Although the book is timely, it is also important that it is sustainable, that it remains relevant in the future. Technology changes so rapidly that there is a danger of instant obsolescence. To that end, I avoid discussion of the particulars of current software or equipment but focus instead on generic tools and ideas that should be relevant in *any* musical situation and for many years to come.

It will be noticed that the 'new technologies' described in the book are predominantly digital but not exclusively so. Neither analogue electronic technologies nor, indeed, mechanical technologies, are necessarily excluded from the picture that emerges. Musicians will always use whatever technology seems appropriate for the given purpose. What has changed is the arrival of these digital technologies, which have shifted our understanding of all other technologies, so much so that music today is assimilated through an inherently digitized culture and mindset. The 'digital musician', therefore, is not one who uses *only* those technologies but is rather a product of the digital culture. This idea will be developed through the book.

Another, literal, interpretation of the phrase 'digital musician', might lead to the assumption that the subject here is machine musicianship, or the computer itself as musician. This possibility is also not excluded: artificial intelligence, algorithmic composition and various forms of automation and are all discussed. However, these are always presented in the context of a human exchange. Once again, the interest lies in the people rather than the equipment. The ambiguity of 'digital musician' is embraced as a positive reflection of the state of these new kinds of musicians.

The phrase 'digital musician' is therefore merely a convenient shorthand to describe musicians working with, or profoundly influenced by, digital technologies.

TO THE EDUCATORS

The Digital Musician is intended first for university and college students who are begin-ning to come to terms with fairly advanced use of technology. Such students have a natural tendency to become obsessed with what their equipment does and how they can best implement the known techniques. By stressing the discovery of an individual voice, I try to open their minds to possibilities that they had not previously considered. In my experience, students will often postpone the creation of interesting work until they own this piece of kit, or that piece of software, or until they have mastered this or that *really cool* technique. It is a premise of *The Digital Musician* that good music can be made at any stage, with any equipment and using any technique.

The book is constructed in such a way as to allow sessions, or series of sessions, to be developed around a particular topic or theme. It will be observed that almost every sub-heading comes with an associated project and some recommended further reading and listening. Inline boxes give some basic technical information as required. Chapters conclude with some questions for discussion.

A major feature of the book is the creative projects, which attempt to apply the key concepts and ideas to a range of practical scenarios with the aim of improving the indi-vidual's ability to interact with their own work and with the work of other people. The projects may be assigned individually or to groups and will also provide good classroom material. They are all capable of repetition, fairly open-ended and should always produce interesting and varied results. They are quite diverse, and are graded by difficulty and amount of time they may take to complete, as follows:

- Elementary (generally may be realized in a single session and require little or no previous work)
- Intermediate (require some advance preparation and may involve an element of public presentation)
- Advanced (a substantial piece of work designed for public consumption).

The projects are mostly designed to be realized with any available equipment and are intended to be capable of adaptation to the particular circumstances of the individual student.

In addition, there are several case studies of digital musicians woven throughout the book. Annotated excerpts from interviews with all of these form the final chapter. These individuals have been chosen to reflect the diversity and range of challenges facing digital musicians, and their comments and experiences are used to illustrate various points along the way. It is interesting to compare them and identify common threads between them. It is hoped that such 'real world' stories will prove inspirational for aspiring musicians.

To summarize, therefore, this book could be used in the following ways, by:

- reading as a stimulus to creative and critical thought and enquiry
- undertaking specific projects and building a session or part of a programme around them
- basing sessions on sections of the book, supplemented by selected projects as sup-porting activities or assessable components.

PART I

Engaging

Creative Identity

WHAT ARE YOU?

In 1897, towards the end of his life, during his extended stay in Tahiti, the artist Paul Gauguin (pronounced 'go-gan') painted *Where Do We Come From? What Are We? Where Are We Going?* It is a very large canvas – 1.39 × 3.74 metres (4' 6' × 12' 4') – and is generally considered his greatest work. Gauguin indicated that the painting should be 'read' from right to left, with the three main groups of figures illustrating the questions posed in the title. The three women with a child represent the beginning of life; the central group symbolizes the daily existence of young adulthood; and in the final group, according to the artist, 'an old woman approaching death appears reconciled and resigned to her thoughts'; while at her feet 'a strange white bird … represents the futility of words'. Beyond this, Gauguin wanted the picture to remain a mystery. 'Explanations and obvious symbols would give the canvas a sad reality', he wrote, 'and the questions asked [by the title] would no longer be a poem.'

The words of the title are profound philosophical questions about life in general and, for Gauguin, the lack of an answer led to a failed suicide attempt soon after the picture was painted. But the way they are addressed in the painting is also an expression of a complex cultural mix. The painting is executed in the Symbolist style, and yet it shows a fascination with the folk art of Tahiti; it is the work of a French artist whose sense of cultural identity has been challenged and extended by his chosen immersion in a foreign culture.

Gauguin's questions are very relevant to today's musicians. The new technologies have transformed the way music is created and heard, composed and performed, produced and distributed. The world that surrounds the musician, the cultural context, has changed in many ways. These changes have created a new musician, who may come from a variety of backgrounds, possess all sorts of musical training and technical skills, have many different kinds of knowledge and opinions, but feels empowered by the new technologies and drawn to making music.

There are, of course, many different musical traditions and many different ways of classifying musicians according to their background. Some classifications are made by musicians themselves, others are made by writers, critics or academics. No single way is really satisfactory, because music tends to seep through its own porous boundaries. It is highly likely that a musician will show characteristics of more than one type.

Many musicians who knowingly work within highly established traditions, such as 'classical' music and certain forms of 'folk' music, take *pitch* as a starting point for their musical training. These musicians generally play an acoustic instrument as their main practice, and they travel a prescribed career path that involves the gradual evolution of technique and musicianship. The criteria for recognizing virtuosity are clearly established, and there is broad agreement among listeners about the level that an individual musician has attained.

Indian *raga*, Javanese *gamelan*, Chinese folk music, Western classical music and some forms of jazz, are all examples of such established traditions. What these systems have in common is an established set of skills and a standard practice. The relationship with pitch is a constant, whether it is the microtonal *sruti* of the *raga*, the harmonious relationship between the instruments of the gamelan orchestra, the modal inflections of Chinese folk music or the twelve notes to an octave of Western music. The first piano lesson generally begins with the note 'middle C', just above the keyhole in the piano frame, the middle of the keyboard. From this fundamental understanding, a pianist's training can begin. The student follows a path prescribed by experts, usually supervised by a teacher who gives 'one-to-one' guidance through the various levels of technical mastery to the full realization of musical potential. So 'technique' is acquired.

Another type of musician may begin with *rhythm*, or at least *beat*. This includes rock and most forms of popular music. Musicians working within this tradition tend to show a relative lack of interest in pitch when compared to the first type, although of course they do not ignore it completely. Bands without some sort of percussion section are rare, and, when they do appear, the instruments often emphasize rhythmic content in order to compensate. There is also general agreement about what constitutes a good musician in this field. The path to success is just as difficult as that for other musicians and is also mapped out by convention and experts.

As you look around the world today, it is clear that this kind of musician is the most prevalent. On the island of Zanzibar, most musicians are drawn to rap, rather than the traditional *Taarab*; in Bali, the young people perform punk rock in shopping malls, in preference to gamelan under pagodas; in Iran, the underground-rave and heavy-metal scenes flourish in spite of attempts by the regime to limit expression to traditional Iranian forms such as the *Radif*. But in many of these cases, the musicians are concerned to introduce traditional instruments and sounds into the more Western forms. Globalization is complex, and there is more going on here than just a Westernization of world culture. A musical commitment to traditional music does not necessarily prevent an involvement in bands, or vice versa. Recent musical history is peppered with examples of 'classically trained' popular musicians or popular musicians who have found a voice in classical forms. Jazz seems to sit somewhere between the two. These categories are not rigid.

A third tradition starts from *timbre*. This type of musician is harder to pin down, for the simple reason that many timbre-focused artists do not consider themselves to be musicians at all, or do not use the word 'music' to describe what they produce. Into this category can be placed the majority of those working in electronic and electro-acoustic[1] music, but also sonic art, sound-art, sound design and various forms of radiophonic[2] and speech-based work. By dealing with *sounds* rather than *notes*, these musicians have changed the nature of music itself, raising questions about what is 'musical'. The conventions of music seem inadequate to describe their activities. These musicians may even begin to challenge music's very existence, since so much of their prime material is *audio* and lacks the expressive intention and cultural baggage of 'music'.

This third type of 'musician' generates and manipulates sound using electronic means. For the majority of the relatively short history of this kind of music, they have done so using non-digital technologies. The fixed elements of the music – the microphone and the loudspeaker – remain (and presumably always will remain) *analogue*, that is to say, transducers that convert sound waves into an electrical signal (in the case of the microphone) or an electrical signal into sound waves (in the case of loudspeakers). The arrival of digital technologies has effected a rapid change in, and expansion of, the techniques available to this musician.

It might be assumed that these 'technological' musicians most naturally fit into the class of 'digital musicians', but in fact this is not necessarily the case. All types of musicians have always worked with technology, and all musical instruments are an example of technological innovation and development. Even the human voice may be thought of as a technology by the singer. For each of the three types of musician described above, a new situation exists, because so many people are now faced with digital technology at some stage in their working lives. The challenge is how, and to what extent, to engage with these technologies.

'Digital musicians' are, therefore, not defined by their use of technology alone. A classical pianist giving a recital on a digital piano is not really a digital musician, nor is a composer using a notation software package to write a string quartet. These are musicians using digital tools to facilitate an outcome that is not conceived in digital terms. However, if that pianist or composer were to become intrigued by some possibility made available by the technology they are using, so much so that it starts to change the way they think about what they are doing, at that point they might start to move towards becoming a digital musician.

The phrase 'digital musician' itself is only descriptive. It is the intention of this book to address a new class of musicians, but not necessarily to rename them. 'Computer musician', 'sound artist', 'sonic artist', 'sound designer', or even just a qualified 'musician' are among the possible names for people from this group. A digital musician is one who has embraced the possibilities opened up by new technologies, in particular the potential of the computer for exploring, organizing and processing sound, and the development of numerous other digital tools and devices which enable musical invention and discovery. This is a starting point for creativity of a kind that differs from previously established musical practice in certain respects, and requires a different attitude of mind. These musicians will be concerned not only with *how* to do what they do, or *what* to do, but also with *why* to make music. A digital musician, therefore, has a certain curiosity, a questioning and critical engagement that goes with the territory.

Although the digital musician could not have existed without the new technologies, that does not mean that he or she uses them exclusively. A digital musician might play an acoustic instrument, or use a non-digital electronic device, as part of their activities. In fact, this will almost certainly happen and be advantageous when it does. The difference is that those technologies will be used in conjunction with or *informed by* the digital. This 'informing' is a consequence of the changes in the state of the mind of the musician outlined above.

So what specifically distinguishes 'digital musicians' from other musicians? What skills do they possess? To be a digital musician requires:

- *aural awareness* (an ability to hear and listen both widely and accurately, linked to an understanding of how sound behaves in space and time)
- *cultural knowledge* (an understanding of one's place within a local and global culture coupled with an ability to make critical judgements and a knowledge of recent cultural developments)
- *musical abilities* (the ability to make music in various ways – performance, improvisation, composition, etc. – using the new technologies)
- *technical skills* (skill in recording, producing, processing, manipulating and disseminating music and sound using digital technologies).

These are not absolute categories: 'aural awareness' may be considered 'musical', acquiring 'cultural knowledge' will require some 'technical skills' and so on. Their interdependency is crucial, and the digital musician will not neglect any one of them. In all respects, the digital musician will be distinguished by *creativity*.

This creativity seems closest to sculpture, as the musician finds and shapes, manipulates and processes, sonic materials. To borrow the title of a book by the great Russian film-maker, Andrei Tarkovsky, it might be called *sculpting in time*. Tarkovsky himself remarked about music: 'I feel that the sounds of this world are so beautiful in themselves that if only we could learn to listen to them properly, cinema would have no need of music at all.' The creative process perhaps also resembles alchemy: combining and recombining sounds, transforming them all the while, seeking the right mixture, the ideal combination.

These are musicians in a digital world and a digital culture in which sound has joined image and text as information or data, capable of endless mutation and transformation. They are musicians brought together by shared interests in a particular musical idea or form, often regardless of national boundaries or cultural heritage. The main medium is digital technology: the personal computer in all its many manifestations, from the desktop machine to the mobile phone; the network, from local area networks to the Internet; virtual worlds and artificial intelligence; multimedia and new media; software instruments and modified hardware.

Today's digital sound recording and its associated distribution and dissemination media has made all sorts of music readily available. This is far more than just a curious by-product of the development of digital media. It has fundamentally changed the cultural landscape. It affects all types of musician, but the digital musician will be the first to take this for granted, the first for whom the digital world is as 'given' as the physical world around them. For the digital musician, it is not just the technologies that are defining, it is the way they are used.

The world the digital musicians inhabit is both a perpetual horizon and a labyrinth of connections or links to the next meaningful encounter. The great challenge is to have *integrity*, to know who they are, where they are, what they are. They are on a journey without a clear destination. Perhaps they will come to a stop one day, but probably not today. The next encounter looks too intriguing, too exciting, to stop now, to stop here.

Driven on by a relentless curiosity, the snail trail of their progress maps their identity as they accumulate ideas, information, stimulations and music. They move perpetually from the known to the unknown. This is what digital musicians are.

FURTHER READING

- Cox, C. and Warner, D., *Audio Culture: Readings in Modern Music*, New York: Continuum, 2006.
  A collection of writings about and by musicians that provides many insights into their creative identities.

- Duckworth, W., *Talking Music*, New York: Schirmer, 1995.
  Seventeen interviews with, and profiles of, leading American experimental composers, containing some revealing personal vision statements.

- Tarkovsky, A., *Sculpting in Time*, Austin, TX: University of Texas Press, 1986.
  An inspiring text about film-making that manages to convey an intensely personal and poetic vision and at the same time say a lot about music.

Project 1 (Elementary): Elevator Pitch

Introduction
An 'elevator pitch' is so called because it is a short summary of the value of something that may be delivered in the time it takes to travel in an elevator, typically 30 seconds. Its purpose is to convey succinctly the value of its subject, be that a product or a service, an organization or an individual.

The Project
Write an elevator pitch of not more than a few sentences that accurately and succinctly sums up your value as an artist. Be ready to deliver this pitch in under 30 seconds to an audience of one.

Notes
Aim for between 70 and 90 words, and bear in mind that the key aspects of what you do need to stand out. There is no time for detailed elaboration. The person listening to the pitch needs to be sufficiently engaged and impressed to want to take this further!

Here is an elevator pitch written by one of the case study artists, Synthia Payne. Notice how it mixes fun with some impressive statements:

> Hello, my name is Synthia Payne and I have advanced skills in technical and artistic media production. Recent projects are real time multi-location, multi-player networked collaboration events. Ongoing collaborators include Stanford University and New York University, as well as many thousands of anonymous players online 24 hours a day, seven days a week. People say I'm always thinking, so let me think up something for you. Thank you.

PROJECT 1

WHERE HAVE YOU COME FROM?

The intriguing answer to Gauguin's question is: it does not matter where you come from. This is the most significant change produced by the new technologies: they are pervasive. They cut across national, cultural and musical boundaries. If the classical musician may be seen as 'highbrow' and the band musician as 'lowbrow', then right now a 'middlebrow' or 'nobrow' musician is emerging.[3] No form of musical knowledge, understanding or ability will be a handicap to these musicians, provided they are willing to embrace the possibilities offered by new technologies.

This applies equally well to the 'technological' musicians, for whom the process of accepting new technologies is a natural evolutionary step. Here, the challenge is to develop the *musicality* of what they do. While it is true that technology has enabled the creation of many new forms of music, this does not mean that the knowledge and understanding accumulated by the other established forms of music is now obsolete.

The challenges posed to art by technological innovations has been a recurring theme throughout history. Music is a technology-based art form, but its technologies are traditionally seen as something to be mastered in order to produce sounds that seem 'natural'. Musicians struggle with the inbuilt resistance of their instruments in order to achieve even greater heights of expressivity. Extracting more extraordinary and beautiful sounds from an apparently limited instrument has provided some of the most powerful moments in music. The arrival in the late nineteenth and twentieth centuries of first electronic and then digital music technologies seemed to some to undermine the very essence of this artistic expression. People could see that a profound change was taking place, and were deeply divided about its implications.

In his classic polemical essay 'The Work of Art in the Age of Mechanical Reproduction' (1936), for example, Walter Benjamin made the following argument about the effect on art of the technologies of reproduction, including sound recording. The 'ritual' to which he refers is the performance, a unique set of circumstances under which an individual or a group experiences a work of art: 'for the first time in world history, mechanical reproduction emancipates the work of art from its parasitical dependence on ritual. To an ever greater degree the work of art reproduced becomes the work of art designed for reproducibility.'[4]

This is a controversial yet influential view which still divides opinion today. The extent to which reproducibility really represents an 'emancipation' from performance is a matter for debate. The extent to which such emancipation may be desirable is even more debatable. On the other hand, Benjamin seems to anticipate one of the main characteristics of digital technology: its ability to create countless exact copies of itself. In some ways, the sense of crisis that this implies persists today.

The age of mechanical reproduction really began with the first magneto-electric devices, which were telephone transmitters made by Elisha Gray and Alexander Graham Bell, but Emile Berliner is usually credited with the invention of the first true microphone in 1877. However, when Thomas Edison invented the carbon microphone later in the same year, his was the first to become commercially available.

Edison also invented the phonograph in 1877, although a Frenchman, Charles Cros, came up with a similar idea independently and slightly earlier. The phonograph was not an electrical device but used a similar principle to the earlier 'phonautograph', which 'wrote' sound onto lamp-blackened glass plate or paper. The phonautograph could not play back sound, however, whereas the phonograph achieved this by drawing grooves into a relatively soft material (wax, tin foil or lead). These grooves could then be retraced by a needle and amplified mechanically. It was not long before this system was mass produced. In 1887, Emile Berliner patented a phonographic system using flat discs rather than cylinders, called the gramophone.

Loudspeakers were invented independently by Ernst Werner von Siemens (in 1877) and Sir Oliver Lodge, who patented the design of the modern moving-coil loudspeaker in 1898. These, combined with both the electromechanical and the magnetic systems described above, evolved rapidly. By the early 1930s, electrical recordings became a viable medium thanks to the invention of magnetic tape recording in 1928 by Fritz Fleumer in Germany. These technologies have all improved since, but their fundamental designs have remained unchanged.

The impact of recorded and reproducible sound on music in general has, of course, been enormous. However, it was some time before composers and musicians began to realize the creative potential of this new medium. With a few exceptions, such as Ottorino Respighi's inclusion of a phonograph (playing bird-song) in his orchestral composition *Pini di Roma* (*Pines of Rome*) in 1924, the technologies were used purely for the reproduction of live sounds or musical performances. The artistic exploration of tape, for example, had to wait until the early 1950s, when Pierre Schaeffer moved on from working with 78 rpm discs.

However, even those composers who did not directly use electronic technologies seemed to be influenced by the possibilities they suggested. In the movement entitled 'Farben' (Colours) from his *Fünf Orchesterstück* (*Five Orchestral Pieces*) Op. 16, composed in 1909, for example, Arnold Schoenberg wrote music that had neither melodic contour nor harmonic direction but rather featured a fairly static sound-mass built from a single chord which changed timbre, or colouration. In 1913, Igor Stravinsky struggled against the limitations of conventional orchestral writing to realize the extraordinary sounds he could 'hear', in his work *Le Sacre du printemps* (*The Rite of Spring*), and in 1924 the composer Alfredo Casella noted in an article that the music of the future would consist of '*any* coordinated succession of sonorities in time'.[5]

For some composers, the expressive potential the new technologies seemed to offer led to a sense of frustration with existing instruments. One such was the pianist-composer Ferruccio Busoni (1866–1924), whose dissatisfaction with the limits of the twelve-notes-to-an-octave tuning system struck at the heart of the concepts of harmony that underpinned classical music. He could see the potential in a new technological solution, even though he had not seen the 'apparatus' itself. In the essay 'Sketch of a New Aesthetic of Music' (1907),[6] he wrote:

> We have divided the octave into twelve equidistant degrees because we had to manage somehow, and have constructed our instruments in such a way that we can never get in above or below or between them. Keyboard instruments, in particular, have so thoroughly schooled our ears that we are no longer capable of hearing anything else – incapable of hearing except through this impure medium. Yet Nature created an infinite gradation – *infinite!* Who still knows it nowadays? ... While busied with this essay I received from America direct and authentic intelligence which solves the problem in a simple manner. I refer to an invention by Dr. Thaddeus Cahill. He has constructed an apparatus that makes it possible to

transform an electric current into a fixed and mathematically exact number of vibrations. As pitch depends on the number of vibrations, and the apparatus may be 'set' on any number desired, the infinite gradation of the octave may be accomplished by merely moving a lever corresponding to the pointer of a quadrant.

Even more antagonistic were the ideas of the short-lived and inflammatory Futurist movement. This was founded in Italy in 1909 with a manifesto by Filippo Tommaso Marinetii which proclaimed a violent belief in new technology and contempt for the art of the past:

We declare that the splendour of the world has been enriched by a new beauty: the beauty of speed. A racing automobile with its bonnet adorned with great tubes like serpents with explosive breath … a roaring motor car which seems to run on machine-gun fire, is more beautiful than the Victory of Samothrace.

(The 'Winged Victory of Samothrace' was an ancient Greek statue that was regarded as one of the most important and beautiful works of art of Western civilization.) Such attitudes, extreme as they may have been, do illustrate the sense of both energy and bewilderment that the new technologies produced.

In keeping with this radical and iconoclastic spirit, the inventor-musician Luigi Russolo (1885–1947) set about making music from all those sounds that the classical tradition excluded. In his manifesto *L'arte dei rumori* (*The Art of Noises*), written in 1913, he made an attempt to categorize those noises and treat them as potential music. While the list is too crude to be useful today, it is interesting as an early example of a typology of sound:

1. *rumbles:* roars, explosions, crashes, splashes, booms
2. *whistles:* hisses, snorts
3. *whispers:* murmurs, mumbles, grumbles, gurgles
4. *screeches:* creaks, rustles, buzzes, crackles, scrapes
5. *noises* obtained by percussion on metal, wood, skin, stone, terracotta, etc.
6. *voices of animals and men:* shouts, screams, groans, shrieks, howls, laughs, wheezes, sobs.

Russolo made his artistic intentions clear in the following passage:

Although it is characteristic of noise to recall us brutally to real life, the art of noise must not limit itself to imitative reproduction. It will achieve its most emotive power in the acoustic enjoyment, in its own right, that the artist's inspiration will extract from combined noises.[7]

He duly built a Futurist orchestra consisting of intonarumori ('intoners' or 'noise machines') and gave several performances during 1914 in Milan and London. The only surviving recordings of Russolo's music were made in 1921 by his brother Antonio, and feature a conventional orchestra 'accompanied' by the noise machines, giving them a strangely romantic quality that rather contradicts the radical aspirations of Futurism.

The Futurists actively sought controversy and polarized opinion, which had a galvanising effect upon the wider culture. The composer Edgard Varèse (1883–1965), who had studied with Busoni, complained bitterly: 'in music we composers are forced to use instruments that have not changed for two centuries'. However, Varèse was a composer who tried to build upon, rather than dismiss tradition. He expanded the orchestra, especially by augmenting the percussion section, and wrote music that anticipated electronic composition until technologies became available to him that were capable of realizing his ideas. In his manifesto *The Liberation of Sound*, published in 1936, he wrote:

> The raw material of music is sound. That is what the 'reverent approach' has made people forget – even composers. Today when science is equipped to help the composer realize what was never before possible ... the composer continues to be obsessed by traditions which are nothing but the limitations of his predecessors.
>
> ... As far back as the twenties, I decided to call my music 'organized sound' and myself, not a musician, but 'a worker in rhythms, frequencies, and intensities'. Indeed, to stubbornly conditioned ears, anything new in music has always been called noise. But after all what is music but organized noises? And a composer, like all artists, is an organizer of disparate elements.
>
> ... The electronic medium is adding an unbelievable variety of new timbres to our musical store, but most important of all, it has freed music from the tempered system, which has prevented music from keeping pace with the other arts and with science. Composers are now able, as never before, to satisfy the dictates of that inner ear of the imagination.[8]

With such passionate (even Romantic) views, and such a strong creative identity, it is no surprise that Varèse encountered constant obstacles to his musical expression. He created a new musical style, but composed only a handful of works, for which he experienced rejection both by the general public and by his professional colleagues (including Schoenberg). His attempts to convince Bell Laboratories to allow him to research electronic music during the 1920s and 1930s failed. It was only when in his seventies that the musical world and the technological world caught up with Varèse. He composed *Déserts* for orchestra and tape in 1950–1954, supported by Pierre Schaeffer who provided facilities at the Radio-diffusion-Television Françaises (RTF) studios, where he was working on musique concrète.[9] Finally, in 1958, Varèse was invited by the architect Le Corbusier to create *Poème Electronique* for the Philips Pavilion at the 1958 World's Fair. This was essentially a sound installation, which used 400 loudspeakers to create a walk-through sonic experience that combined synthesized, recorded and processed sounds.

Another pioneer was John Cage (1912–1992), a composer who once again emerged from the classical tradition, yet challenged its fundamental precepts. Cage was influenced by Varèse and studied with Schoenberg, who described him as 'not a composer, but an inventor – of genius'. Part of Cage's vision was the idea that all sounds have musical potential: we just need to open up our ears to that possibility. In the 1930s, this was a radical idea that required both conviction and commitment to defend. Fortunately, Cage was skilled at articulating his theories with both wit and charm. In 1937, he delivered a lecture in Seattle entitled 'The Future of Music – Credo', which included the following passage:

I BELIEVE THAT THE USE OF NOISE

Wherever we are, what we hear is mostly noise. When we ignore it, it disturbs us. When we listen to it, we find it fascinating. The sound of a truck at 50 m.p.h. Static between the stations. Rain. We want to capture and control these sounds, to use them, not as sound effects, but as musical instruments. Every film studio has a library of 'sound effects' recorded on film. With a film phonograph it is now possible to control the amplitude and frequency of any one of these sounds and to give to it rhythms within or beyond the reach of anyone's imagination. Given four film phonographs, we can compose and perform a quartet for explosive motor, wind, heartbeat, and landslide.

TO MAKE MUSIC

If this word, music, is sacred and reserved for eighteenth- and nineteenth-century instruments, we can substitute a more meaningful term: organization of sound.

WILL CONTINUE AND INCREASE UNTIL WE REACH A MUSIC PRODUCED THROUGH THE AID OF ELECTRICAL INSTRUMENTS ...

The special property of electrical instruments will be to provide complete control of the overtone structure of tones (as opposed to noises) and to make these tones available in any frequency, amplitude, and duration.[10]

This text clearly draws on the ideas of Varèse and others, but also anticipates many of the techniques that are available to digital musicians today. Cage was one of a number of experimental composers who used computers in his composition, most notably in the work HPSCHD (1969), created in collaboration with Lejaren Hiller,[11] but also throughout his career as a means of generating random numbers based on the Chinese 'Book of Changes' or I Ching, and texts such as 'mesostics' in which a vertical phrase intersects horizontal lines of writing.[12]

The first significant use of computers for music seems to have taken place in 1957 at the Bell Telephone Laboratories in New Jersey, where Max Mathews created a program to manipulate and process sound. In the same year, the first computer-generated compositions appeared, including the *Illiac Suite*, created at the University of Illinois by Lejaren Hiller and Leonard Isaacson. Europe was relatively slow to seize upon the potential of computers for music, but the establishment of the Institut de Recherche et de Coordination Acoustique/Musique (IRCAM) in Paris, France, in 1976 seems to represent a turning point in these developments.

Of even more importance to digital musicians were: the release in 1977 of the Apple II, the Commodore PET, and the Tandy TRS-80 computers, all forerunners of today's desktop machines; the creation of the first computer network by the Advanced Research Projects Agency (ARPA, later known as the Defense Advanced Research Projects Agency, or DARPA) in February 1958, leading to the first wide area network, which was operational by 1983; the development of Digital Signal Processing (DSP) techniques for audio in the 1960s; the general adoption of the MIDI (Musical Instrument Digital Interface) specification in the early 1980s; and the creation of the World Wide Web in 1991 at the Swiss/French particle physics laboratory Organization européenne pour la recherche nucléaire, commonly known as CERN.

It is interesting to note that, even at the very origins of computer science, the musical possibilities offered by number-crunching machines were realized. In 1843, Lady Lovelace (Ada Byron) (1815–1852) wrote 'The Sketch of the Analytical Engine' about a calculating machine conceived by Charles Babbage at Cambridge. Babbage had already partially built a 'Difference Engine', and was planning the more sophisticated 'Analytical Engine'. This was an early model of a programmable computer, and Ada Byron immediately recognized the potential for 'universality' of the device. In the essay, she describes all aspects of Babbage's machine, including this passage about its musical application:

> Again, it might act upon other things besides number, were objects found whose mutual fundamental relations could be expressed by those of the abstract science of operations, and which should be also susceptible of adaptations to the action of the operating notation and mechanism of the engine … Supposing for instance, that the fundamental relations of pitched sounds in the science of harmony and of musical composition were susceptible of such expression and adaptations, the engine might compose elaborate and scientific pieces of music of any degree of complexity or extent.[13]

FURTHER READING

- Braun, H.-J., *Music and Technology in the Twentieth Century*, Baltimore, MD: Johns Hopkins University Press, 2002.
  A compilation of essays covering a very wide range of topics, including production and recording and the economic and social factors that have shaped the music industry.

- Holmes, T., *Electronic and Experimental Music: Technology, Music, Culture*, New York: Routledge, 2012.
  An authoritative introduction to the history of the marriage between music and technology, from the earliest developments through the arrival of computers to the present day.

- Kahn, D., 2001, *Noise, Water, Meat: A History of Sound in the Arts*, Cambridge, MA: MIT Press, 2001.
  An interdisciplinary history that explores aural activities in literature, music, visual arts, theatre, and film.

WHERE ARE YOU GOING?

There is a danger, when contemplating the evolution of digital technology, of sounding, or even of actually becoming, utopian. It should be stated that these new 'digital' musicians are not inherently superior to the old musicians, and we are not heading for

Figure 1.1   Night on Earth © NASA

utopia. The phrase 'the digital world', with its global implications, seems to imply a state of affairs that holds good for everybody everywhere. This is not the case, as contemplation of a few statistics will quickly reveal.

About a quarter of the world's population does not have any access to electricity.[14] Figure 1.1 shows a picture of the Earth at night,[15] seen from space, and illustrates the distribution of electrical light. The number of computer users is, therefore, a subset of that, and the number of computers connected to the Internet even smaller. The number of internet users in the world in 2011 stood at just over two billion,[16] compared to a world population of more than six billion.[17] These statistics and images give only a loose impression of the overall picture and, of course, are subject to daily fluctuation, but the main point remains: the digital 'world' is accessible only to relatively few people. In the early days of the Internet, these people were sometimes called the 'digerati'. *The Edge* gives the following definition: 'Who are the "digerati" and why are they "the cyber elite"? They are the doers, thinkers, and writers who have tremendous influence on the emerging communication revolution. They are not on the frontier, they *are* the frontier.'[18]

The numbers of the so-called digerati have now swelled considerably to include many people in the digital world, but these are still a technologically literate elite in comparison with the world's population taken as a whole. What makes the digital world so extraordinary is the way it defies geographical and national boundaries and can compress or expand time and space. The technology of the Japanese digital musician is mostly indistinguishable from his or her European counterpart, and they can and do share files across the Internet without noticeable difficulty.

It seems fairly clear that there will be a greater proliferation of digital technologies; although this will not necessarily make a better world, it does seem more or less inevitable. It also seems clear that it will rapidly become irrelevant that these are *digital* technologies; in other words, that the novelty of digitization will be replaced by a set of assumptions about their capabilities. This is in fact already happening, and many domestic appliances use computer technology for their operation without this being apparent to the consumer.

The digital music culture is increasingly an *aural* culture. Notation has a place within this culture, but the primary musical exchange is based on sounds. Since these sounds are held in digital form on digital media, their existence is abstracted even to the point of leaving no trace. The contents of a computer hard drive may be erased with ease, without destroying the drive itself. They may also be transformed into some other kind of data, modified so that their nature as sounds is changed. So the culture is based on what is heard, rather than on the written artefact. Performers devise music in real time, or over networks. Composers create music from sound recordings to be played back through loudspeaker systems. None of this is written down on paper.

One consequence is that the tendency to make a grand narrative out of the evolution of music itself will have to cease. The drawing of a single evolutionary line through classical music (Bach, Beethoven, Wagner, and so on through the breakdown of tonality), or popular music (where the blues leads to rock, where The Beatles develop beyond Gerry and the Pacemakers, where trance evolves from techno), will become a less viable method. In a world where all these musics are as accessible and available as any other, where the most 'extreme' music is equivalent to the most 'conventional' as pure digital information, evolutionary lines must be drawn in many different directions at once.

Today's musician is faced with a bewildering and exciting diversity. The full range of sound, from pure noise to a single pitch is available, as is the full range of human music. Every kind of means to manipulate these sounds is at the fingertips and often for relatively little cost. The channels of dissemination are open, and an individual working in isolation anywhere may reach a global audience. This all means that the musician needs to develop *sensitivity*, *integrity* and *awareness*. These are expressed not just in words, but in the sound itself and through the music. This requires intelligence; it requires critical reflection; it requires knowledge and understanding. The study and analysis of music is becoming increasingly relevant to the actual practice of making music.

The music to be made may 'sound like' anything at all, but the sound must be *distinct*. It is not enough merely to reproduce what has already been done. The music is a voice, a way of articulating in sound. The diversity of digital culture throws into relief the individual identity of the voice that wants to be heard. The technology of endless reproduction emphasizes the need for consistent originality.

Given the breadth of these statements, the diversity of the culture, the problem of the lack of linear progression, the absence of 'tram-lines' down which to travel, the unfamiliarity of much of the terrain, and the apparent disintegration of known musical values, it might be concluded that the digital musician faces an impossible and unrewarding task. The compulsion to make something musical that 'speaks', that shows itself to be relevant to human existence, remains, even if the means and the language with which to do this has vastly expanded.

The skills that the digital musician should possess are many and varied. These skills are currently being taught largely through 'music technology' programmes, although often with other subjects or in an interdisciplinary way. The breadth of skills required means that at some point the digital musician must make choices about which to pursue further if real depth is to be achieved. Part of the basic skill set, therefore, is the

acquisition of sufficient musical knowledge, self-understanding and powers of discern-
ment to be able to make those choices.

At any point in the process of becoming a digital musician, there will be many
things you *could* know, a number of things you *should* know and several things you *must*
know. Age is not a factor: it is a characteristic of this kind of music that even the most
experienced practitioner in one aspect may be a beginner in another. Someone may be
amazingly skilled at digital signal processing but cannot play an instrument, or an expert
in sound recording but a beginner in computer programming, or work extremely well
with sound alone but lack the technique to combine sound with visual imagery. Yet, a
student of music technology is expected to have some ability in all of these. The digital
musician is a 'jack of all trades' and a master of *some*.

FURTHER READING

- Gauntlett, D., *Creative Explorations: New approaches to identities and audiences*,
  New York: Routledge, 2007.
  Draws on experimental evidence from people modelling their identities using visual
  methods, such as Lego, to investigate creativity.

- Kurzweil, R., *The Age of Spiritual Machines*, New York: Viking Adult, 1999.
  Ray Kurzweil is generally regarded as the most prominent techno-utopian. He is
  also a digital musician and inventor of a range of keyboards, as well as speech
  synthesis technologies and much more. This book elaborates his futuristic ideas of
  the 'singularity': the moment when computers exceed human intelligence.

- Lanier, J., *You Are Not A Gadget: A Manifesto*, London: Penguin, 2011.
  A controversial critique of collectivism in the digital age by the musician, philosopher, and inventor of the term 'virtual reality', Jaron Lanier. In many respects, this is
  the polar opposite of Kurzweil's utopian vision.

INTRODUCTION TO THE CASE STUDIES

The final chapter of this book consists of an annotated collection of interviews with
musicians who have all, in their different ways, grappled with these issues and questions throughout their careers. They have been chosen to represent, as far as possible,
the diversity and range of backgrounds of digital musicians, from the classically trained
to the pop musician, from the (multi)media artist to the interactive performer, from the
software engineer to the 'born-digital' electronica artist, from the young to the old, from
the academic to the commercial, and so on. Comments from these musicians will be
used to illustrate some of the key ideas that crop up during the book. The interviews are
preceded by biographies, short summaries of which are given below. The one thing they
all have in common is a clear sense of their own creative identity, in some cases forged
over many years.

- *Oswald Berthold* is a German electronica artist and programmer who formed a pioneering band called Farmer's Manual and has subsequently moved into installation work.
- *Nick Collins* is a programmer and musician with an interest in machine listening, live coding and interactive systems.
- *Julio d'Escriván* is a Latin-American composer who works with film and video, and researches the 'traditional' literacies of non-traditional digital musicians.
- *Ambrose Field* is a composer who studies the impact of interactive digital technology on musical performance and has worked in many multichannel formats. He also founded the Worldscape Laptop Orchestra.
- *Rob Godman* has worked with orchestras and community groups and has particular interests in installation work, collaborative composition, and 'returning to his roots' in live performance.
- *Chris Joseph* works primarily with digital text and has created a number of interactive multimedia stories, including 'Inanimate Alice'.
- *Thor Magnusson* is an Icelandic writer, musician and artist/programmer who writes his own musical software. His academic background is in philosophy of mind, language and aesthetics, with a focus on Indian philosophy.
- *Kaffe Matthews* is a pioneer of live improvisation, working with self-devised software and violin. She has also made many site-specific works and installation pieces, including the Sonic Bed and the Sonic Armchair.
- *Randall Packer* is an authority on multimedia, as well as being a leading composer and artist. His recent work has strong political content and involves live theatre.
- *Pauline Oliveros* has influenced American music extensively in her career spanning more than sixty years as a composer, performer, author and philosopher. Her research interests include improvisation, special needs interfaces and telepresence teaching and performing.
- *Synthia Payne* is an expert in online music collaboration, and experienced in audio and video production and editing, game sound design, teaching, and event coordination. Her recent projects are real-time multi-location multi-player networked collaboration events.
- *Quantazelle (Liz McLean Knight)* is immersed in technology, fashion, music and the often-surprising overlaps between them. She is a DJ and produces her own versions, and throws events related to the aforementioned interests.
- *John Richards'* work explores performing with self-made instruments and the creation of interactive environments. He is the director of the Dirty Electronics Ensemble and a member of the post-punk band Sand.
- *Sophy Smith* trained as a classical musician and began working with technology at university. She now composes for dance and theatre and runs a Live Art company called Assault Events. She has a PhD in team-turntablism.
- *Atau Tanaka* is a Japanese/American composer and researcher who creates sensor-based instruments in a quest for the idiomatic voice in the interface. He composes for network systems, handheld devices and makes gestural sound-image performance.
- *Martyn Ware* was a founder member of synth-pop bands The Human League and Heaven 17 and is a producer and composer who writes for film, TV, theatre and radio. He also makes original audio-visual soundscapes with his long-term collaborator Vince Clarke through The Illustrious Company.

To listen to works by the case study artists, read the complete interviews, or download original creative projects by them written specially for this book, please visit the website.

Project 2 (Intermediate): Personal Vision Statement

Introduction

Being able to describe your personal vision is something which will stand you in good stead throughout your career. It is surprising how often this ability is required, not just in job applications or before and after performances, but also in more casual situations. It is surprising how many artists seem to be incapable of doing it! A personal vision statement should set out in a few paragraphs the essence of what is distinctive about your work, your areas of interest, and your view of the wider context. The 'vision' aspect clearly implies an eye to the future, so some predictions about how things might develop both in the world at large and for yourself as an individual are welcome. Every vision statement will become a record of how you saw yourself at a given moment, so over time these will build into a kind of diary of your evolution as an artist.

The Project

Write a personal vision statement of approximately 500 words.

Notes

This can be an intimidating exercise if you are just starting out, so here are some helpful tips:

- Start with the wider context and comment on the musical and artistic world you inhabit. However, try to avoid making just a catalogue of likes and influences. They will tell the reader *something* about you, but not enough to identify your unique creative identity. Home in on those aspects of your own work which mean the most to you and which can provide the strongest evidence of your abilities. What do they have in common? Is there something you can point to that seems to define your work in general?

- Consider the future. How would you like to develop? How do you think things *should* develop? What is the likelihood of that happening? What are the obstacles? You may think of this project as a kind of SWOT analysis: strengths, weaknesses, opportunities, threats. Perhaps a way to begin is to make a list under those four headings and then try to develop the points they raise into a vision statement.

- Often the hardest aspect of the exercise is to find the language effectively to describe something in your vision. There are several solutions here. One is to write in an intensely personal way, a bit like a manifesto. This has the advantage of a direct expression, but can run the risk of being self-indulgent and so become off-putting to read. Another approach is to stand back from yourself and write as objectively as possible. This has the advantage of coming across as clear and considered, but the potential disadvantage of being too cold or even boring to read. Clearly some mid-point is probably best to aim for, but the main thing is to be consistent in the written style.

PROJECT 2

Discussion Questions

- What are you?
- Where do you come from?
- Where are you going?

Aural Awareness

The entire music industry is deaf. Including journalists. And a lot of musicians.
—(John Richards, conversation with the author, 2005)

LISTENING

The ear is the most important attribute of the digital musician. The more music has become a matter of the manipulation of *sounds* rather than *notes*, the more central the aural aspects have also become. What musicians do with their ears, rather than their instruments, has been a relatively neglected aspect of musical training up until now. Traditional aural skills, such as interval recognition, chord identification, aural transcription, score-reading, sight-singing, and so on, while useful in certain musical situations, only go part of the way towards the kind of aural awareness necessary for digital music.

A small survey undertaken for this book asked fifteen leading academics in music technology the following questions. Should a digital musician be able to:

a)   distinguish between the sound of rain and the sound of fire? (This is not so easy as it might seem without a visual cue.)

b)   recognize a dominant seventh chord by ear? (This is a traditional aural skill in music training.)

The answers to question a) were unanimous: 'yes – that's essential'. The answers to question b) were a lot less certain. There are obviously some situations where such a skill might be useful, but it could be preferable to be able to recognize the general character-istics of the interval of a seventh chord *wherever* they might occur. This would include many natural sounds and certain types of non-Western and folk music. The dominant seventh chord, in itself and accompanied by all the 'rules' of tonal harmony, is problem-atic: its harmonic function almost (but not quite) removes its status as a sound.[1]

Listening Modes

These responses highlight the importance of the aural abilities of the digital musician: what matters most is *how they listen*. It is surprising how little this vitally important topic has been discussed in musical history. It is only during the twentieth century, with the advent of recording technologies, and, hence, the possibility of repeated listening, that 'aural awareness' seems to have become recognized. Even then, there have been relatively few attempts systematically to examine it with regard to musical concerns, outside the science of acoustics. Probably the first serious musical study of the subject was published in 1966, by the composer Pierre Schaeffer. He identified four *modes of listening*, defined by French words that have more shades of meaning than are available in English:

1   *Écouter* is 'listening to someone, to something; and through the intermediary of sound, aiming to identify the source, the event, the cause', thus 'treating the sound as a sign of this source, this event'. Example: 'I hear the sound of a car and do not cross the street.' This may also be called *causal* listening.

2   *Ouïr* is 'perceiving by the ear, being struck by sounds'. This is 'the crudest, most elementary level of perception; so we "hear", passively, lots of things which we are not trying to listen to or understand'. Example: 'Traffic noise is continuous outside my window, but I am not aware of it.'

3   *Entendre* involves aural discrimination or, as Schaeffer puts it: 'showing an intention to listen [*écouter*], and choosing from what we hear [*ouïr*] what particularly interests us, thus "determining" what we hear'. Example: 'That sound has a texture which changes in a really interesting way.'

4   *Comprendre* is essentially *understanding*, or 'grasping a meaning, values, by treating the sound like a sign, referring to this meaning through a language, a code'. Example: 'That piece of music made real sense to me and I enjoyed it.' This may also be called *semantic* listening.[2]

Schaeffer remarked: 'The four modes can be summed up more or less in this sentence: I heard (*ouïr*) you despite myself, although I did not listen (*écouter*) at the door, but I didn't understand (*comprendre*) what I heard (*entendre*).'[3] These thoughts led Schaeffer to his most famous notion: *reduced listening*. This means listening to a sound for its own sake, *in itself*, as what Schaeffer calls a 'sound object', by removing its real or supposed source and any meaning it may convey. A sound can have inherent value on its own and not just because of what it may appear to represent. Schaeffer recognized that this is different from ordinary listening and is, therefore, somewhat unnatural. The benefit of listening in this way is that we can understand sonic phenomena for themselves and in themselves.[4]

Listening Purposes

All these listening modes are interesting to the musician, but the most commonly used in musical situations are those which involve discrimination and understanding. Whereas sound *can* be used simply for information ('What is it? Who is it? What is happening?'), the musician often listens *past* the immediately obvious aspects of a sound and seeks to unlock something more from its sonic characteristics. As Schaeffer explained: a more sophisticated listener 'turns away (without ceasing to hear it) from the sound event and the circumstances which it reveals about its source and uses it as a means to grasp a message, a meaning, values'.[5]

Schaeffer's ideas have greatly influenced subsequent work on listening to music created with electronic technologies. In particular, the idea of 'reduced listening' has informed much electro-acoustic music. The 'sonic object' itself has become the focus of musical attention, as artists and others seek new ways to discover and manipulate sonic material. Whereas tape and electronic media allowed some extraordinary manipulations, digital technologies have enabled the listener to 'enter' the sound to a level previously unimaginable, even to the point of being able to extract and edit the smallest constituents and sonic particles.

This kind of listening can sometimes go too far. The electro-acoustic composer Denis Smalley has identified what he calls 'technological' listening and observed: 'Technological listening occurs when a listener "perceives" the technology or technique behind the music rather than the music itself, perhaps to such an extent that true musical meaning is blocked.'[6] Another way of describing this is 'recipe listening'; in other words, a tendency for the listener to be disproportionately interested in *how* something was made, rather than the musical or sonic outcomes. To listen well, then, requires not only an awareness of the modes, but also an ability to move between them and to discriminate appropriately at a given time, focusing upon the musical and sonic aspects as well as the technical processes that lie behind them, in a balanced way.

Listening is done for many different reasons and in many different ways. These are affected by the situation and motives of the listener at a given moment. The musician will often listen in a different way and with a different *purpose* to other people. Understanding this purpose is a crucial aspect of aural awareness. It begins with an awakening to the listening situation, both in a musical context and in daily life. This is followed by an increased sensitivity to the modes of listening, the ways in which one listens. Finally, 'active listening' summarizes a state of heightened perceptive or receptive aural awareness that will be invaluable in most musical situations.

FURTHER READING

- Mathieu, W. A., *Listening Book: Discovering Your Own Music*, San Francisco, CA: Shambhala Publications, 1991.
  A playful book aimed at helping us appreciate the connection between sound, music and everyday life.

- Norman, K. 'Real-World Music as Composed Listening', *Contemporary Music Review*, 15:1, 1996, 1–27.
  Analyses the use of sounds from the real world as musical material in the works of various writers, composers, movie directors and other non-sonic arts specialists.

- Schaeffer, P. and Chion, M. (Dack, J. and North, C. trans.) (1983) *Guide to Sound Objects*. Online. Available HTTP: http://www.ears.dmu.ac.uk (accessed 30 August 2011).
  Vast and somewhat controversial text that nevertheless contains some important theorizing that has profoundly influenced digital music. The discussions of 'acousmatic' and 'reduced' listening are both in Section I.

- Schafer, R. Murray, *A Sound Education: 100 Exercises in Listening and Sound-Making*, Ontario: Arcana Editions, 1992.
  Aims to engage people with their soundscape and increase awareness of acoustic design.

- Smalley, D. 'The Listening Imagination: Listening in the Electroacoustic Era', *Contemporary Music Review: Live Electronics*, 13:2, 1995, 77–107.
  An examination of listening, informed by Schaeffer's theories.

LISTENING SITUATIONS

The composer John Cage declared: 'let sounds be themselves', and did so in the belief that *there is no such thing as silence*. He liked to tell this famous story of his visit to an anechoic chamber, which is, literally, a room without echo reflections, in other words: completely without reverberation. It is the ideal 'neutral' space for work in acoustics:

> It was after I got to Boston that I went into the anechoic chamber at Harvard University. Anybody who knows me knows this story. I am constantly telling it. Anyway, in that silent room, I heard two sounds, one high and one low. Afterward I asked the engineer in charge why, if the room was so silent, I had heard two sounds. He said, 'Describe them'. I did. He said, 'The high one was your nervous system in operation. The low one was your blood in circulation.'[7]

One outcome of this experience was Cage's notorious 'silent' piece: *4' 33"*. The point of this piece is, of course, that there is no silence, but that one should instead pay attention to the surrounding environmental sounds. Cage used the device of a musical time frame (usually presented by a performer making no sound in three distinct 'movements', the score showing *tacet*, which means 'make no sound', for each) to force our attention elsewhere. There is no need to witness a performance of this piece to learn the lesson: the environment can be listened to at any time.

Contrast this with a concert given in a blacked-out theatre or concert hall, through loudspeakers only. This is the *acousmatic* situation, in which *only* audio information, without visual cues, is available. The word 'acousmatic' derives from an Ancient Greek practice attributed to Pythagoras (sixth century BC), of teaching from behind a curtain, so that students (called *akousmatikoi*, or 'listeners') would be forced to pay attention to what they heard, rather than being distracted by the physical presence of the teacher. The term was revived in 1955 by Jérôme Peignot and subsequently taken up by Pierre Schaeffer and others working in electronic music. Because the loudspeakers fail to provide the listener with any visual indication of the sources of the sounds heard, the imagination of the listener may in theory be thoroughly engaged. No musical performer, no visible sound source, just listening. This is an enforced listening situation that, once again, produces a state of heightened aural awareness.

In fact, despite their superficial differences, these two listening situations have a great deal in common. Both find ways of making the listener focus upon the sounds that surround them, and both structure and shape that experience to carry musical and artistic intentions. These two extreme examples are deliberately chosen to make a point about aural awareness. The reader's normal listening is likely to involve oscillations between various modes and states and depend on the situation. The important thing is to be as aware as possible of listening at any given moment. This can be tested by listening to speech, to music, to nature, to machinery, to the body and noting what is heard in different listening states. Similar sounds can be heard differently in different situations and with a variety of meanings. Understanding these differences is the goal.

PROJECT 3

Project 3 (Elementary): Listen, Listen

Introduction

This project may be graded 'elementary' but it is nevertheless hard to do well and will always be useful if practised on a regular basis. There have been many versions of it published over the past fifty years or so. It was a staple of the 'acoustic ecology' movement, founded by R. Murray Schafer, and has appeared in numerous other contexts, but its familiarity should not hide its importance.

The Project

1   For a predetermined period of time (less than 5 minutes is best) listen intently to the sounds around. Become aware of sounds not normally noticed.
2   Follow the first instruction again, but this time try to write down what is heard using a system of symbols. A good way to start is to draw out a timeline on graph paper first.

Notes

The project can be done using only the first instruction. It can also be adapted to specific situations, for example near a major road. In this case, the process of notation becomes particularly challenging.

THE SOUNDSCAPE

The general level of noise in the world around us has dramatically increased. Never has the contrast between the interior and exterior acoustic worlds, or sonic environments, been greater. In his book *Acoustic Communication*, Barry Truax observes:

> [Listening] is a set of sophisticated skills that appear to be deteriorating within the technologized urban environment, both because of noise exposure, which causes hearing loss and physiological stress, and because of the proliferation of low information, highly redundant and basically uninteresting sounds, which do not encourage sensitive listening.[8]

Truax identifies three levels of listening: *listening-in-search*, which is 'the ability to focus on one sound to the exclusion of others';[9] *listening-in-readiness*, which is the process whereby we can receive 'significant information, but where the focus of one's attention is probably directed elsewhere';[10] and *background-listening*, which is when the 'sound usually remains in the background of our attention'.[11]

Truax himself is part of a group of artists and scientists, musicians and composers, who are particularly interested in the sounds of the environment. The term 'soundscape' was coined by the Canadian, R. Murray Schafer to describe the acoustical environment. His book *The Soundscape: Our Sonic Environment and the Tuning of the World*, first published in 1977, significantly extends the notion of music to include *all* sounds and describes the cosmos as a continuously unfolding musical composition to which we are partial listeners.

Murray Schafer identifies *keynote sounds* (that are not heard consciously but give a 'tonality' to a soundscape), *signals* (foreground sounds that are listened to consciously) and *soundmarks* (specially noted sounds that function as acoustic landmarks). He also distinguishes between two different types of music: the Apollonian, which 'arises with the discovery of the sonic properties in the materials of the universe', and the Dionysian, which is 'an internal sound breaking forth from the human breast' and 'arises as a subjective emotion'.

Attracted by these ideas, but with her own 'take' on listening, the composer Katharine Norman defined it in 1996 as a 'complex, multi-layered activity' and observed (once again) three types: *referential* listening, which connects sounds to objects; *reflective* listening, which involves an enthusiastic appraisal of the sound for its acoustic properties; and *contextual* listening, which relates the sound to the context of the listener's individual history and memory.

Pauline Oliveros, on the other hand, writing in the 1960s for *Source* magazine, preferred not to theorize but simply to listen attentively, open herself up to, and describe, the sounds around her:

> The bulldozer starts again moving the air like an audible crooked staircase before reaching its full power. As I lean on my wooden table, my arm receives sympathetic vibrations from the low frequencies of the bulldozer, but hearing seems to take place in my stomach. A jet passes over. Some of its sound moves through my jawbone and out the back of my neck. It is dragging the earth with it.

> I would like to amplify my bowl of crackling, shaking jello. (Once in 1959 a bull-dozer came through the side of my house while I was eating lunch. The driver looked at me, backed out, and continued to operate the bulldozer.) I would like to amplify the sound of a bull dozing.[12]

Notice how she makes connections between present sounds and imaginary or remembered sounds, even between materials (staircase/wood) and words (bulldozing/bull dozing).

Awareness of external sounds goes hand in hand with an increased concentration on internal sounds. The phenomenon of the in-ear listening system, for example, throws attention away from the environment to the sound world inside our own heads. The unique playlist, with its individually selected sounds, forms a kind of soundtrack to our lives, both blotting out the sonic environment and yet forcing us to engage with it in a different way. It throws us into a highly individualized state, each travelling around the environment in our own time and in our own sonic world.

This is a profound change from the world before recording technologies, when music was heard simultaneously by many people in a single hall and, generally, only once. Walter Benjamin's remarks about the emancipation of the work of art from its dependence on performance ritual is particularly exemplified by Muzak and other 'ambient' music which is created *not* to be listened to, but rather, in Brian Eno's words, to be 'a place, a feeling, an all-around tint to my sonic environment'.[13]

This artificial, or virtual, soundscape, created by oneself or others (or both in collaboration) fluctuates in its relationship to the 'natural' environment. In an extreme situation, such as the concert hall or the headphones, it overpowers it almost completely; at other times (in an airport, or a restaurant, perhaps), it drifts in and out of significance. 'Ambient Music' has, interestingly, made a transition from the kind of almost unnoticed aural wallpaper envisaged by Eno and others, to a distinctive musical genre in its own right, which exhibits different characteristics from other music and is designed to be listened to in a quite specific way. The 'chill-out' room is a good example, reinstating an element of ritual into ambience.

FURTHER READING

■ Schafer, R. M., *The Soundscape: Our Sonic Environment and the Tuning of the World*, Rochester, VT: Destiny Books, 1977, 1994.
   The classic introduction to the idea of soundscape, and still full of relevant ideas.

■ Truax, B., (ed.) *Handbook for Acoustic Ecology*, Vancouver: Cambridge St Publishing, 1999.
   Covers all the key theoretical and technical ideas relating to soundscape.

■ Truax, B., *Acoustic Communication*, Westport, CT: Ablex, 2001.
   Particularly good on the ways in which digital technologies have completely redefined listening and the consumption of patterns of sound.

■ Wishart, T., *Sounds Fun*, London: Universal Edition, 1977.
   Trevor Wishart is a digital music pioneer. This collection of games and exercises for ten to forty people is specifically designed to encourage active engagement in listening.

Project 4 (Intermediate): Soundwalk

Introduction

The *Handbook for Acoustic Ecology* defines a soundwalk as follows:

> A form of active participation in the soundscape. Though the variations are many, the essential purpose of the soundwalk is to encourage the participant to listen discriminatively, and moreover, to make critical judgments about the sounds heard and their contribution to the balance or imbalance of the sonic environment.[14]

A soundwalk is, therefore, a walk that is led by the ears rather than the eyes. It may be short or long, highly structured or free, varied or repetitive, and take in a range of environments or just stick to a single area.

The Project

Make a soundwalk. Think about every aspect of the aural experience. The soundwalk may be prescribed (with a fixed beginning, middle and end) or it may be free.

Notes

One way to approach to this project is to identify *soundmarks*, which are the aural equivalent to landmarks. These are prominent sounds which have a high importance to the local area. The soundwalker can navigate the aural landscape using these sounds. A different approach is more freely to explore a given geographical area, with the ears 'wide open', perhaps recording both what is heard and reflections upon what is heard. Hildegard Westerkamp, who is probably the foremost exponent of soundwalking, remarks:

> A soundwalk can be designed in many different ways. It can be done alone or with a friend (in the latter case the listening experience is more intense and can be a lot of fun when one person wears a blindfold and is led by the other). It can also be done in small groups, in which case it is always interesting to explore the interplay between group listening and individual listening by alternating between walking at a distance from or right in the middle of the group. A soundwalk can furthermore cover a wide area or it can just centre around one particular place. No matter what form a soundwalk takes, its focus is to rediscover and reactivate our sense of hearing.[15]

> Another approach is a mediated soundwalk, done several times along the same route wearing a portable music player and headphones, with a different playlist each time. Observe how the playlist alters perceptions of the world around, of space and of time. Relationships with the buildings, or other people, seem to change.

PROJECT 4

Soundscape Composition

Soundscape composition was developed by (amongst others) the World Soundscape Project at Simon Fraser University, Vancouver, Canada, with the aim of invoking 'listener's associations, memories and imagination related to the soundscape'.[16] In the early days it consisted simply of a recording of environmental sounds taken out of context (usually played in a concert). There was little editing beyond the selection of the mate-rial to be played and sometimes a cross-fade. In recent years, sound transformation and manipulation has played an increasing role in soundscape composition, but always with the aim of revealing aspects of the sound without making it unrecognizable.

Probably the best way to understand and appreciate soundscape composition is to listen to some examples and undertake a project of one's own. The following are some varied examples of ways in which the soundscape has been recorded and transformed into musical compositions. They are followed by a composition project.

RECOMMENDED LISTENING

▶ World Soundscape Project (1973) *The Vancouver Soundscape* [CD]. Vancouver: World Soundscape Project, CDI.
A collection of original recordings from the World Soundscape Project, including an introduction to the science and art of composing the soundscape, narrated by R. Murray Schafer.

▶ Luc Ferrari (1967–70) *Presque Rien ou le lever du Jour au Bord de la Mer* (Almost nothing or daybreak at the seaside).
A tape piece prefiguring soundscape composition. It portrays a fishing village com-ing to life at daybreak.

▶ World Soundscape Project (1996) *Soundscape Vancouver 1996* [CD]. Vancouver: World Soundscape Project, CDII.
Contains original digital soundscape compositions by Darren Copeland, Sabine Breitsameter, Hans Ulrich Werner, Barry Truax and Claude Schryer.

▶ Barry Truax (2001) *Islands* [CD]. Cambridge Street Records, CSR CD-0101.
'Train rides lead to restful escapades away from the stress of the workday, an afternoon nap invites a sonic meditation with cicadas and Italian water fountains … along with other natural soundscape elements, providing the makings of a magical place of wonder and rest. I think the implicit statement of this CD is that our society is in need of islands of rest and contemplation.' Darren Copeland, *Musicworks* 82.

▶ Katharine Norman (2002) *London* [CD]. NMC Recordings, NMC D034.
London is ambient, environmental story-telling – a true underground sound. Its three soundscapes were inspired by the people of London – working, talking, laughing or crying, their lives forming a complex pattern of sound.

▶ John Levack Drever (2006) *Cattle Grids of Dartmoor* [CD]. Pataphonic (SM06-05CD).
Field recordings of cars, horses and others passing over cattle grids. Drever's work is concerned with the minutiae of everyday soundscapes, residual noise and the built and natural environments.

▶ Hildegard Westerkamp (2010) *Transformations* [CD]. Empreintes DIGITALes, IMED 1031.
Pauline Oliveros comments in the sleevenotes to this collection of soundscape compositions spanning nearly two decades: 'One can journey with her sound to inner landscapes and find unexplored openings in our sound souls. The experience of her music vibrates the potential for change. Her compositions invite interaction – a chance to awaken to one's own creativity.'

Project 5 (Advanced): Soundscape Piece

Introduction

In his article 'Genres and Techniques of Soundscape Composition as developed at Simon Fraser University',[17] Barry Truax identifies a range of general characteristics of this project, as follows:

> FIXED PERSPECTIVE: emphasizing the flow of time; or a discrete series of fixed perspectives.
> Variants: time compression; narrative; oral history
> Techniques:

- layering in stereo; layering in octophonic
- found sound (with or without time compression)
- narrative; poetry; oral history
- transitions between fixed perspectives.

> MOVING PERSPECTIVE: smoothly connected space/time flow; a journey
> Variants: simulated motion; real ◄———► imaginary/remembered
> Techniques:

- classical cross-fade and reverb
- parallel circuit cross-fade
- layering part and whole
- layering untransformed and transformed.

> VARIABLE PERSPECTIVE: discontinuous space/time flow
> Variants: multiple or embedded perspectives; abstracted/symbolic
> Techniques:

- multi-track editing – 'schizophonic'* embedding
- abstracted perspective.

(*'Schizophonia' refers to the split between an original sound and its recorded reproduction in the context of a digital work.)

The sounds themselves will exist on a sliding scale between 'found sound' and 'abstracted sound'; in other words, there are those sounds that are just straightforwardly recognizable recordings, and those that seem to have no source, and probably many in between the two.

The Project

Make a soundscape piece of between 5' and 10' duration, following the guiding principles outlined by Barry Truax, as follows:

PROJECT 5

- listener recognizability of the source material is maintained
- listener's knowledge of the environmental and psychological context is invoked
- composer's knowledge of the environmental and psychological context influences the shape of the composition at every level
- the work enhances our understanding of the world and its influence carries over into everyday perceptual habits.

Notes

The steps towards this composition will involve an initial period of gathering sounds, either through field recordings or by sourcing appropriate sounds (N.B. always obtain permission for copyrighted sounds). This phase is very important, since without good-quality initial sounds, a good-quality result is unlikely to emerge. It will probably take a few weeks to undertake this exercise.

The second phase will be experimental: working with combinations and transformations of these sounds. Remember the basic principles outlined above. Achieving a coherent perspective for the listener is crucial, whichever of the approaches described above is adopted. This phase of composition may be shorter or longer, depending on the complexity of the material. However, it is important to allow a time lapse between this phase and the following phrases.

Phase 3: critical reflection. Coming back to the work with 'fresh ears' after a period away.

Phase 4: performance. This is the goal and should be born in mind from the start. What will be the performance situation? Will it be stereo, or will a multi-channel set-up be available? Will it be acousmatic, or will there be visual distraction?

The process of composition will probably take a minimum of six weeks, but may take much longer.

HEARING

Hearing is the means whereby we listen. The complexity of the act of hearing is best appreciated when taken out of the laboratory and analysed in the real world. The 'cocktail-party effect' is a good example: listening to a single person's speech in a room full of loud chatter or subconsciously monitoring the sounds around so that when someone mentions something significant the ear can immediately 'tune in' and listen. This is an example of *selective attention* and is normally done with relatively little apparent effort, but, in fact, it is a highly complex operation. First of all, the desired sounds must be separated from what is masking them.[18] This is achieved by using both ears together to discriminate. Second, the words must be connected into a perceptual stream. This is done using a process called *auditory scene analysis*, which groups together sounds that are similar in frequency, timbre, intensity and spatial or temporal proximity. The ears and the brain together act as a filter on the sound.

However, the ears are not the only way to register sound. In an essay on her website, the profoundly deaf percussionist Evelyn Glennie discusses how she hears:

Hearing is basically a specialized form of touch. Sound is simply vibrating air which the ear picks up and converts to electrical signals, which are then interpreted by the brain. The sense of hearing is not the only sense that can do this, touch can do this too. If you are standing by the road and a large truck goes by, do you hear or feel the vibration? The answer is both. With very low frequency vibration the ear starts becoming inefficient and the rest of the body's sense of touch starts to take over. For some reason we tend to make a distinction between hearing a sound and feeling a vibration, in reality they are the same thing. ... Deafness does not mean that you can't hear, only that there is something wrong with the ears. Even someone who is totally deaf can still hear/feel sounds.[19]

She goes on to explain that she can distinguish pitches and timbres using bodily sensation. This can be equally true when there is a direct connection to the human body. Antonio Meucci (1808–1889) was probably the first scientist to explore its sound-transmitting and -receiving properties, as part of his research into electromedical treatments. Meucci connected an electrode to a patient's mouth, then placed a similar device in his own mouth while standing in another room. When he passed a current through the two connected electrodes, his patient cried out in pain. This was unheard by Meucci's ears but, to his surprise, he 'heard' the sound through his tongue, in a so-called 'electrophonic' effect that he dubbed 'physiophony'.

Some digital musicians have taken this idea a stage further, to the extent of exploring the sonic properties of the human body itself. An extreme example is Stelarc, a performance artist whose work has included surgical interventions and body modification. His piece *pingbody* (1996) 'heard' electrical stimuli sent via the Internet which stimulated his wired muscles to involuntary motion. Part of his project to create a 'cyborged' body is focused on hearing, and he has had a networked ear surgical grafted onto his arm. The purpose of the extra ear is to emit sounds as well as to hear differently. He asks the question, 'Why an ear?' and answers, 'The ear is a beautiful and complex structure ... it not only hears but is also the organ of balance. To have an extra ear points to more than visual and anatomical excess.'[20] Clearly, he sees the ear itself as an aesthetic object.

FURTHER READING

- Bregman, A. S., *Auditory Scene Analysis: The Perceptual Organization of Sound*, Cambridge, MA: MIT Press, 1990.
  Explores hearing in complex auditory environments, using a series of creative analogies to describe the process required of the human auditory system as it analyses mixtures of sounds to recover descriptions of individual sounds.

- Yost, W., *Fundamentals of Hearing: An Introduction*, San Diego, CA: Academic Press, 2000.
  Examines the fundamentals of acoustics and hearing science from a communication studies perspective.

Project 6 (Elementary): Speech Patterns

Introduction

Musicians have always been fascinated by the patterns of human speech. The composer Leos Janácek (1854–1928), for example, would jot down 'speech-melodies', which he heard around him, in a process rather similar to the one described in this project. More recently, Steve Reich has used recordings of spoken text to generate short melodic phrases in a number of works, including *Different Trains* (1988) and *The Cave* (1994). The word–phrase–sentence structure of speech is replicated in much music, particularly where the human voice is the basis of the melodic construction. This is even true in some electronic music, where the limitations of the instrument are not normally a factor in determining the lengths of phrases. There is something fundamental to musical communication in the patterns of speech, even if direct comparisons with *language* are not always helpful.

The Project

Sit in a crowded café or restaurant and listen carefully to the patterns of human speech. Try not to understand *what* people are saying, just the sound they make when they say it. Just the same, ask if you can hear meaning in the sound? Are there recognizable rhythms and shapes? How long do these go on? In what ways does the overall level of activity vary? Document the sessions in writing and do several sessions in different locations on different days.

    The same exercise can be tried using recording. It is interesting to note the difference between what the ear hears and what the microphone 'hears': the two are not necessarily the same.

Notes

This could become more of the basis for a piece than just an exercise. The transcriptions, either recorded or notated, could form the basis of a complex texture, or individual patterns could be drawn out to form musical shapes. One interesting approach in this case is to think about spatialization. Can the location of the pair of ears that is hearing be accurately reproduced using spatial tools? Likewise, can the resonance of the space be so reproduced? The human ear is a directional device, so clearly this is important.

PROJECT 6

THE EAR–BRAIN CONNECTION

The scientific study of hearing is called *audiology*, a field that has made great advances in recent years, especially with the advent of new technologies such as digital hearing aids and cochlear implants. For musical purposes, an awareness of the basic aspects of hearing is usually sufficient, but a deeper investigation of the human auditory system can be inspiring and even technically useful. In particular, experiments with sound localization and computer modelling of spatial effects derive to some extent from these understandings.

INFORMATION: THE MECHANICS OF HEARING

The human ear is divided into three sections. The outer ear comprises the external flap (*pinna*) with a central depression and the lobe. The various furrows and ridges in the outer ear help in identifying the location and frequency content[21] of incoming sounds, as can be verified by manipulating the ear while listening. This is further enhanced by the acoustic properties of the external canal (sometimes called the *auditory canal*), which leads through to the eardrum, and resonates at approximately 4 kilohertz (kHz). The final stage of the outer ear is the eardrum, which converts the variations in air pressure created by sound waves into vibrations that can be mechanically sensed by the middle ear.

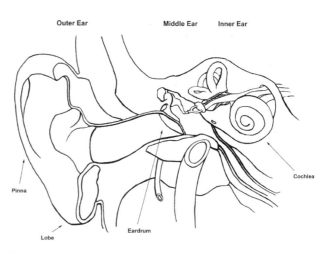

Figure 2.1   The Human ear © Nina Sellars

The middle ear comprises three very small bones (the smallest in the human body), whose job is to transmit the vibrations to the inner ear. This contains various canals that are important for sensing balance and the *cochlea*, a spiral structure that registers sound. Within the cochlea lies the *organ of Corti*, the organ of hearing, which consists of four rows of tiny hair cells or *cilia* sitting along the *basilar* membrane.

Figure 2.2 shows the sensory hair bundle of an inner hair cell from a guinea pig's hearing organ in the inner ear. There are three rows of outer hair cells (OHCs) and one row of inner hair cells (IHCs). The IHCs are sensory cells, converting motion into signals to the brain. The OHCs are more 'active', receiving neural inputs and converting them into motion. The relationship between the OHCs and the IHCs is a kind of feedback: an electromechanical loop that effectively amplifies the sound. Vibrations made by sound cause the hairs to be moved back and forth, alternately stimulating and inhibiting the cell. When the cell is stimulated, it causes nerve impulses to form in the auditory nerve, sending messages to the brain.

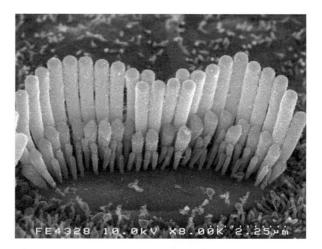

Figure 2.2   Hair cells, or 'cilia', in the inner ear (of a guinea pig)
© Dr David Furness/Wellcome Trust Medical Picture Library

INFORMATION

The cochlea has approximately 2.75 turns in its spiral and measures roughly 35 millimetres. It gradually narrows from a wide base (the end nearest the middle ear) to a thin apex (the furthest tip). High frequency responsiveness is located at the base of the cochlea and the low frequencies at the apex. Studies[22] have shown that the regular spacing of the cilia and their responses to vibrations of the basilar membrane mean that a given frequency f and another frequency $f \times 2$ are heard to be an octave apart. Some of the most fundamental aspects of musical perception, such as pitch, tuning, and even timbre, come down to this physical fact.

The way in which the brain deals with the acoustical information transmitted from the ear is still not fully understood. The study of this part of the hearing process ranges across several disciplines, from psychology to neuroscience or, more precisely, *cognitive* neuroscience.[23] The latter uses biological findings to build a picture of the processes of the human brain, from the molecular and cellular levels through to that of whole systems. In practice, neuroscience and psychology are often combined and interlinked.

To simplify considerably: the cilia transmit information by sending signals to the *auditory cortex*, which lies in the lower middle area of the brain. Recent techniques such as PET scans[24] and Functional MRI scans[25] have enabled scientists to observe brain activity while hearing, seeing, smelling, tasting and touching. The locations of hearing and seeing activity, for example, are quite different, and in fact are even more complex than this implies, because different *types* of hearing stimulate different parts of the brain. Music itself can stimulate many more areas than just those identified with different types of hearing, as emotions, reasoning and all the other facets of human thinking are brought into play.

MACHINE LISTENING

Various attempts to build computer models of the auditory system have had some impact on digital music. Computational auditory scene analysis, for example, tries to extract single streams of sound from more complex polyphonic layers, which has had consequences for perceptual audio coding, such as in compression algorithms like mp3. Feature extraction techniques have enabled fairly reliable detection of musical features such as pitch and beat. Machine listening still has some distance to travel before it can reach the ideal of being able to produce a score automatically from a single hearing of a piece, but there has already been some limited success with recordings of piano music. However, there remains a major challenge in achieving a machine listener that 'understands' the causal way in which human beings hear in real time.

Like the other parts of the cerebral cortex, the auditory cortex processes sensory information by organizing its *neurons*, or nerve cells, into areas. Neurons are networked together and communicate with one another using chemical and electrical signals called *synapses*, which constantly fire during any brain process. These carry messages about the causal relationships between perceived sounds, both past and present. Although the networks of neurons in the auditory cortex register and process sound itself, other parts of the brain contribute to deciding about characteristics such as its musical or aesthetic

Figure 2.3   A network of neurons © Q.-L. Ying and A. Smith/Wellcome Trust

value. The nerve impulses are also important in determining the localization of sound in space.

These neural networks or 'neural nets' have been modelled in various ways, both intentionally and unintentionally.[26] This is highly demanding on computational power, and so often uses parallel distributed processing (PDP) to make its models of human cognition. The Connection Machine, built at the Massachusetts Institute of Technology in 1987–1988, was one such that has sometimes been used for music. The main use of such models has been to identify patterns in vast and unstructured sets of data, such as weather forecasts, image and speech recognition and even in computer games. However, they have also been applied to perception of musical characteristics such as pitch, rhythm or melody, or for more intuitive human–computer interfaces, or to model the creative process itself. There has consequently been an awakening of interest in 'connectionist' models of music.

One typical example is the CONCERT network, which 'is trained on a set of pieces with the aim of extracting stylistic regularities'. CONCERT can then compose new pieces that mimic the learned styles by predicting the likelihood of the next event based on its stored knowledge of preceding examples. A central ingredient of CON-CERT is the incorporation of psychologically grounded representations of pitch, duration and harmonic structure.[27] In a similar vein, the ALICE computer repeatedly 'listens' to music, extracts the key features, and then tries to create its own original pieces in a similar style.[28]

However, there are ways of applying our knowledge of the ear–brain connection that are both less driven by technical challenges and more musically adventurous. During the composition and realization of their 2002 work *Construction 3*, for example, Tony Myatt and Peter Fluck used neural nets to map gestures by the performer onto the computer.[29] The work is an interactive multimedia composition for computer, computer-enhanced saxophone and computer graphics projected onto irregularly shaped screens. The work 'hears' the gestures made by the performer, although, as Myatt noted: 'The success of the technique relies upon a clear and appropriate attribution of meaning to each gesture and to generate information and an appropriate mapping of this generative data to musical parameters'.

Figure 2.4 Performance configuration for *Construction 3* by Tony Myatt and Peter Fluck © Tony Myatt and Peter Fluck

FURTHER READING

- Martin, F. N. and Clark, J., *Introduction to Audiology*, Boston, MA: Allyn and Bacon, 2003.
  The standard introduction to hearing and hearing disorders.

- Griffith, N. and Todd, P. (eds), *Musical Networks: Parallel Distributed Perception and Performance*, Cambridge, MA: MIT Press, 1997.
  A study of connectionist models of music, covering pitch perception, tonality, musical streaming, sequential and hierarchical melodic structure, composition, harmonization, rhythmic analysis, sound generation, and creative evolution.

- Todd, P., *Music and Connectionism*, Cambridge, MA: The MIT Press, 1991.
  Examines the techniques of connectionism and parallel distributed processing in a wide range of topics in music research, from pitch perception to chord fingering to composition.

- Wang, D. and Brown, G. J., *Computational Auditory Scene Analysis: Principles, Algorithms and Applications*, Hoboken, NJ: John Wiley & Sons/IEEE Press, 2006.
  A summary of the current state of research in this area. See also the website http://www.casabook.org

Discussion Questions

- How does working in digital music influence the act of listening? Is it different from listening in other situations? If so, in what way?

- What sounds should a digital musician be able to identify by ear? Are there any sounds which are irrelevant to digital music?

- What do you understand by the phrase 'acoustic ecology'? What are the key issues in this field?

- To what extent is reduced listening possible? Is it desirable to remove a perceived sound from its source? What are the implications of doing so, both in music for the ears alone and in music with image?

- What is the role of artificial intelligence in music? What would be the ideal? And what is likely to be the reality?

Exploring Sound

I was always into the theory of sound, even in the 6th form. The physics teacher refused to teach us acoustics but I studied it myself and did very well. It was always a mixture of the mathematical side and music.
—(Hutton, J. 2000 *Radiophonic Ladies: Delia Derbyshire* (interview). London: Sonic Arts Network)

ACOUSTICS AND PSYCHOACOUSTICS

Delia Derbyshire (1937–2001) worked at the BBC Radiophonic Workshop[1] and was famously responsible for the distinctive electronic arrangement of Ron Grainer's theme tune for the television series *Doctor Who*,[2] among many other things. She used tape loops, oscillators and early synthesizers to create music and sound-tracks. She was a typical example of a technological musician, qualified in music but making 'special sounds' derived from an understanding of sound through the science of acoustics, combined with a belief in the supremacy of aural perception and the brain in shaping music.

Some of the basic elements of music are, traditionally: rhythm, pitch, dynamics and timbre. The basic elements of sound, on the other hand, include: duration, frequency, amplitude and spectrum. The two have much in common, of course, but the match is not exact. For example, rhythm in music is perceived in relation to pulse, beat or tempo, whereas the duration of a sound is usually measured in seconds, with little reference to its 'rhythmic' relationships. Likewise, 'pitch' arises from a subjective perception of the dominant frequency of a given sound, whereas 'frequency' is expressed in vibrations per second and is objectively measurable; 'dynamics' are relative, whereas 'amplitude' is fixed, and 'timbre' is the perceived quality of a sound, whereas 'spectrum' is a detailed account of its harmonic (or partial) components and their changing relationships.

The scientific study of sound takes in both *acoustics* and *psychoacoustics*. Where psychoacoustics concerns itself mainly with the human perception of sound, acoustics traditionally begins with the study of sound itself. Psychoacoustics is relatively new compared to acoustics, which is an established and vast field incorporating many sub-disciplines, such as:

- *aeroacoustics* (aerodynamic sound)
- *architectural* and *vibration* acoustics (how sound behaves in buildings and structures)
- *bioacoustics* (the use of sound by animals such as whales, dolphins and bats)
- *biomedical* acoustics (e.g., ultrasound)
- *speech* communication
- *underwater* acoustics
- *physical* acoustics, which explores the interaction of sound with materials and fluids, e.g., *sonoluminescence* (the emission of light by bubbles in a liquid excited by sound) and *thermoacoustics* (the interaction of sound and heat).

Some sub-disciplines of acoustics deal explicitly with musical concerns, including the study of the physics of musical instruments, and *acoustic engineering*, which investigates how sound is generated and measured by loudspeakers, microphones, sonar projectors, hydrophones, ultrasonic transducers, sensors and other electro-acoustical devices.

Acoustics has provided an objective, scientific, way of understanding sound, and most of the new technologies take that as their starting point. Some software may superimpose 'musical' characteristics to make the interface more acceptable to musicians, but the underlying processes remain mathematical. A computer is a number-crunching machine, which is very capable of extremely precise and sophisticated measurement and processing of the elements of sound. The kind of subjective perceptions and relative judgements required by 'music' is an additional layer which is partially built upon an understanding of psychoacoustics. Thus, for example, pitch and time processes, spatialization and reverberation filters, and so on, rely upon listener perception as much as any scientifically measurable properties of sound behaviour.

One important practical aspect that affects musicians working with such techniques is the phenomenon of 'psychoacoustic fatigue', which is described by David Howard and James Angus as follows:

> This arises because the ear and brain adapt to sounds. This has the effect of dulling the effect of a given timbre modification over a period of time. Therefore one puts in more boost, to which the listener adapts, and so on.[3]

As they observe, the only way to compensate for this problem is to take frequent breaks during the musical process.

INFORMATION: *FUNDAMENTALS OF ACOUSTICS*

Sound is a disturbance in a medium such as air, water or even a solid, and it travels in waves. A sound wave has three main and related characteristics: frequency, amplitude and velocity. Velocity will depend on a number of factors, including the *density* and *elasticity* of the material through which the wave passes. Elasticity is the ability of a material to regain its shape after deformation from some force. The elasticity of steel and glass is much greater than that of water or air, so sound will travel faster through solids than through liquids or gases. The density of a material refers to its mass per unit volume.

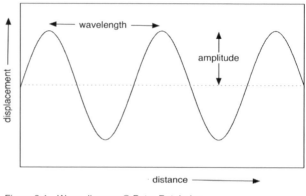

Figure 3.1   Wave diagram © Peter Batchelor

Raising the temperature (which decreases its density) has the effect of increasing the velocity of sound through the medium. Sound travels through air at a rate of roughly 343 metres (1125 feet) per second (ms^{-1}) in a dry room at 20°C (68°F), but this figure will vary. At 0°C (32°F) in the same room, its speed will be roughly 331 ms^{-1} (1086 fs^{-1}), whereas in breath, which is not dry, at 25°C (77°F) it will travel at approximately 346 ms^{-1} (1135 fs^{-1}).

Amplitude is the measure of maximum disturbance in the medium during a single cycle. The amplitude of sound waves is normally measured in units of pressure called pascals (Pa).[4] Frequency is the rate of change in a phase[5] of a wave and is equal to the velocity of the wave divided by its wavelength. The frequency of waves remains exactly the same when they pass through different media, and only their wavelength and velocity change. Frequency is measured in hertz,[6] which indicates the number of cycles (or periods) per second passing a fixed point. Figure 3.1 shows a typical wave form. The displacement of a particle in the medium is shown up the y-axis and the distance travelled by the wave along the x-axis.

Travelling waves are moving and make a disturbance that varies across distance and time. *Standing waves* result from the interference of two travelling waves and appear to stay in one place; for example, the vibrations of a bass guitar string. *Longitudinal* sound waves vibrate directly along, or parallel to, their direction of travel, as opposed to a *transverse* wave, which oscillates perpendicular to its direction of travel. The vibrating bass guitar string is an example of a transverse wave, and a sound wave in a tube is an example of a longitudinal wave. One crude way to visualize the difference is to imagine a 'slinky' laid out on a table. If pushed back and forth from either end, a longitudinal wave is created. If moved from side to side, a transverse wave is the result.

A longitudinal wave compresses the air in between molecules, which then reacts by expanding according to the elasticity of the substance. This longitudinal motion generally happens in three dimensions, as unconstrained sound waves radiate in all directions in an expanding sphere. The wave form is, thus, a result of the displacement of particles in the medium (e.g., air molecules) as it moves from its state of rest. These variations in molecule displacement lead to related variations in pressure. The *wavelength* is the distance between any two equivalent points along a wave and is measured in metres, so audible sounds will have wavelengths of between about 1.7 centimetres (0.021 inches) and 17 metres (18.6 yards). The lower the pitch of a sound, the longer the wavelength.

FURTHER READING

■ Campbell, D. and Greated, C., *The Musicians Guide to Acoustics*, London: Dent, 1987.
A classic text which sets out the basic information clearly and authoritatively.

■ Howard, D. and Angus, J., *Acoustics and Psychoacoustics*, Oxford: Focal Press, 2001.
As the title suggests, this reflects recent research into psychoacoustics and takes account of developments in the digital domain.

SOUND STRUCTURES

Cognitive psychology and cognitive neuroscience have produced abundant evidence that human beings have a natural tendency to try to make sense of complex or ambiguous information through pattern recognition. *Gestalt* theory (the word means 'essence' or 'complete form') suggests that our brains will generate whole forms from haphazard collections of shapes or structures. This idea has been used, for example, in computer interface design, where the laws of similarity (the mind groups similar elements into collective entities or totalities) and proximity (spatial or temporal proximity of elements may induce the mind to perceive a collective or totality) have influenced the arrangement of desktops, menus and buttons.

The same ideas hold good in sound. We tend to group together proximate or similar sounds as we seek to make sense of sonic structures. Psychoacoustic perceptions are the basis for such groupings, and pattern–recognition is the means whereby we construct meaning from them. This can apply at a very local level, say moment to moment within a composition, or at a larger scale, as we perceive relationships between the parts of a whole piece. Musical interest often derives from the shifts in perception that take place during the process of forming these understandings. In digital music, the sonic structures that are present at every level, from an individual sample to the overall composition, may be similarly analysed and understood by the computer. This offers unparalleled opportunities for access to the natural processes of the human brain and therefore to greater expressivity and communication.

Since digital music is largely disembodied, a perceptual approach to sonic structures tends to dominate our listening. In other words, whereas instrumental music was the result of direct physical actions on to a resonating body (the bowing of a violin, the blowing of a trumpet, the striking of percussion, etc.), digital music may be produced without physical intervention and through remote loudspeakers. Consequently, we listen to the sounds of this music as structures in their own right, regardless of source (as in Schaeffer's reduced listening) and try to make sense of them in relation to one another and in the context of the work as a whole. This may even apply when the sound source comes from nature or indeed a musical instrument. Digital musicians will find themselves listening differently to such sounds as their *gestalt* awareness becomes heightened over time.

Twentieth-century music, from the 'cloud' pieces of György Ligeti to the chance compositions of John Cage, have exploited these tendencies. A recent example of a work that explicitly explores similar ideas, but uses live interactive digital sound during the performance, is Daniel Schachter's *FlaX* (2002) for flute, fixed electro-acoustic material and live processing. The flautist is offered a menu of fragments of material or musical gestures in each section of the piece, which may be ordered in any way. The fixed material is organized into a series of key structural moments, which the flautist will recognize. Schachter expects the flautist to rely on his/her *gestalt* perceptions in combining and recombining the gestures with the live sound and the processed sounds. He accordingly groups the gestures in categories according to what he calls their 'perceptive pregnance' (impulses, crescendi, frullati (flutter-tongues), iterations, phrases, rough sounds). The real-time processing is done by another performer, who similarly has various options available during each section. The overall aim is to create a dialogue between the performers, as well as between the piece and the audience.

FURTHER READING

- Leman, M., *Music, Gestalt, and Computing: Studies in Cognitive and Systematic Musicology*, Berlin and New York: Springer-Verlag, 1997.
  A collection of essays that explores everything from theoretical musicology to interactive computer systems from a *gestalt* perspective.

RECOMMENDED LISTENING

- ► Schachter, D. (2002) '*FlaX* for flute, electroacoustic sounds and live processing' on *... riccordo ...* [CD] Buenos Aires: Schachter.
  The title comes from *flauta*, the Spanish word for flute, and X as an indication of the sound processing.

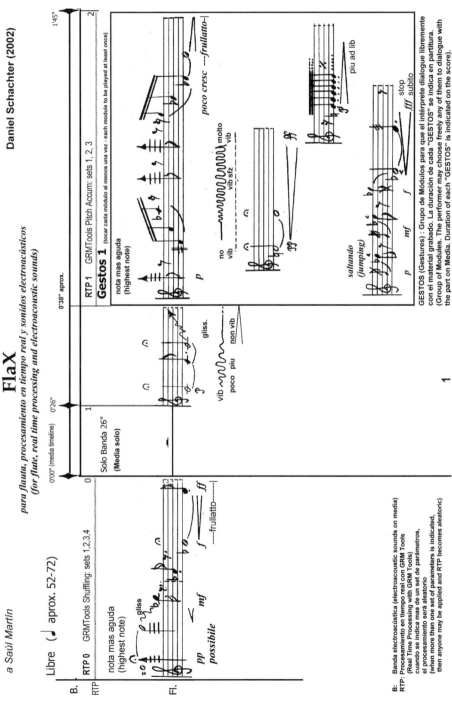

Figure 3.2 FlaX by Daniel Schachter: Page 1 of the score © Daniel Schachter

Project 7 (Intermediate): Sound Structures

Introduction

This project encourages you to examine the structures of sounds, looking for key characteristics, recognizable patterns and relationships. It may be extended into a complete composition, but begins with a classification of sound types. This project is surprisingly difficult,
and will waken up the ears to previously unconsidered aspects of the sounds.

The Project

Make or download a collection of up to six sounds. Find sounds that are as different as
possible from one another. Listen to them repeatedly under studio conditions or on headphones. Try to hear every last detail of the sound.

- *Step 1.* Identify by ear the key features of the sonic structures of each sound. These
  can be noted down either in words or in a (self-devised) graphical form.

- *Step 2.* Classify the sounds according to what they *are*.

- *Step 3.* Classify the sounds according to what they are *not*.

- *Step 4.* Now try to combine and recombine the sounds in a musical way that reflects
  and draws out the relationships identified in the earlier steps. No processing or manipulation allowed – only placing the sounds in time. Layering is permitted.

Notes

Of course, sound is not really divided into 'objects' but is rather a continuum. One question to
ask during this project is to what extent the recording or sampling of these sounds removes
this sense of continuum. Also, ask whether Schaeffer's concept of a 'sonic object' is useful.

DURATION

Digital techniques have opened up duration to a degree unimaginable before now. In
his important book *Microsound* (2001), Curtis Roads identifies nine time scales of music,
as follows:

1   *Infinite.* The ideal time span of mathematical durations such as the infinite sine waves
     of classical Fourier analysis.
2   *Supra.* A time scale beyond that of an individual composition and extending into
     months, years, decades and centuries.
3   *Macro.* The time scale of overall musical architecture or form, measured in minutes
     or hours, or in extreme cases, days.
4   *Meso.* Divisions of form. Groupings of sound objects into hierarchies of phrase struc-
     tures of various sizes, measured in minutes or seconds.
5   *Sound object.* A basic unit of musical structure, generalizing the traditional concept of
     note to include complex and mutating sound events on a time scale ranging from a
     fraction of a second to several seconds.

6 *Micro*. Sound particles on a time scale that extends down to the threshold of auditory perception (measured in thousandths of a second or milliseconds).
7 *Sample*. The atomic level of digital audio systems: individual binary samples or numerical amplitude values, one following another at a fixed time interval. The period between samples is measured in millionths of a second (microseconds).
8 *Subsample*. Fluctuations on a time scale too brief to be properly recorded or perceived, measured in billionths of a second (nanoseconds) or less.
9 *Infinitesimal*. The ideal time span of mathematical functions such as the infinitely brief delta functions.[7]

With the exception of time scales 1 and 9, which are really only theoretical possibilities, these are now all practically available to the digital musician. Roads develops an analogy with the science of matter by considering the properties of waves and particles, a debate that goes back to Ancient Greece and beyond and continues today in the field of quantum physics. He concludes with the comment: 'Sound can be seen [as] either wavelike or particle-like, depending upon the scale of measurement, the density of particles, and the type of operations we apply to it.'[8]

Many of the time-based modifications made to single sounds by digital technologies carry implications for longer-term musical structures. The action of digitally 'stretching' a sound, for example, simply fills the newly extended duration with additional data which may (or may not) give an aurally convincing impression of a stretch but nevertheless resembles the old data in that it consists of a certain number of samples per second. Each individual sample (or even smaller unit) contains a certain amount of frequency information, however imperceptible, which when added together over time creates the sonic effect.

The two best-known examples of such digital manipulations of sound through time are *pitch-shifting* and *time-stretching*. The latter affects the duration of a sound without changing its pitch, the former changes the pitch without altering duration. These techniques are often used in the recording studio to correct small errors of pitching or timing in human performance. However, their creative potential extends beyond mere error correction into sound transformation. Both these techniques may be time-varying, that is to say, applied in varying amounts to portions of a sound file. Some software allows for hand-drawn or oscillator control or even control by dynamic envelopes extracted from the sound itself or from other sounds. The processes can be applied to any sounds or events or even to whole pieces of music.

Duration is more than just a measurable time span. It is a perceptual consequence of the passage of time and is in many ways the stuff of music itself, since auditory events have an effect upon that perception. As sonic experiences constantly pass into memory, their remembered existence influences the perception of the present. The pace at which the present experience unfolds and the perceived relationships between that and other rates of change is largely responsible for excitement and interest in a piece of music. If a 'natural' duration is one in which the duration of the sound appears to be consistent with the nature of the sound source, then in digital music there is great potential for exploiting unnatural, even unfeasible, durations. A piece of music may even set up a counterpoint, or argument, between the 'natural' and the 'unnatural'. This has greatly expanded both the language of music itself and the dramaturgy available to musicians (where 'dramaturgy' refers to both the timing and the character of the appearances of sounds within a composition).

PROJECT 8

Project 8 (Elementary): Extended Duration

Introduction

On the face of it, this is quite a simple project. However, it has the potential to develop into an entire extended musical composition. It will require some audio editing software, but this need not be particularly sophisticated. Some of the free downloadable software will do perfectly well.

The Project

Find a sound with a natural decay (e.g., a gong, or a piano) and use digital processes to extend its length to at least twice its original duration, *without losing interest in the sound*.

Notes

This is more than just a technical exercise. The last part of the instruction contains a hint of how this could develop further. Keeping up interest in the sound implies some amount of transformation or development in what is heard.

FURTHER READING

■ Roads, C., *Microsound*, Cambridge, MA: MIT Press, 2001.
  Below the level of the musical note lies the realm of microsound, of sound particles lasting less than one-tenth of a second.

RECOMMENDED LISTENING

▶ Leaf Inge (2002) *9 Beet Stretch*. Online. Available HTTP: http://www.expandedfield. net/ (accessed 8 October 2011).
  A recording of Beethoven's Ninth Symphony (Nicolaus Esterházy Sinfonia and Chorus/Drahos (Naxos 8.553478)) is stretched digitally to a duration of 24 hours with no distortion or pitch shifting.

▶ Curtis Roads (1987) *nscor* [CD] Wergo, 2010-50.
  One of the earliest examples of microsound, that explores sounds of extremely short duration. The piece was written using various computer programs, including G. M. Koenig's 'Project 1', the 'Sound Synthesis Program' (SSP) by Paul Berg, and 'Music 11' by William Buxton.

▶ Horacio Vaggione (1996) *Schall* [CD] Chrisopée Electronique, LCD 278 1102.
  A work that explores the relationship between thousands of extremely short sounds, derived from piano notes, and longer sounds from the same source. This is essentially a study in varying durations, but also in the resulting textures that emerge.

PITCH AND TUNING

Given that melody is a succession of pitches, and harmony an aggregation of pitches, it may be concluded that the main contribution of digital technologies to the pitch domain is *facility*. It is certainly true that it is now much easier and quicker to create melodies and harmonies, including those that use non-standard tunings, inflections and *glissandi*, timbral nuances, and so on. A wide range of interactive devices and new digital instruments offer control over the expressive potential of these most prominent elements of music. Automation too has focused a great deal on pitch as a primary means of organizing music, so machines devote much computational time to understanding and predicting pitch sequences.

However, the role of pitch itself in digital music has also changed. Traditional music gave primacy to pitch and the sounds called *notes* were defined first and foremost by their fundamental pitch. But *all* sound, apart from certain types of noise, contains some pitch. What has changed in music made with new technology is that the pitch is no longer always the most important aspect of the sound. This does not necessarily mean that digital music has rejected the idea of a 'note'. It is embedded in MIDI systems, for example, and in music that combines traditional instruments with digital sound. But it does mean that digital music tends to treat pitch merely as one aspect of a sound that may be investigated.

Pitch is very much a matter of human perception, based upon what is heard to be the dominant frequency in a given sound. As discussed earlier, this has a physical basis in the vibrations within the ear, but there is also a psychoacoustical aspect. Where the pitch perception is fairly unambiguous, the wave form is normally periodic; that is to say, it repeats in cycles per second (hertz) over time in a perfectly ordered way, producing a single pitch. An *aperiodic* wave, by contrast, never repeats itself but moves randomly (and noise is simply an unpitched aperiodic wave).

The resulting number corresponds to the pitch of the note, so the A above 'middle C' repeats at 440 Hz. A change in frequency normally means a perceptible change in pitch, but slight changes to the dominant frequency of a note (e.g., in vibrato) will not. The perception of pitch also depends partly on amplitude and other factors. When a given note is played on different instruments, the pitch may be recognizably the same, but the wave forms look quite unlike one another. This is because each instrument has its own distinct physical and acoustical properties which produce a unique timbre.

The systematization of pitch which is familiar in the Western world, comprising twelve equal steps to an octave, is by no means universal and is also somewhat controversial. It is a mathematical reinterpretation of the phenomenon of the *harmonic series*, designed to create a standardized system of tuning for keyboard instruments in particular.

INFORMATION: *THE HARMONIC SERIES*

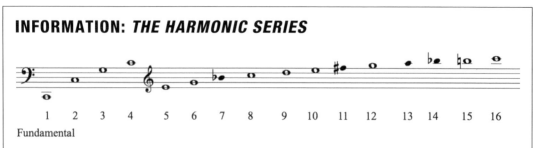

1 2 3 4 5 6 7 8 9 10 11 12 13 14 15 16

Fundamental

Figure 3.3   Harmonic Series (musical notation) © Andrew Hugill

The discovery of the harmonic series is usually credited to the Ancient Greek Pythagoras, although there is evidence that the Chinese and other civilizations knew about it much earlier. Pythagoras observed that a vibrating string touched exactly halfway down its length produces a partial tone, which sounds similar to, but higher than, the one produced by the whole length of the untouched string. The point at which the string is touched is called a *node*, and the sound it produces is called a *harmonic*. Harmonics were historically known as *overtones*, and the open string vibration as the *fundamental*. Both terms are still used quite often today.

Figure 3.4 shows a vibrating single string, or monochord, attached at both ends, with stationary points (nodes) at the ratios 1:1, 2:1, 3:2, 4:3. These nodes are distinct from the antinodes, or maximum moving points, between them.

This halfway division is in the ratio 2:1 and the resulting pitch is an 'octave' higher than the open string. The next sub-division that produces a clearly audible pitch is at 3:2, which sounds a 'fifth'. The one after that is in the ratio 4:3, then 5:4, 6:5, 7:6, and so on. The same phenomenon is equally apparent in a vibrating column of air. A flute, for example, is a vibrating column of air whose harmonic series is exploited by the flautist.

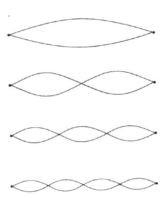

Figure 3.4   Vibrating monochord © Andrew Hugill

The intervals of the octave, perfect fifth, perfect fourth, major third, minor seventh, and the rest, as they appear on the piano keyboard, therefore correspond roughly, but *not* exactly, to the nearest relevant whole number ratios in a Pythagorean system. This detuning from nature begins with the so-called 'perfect fifth', which is not *quite* a ratio of 3:2. (Note that in this list the intervals indicate the distance from the previous pitch.)

Fundamental (Harmonic 1) = Unison = 1:1

Harmonic 2 = Octave = 2:1

Harmonic 3 = Perfect fifth = 3:2

Harmonic 4 = Perfect fourth = 4:3

Harmonic 5 = Major third (4 semitones) = 5:4

Harmonic 6 = Minor third (3 semitones) = 6:5

Harmonic 7 = Lowered (flattened) Minor third = 7:6

Harmonic 8 = Raised (sharp) Major second = 8:7

Harmonic 9 = Major whole tone (2 semitones) = 9:8

Harmonic 10 = Minor whole tone (1 semitone) = 10:9.

In practice, it is fairly easy to hear up to Harmonic 6 in most sounds, and the seventh harmonic is particularly clear in highly resonant instruments or spaces.

There is no particular reason to subdivide the octave into twelve steps, and many cultures around the world use either many more subdivisions (Indian classical music, for example) or many fewer (Japanese folk music, for example). Nor is it necessary to have equal steps. By using 'just intonation' (i.e., only whole number ratios), an octave containing over forty 'pure' yet uneven steps may readily be achieved. The octave itself may be challenged: systems exist where the 2:1 is not the theoretical end of a given series of subdivisions. Even if the restriction of equal temperament is retained and only seven-step scales within an octave are used, there are still many alternative sequences to the one 'major' and two 'minor' used in traditional tonal music. Alternative tuning systems, therefore, offer up a host of musical possibilities based on pitch alone.

Harmonicity and Inharmonicity

When the harmonics in a sound exist in a stable relationship to one another, so that a pitch (usually the fundamental) is perceived, they are said to exhibit *harmonicity*. In many sounds, however, the overtones have fluctuating and dynamic relationships that change over time, and many of the overtones that are not characterized by whole-number ratios have a significant role in contributing to the whole character of a sound. Typical examples are bells, or the high notes on a piano, where the physical con-struction of the sound-producing object or instrument may cause deviations from a predictable whole-number ordering of partials. This is called *inharmonicity*, and the amount of deviation from this ordering determines the degree of inharmonicity. Thus, an unpitched instrument such as a cymbal generates many partial tones, but their lack of obvious whole number relationships makes them inharmonic. Many digital manipulation techniques exploit the inharmonic characteristics of sounds that have unstable pitches.

For physical modelling in computers, such variables present many technical chal-lenges, which have largely been overcome today, resulting in some highly convincing virtual instruments. Digital analysis techniques have enabled a detailed examination of the behaviour of every partial in a given sound. Digital synthesis has allowed the creation of new sounds based on complex interactions of overtones. Pitch material, in the form of sinusoids (simple harmonics) may be examined, extracted, manipulated, processed, transformed and recombined with ease. The facility offered by computers has extended beyond the creation of sequences of notes into the creation of pitch itself.

RECOMMENDED LISTENING

▶ Warren Burt (1992–98) *Music for Microtonal Piano Sounds* [CD] Tall Poppies, TP093.
A collection of experimental pieces for computer, synthesizer and MIDI controller that explore the gaps between the piano keys.

▶ Wendy Carlos (1986) *Beauty in the Beast* [CD] East Street Digital, ESD 81552.
'I've taken ideas from many disparate cultures, heeding Debussy's dictum: "whatever pleases my ear," and filtered it through all the wonderful new musical means at my disposal and through my decidedly Euro-American post symphonic composorial skills' (from the sleevenotes). The album uses many different tuning systems.

▶ John Chowning (1977) *Stria* [CD] Wergo, WER 2012–50.
A digital composition that is organized around eight pseudo-octaves, three above and five below the central frequency (f=1000Hz), based on the golden ratio 1.618:1 rather than the 2:1. Chowning invented FM synthesis and his work often explores inharmonicity.

▶ Jonathan Harvey (1980) *Mortuos Plango, Vivos Voco* [CD] Computer Music Currents vol. 5, Wergo, WER 2025-50.
A classic work of computer music, created at IRCAM in Paris, and focused on the partials and pitches of the great bell at Winchester Cathedral and the voice of the composer's own son singing the text inscribed on the bell: 'Horas avolantes numero mortuos plango vivos ad preces voco.' ('I count the fleeting hours, I lament the dead, I call the living to prayer.')

PROJECT 9

Project 9 (Advanced): Drone Piece

Introduction

The drone is a fundamental aspect of much of the world's music, providing a stable reference point against which to hear the pitches of a melody. This is especially important where the expressive intentions of the music rely upon microtonal inflections. A drone may be purely pitch-based or may also include a rhythmic element, when tuned percussion instruments are used. Either way the purpose of a drone is to be constantly present and to unify a piece.

Despite their relatively humble limitation to one (or sometimes two) 'notes', drones frequently contain great interest in their own right. Often they exploit overtones or harmonics, or the beating that results from close spectra, or changes in timbral colour over time. They can provide a sense of space or of rhythmic change that is structurally important to the whole composition.

The Project

Create a digital drone lasting at least five minutes. It should aim to retain the listener's attention, but without introducing any additional material such as melody or harmony. However, timbral variation resulting from spectral changes is permissible, and the basic sound itself may change character, so long as it remains on the same pitch (or pair of pitches). Rhythm may also be introduced, but only as part of the drone, not as an end in itself. Volume levels may change considerably during the composition.

Notes

If you are stuck for an initial sound source, try using your own voice. Sing vowel sounds: a–e–i–o–u (pronounced aah, ay, eeh, oh, uh) in a continuous rotation. The word 'why', sung slowly and extending all the vowel sounds, also works well (especially in a bathroom!). Sing through the nose somewhat, and gradually awaken the harmonics present in the voice. A buzzing safety razor held against the cheek can also boost the effect. The sound can be extended and developed in the computer.

This project requires a lot of work to succeed. It is easy enough to generate five minutes of droning, and to add a few effects with a standard software package. However, this will be unlikely to satisfy all the musical requirements. You should engage in a series of critical listenings over a period of a few weeks. Try to identify where the musical interest slackens and why. Repetition is not necessarily a problem in a drone, but too much repetition leads a certain monotony which (perhaps surprisingly) is not necessarily welcome! It is all a question of playing with listener expectations, of introducing some new non-repetitive element at the right time, of making the most of the basic materials. This may appear to be a piece about pitch, but it is in fact as much about *timing*, which is thrown into relief when the pitches are so limited.

FURTHER READING

- Sethares, W., *Tuning, Timbre, Spectrum, Scale*, London: Springer-Verlag, 2004. A comprehensive account of the subject that relates tuning to timbre and spectrum by employing local consonance, and sees no discontinuity between these elements.

FROM NOISE TO SILENCE

Digital technologies have made available the full audible, and inaudible, range of sounds. Amplification is a fact of life in digital music and its capability to deliver extremes of loudness or quiet have resulted in whole new genres of music. One of the case studies, Atau Tanaka, cut his digital teeth in the field of Japanese noise music which, inspired by free improvisation, punk and industrial music, tries to go beyond the conventional boundaries by exploiting extreme levels of sound to create a visceral experience that, as he recalled recently 'often leaves the audience members curled up in a foetal position'. At the opposite end of the spectrum, and no less radically, 'lowercase' music generally comprises extremely quiet recordings of small or overlooked sounds of extremely short – up to 100 milliseconds' – duration. Some lowercase albums are mostly inaudible: the sound is *felt* rather than heard. What these extreme examples show is a general fascination of digital music with a scale that ranges from noise to silence, from extreme loudness to extreme quiet.

In musical situations, sound is heard in relation to silence. A piece of music normally begins and ends with a notional 'silence' and may contain silences as formal devices, dramatic gestures, or moments of contrast. However, as Cage's visit to the anechoic chamber makes clear, silence is only a relative concept, since there is always *some* sound to be heard. *Digital* silence, though, is quite different from its acoustic equivalent, for two main reasons. First, an absence of data, or sound information, in a stream represents a violent discontinuity: the contrast is abrupt and the silence absolute. Second, there is none of the noise, hiss, crackle and rumble produced by analogue equipment, which forms a sometimes–unwelcome backdrop to some recorded sound. A digital silence throws the listener suddenly out of the sound world of the machinery and into the natural world of the surrounding acoustic of the auditorium.

There have been many creative solutions to this 'problem' of digital silence, ranging from the addition of an 'ambient' resonance track to create an artificial acoustic within which the digital music can apparently reside, to the use of synthetic digital resonance to maintain the acoustic illusion. There is even software to produce artificial analogue hiss, crackle and so on. Some artists deliberately exploit the extreme contrast of digital silence and seem to relish the 'blackout' effect it produces. The important point is that an absence of sound can be just as musically significant as the presence of sound, and this is heightened in digital music.

INFORMATION: *NOISE AND LOUDNESS*

'Noise' is both an aesthetic and a technical term. Technically speaking, it refers to a signal without meaning or, in audio, a sound without pitch.

Noise comes in several 'colours'. 'White' noise sounds like the 'whoosh' of the sea (although without its fluctuations) and contains every frequency within human hearing (generally from 20 Hz to 20 kHz) to equal power over ranges of equal width. However, the human ear normally perceives this to have more high-frequency content than low. The range from 10 to 20 Hz is heard to be equivalent to the range from 100 to 200 Hz. 'Pink' or 1/f noise filters white noise by reducing the levels per octave. Such 1/f noise occurs in nature, astronomy and even economic systems. 'Brown', or 'red', noise is the kind of signal produced by Brownian motion (the random motion of molecules) and is a more extreme version of pink noise that emphasizes the lower octaves by reducing power octave by octave by 6 dB. The opposite of brown noise is 'purple' noise, which increases power per octave (also by 6 dB). 'Grey' noise exploits a psychoacoustic loudness curve to deliver a more accurate *perceptual* white noise to the listener. So-called 'black' noise has a power level of zero in all frequencies, apart from perhaps a few narrow bands or 'spikes'. Black noise is, technically, silence.

Although noise is generally thought to be loud, it is not necessarily so. In fact, loudness is another property altogether, which is also important to the digital musician. A famous research project conducted[9] at the Bell Laboratories by Harvey Fletcher and W. S. Munson in 1933 asked many people to judge when pure tones of different frequencies were the same loudness. The averaged results gave a set of 'equal loudness curves' which reveal that, under laboratory conditions, the perceived loudness of a sound is, surprisingly, not directly equivalent to the amplitude of its pressure. This is because the sensitivity of human hearing varies according to the frequency of a sound wave.

Loudness can be measured in three different ways. The sound intensity level (SIL) is the flow of energy through a unit area in a particular direction, given in watts per square metre.[10] The sound pressure level (SPL) is the average pressure exerted by a sound at a particular point in space, given in pascals (where 20 micropascals (µPa), is the threshold of audibility and 20–30 Pa is roughly the pain threshold for most humans). The sound power level (SWL or PWL) is a theoretical total of acoustic power radiated in all directions calculated in comparison to a specified reference level (usually decibels relative to 1 watt, or dBW).

The decibel scale, sometimes abbreviated to dBSPL, is based on the fact that humans only register the SPL. Decibels are not a direct measure of the loudness of a sound, but are given relative to a zero level, which is (normally) the threshold of human hearing. This means that doubling the decibels does not automatically result in a doubling of loudness: 85 dB is considered harmful, 120 dB is unsafe, and 150 dB will cause actual damage to the human body.

In aesthetic terms, noise refers to any unwanted or uncomfortable sound. Perhaps John Cage's silent piece *4' 33"* was the first example of noise music, since it contained only those sounds that would not normally be wanted during a concert. Western music history has seen the gradual inclusion of sounds that are initially dismissed as 'noise' into mainstream musical practice. So, for example, increasingly huge amounts of percussion have been used in orchestras, including a range of tuned instruments, unusual or exotic untuned instruments, and many effects. Igor Stravinsky's *Le Sacre du Printemps* (*The Rite of Spring*), premiered in 1913, included timpani, triangle, tambourine, guiro, two antique cymbals, cymbals, bass drum, tam-tam (as well as quadruple woodwind, including two bass clarinets, and a large brass section) and by 1926, Edgard Varèse included thirty-nine tuned and untuned percussion instruments in his massive orchestra for *Arcana*. Into this mix has been added many electronic sounds and instruments. On many occasions, when an unfamiliar sound is added to the palette, audiences and critics have reacted in a hostile way, dismissing the new music as 'noise'.

This understanding of noise as an inappropriate sound in a given context persists in digital music, but in a rather inverted form. So, for example, the Japanese noise musician Merzbow, whose work would shock many listeners in its embracing of extremes of loudness, has remarked: 'If by noise you mean uncomfortable sound, then pop music is noise to me.'[11] Paul Hegarty makes the point that noise music is 'constantly failing – failing to stay noise, as it becomes familiar, or accepted practice.'[12] It nevertheless persists, and part of its appeal lies in its impact on the body, while on a more intellectual level it seems to make a comment on the environment we inhabit today.

In the wider environment, noise is pervasive. The noise that causes so much irritation and distress, giving rise to hundreds of complaints a day to government organizations, to the creation of noise maps and attempts to quieten the soundscape, is made worse by the individual's feeling of powerlessness to control their situation. In the context of acoustic ecology, noise pollution becomes a political matter and occasions struggles and protests. In the 1970s this kind of noise was first formally recognized as more than just a nuisance, with the publication of the Portland Noise Code (1975), which has been the model for many similar sets of regulations since. Even so, noise continues to have considerable negative impact on human and animal life. The extent to which digital music adds to or shields us from this impact is a matter for debate, as listeners to both sides of a loud mp3 player on a crowded train will readily understand.

To summarize, we may observe that pitch and noise represent opposite ends of a continuum:

Pitch ———————— Noise

Every sound sits somewhere on this line, although often varying its position. The extent to which the role of pitch has changed may be understood by comparing it with another continuum:

Music ———————— Sound

Until fairly recently, it would have been assumed that the two lines were essentially the same, that 'music' was about 'pitch' and that 'sounds' were mostly 'noise' (in a musical context). Recent advances have blurred this distinction so that music, sound, pitch and noise all inhabit the same field, and artistic expression may exploit our appreciation of the qualities of all and the relationships between them.

PROJECT 10

Project 10 (Advanced): Incomplete Silence

Introduction

There is a tradition of 'silent' pieces of music, of which the most famous is John Cage's *4' 33"*. However, that was not the earliest example: the first was probably the humorously titled 'Funeral March for the Obsequies of a Large Deaf Man' composed in 1884 by Alphonse Allais. In recent years, new technologies have enabled the creation of all sorts of music that is not exactly silent but extremely quiet, including sounds that sit outside the range of human hearing.

The Project

Make a digital piece lasting exactly one minute that consists only of extremely quiet or inaudible sounds. The audible level should never rise above 10 dBPSL. Try to work towards as much silence as possible, without losing atmosphere. However, at no point should there be total silence. The aim is keep the listener's attention with the least possible information. At what point does the listener lose contact with organized sound and connect with environmental sound? Can this be controlled?

Notes

You may wish to explore extremely low or extremely high sounds. These will have an effect without being directly audible. They will also affect any audible sounds that are present. You will also need to consider the listening situation. Headphones may provide the best acoustic isolation, but may detract from any intended interactions with unpredictable environmental sounds.

One way of approaching this composition is to begin by listening to complete silence, then to start to add sounds. Repeated listenings will gradually build an appreciation of what little is heard. However, do be very careful of psychoacoustic fatigue. Intense listening of this type can be very tiring. Take frequent breaks.

FURTHER READING

- Hegarty, P., *Noise Music: A History*, New York: Continuum, 2007.
  Argues that noise is a judgement about sound and that what was once considered noise can become acceptable as music.

- Cage, J., *Silence*, London: Marion Boyars, 1968.
  A seminal text that has influenced an entire generation of experimental musicians.

RECOMMENDED LISTENING

▶ Bernhard Günther (1993) *Un Peu de Neige Salie* [CD] Trente Oiseaux, TOCSE01.
  Haiku-influenced work that can be very intricate while, at the same time, extremely minimal.

▶ Merzbow (1997) *Merzbox Sampler* [CD] Extreme, XLTD 003.
  A survey that includes some earlier electronic tracks from the best-known Japanese noise musician.

▶ Merzbow (2004) *Merzbird* [CD] Important Records, imprec040.
  Entirely digital and populated with some more beat-based material alongside the usual harsh noise.

▶ Steve Roden (2000) *Four Possible Landscapes* [CD] Trente Oiseaux, TOC 00.
  Extremely quiet at times, but never completely inaudible, and populated with very delicate melodies, clicks and textures.

▶ Various (2002) *lowercase sound 2002* [CD] Bremsstrahlung Records.
  A two-disc set comprising field recordings and digital compositions including Francisco Lopez's almost silent 'Untitled #118'.

TIMBRE

Timbre has always been an important feature in music, but especially so during the twentieth century, when composers began to create pieces that focused almost exclusively on its expressive potential, sometimes at the expense of melody, harmony and rhythm. Electronic music may even be said to consist entirely of timbres, since melodic, rhythmic and harmonic content are all treated in exactly the same way, as sound material.

However, timbre is multi-dimensional and has no single definition. It may be summarized as the characteristics that allow us to distinguish one sound from another. In other words, its various dimensions add up to the perceived quality of a sound. One dimension of timbre is based on the observation that the physical properties of a sound-producing body give rise to 'formants', which help to shape the sound's spectrum. Formants are concentrations of acoustic energy or spectral strength within a particular invariant frequency range.

Timbre is shaped by the *envelope* of a sound. The envelope is commonly described as having three stages:

- *attack* (initial or starting transient) – the result of the means by which the sound was initiated
- *body* (continuant) – how and whether the sound is sustained
- *decay* – the result of the damping in the system after any energy input has ceased.

Any sound has an overall envelope, and each and every partial tone also has its own envelope. Where pitch predominates, the timbre of a sound may be varied as long as the pitch remains the same. Thus, a musically expressive 'note' may contain all sorts of variations in timbre and even some slight variations in pitch (such as vibrato), provided the fundamental pitch remains audible and dominant. However, if timbre replaces pitch as the dominant characteristic of a sound, such variations become less important.

However, the timbre of a sound usually changes over time. A complex sound, containing many competing partials (a bell, for example) is difficult to summarize, to hear accurately and to describe. How much easier it is to say 'that's an A on a piano' than 'that's a complex spectrum of shifting tones in which the fundamental appears to be around 440 Hz, but the sixth partial seems particularly strong after 10 milliseconds'. The difficulty of the challenge must not be allowed to deflect the digital musician, for whom an ability to hear spectral detail is essential.

The question posed earlier ('Is it necessary to be able to recognize a dominant seventh chord?') now comes to the fore. It *is* necessary to be able to recognize the seventh harmonic in the series, which gives an interval that is nearly (but not quite) a minor seventh above the octave above the fundamental. What's more, the intervening harmonics describe a kind of dominant seventh chord. Therefore, it is necessary to be able to recognize the characteristic sound of the seventh, because this is present in most sounds to some degree. The dominant seventh chord, on the other hand, has a functional value in a harmonic system, which may not always be relevant to the musical endeavour. There are still further complexities here. The individual envelope of each partial (or harmonic) in a periodic pitched sound may be analysed separately and, once again, there are changes over time. The inharmonic spectrum of aperiodic sounds contains unstable components. All this makes up timbre.

This is a discussion to which we shall return in subsequent chapters, as we tackle topics such as sound processing and transformation, composition and spectromorphology. For the purposes of the present section, it will suffice to observe that timbre is the very stuff of digital music and that an ability to explore its constantly changing detail is an essential skill. However, it is a rather imprecise term that has probably outlived its usefulness. Digital technologies permit one to 'enter' the sound in ways that were simply not possible before, and to manipulate both the harmonic and the inharmonic content of the spectrum. All sounds exhibit timbral characteristics that may be analysed and represented by the computer.

RECOMMENDED LISTENING

▶ Bernard Parmegiani (2000) *De Natura Sonorum* INA-GRM, INAC3001.
   Only one piece of recommended listening to conclude this chapter, but it is a monumental one. This is a twelve-movement composition that explores the nature of sound materials in comprehensive depth.

FURTHER READING

■ Smalley, D., 'Defining Timbre, Refining Timbre', *Contemporary Music Review*, 10:2, 1994, 35–48.

Project 11 (Intermediate): Timbral Study

Introduction

The use of computers to analyse sounds spectrally has great musical potential, because music is all about repetition and variation. The creative potential of spectral analysis resides in an understanding of how sound behaves through time.

The Project

This project begins with finding some objects that have interesting sonic properties. These could be natural objects, or pieces of junk, or indeed musical instruments.

   The first step is to try to describe each sound. Is it periodic or aperiodic? What are its timbral characteristics? How does the sound change over time? Try to make a diagram of the envelope of the sound. How does it begin and end?

   Now listen closely and try to deduce spectral information. Are the harmonics true, or partial? Or a combination of these? Is there variation over time in the harmonics, or do they seem stable? Can individual harmonics be identified and do any take precedence during the sound?

PROJECT 11

Finally, make a recording of the sound. Try cutting off the attack – is it still recognizable? Now consider the complete sound: look at the waveform and then at a spectrogram. To what extent does this confirm the impression gained by your ears? Are there any obvious differences?

Apply this process to a number of 'sonic objects' and compare the differences and similarities between them. Can you classify the results or divide the sounds into meaningful groupings?

Notes

This can be a useful substitute for stage 1 of Project 32 … *From Scratch*, if that is being undertaken.

Discussion Questions

• How do you make sense of music? What are the key elements that combine to give it meaning?

• Given that digital music has no score, what is the role of acoustic perception in enjoyment and understanding? What is the relationship between the digital elements and the physical sensation of sound?

• Is it possible to separate pitch from duration, or frequency from time? What are the implications for music, whichever way you answer the first question?

• What are the effects of noise in the world today? Is there too much music? Why make music when there is so much of it about?

CHAPTER 4

Listening to Music

The overall aim of this chapter is to help the musician prepare to listen effectively to the vast and varied range of work that falls under the broad heading of 'digital' or 'electro-acoustic' (or even 'electronic') music. Listening here refers to the act of both listening as an audience member and partcipatory listening as a musician.

This is a lifetime's activity, of course, and each individual will develop their own strategies and preferences. Nevertheless, there are certain common features that are important in all situations, beginning with preparing one's own ears (and observing some basic safety procedures in doing so) and becoming aware of certain phenomena which affect both listening and digital creativity, before plunging into the highly diverse and extensive body of repertoire that distinguishes this form of music. Developing active and critical listening skills are essential, and this chapter attempts to show how that might be done, leading to some specific exercises using a selected work, Jean-Claude Risset's *Sud*, which contains a fascinating interplay between natural and synthetic sounds.

The chapter should be read in conjunction with the Historical Listening List provided in the Appendix, for which a playlist is provided on the book's accompanying website. This amounts to a preliminary repertoire list for digital music, which is not to say that all the music it contains was made using computers, but rather that it describes the evolution of the aesthetics and techniques that have informed digital music-making.

THE MUSICIAN'S EAR

Consideration of the musician's ear should begin with an important health and safety warning. Given the delicacy and complexity of the human auditory system, and the importance of a 'good ear' to a musician, it pays to be aware of the potential risks to hearing. The main danger is excessively loud (or intense) sound. Digital musicians generally work with some kind of amplification and often explore unusual properties of sound, sometimes at extreme levels. Prolonged exposure to loud sounds can have the effect of flattening out the delicate cilia in the organ of Corti. The consequences of this are a generalized hearing loss and, more damaging still for a musician, a loss of hearing *acuity*, which is the ability to distinguish different frequency bands. A third possible consequence is *tinnitus*, a disturbing and still insufficiently understood condition in which the cochlea generates noise. People often notice a ringing in the ears after a loud concert: this is tinnitus. For most young people, it will disappear after a time, but prolonged and repeated exposure to the source may lead to it becoming permanent.

A healthy young person can hear an average frequency range of between 20 Hertz (Hz) and 20 kHz. It is a fact of life that this range starts to diminish from the teenage years onwards. A typical 60-year-old may well have lost 12 kHz of hearing from the upper register. This is natural and to be expected, but prolonged exposure to loud sounds could accelerate the process, and hearing might be severely damaged without adequate protection. What constitutes a 'loud sound' is somewhat subjective and will vary from person to person and from situation to situation. When it senses loudness, however, the ear will attempt to protect itself against pain by using an acoustic reflex, which is an involuntary muscle contraction in the middle ear. This decreases the amount of vibration transmitted to the brain and can be felt quite clearly when a sudden loud or intense sound is heard. One unfortunate consequence for musicians is that they will often *increase* loudness levels in order to compensate and 'hear the sound better'.

Where the musician is in control of the sound levels (headphones, speakers, playing an instrument, and so on), then it is a good idea to be aware of the acoustic reflex. It is advisable to turn the volume level *down*, rather than up, in order to hear things more clearly. This might seem odd, but the result is that the acoustic reflex is disengaged, allowing closer listening. Where the musician is *not* in control of the levels, the only thing to do is to wear in-ear protection. Good quality earplugs will have a 'flat' attenuation, which will only reduce the overall level, without affecting the sound balance. These should be a standard item of personal equipment for digital musicians who are looking, above all, to control the sound they make.

These remarks should not, however, be allowed to prevent experimentation and exploration of the limits of sonic experience. With proper and appropriate safety measures and due consideration, some very extreme aspects of hearing can be creatively exploited. To give two examples, both *ultrasound* and *infrasound* have been used in musical situations. Ultrasound refers to sounds above the upper limit of normal human hearing and is used a great deal in medical sonography to produce images of foetuses in the womb, for example. Infrasound is the opposite, consisting of sounds below the normal range of human hearing.

In 2003, a team of researchers led by Sarah Angliss of the *Soundless Music* project, and the pianist GéNIA, performed a concert at the Purcell Room, London, in which two pieces were 'laced' with infrasound (below 20 Hz). Audience questionnaires revealed a change in the musical experience when the infrasound was added. Up to 62 per cent of the audience reported having 'unusual experiences' and altered emotional states. The results were not completely conclusive, but there were strong indications that an unheard phenomenon could produce a different musical experience.[1] Ultrasound and, to a lesser extent, infrasound, have also been used in music-therapy treatments, with some success.

AURAL PHENOMENA

The musician will also need to be aware of a range of aural phenomena with musical applications. Take, for example, the phenomenon of *beats*, which has long been used to tune musical instruments. When two pitched notes are sounded together, a periodic and repeated fluctuation is heard in the intensity of the sound, resulting from interference between the two sound waves. Eliminating these beats will enable a piano tuner to tune a note to a unison. String players use a similar phenomenon to tune their strings to the interval of a fifth, where there is a clear mathematical relationship between the frequencies in the sound. Some composers have used this beating as the basis for their music, but mostly it is just a useful device for preparing to play. The digital musician has access to many new sonic phenomena and aural illusions that can provide the basis for musical explorations. Some of these are embedded in software or take the form of plug-ins to modify the sound or create effects. Well-known examples, such as the *Doppler* effect[2] or *difference tone*,[3] can be used to add acoustic interest and excitement to a piece of digital music.

Aural phenomena normally exploit the natural tendency of the ear–brain connection to try to make sense of what it hears. This can give rise to convincing illusions based on patterns in which the listener fills in the gaps that apparently exist. The aural illusion of 'phantom words', for example, derives from the spatial locations of a collection of meaningless spoken fragments. After a while, listeners will naturally piece them together to hear words and phrases, in their own languages, that are not actually there. These illusions have been quite thoroughly researched,[4] and, interestingly, the results have tended to show that the ways the two hemispheres of the brain interact are a factor in their perception. The idea that the left brain is logical, sequential, rational, analytical and objective and understands parts of things, whereas the right brain is random, intuitive, holistic, synthesizing and subjective and understands wholes has been challenged by recent neuroscience. It seems that the relationships between the two halves of the brain are more complex than that, with both having a part to play in the formation of perceptions and understandings. Nevertheless, individuals do tend to favour one side or another, and the way in which certain patterns are perceived can therefore depend upon which side of the brain dominates or whether the individual is left- or right-handed, or even what language they speak.

One aural illusion which may be regarded as a curiosity, but nevertheless a revealing one, is called the *Shepard tone* or *Shepard scale*, after the man who discovered it in 1964. This is one of those phenomena that are much harder to explain than to understand aurally. What is heard is a musical tone or scale that appears to continuously ascend or descend without ever actually getting higher or lower. The effect is achieved by superimposing tones with carefully controlled loudness levels to give the impression of continuous motion within an octave.

To summarize: the digital musician's ear, like that of any musician, is a key attribute and needs nurturing and care. The kinds of aural phenomena and illusions that are familiar to most musicians are also important to the digital musician. Digital sound manipulation techniques, however, have opened up some new and potentially creative possibilities in this area, and the ear needs to develop in order to exploit those. In digital music, the ear has primacy and the subjective ability to be able to hear accurately and with awareness is crucial.

FURTHER READING

■ Risset, J.-C., 'Paradoxical Sounds', in Mathews, M. V. and Pierce, J. R., *Current Directions in Computer Music Research*, Cambridge, MA: MIT Press, 1989.

RECOMMENDED LISTENING

▶ Diana Deutsch (2003) *Phantom Words and Other Curiosities* Philomel Records.
   An exploration of aural illusions and sound perception, including 'phantom words' that the brain generates from a collection of meaningless sounds.

▶ Missy Elliott (2005) *Lose Control* Atlantic Records, 7567–93765–2.
   Hip-hop track featuring an ascending Shepard scale throughout.

▶ Christian Smith and John Selway (2008) *Total Departure* Drumcode Records, DC41.
   A techno track that exploits an ascending Risset tone. The continuous glissando was developed by the composer Jean-Claude Risset.

▶ James Tenney (1969) *For Ann (rising)* Artifact Records, 1007.
   An early digital composition created from a set of rising glissandi similar to Shepard tones by a pioneer who worked with Risset. Philip Corner commented: 'It must be optimistic! (Imagine the depressing effectiveness of it – he could never be so cruel –downward.)'

ACTIVE LISTENING

For the *musician*, as opposed to the general listener, listening to music is a special activity characterized by an interest not just in the superficial effects of the music but also in certain factors of relatively little importance to the non–musician, such as: Why was it made? How is it constructed? What does it resemble? Where does it come from? How much can I learn from it? and What does it mean? In his book *When Music Resists Meaning*, Herbert Brün argues passionately for the possibility of a genius listener. He sees the experience of music being created mutually by the composer (who causes the music) and the listener (who causes the effect of the music). He says:

> There are three kinds of music for three kinds of listener.
>
> 1   First the music which reorganizes already established music elements into new patterns. This is music for the listener who enjoys the status quo, to be looked at from different angles.
> 2   Second there is the music which enlivens old patterns with new musical elements. This is music for the connoisseurs, the listeners who enjoy looking at themselves from different angles.

3   And last, but not least, there is the music in which new musical elements create their new patterns. This is music for listeners who are still conscious of the fact that, after all, they had once created the need for music in their minds, and who now are happy and gratified if this need is met, in that at last they can hear what they never had heard before.[5]

Perhaps a less complicated way of saying the same thing is that there is a difference between the *active* and the *passive* listener. The active listener is curious and engages fully with the experience of the music by *seeking to understand*. Passive listeners are content merely to hear and pass on (possibly making a simple judgement about the quality of the experience as they do so). For the digital musician, active listening is essential. This is a hard lesson, because it might involve listening to things that are disliked. Why would anyone want to listen to something they do not like? Because this is part of the process of understanding that develops the individual's aural awareness. It may even lead to a reappraisal, a new appreciation, of the disliked music. At least, it will encourage an objective, impartial approach to the business of making judgements. This is not easily taught and is something for which the individual musician must take responsibility.

Active listening can take place when attending a concert or listening to a recording, but it is also a feature of both musical performance and musical creation. In the performance situation, responsiveness to other musicians is dependent upon active listening. This is especially true during improvisation, which is why that is such a useful practice for the digital musician. The ability to both hear accurately and understand the musical activities of others is essential to making your own contribution effective and relevant. In the creative or compositional situation, the technology allows the musician to listen and relisten time and again to the same material, which presents a uniquely active opportunity. Here, the aural awareness becomes highly focused until an extreme discrimination may be reached. This can lead to obsessive listening and often the key is to know when to *cease* listening and move on.

It might be argued that, since most recordings today are digital, listening to anything other than live music is an inherently digital experience. Even in live situations, the musical experience may well be digitally mediated, and the act of listening may involve more than simply hearing and appreciating the music, especially when some form of interactivity is involved. Nevertheless, the listening behaviours of digital musicians will be rather similar to their counterparts, albeit drawing on a somewhat different body of repertoire and responding to certain unique features that characterize this kind of music.

One early debate that almost inevitably arises when confronted with music that does not conform to the familiar note-based patterns and structures may be summarized by the question: *what is music?* This discussion on the whole generates more heat than light, but is probably necessary to have just the same. The standard definition of music, and the one that is accepted in this book, is Varèse's 'organized sound'. A definition exists to be applied as far as possible in a universal way in all situations. Notice that 'organized sound' makes no judgement about quality. Listening to digital music will almost certainly involve encountering and accepting sounds that are not recognizable as 'music' in the conventional sense. It is therefore fundamental that digital musicians be able and willing to extend their listening habits beyond the familiar. The challenge is first to be open to new musical experiences, and second to develop an ability to discriminate and so make considered judgements about the quality of those experiences.

FURTHER READING

■   Brün, H., *When Music Resists Meaning*, Middletown, CT: Wesleyan University Press, 2004.
Brün was a pioneer in the development of computer music, with a particular interest in the social functions of composer and listener, communication, originality and the human implications of various compositional processes.

CRITICAL LISTENING

The scientist David Bohm once wrote:

> The expression of the new quantum concepts is beset with severe difficulties, because much of our customary language and thinking is predicated on the tacit assumption that classical concepts are substantially correct.[6]

This is also true in digital music, where the use of a traditional critical method is inappropriate to the subject and yet often there is no clear substitute. To avoid making the mistake Bohm identifies, it is necessary to start first with the sounds themselves. Digital music is very often built from the smallest element upwards, rather than from the larger structure down. In other words, artists will tend to work directly with sonic materials when building a musical composition, rather than sitting down to create, say, a symphony.

So, critical listening begins with an ability to listen accurately and well to sounds themselves. In digital music, this is not so easy as might be imagined. Sounds are generally subject to manipulations and processes which may be more or less complex but which will always introduce a level of abstraction into the listening experience. In other words, it may not be obvious what the sounds *are* or where they have come from. Now, the musician is faced with having to discriminate qualitatively between sounds of uncertain origin. Determining an appropriate critical response to such sounds can be very difficult indeed. Musicians must use their understanding and perception of the context and intention of the work, as well as their innate sense of musicality. This is critical listening. Forming judgements is a necessary part of this kind of listening, so it may be observed that the purpose of critical listening is twofold: to increase one's understanding of the technical and creative aspects of the music and to improve one's own musical skills. It is clear, therefore, that developing abilities in this will be immensely beneficial.

Critical listening is also essential to the way in which one understands the cultural aspects of music. It is almost a cliché of cultural studies that, for example, a division exists between 'popular' music and 'art' music. It is a central argument of this book that (at last!) this distinction is being eroded in digital culture. Whereas, in the past, a 'highbrow' musician was usually 'classically trained' and a 'lowbrow' musician was not, the new technologies are enabling the emergence of a new kind of musician, whose work resists easy classification in either sector and who may move comfortably into a range of situations. These new musicians have greatly increased access to techniques and equipment that were previously only available to a few. Excellent results can be achieved with readily available hardware and software, and many of the obstacles to making good music are effectively being removed. To be sure, the need to practice, to develop, to evolve as a musician is as important now as it has ever been, but the easy classification of musicians into those with a 'proper' technique and those without is being exposed as too simplistic.

There are historical reasons for this. At one time, it was commonplace to assume that art music blazed an experimental trail which popular music then exploited. In many instances that was true, but the reverse also occurred. Today, there is simultaneity of discovery, such that it is really impossible to claim the lead for either side of the supposed divide. In fact, digital musicians will be able to exploit their work commercially as well as making ground-breaking musical discoveries. The distinctions that prevailed in the analogue world at this point are no longer so relevant. A digital soundfile is fundamentally data and might just as well be a recorded sound as an electronically generated sound.

The emergence of the new technologies has filled a gap between 'art' and 'popular' musics. By placing the full range of audio-processing techniques in the hands of a mass market for a relatively low price, the digital revolution has rendered all kinds of musical activities equivalent. Now the only thing that determines whether a particular technique is used is the limits of the musician's imagination or technical abilities. This began to emerge when The Beatles enthusiastically embraced *musique concrète* techniques in the recording studio or when minimalism swept all before it in the art houses of the 1970s and 1980s, with its motoric beats and harmonic simplicity.

In Indonesia now, a new genre called 'brutal ethnic' combines traditional Javanese melodies and rhythms with Indian film musics and death metal. In Nepal, studio artists deliberately juxtapose music from different traditions and cultures in complex mixes that might include various types of Asian folk and film music alongside reggae and rap, classical and disco. Australian studio engineers use 'secret' techniques to enhance *dijeridu* recordings, the technical challenge being to conceal the 'artificial' element to the point at which the listeners believe they are hearing a purely 'natural' *dijeridu* sound. In their different ways, each of these represents an example of the way in which 'popular' and 'art' practices have become blurred through the creative use of digital technology.

Finally, critical listening is the decisive factor in the construction of history. This is not a history book, nor is there enough space to recount the whole of the history of electronic and digital musical evolutions in the past century. On the other hand, our critical listening is greatly improved by an understanding of at least some key points of those evolutions. Given their importance, it is surprising that they have not been documented more thoroughly, and in many cases they seem to have been seen more as marginal notes in the history of notated instrumental music. This is partly due to the nature of the medium. The removal of notation makes them less well suited to academic study and, furthermore, the music itself tends to resist classification. Also, it has proved surprisingly difficult to preserve some of this music. The physical medium (usually tape) deteriorates quite rapidly, and even digital formats become unreadable quite quickly.

Another problem is that the history of the musical evolutions is so closely linked to the history of developments in technology. This means that historical accounts often read like a catalogue of technological innovation, with the artists apparently running along behind, forever trying to keep up with what the engineers have developed. It is certainly true that the present culture would not exist were it not for developments in technology, but musical innovations are more important to the musician. Critical listening, therefore, has to hear beyond the technology itself and into what is being expressed musically. Once again, this can be challenging when the novelty of this is that technique or piece of equipment is such a prominent feature of a work.

RECOMMENDED LISTENING

The following recommendations are all examples of digital music that seem to have their roots either on the 'popular' or the 'art' side of the fence, but which show clear evidence of a convergence and cross-fertilization, to the point that the distinction itself starts to break down.

▶ Aphex Twin (1994) *Selected Ambient Works Vol. 2* [CD] Warp 21.
Richard James, aka Aphex Twin, is a DJ and electronica artist, although this album is at times difficult to connect with that world.

▶ Autechre (1994) *Amber* [CD] Warp 211.
Rob Brown and Sean Booth (Autechre) are UK artists whose roots lie in techno and hip-hop, but whose work has steadily moved into more experimental areas. This was their second album and already shows signs of the journey they were to undertake.

▶ The Chemical Brothers (1999) *Surrender* [CD] Virgin Records, XDUSTCD4.
Clearly club music, but the attention to detail and intricate handling of digital sound seems to root this music elsewhere.

▶ DJ Spooky (1996) *Songs of a Dead Dreamer* [CD] Asphodel, ASP0961.
A New York DJ producing music that sounds quite unlike dance music, connecting with dub reggae and ambient music.

▶ Frank Zappa (1986) *Jazz from Hell* [CD] Rykodisc, RCD 10549.
Almost entirely created on the synclavier, and the only all-instrumental album ever to have a 'parental advisory' warning attached!

FURTHER READING

■ Greene, P. and Porcello, T. (eds), *Wired for Sound: Engineering and Technologies in Sonic Cultures*, Middletown, CT: Wesleyan University Press, 2005.
A thorough discussion of how sound engineering techniques have influenced all aspects of culture.

■ Middleton, R., *Studying Popular Music*, Philadelphia, PA: Open University Press, 1990.

Contends that popular music can be properly understood only through interdisciplinary study methods. He demonstrates this through a critical analysis of issues
from the political economy of popular music, its history and ethnography, to its
aesthetics and ideology.

- Jones, A., *Plunderphonics, 'Pataphysics and Pop Mechanics: An Introduction to
  Musique Actuelle*, Wembley, Alberta: SAF Publishing, 1995.
  Surveys the fringes of popular music, from left-wing movements to left-field experi-
  mentalists, including some involved in digital music.

LISTENING TO ELECTRO-ACOUSTIC MUSIC

The project that follows is designed to encourage and develop critical listening skills for
electro-acoustic music. It draws upon three recent pieces of research. The first appeared
as part of a series of composer portraits created by the Groupe de Recherches Musicales
in Paris, entitled *Portraits Polychromes*. Leigh Landy recounts that Jean-François Lagrost:

> invited thirteen participants aged 15 to 60, all involved in some way with music, to
> listen to the first of the three movements of [Jean-Claude Risset's] *Sud* twice, once
> just listening and the second time writing, making annotations. After each listening,
> the individuals discussed their experiences with the author. These interviews were
> recorded. The participants were asked to pay particular attention to the following
> four categories: materials, space, light, and evolution.[7]

The second piece of research was conducted during 2002–2006 by Landy himself, along
with Robert Weale, and involved many participants from a range of musical and non-
musical backgrounds. This was called the *Intention/Reception Project*. Landy explained:

> Through repeated listening and the introduction of the composers' articulation of
> intent (through a work's title, inspiration, elements that the composer intends to
> be communicated, eventually elements of the compositional process itself) listen-
> ing responses are monitored. The purpose of the project is to investigate to what
> extent familiarity contributes to *accessibility* and *appreciation* and to what extent
> *intention* and *reception meet* in the very particular corpus of electro-acoustic
> music.[8]

The third piece of research is an analysis of *Sud* by Giselle Ferreira that was first published
in 1997.[9] This suggests that 'meaning is a multi-layered construct that relates musical
and worldly experiences. From this perspective, *Sud* may be perceived as an encounter
between human imagination and nature in two of its most powerful symbols: the sea, …
and the forest.' The analysis therefore uses a perceptual approach rather than traditional
means such as pitch, timbre or durational information. As Ferreira remarked: 'When any
sound is potentially musical, the actual musical value of a sound is redefined within each
composition, and its identity is constantly reinvented.'

Project 12 (Elementary): *Sud*

Introduction

This critical listening project is probably best conducted in a single session divided into two parts, with a clear break between the two. It also requires some careful execution, since it is important that the information about the piece given in the second step below is not read until *after* the first listening. This piece will also form the basis of a more extended analysis project in a later chapter, so although the project is graded 'Elementary', it may be taken as preparation for a much more substantial piece of work to be undertaken on another occasion.

The Project

Step 1. *Important: do NOT read the contents of Step 2 until AFTER Step 1 has been completed.*

    Listen to the first section or movement of Jean-Claude Risset's *Sud* (1985). Having listened to the piece, discuss it with other listeners (if no other listeners are available, then record your thoughts). In particular, examine the relationships between the various elements in the work. Pay particular attention to *motion* and to *spatial imagery*. How does the work cohere, indeed *does* it cohere? Is there a structure? What are the musical materials? What are the main contrasts in the piece? What musical purpose do they serve? How do sounds transform? What is the character of the music? What does it all mean? How may you judge its effectiveness?

Step 2. Read the following programme notes by Risset, then listen to the work again and engage in a similar discussion. Has anything changed this time? Has your appreciation altered? Does the composer's stated intention come across? Is there more to this than meets the ear? Try to go beyond Risset's description towards a more critical analysis. Is that possible, and how does it help?

> *Sud* (South) … uses mainly sounds recorded in the Massif des Calanques (a rugged region of France) and also sounds that were digitally synthesized in Marseille. These sounds were processed by computer at the GRM, using programs developed by Benedict Mailliard and Yann Geslin. From the start, and throughout, the piece takes the form of 'phonography' – but the sounds are generally altered by digital processes. Thus the dynamic profile of the waves, which open the piece, permeates all the movements. The piece is built from a small number of 'germinal' sounds: recordings of the sea, insects, birds, wooden and metal chimes, of brief 'gestures' played on the piano or synthesized in the computer. I proliferated this material by using various transformations: modulation, filtering, colouration, Spatialization, mixing, hybridizing. Cézanne wanted 'to unite curves of women with the shoulders of hills'. Similarly, hybrid synthesis allowed me to work 'in the very bone of nature' (Henri Michaux), to produce chimeras, hybrids merging birds and metal, or wood and sea sounds. I used this procedure mainly to transpose profiles and flows of energy. The pulse of recorded sea sounds is thus imprinted on certain other sounds, whereas at other times sounds reminding of breaking waves are unrelated to the sea.

A pitch scale (G–B–E–F sharp–G sharp), first presented with synthetic sounds, is later used to colour various sounds of natural origin. In the last section the scale becomes a genuine harmonic grid which resonates like an aeolian harp to birds and waves sounds. The manifold sounds produced by computer can be located on a diagram resembling a family tree: their layout in time brings several rhythmic levels into play and implies what might be called a logic of fluxes.

'Sud' comprises three sections. The programme for the first is as follows:

1. (9'45') The sea in the morning. The opening profile permeates the entire piece. Waking birds, from isolated peeps rising to a stretto.Harmonic clouds. Hybrid sounds emerge from the low frequencies.Heat. Luminy, at the foot of Mount Puget real and imagined insects and birds.

FURTHER READING

■ Landy, L., *Understanding the Art of Sound Organization*, Cambridge, MA: The MIT Press, 2007.
Sets out to create a theoretical framework for the subject, defining terms and categorizing works, but also seeking to make the music more accessible to the listener.

Discussion Questions

- Is the distinction between popular and art music still relevant today?

- Choose any one of the works on the Historical Listening List and discuss its aesthetic intentions versus its actual result. How do you judge its success?

- Is there a difference between active and critical listening? If so, what is that difference?

- How might you become a genius listener?

PART II

Creating

Organizing Sound

> *The raw material of music is sound. That is what the 'reverent approach' has made people forget – even composers. … As far back as the twenties, I decided to call my music 'organized sound' and myself, not a musician, but 'a worker in rhythms, frequencies, and intensities'. Indeed, to stubbornly conditioned ears, anything new in music has always been called noise. But after all what is music but organized noises? And a composer, like all artists, is an organizer of disparate elements.*
> —(Edgard Varèse, *The Liberation of Sound* (1936))

The digital musician is one who takes Varèse's visionary statement as axiomatic. Indeed, he or she may decide to agree with Varèse completely and refuse the label 'musician', preferring 'sound artist', 'sonic artist' or even 'sound designer'.

SOUND-ART, SONIC ART AND SOUND DESIGN

'Sound–art' and 'sonic art' have much in common, but there are also some cultural and artistic differences between them. 'Sound–art' flourishes in many countries, and especially

Germany, where it goes under the name of 'Klangkunst', which literally means 'noise art'. However, this word is more often translated as 'sound-art' and occasionally 'sonic art', which conveys the difficulty of giving a single clear definition of the term.[1] Sound-art is understood to emerge from a visual tradition in which sound is, unusually, the leading element of a work. This includes installations, mixed media works and even some types of radio art. Sound-art sometimes involves recontextualization, which means taking something out of its familiar context and presenting it anew as an object of aesthetic contemplation.[2] A typical example of sound-art is Jem Finer's work Longplayer, installed in 2001 in Trinity Buoy Wharf Lighthouse in London's Docklands and made from recordings of Tibetan prayer bowls, looped and stretched by a computer for over 1,000 years' worth of combinations. Finer is also a banjo player with the rock band The Pogues. He commented in an interview:

> I think [Longplayer] is definitely music, and if there's such a thing as sound art then it's certainly sound art as well. Sound is the consequence of an idea, and maybe that's sound art; and if you take that sound and make something else of it then maybe that's music.[3]

The phrase 'sonic art' seems to have come more from the tradition of electro-acoustic music that stretches back to the early days of music made using electronic technologies. At a recent meeting of the UK Sonic Arts Network, it was agreed that the phrase 'sonic art' has no single definition and is really an umbrella term which covers anything made with sound, including conventional music. The most celebrated account of sonic art appears in Trevor Wishart's book On Sonic Art (1996), and some of Wishart's own compositions, in particular the Vox cycle, may be regarded as classic sonic art works. These often explore sound-morphing techniques, such as the '(super)human voice' used in Vox 5 (1986), which transforms into various sounds, including bees and crowds.

'Sound design' has a less 'art-house' association. Sound designers work in film, television, theatre, new media and even museums and theme parks. The term probably originates in the tradition of separating the 'music' track from the 'sound' track in movies (although the most interesting film directors often blur that distinction). One of the most successful sound designers has been Walter Murch, who won one of his three Oscars for the sound-mixing on the film Apocalypse Now (1979, directed by Francis Ford Coppola). In an essay, Murch distinguishes between what he calls 'encoded' and 'embodied' sound in sound design:

> The clearest example of encoded sound is speech. The clearest example of embodied sound is music. ...
>
> What lies between these outer limits? Just as every audible sound falls somewhere between the lower and upper limits of 20 and 20,000 cycles, so all sounds will be found somewhere on this conceptual spectrum from speech to music.
>
> Most sound effects, for instance, fall mid-way: like 'sound-centaurs', they are half language, half music. Since a sound effect usually refers to something specific – the steam engine of a train, the knocking at a door, the chirping of birds, the firing of a gun – it is not as 'pure' a sound as music. But on the other hand, the

language of sound effects, if I may call it that, is more universally and immediately understood than any spoken language.[4]

These artists have much in common, despite the differences in their creative intentions and in the labels that are attached to them. They share a deep understanding of sound and how it behaves. The way in which they organize these behaviours is musical.

FURTHER READING

■ Gibbs, T., *The Fundamentals of Sonic Art and Sound Design*, Lausanne: AVA Publishing, 2007.
   Defines the terms and examines the history and practice of sonic art and sound design.

■ Kenny, T., *Sound for Picture: The Art of Sound Design in Film and Television*, Vallejo, CA: Mix Books, 2000.
   A practical, how-to book, about creating soundtracks for movies.

■ Ondaatje, M., *The Conversations: Walter Murch and the Art of Editing Film*, New York: Knopf, 2002.
   A series of discussions about film editing techniques and aesthetics that has relevance to sound design.

■ Sonnenshchein, D., *Sound Design: The Expressive Power of Music, Voice, and Sound Effects in Cinema*, Studio City, CA: Michael Wiese Productions, 2001.
   Another practical book, underpinned by theoretical discussion of psychoacoustics, music theory and voice study.

■ Wishart, T., *Audible Design*, York: Orpheus the Pantomime, 1994.
   A companion work to *On Sonic Art*, more focused on the practical aspects of sonic art and sound design.

■ Wishart, T., *On Sonic Art*, Amsterdam: Harwood Academic Publishers, 1996.
   A classic work about sonic art, looking at the philosophy and aesthetic aspects of the subject.

RECOMMENDED LISTENING

▶ Trevor Wishart (1986) 'Vox 5' on *The Vox Cycle* [CD] Electronic Music Foundation. Also on DVD: *Metafonie: Cinquanta anni di musica elettroacustica* (DVD01-AV001) from LIMEN classic and contemporary, Milan.

▶ Trevor Wishart (1993–4) *Tongues of Fire* [CD] Golden Nica, Ars Electronica.

Project 13 (Intermediate): Hearing Hearing

Introduction

John Cage wrote: 'one way to study music: study Duchamp'. In many ways, Marcel Duchamp (1887–1968) set the scene for 'sound art'. There are numerous references to the sonic properties of objects in his work, such as *With Hidden Noise* (1916), a ball of string compressed between two metal plates and concealing a mysterious object, which rattles when shaken. There are even some musical compositions, including an early experiment with chance entitled *Erratum Musical* (1913). However, the most useful aspects of Duchamp for the digital musician are his ideas and concepts. In his *Green Box* (published in 1934), for example, he observed: 'one can look at seeing; one cannot hear hearing'.

The Project

Meditate upon Marcel Duchamp's statement 'one can look at seeing; one cannot hear hearing'. Create a technology-based system that hears itself.

Notes

At its simplest, this project suggests some kind of feedback loop. Think about the flow of acoustical information into and through the system. This could be modelled upon the ear–brain relationship. It might take place entirely within a computer, or it might involve external devices. What is actually heard as a result of the process? Can heard hearing be represented? And what is the relationship between music and hearing?

SOUND IN SPACE

In practice, sound is always heard in some kind of space and is subject to various environmental conditions. The reality is that sound, like any other form of energy, decays and degenerates, a process which is hastened or affected by its surroundings. In an ideal world containing no friction, no energy would be lost. The potential, or stored, energy plus the kinetic, or motion, energy would be equal to the total energy input. However, the real world contains friction, and, consequently, energy is lost. The radiation of the sound, too, loses energy.

The creative possibilities opened up by the behaviour of sound in space are evident in *sound diffusion*, where the source material may be sound produced by an instrument or instruments but also may be stereo or multi-channel recordings. Distance perception and a sense of spaciousness can be crucial to the subjective evaluation of the sound qualities of a given diffusion. To be enveloped by sound is often seen as valuable. Compare, for example, the experience of listening to a stereo system with listening to 'surround sound'. At its best, the surround-sound experience is richer because the sounds come from all directions simultaneously, not just in front of the listener. This resembles our experience of sound in nature, and the quality of naturalness seems to be very important. Surround sound tends to be less convincing when it appears too artificial or unnatural.

This raises an important point about both sound diffusion and, indeed, sound-recording: the human ear is the supreme judge of quality, rather than any objectively measurable, acoustical law. It may seem that a recording studio, for example, is where the most developed *technical* skills are required. A typical recording studio certainly conveys that impression, with its forbidding array of lights, buttons and equipment. But this is an illusion. The most important pieces of equipment in the recording studio are the ears of the people using it, and everything else should serve those. The recording studio is a temple to aural awareness, rather than technical skill. It is no accident that some of the most highly developed ears are those possessed by sound engineers. They are used to listening critically and carefully at all times.

In their book *The Musicians Guide to Acoustics*, Donald Campbell and Clive Greated give the following list of maxims that will serve the sound diffuser well in most spaces:

- Sound level should be adequate in all parts of the room
- Sound should be evenly distributed both in the audience and on stage
- Reverberation should be suitable for the particular application
- First reflections should not be excessively delayed.[5]

To develop the final point: one way in which the spatial location of a sound is understood by the listener is as a result of the phase differences, or timings, between the arrival of a signal at the two ears. (Other ways depend on frequency and amplitude.) The human ear can pinpoint the location of a sound with great accuracy up to a maximum phase difference of 0.65 milliseconds. If first reflections take longer than that to arrive, the localization can become confused. This may be desirable in certain situations, but most of the time it is an unwelcome effect.

INFORMATION: BEHAVIOUR OF SOUND IN SPACE

Sound travels in three dimensions, which is often represented using a wave-front diagram (see Figure 5.1).

Here, the distance between the concentric circles gives the wavelength, and so the more tightly packed the circles, the higher the frequency. A *wave-ray* diagram, on the other hand, has the advantage that it shows the *path* of a single ray, but obviously lacks the detail of the total field (see Figure 5.2).

Parallels can be drawn between the behaviour of sound and the behaviour of light. Sound may be *refracted* (i.e., bent) by an object or by changes in temperature in the medium through which it passes. Diffraction occurs when the sound waves are obstructed or laterally restricted. A good example of lateral restriction is making a sound down a cardboard tube. When the sound waves emerge from the tube, they spread out in all directions. Sound may also be *reflected* from, or *absorbed* into, a surface. This will depend upon the rigidity, porosity and flexibility of the surface in question.

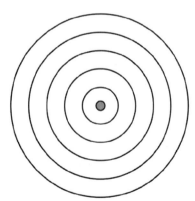

Figure 5.1   Wave-front diagram © Peter Batchelor

INFORMATION

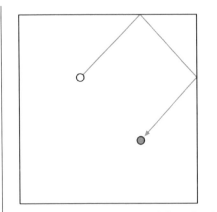

Figure 5.2   Wave-'ray' diagram © Peter Batchelor

The sources of a sound are said to be *correlated* if they deliver the same signal (e.g., two loudspeakers) or if there is a single source but reflections off a wall or other surface mean that more than one signal reaches the ear after a slight delay. *Uncorrelated* sound sources are those that deliver different signals (e.g., several different instruments spread around a room) or where the delay from reflections is so long as to cause an audible difference between signals.

Adding uncorrelated sources together is complicated, because the result does not depend upon the phases of the waves. It is the sound power level (SWL), rather than the sound pressure level (SPL), which is combined, resulting in a much lower increase in apparent loudness. In other words, two uncorrelated sources do not produce double the volume level. This can lead to confusion when using decibels to measure levels and becomes even more complicated and, hence, unpredictable depending on the type of space in which the sound is made.

An *echo* is a long-term reflection of a sound arriving at the ear of the listener a certain time (more than 50 milliseconds) after the sound itself. Echoes usually occur when the reflective surface is rigid, non-absorbent and inflexible. If a surface against which a sound bounces is not flat, then a *diffuse* reflection will have waves bouncing back in different directions. This can be a useful musical effect, and shaped surfaces are sometimes used for focus. Concave shapes, for example, bundle the sound waves together in a predictable way. Such shapes are often found in the construction of churches.

All these characteristics are factors in what is generally called *reverberation*. Studies of reverberation have been instrumental in informing the acoustic design of many halls and spaces. This field of research is in constant development, but there seems to be general agreement that the *early field*, or initial time delay gap (i.e., the time it takes the first reflection to reach the ear of the listener after the arrival of the direct sound) is crucial to the perception of acoustical presence. The arrival of bass sounds will condition the perception of qualities such as 'warmth' and 'strength', and the *reverberant field* creates a perception of immersion in sound. Thus, an initial time-delay gap of between 8 and 25 milliseconds generally produces the best intimacy, or 75–300 milliseconds for the bass or 'warmth' field. As the waves get closer together and weaker, they form the characteristic reverberant *tail* of a sound in a given space. In general, the longer the delay between the arrival of a sound and the reverberant sounds, the more 'distant' the sound seems.

This wave-ray diagram (Figure 5.3) gives an impression of the collection of reflected sounds in a space that go to make up the reverberation. It is clear that factors such as the absorbency or reflection of the walls will affect the reverberation time.

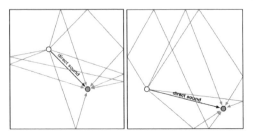

Figure 5.3   Reverberation © Peter Batchelor

Figure 5.4 represents the same information measured against time. The initial direct sound is followed by all the reflected sounds. The early reflected sounds will often be perceived to be more important than the later ones, but the overall reverberation time will nor-mally be the most important

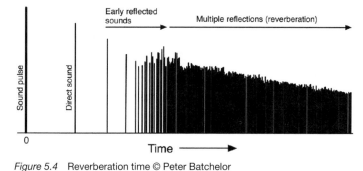

Figure 5.4   Reverberation time © Peter Batchelor

characteristic. Space and time are inextricably linked, and separating them for discussion in this chapter has been done purely for convenience.

The reverberation time of a given space may be calculated using a formula[6] that measures the time taken for the SPL to drop to 60 dB below the level of the original signal. This drop of 60 dB is a somewhat arbitrary figure but works well in many practical situations. The loudest orchestral sound is about 100 dB, whereas the background noise in most auditoriums is about 40 dB.

The musical exploitation of reverberation and the behaviour of sound in space is a characteristic of more or less every live performance and can often be a crucial factor in its success. This is especially important for musicians whose ability to control the sound is central to their existence as artists. Given that digital musicians often perform in spaces which are not conventional concert halls, it is unsurprising that many site-specific works have been created to explore the resonant properties of spaces. One interesting recent example is the *Silophone* (www.silophone.net) by [The User], a Montreal-based project begun in 2000, which:

> makes use of the incredible acoustics of Silo #5 by introducing sounds, collected from around the world using various communication technologies, into a physical space to create an instrument which blurs the boundaries between music, architecture and net art. Sounds arrive inside Silo #5 by telephone or internet. They are then broadcast into the vast concrete grain storage chambers inside the Silo. They are transformed, reverberated, and coloured by the remarkable acoustics of the structure, yielding a stunningly beautiful echo. This sound is captured by microphones and rebroadcast back to its sender, to other listeners and to a sound installation outside the building. Anyone may contribute material of their own, filling the instrument with increasingly varied sounds.

PROJECT 14

Project 14 (Intermediate): Diffraction Installation

Introduction

This project demonstrates diffraction, which also acts as a stimulus for the creative potential of working in a space.

The Project

The aim is to create a controlled installation using only sine tones.

First, set up a sine tone generator feeding a single easily moveable loudspeaker. Place the loudspeaker in front of an obstacle, such as a piece of furniture. Vary the frequency of the tone, and observe how audible it is. Wavelengths longer than the width of the obstacle should diffract better than shorter ones. Confirm this by using the formula wavelength = speed of sound ÷ frequency.

Do the same experiment with a speaker directed at a doorway or other opening, and see what happens to the sound as you move past the doorway.

Now add two or more loudspeakers delivering sine tones into the installation in a similar way. Remember that the objective is to create a controlled environment that demonstrates diffraction. What are the effects of the additional sine tones? How might these be controlled?

Finally, observe what happens when a human presence is introduced into the installation. How does this change the nature of the diffraction? Can this be controlled in some way?

Notes

Although this is mainly a technical experiment, it might also suggest more creative possibilities. Can you go beyond sine tones to create an installation that is highly controlled yet musically meaningful?

FURTHER READING

■ Blesser, B. and Salter, L.-R., *Spaces Speak, Are You Listening?: Exploring Aural Architecture*, Cambridge, MA: MIT Press, 2007.
   Explores the acoustic architecture of many different spaces, from prehistoric caves to classical Greek open-air theaters, from Gothic cathedrals to the acoustic geography of French villages, from modern music reproduction to virtual spaces in home theatres.

■ Newell, P., *Recording Spaces*, Oxford: Focal Press, 2001.
   A technical guide to recording studio design.

■ Barrett, N., 'Spatio-musical composition strategies', *Organized Sound*, 7:3, 2002, 313–323.
   Spatial elements in acousmatic music are inherent to the art form, in composition and in the projection of the music to the listener. But is it possible for spatial elements to be as important carriers of musical structure as the other aspects of sound?

■ Oliveros, P., 'Acoustic and Virtual Space as a Dynamic Element of Music', *Leonardo Music Journal*, 5, 1995, 19–22.
The author provides an overview of her background as a performer and composer interested in acoustics and technology. Her discussion ranges from a description of her practice of 'deep listening' to her work developing the Expanded Instrument System – which allows the performer greater control over acoustic space – to her collaborations with other composers and instrument builders.

NETWORK SPACE

Network space is becoming increasingly active as broadband speeds improve. The nature of the network space is characterized, of course, by physical separation, but also by certain inherent technical issues such as latency (signal delay) and loss (signal error). Interactions between remotely located musicians may often be unstructured or uncoordinated, informed by, rather than reproducing, offline and geographically located practices.

The musicians' conceptions of the nature of the network space in which they are playing may vary widely, in ways that are often expressed metaphorically (the network as a sea, as a void, as nature, etc.). Some network spaces appear to merge the acoustic characteristics of the physical spaces that are connected to them, others emerge from the acoustic properties of the samples or soundfiles that are used within them, and still others are digitally 'clean' spaces populated by synthesized sounds. The possibility also exists to change the user's perception of the space during the musical exchange; in other words, a virtual space may have any or many different acoustic properties. These observations apply just as well in virtual worlds and gaming spaces, which are increasingly being used for creative and performative work.

Pauline Oliveros has worked in tele-musical performance since the early 1990s, and clearly sees value in the capability of network space to bring together remote spaces:

> 'Space is the place' said Sun Ra. I agree. We make space, take space and give space in order to perturb, disturb and reverb. Network space is a newer frontier though we have inhabited it for more than a hundred years on the telephone. Now we have the opportunity to bring spaces from distant locations into public interactivity out of the ear of the listener into the ears of collectives in virtual spaces. We can create and perform in virtual space or in mixed realities. Most important will be the ability to create the sensation and feeling of distant spaces locally and interactively so that inhabiting virtual space will be no different to that real or local space.[7]

Synthia Payne similarly sees network space as a place where an unusual mix of musicians can work together. She describes her use of network space in the *Cyberjammer* project:

> I wanted to create a 'networked arts environment' with all of the functionality of an offline performance and recording studio, i.e. sound system, good acoustics, audience seating, set design, cameras and visual projection. The networked space being an extension or a bridge to connect different spaces around the world and beyond, rather than a place of disorientation. … So I did not intentionally say okay

worn in-ear. One consequence of this is that the sound is best heard through head-phones, although in recent years convincing 'spatial equalization' between loudspeakers in binaural systems has been achieved. Binaural stereo can give an excellent sense of 3D, and is particularly useful in virtual-reality simulations and computer games, where the listener has an isolated acoustic experience. Algorithms for binaural sound-processing are built into a number of software packages and standard plug-ins, so the opportunity to manipulate sound in this way is readily available.

Multichannel Sound Diffusion

The 1970s saw an attempt to introduce a commercial four-channel system, known as 'quadraphony'. Although this format failed to achieve public acceptance, variations of one-channel per loudspeaker, or multi-channel systems, are still around. Eight-channel, or octophonic, systems are in frequent use for acousmatic and electro-acoustic concert music. There are many different configurations and speaker layouts used in such concerts.

A complex system might increase the number and variety of loudspeakers and include 'tweeter-trees', which resemble the hub and spokes of cartwheels with small speakers attached, suspended over the heads of the audience. This kind of system can achieve great accuracy in both localization and spatialization but is still something of a specialist set-up. A highly complex system might comprise an automated seventy-six-channel mixer feeding an array of fifty or more loudspeakers. However, it is not essential to work in such enormous surroundings to achieve good sound diffusion. A reasonably portable sound diffusion system can readily be assembled and configured to suit unusual spaces. This form of music-making is greatly on the increase as equipment falls in price and artists seek to take control of their own sound.

INFORMATION: SPATIALIZATION LAYOUTS

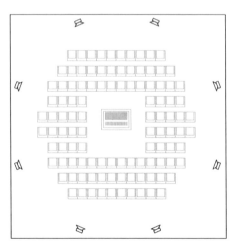

Figure 5.6   The 8-channel 'Stonehenge' layout ©
Peter Batchelor

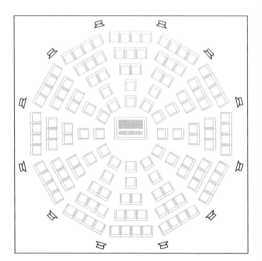

Figure 5.7   A 12-channel layout © Peter Batchelor

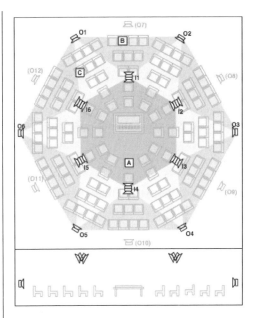

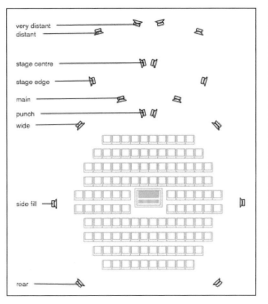

Figure 5.8   A layout including overheads © Peter Batchelor

Figure 5.9   A 'theatrical' diffusion rig, designed to create a range of effects © Jonty Harrison

A more familiar, and generally commercial, solution to spatialization is offered by 5.1 (and more recently 6.1 and 7.1) *surround sound*, which is found in many cinemas and increasingly in the home. A typical 5.1 system has five channels playing back through five main speakers: three at the front (stereo left and right, plus centre mono), and two at the side or rear (stereo left and right); plus a sub-woofer for bass sounds. The 7.1 system uses two more speakers, 6.1 one extra, and so on. The underlying concept of 5.1 surround is in fact 3.2 stereo, which means that the front three speakers are providing the stereo sound image, and the side/back speakers are delivering ambient or supporting sounds. This can produce an unconvincing effect, most usually because the speaker placement is problematic and stereo signals delivered through three loudspeakers can be confusing. For 5.1 to work successfully, therefore, generally requires an acceptance of these limitations. If the effect desired is a true 360-degree surround, then these formats are not ideal. Note also that the subwoofer, or .1 loudspeaker, is optional and so should be treated as an additional effect. The 5.1 surround mix should work effectively without this speaker, which can only handle very low frequencies (generally below 120 Hz).

Ambisonics is an extremely thorough system that aims to provide a comprehensive solution to all aspects of directional sound, including recording, transmission and reproduction. Unlike other systems, which tend to favour sounds from the front, it treats all sounds from whatever direction as equal. It works by recording the loudness and spatial location of a signal onto separate channels, using a special microphone array that bunches capsules in a spherical formation resembling a human head. The system therefore needs four or more loudspeakers and a decoder to achieve full 3D 'periphony' in playback. At the University of York, for example, the Arthur Sykes Rymer Auditorium is equipped with a sixteen-speaker ambisonic rig consisting of four high speakers, eight horizontal speakers and four speakers below the audience. Ambisonics gives as close to a realistic 3D sound as is possible and there seems to be little doubt that it is the most effective surround-sound system in existence.

Wave-field synthesis derives from the Huygens Principle,[11] which states that a sound wave front contains an infinite number of small sound sources that in turn form smaller waves that make up the next wave front. Since this process can be predicted, it is possible to synthesize the wave front such that a listener could not tell the difference between the real and synthetic waves. In other words, it does not create a psychoacoustic illusion but rather a physical wave field, using precise delays between signals. A large array of loudspeakers, arranged in a line or a circle around the listener, is required to convert this into a practical reality, but the possibilities it offers for precise localization of sound are great. Consequently, it has proved attractive to large installation-base theatres such as those at Disney World or the Odysseum Science Adventure Park in Cologne.

As these descriptions demonstrate, one very practical problem with spatialization is that it usually requires a quite specific or controlled listening environment. Even within standardized set-ups there can be considerable variation in listening experience, often based on the extent to which the listener's seating position varies from the 'sweet spot', the point of optimum listening. Given that the digital musician is seeking to create a unique sound, including its position (or apparent position) in space, this variability and lack of control of the listening situation can present a challenge. Many different solutions have been adopted, ranging from an extreme precision (fixed listening position) to an extreme lack of precision (the ambulant listener). It is an important aspect of any music-making that involves loudspeakers to consider the listening experience and, hence, the spatialization.

The challenges of spatialization have been a key focus of electro-acoustic music over many decades, and there have been numerous works designed for highly specific set-ups.

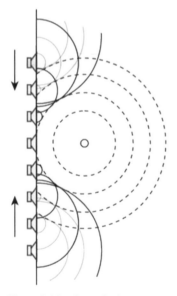

Figure 5.10 A synthetic wave-field created from parts © Matt Montag

Figure 5.11 A typical speaker array used in wave-field synthesis © Matt Montag

The collapse of these pieces onto stereo CD can be damaging to the concept, and a live experience is preferable. The Canadian composer Robert Normandeau explicitly sets out to create what he calls 'cinema for the ears' in which the spatialization is integral to both the sound quality and the meaning of the music. In his work *Clair de Terre* (1999), for example, the concept derives explicitly from photographic imagery of the Earth seen from outer space. Normandeau wrote:

> This work is divided into twelve movements that systematically explore elements of the grammar of cinematography that have been transposed into the language of electro-acoustics. Preceded by an overture – Ouverture – each of these twelve movements are composed of a soundscape, an object's sound, the sound of a musical instrument, and vocal onomatopoeias. All of these sound elements are drawn from the sound bank that I have built up over the last ten years.[12]

Normandeau has recently become interested in the possibilities offered by audio DVD formats, which allow multichannel control within a standard system.

Project 16 (Advanced): Types of Space

Introduction

Consider the notion of 'space' in music. 'Outer space' is one of several types of space. Inner space, or the space of the imagination, is another. Personal space is a familiar concept from psychology: the area that is felt to be the property of the individual, which can be 'invaded' by others. A private space suggests something intimate, secret. A piece of music itself could also be said to occupy a 'cultural space'; in other words, it represents something about the culture from which it has emerged. Finally there is the sense of 'spaciousness' that you might get from contemplating a natural phenomenon such as the Grand Canyon, or a cloud. Given that music is a time-based art form, these ideas of space are difficult to imagine made in sound. And yet they can, and have, been conveyed. To hear examples from history, listen to the following:

- Outer Space (1): Richard Strauss *Also Sprach Zarathustra*, which carries all kinds of associations, and all the moon-shots, was used in Stanley Kubrick's *2001: A Space Odyssey*.
- Outer Space (2): Louis and Bebe Barron's music for the film *Forbidden Planet*. This film was the first motion picture to feature an electronic music score. Here 'outer space' is evoked by 'otherworldly' sounds.
- Inner Space: Erik Satie Gymnopédie No. 1. This manages to convey an inner world by restricting the amount of musical material and adopting a direct simplicity of style.
- Personal Space: Alvin Lucier *I Am Sitting In a Room*. This is a classic meditation on the relationship between an individual and his surroundings.
- Private Space: Luciano Berio *Visage*. A disturbing insight into a private imaginary world.

PROJECT 16

- Cultural Space: Karlheinz Stockhausen *Hymnen*. Stockhausen's attempt to explore the music of the world, which ends up revealing a great deal about his particular time and space.
- Spaciousness (1): Gustav Mahler Symphony No.1, specifically the opening of the first movement for an illustration of natural space.
- Spaciousness (2): György Ligeti *Atmosphères*, a good example of a cloud-like space.

What is impressive about all these works is the way in which they successfully map the evident musical imagination of the composer. Their intention seems to match the outcome (even in the case of the Stockhausen).

The Project

Choose one of the types of space (or find another of your own) and make a short acousmatic piece that creates that space for the listener.

Notes

This is a project about intention and result, so it will be measured in terms of its ability to communicate its ideas through sound alone, hence the acousmatic (loudspeakers only) brief. Gathering audience responses, perhaps through a simple questionnaire, could be an interesting way of testing this.

The project will take a few weeks to complete, and should be delivered to an audience in a formal listening situation that is not encumbered with distractions. It is essential that the audience listens carefully to the music.

FURTHER READING

- Rumsey, F., *Spatial Audio*, Oxford: Focal Press, 2001.
  Explores the principles and practical considerations of spatial sound recording and reproduction. Particular emphasis is given to the increasing importance of multichannel surround sound and 3D audio, including binaural approaches, without ignoring conventional stereo.

- Malham, D., *Primer on Basic Ambisonics: Spatial Hearing Mechanisms and Sound Reproduction*. Online. Available HTTP: http://www.york.ac.uk/inst/mustech/3d_audio/ambis2.htm (accessed 1 September 2011).
  Discusses the principles and technology of ambisonics.

SOUND THROUGH TIME

Much of the previous discussion is equally relevant to the behaviour of sound through time. In fact, it is fairly meaningless to talk about sound without reference to time. The same is equally true of silence. As John Cage observed: the thing that sound and silence have in common is duration.

There are only two ways of putting sounds together. The first is to hear them successively, one after another. This may be called *horizontal* composition, in the sense that time travels along an imaginary horizontal axis. The other is to combine them simultaneously, which may be called *vertical* composition. Most music mixes these approaches in some way.[13] It could be argued that even purely horizontal composition is in fact both horizontal *and* vertical, because music is a time-based art form and any one sound might be understood as a combination of many smaller sounds in varying relationships.

In a horizontal composition, layers of related sounds may develop in ways that the listener can perceive. Often, four layers is the maximum number that can be separately and simultaneously followed. In a vertical composition, the emphasis will generally be more upon overall texture. A composition need not restrict itself to one approach or the other, and often the musical interest derives from the interplay of the two. The drama of music comes from the way in which the various musical elements interact. Having a sense of how to handle these interactions is the mark of a good composer.

The passage of time, or rather the perception of the passage of time, is part of the essence of music. This is why the sections of classical works are called 'movements'. Any composer, therefore, must think about questions of rupture and continuity. A repetitive or continuous element may bind the music together, but may also create a sense of stasis. Fragmentation may give an early impression of movement, but too much of it can rapidly leave the listener disorientated, at which point stasis is once again the result. Now, stasis may be exactly what is required by some artistic concepts, so these are not inherently *wrong*. However, they do need to be handled with awareness and care so that the sounding result matches the intention of the work.

In digital music, the timing of sounds can be highly precise, even sometimes over-precise in the way that computationally exact processes tend to be. Part of the challenge facing the musician is to make digital processes *sound* natural – or sound characteristically unnatural if that is the aim of the composition. Much of this comes down to handling timings, and the listener will quickly perceive any inconsistency between the apparent aim of the composition and the sounding result as shortcomings.

Spectromorphology

One organizational approach to this aspect of digital processes goes under the (rather cumbersome) name of spectromorphology. This is based on inharmonics, where the individual digital sample represents a vertical snapshot of time-based relationships. The idea of the horizontal and the vertical in this situation can be extended to both the shortest possible sonic event and the largest musical structure. The word 'spectromorphology' therefore refers literally to the way sound spectra (spectro-) are shaped (-morphology) over time. It may be defined as 'an approach to sound materials and musical structures which concentrates on the spectrum of available pitches and their shaping in time'.[14]

Since sounds are the content of these shapes, and every sound must *have* a shape, it can be said that the two elements are indissolubly linked. The spectrum of a sound that lacks a fixed pitch changes so much over time that its morphology is often unstable and *dynamic*. The various elements are in transition, or moving. Most natural and environmental sounds fall into this category. Motion is therefore a key focus of music that exhibits spectromorphological thinking.

Sounds may be classified by their behaviour through time, as follows:

- *discrete* (single, short, separated)
- *iterative* (rapidly repeated, like a drum roll)
- *continuous* (sustained, continuations of sounds).

Musical situations often contain combinations of all three, but there is always motion from one type to the next. In his essay on spectromorphology, Denis Smalley introduces a concept of correspondence to describe these moments of shift from one morphology to another. He describes an attack which:

> sets in motion a resonating spectrum which we might expect to decay gradually. The further away we travel from the attack point the more we may be coaxed into observing how the spectral components of the continuant phase proceed, and the less interested we shall be in the generic role of the initial impact.[15]

This example is typical of spectromorphological thinking, and Smalley goes on to elaborate how it might form a structuring principle for composition. Even at the relatively short-lived level of this example, a composer might use digital technology to manipulate, say, inharmonic elements of the decay, to begin its transformation into another sound type.

Just as the organization of sound in space connects to its passage through time, so time-based manipulations reconnect to space. In his electro-acoustic piece *Valley Flow* (1992), Smalley explores this connection:

> The formal shaping and sound content of Valley Flow were influenced by the dramatic vistas of the Bow Valley in the Canadian Rockies. The work is founded on a basic flowing motion which is stretched or contracted to create floating and flying contours, panoramic sweeps, and the flinging out of textural materials. Special attention is paid to creating spatial perspectives – gazing out to the distinct horizon, looking down from a height, the impact of mountain bulks and the magnified details of organic activity.[16]

The result is a kind of sonic landscape which seems to link directly with a visual experience. The piece is layered and striated, just like the landscape it depicts, but also sweeps in a speeded-up version of the activity that formed the Bow Valley itself or the passage of the eye across its various features. The detailed manipulation of the sound through time, however, also creates a psychological effect that seems to correspond to the sense of awe experienced in the presence of such large geological formations.

RECOMMENDED LISTENING

▶ Denis Smalley (1982) *Vortex* [CD] Ode Recordings, CDMANU1433.
▶ Denis Smalley (1992) *Valley Flow* [CD] Empreintes Digitales, IMED-9209-CD.

FURTHER READING

■ Smalley, D., *Spectro-morphology and Structuring Processes*, in Emmerson, S. (ed.) *The Language of Electroacoustic Music*, London: Macmillan, 1986, pp. 61–93.
An important chapter summarizing the main ideas of spectromorphology.

■ Smalley, D., 'Spectromorphology: Explaining Sound-Shapes', *Organized Sound*, 2:2, 1997, 107–126.

■ Young, J., 'Sound Morphology and the Articulation of Structure in Electroacoustic Music', *Organized Sound*, 9:1, 2004, 7–14.
Focuses on the potential for the morphology of sound structures to function at different structural levels within a musical argument.

Project 17 (Advanced): Quintessence

Introduction

This is a large-scale composition project for fixed media, intended for public performance. It is designed to explore sound through time and sound in space, using spectromorphology as a guiding principle.

The Project

Many ancient civilizations identified four elements: earth, air, water, fire. Aristotle suggested that air is primarily wet and secondarily hot, fire is primarily hot and secondarily dry, earth is primarily dry and secondarily cold, and water is primarily cold and secondarily wet. In Japanese tradition, earth represents things that are solid, water represents things that are liquid, fire represents things that destroy, air represents things that move. There are similar concepts in Chinese philosophy, Buddhism, Hinduism, ancient Egyptian beliefs, Babylonian culture, and so on.

A fifth element, called the *quintessence*, is also described in many of these traditions. This seems to lie beyond the terrestrial elements, filling the heavens (aether), or to represent things not of our daily life (spirit).

The aim of this project is to create a 5–10 minute electro-acoustic piece that evokes the quintessence through the interactions of sounds that represent the four basic elements.

Notes

This project could take a few months to complete. The first step is to assemble suitable sounds, either by making original recordings or by finding good quality source materials. Quality is essential. For the piece to be effective, the sounds must have inherent interest in their own right and be well recorded so as to enable effective transformations.

The next step is to find ways to extend and develop the sounds. The ideas of spectromorphology should be the guide. In particular, concentrate on layering, texture, transition, gesture and motion. How may the sounds be shaped into musical materials that engage and express dramatically the higher goals of the composition?

PROJECT 17

Finally, attention should be paid to the performance situation. Spatialization will be a very useful tool regardless of the equipment used. In stereo, a good stereo image and effective use of foreground, background and panning, will support the compositional approach. This will be magnified if a multi-channel set-up is available.

This should normally be an audio-only project.

Discussion Questions

- What are the differences between sonic art and sound design and why do they matter?
- To what extent is music a product of the space in which it is heard or produced? How does this translate into digital music?
- What is 'network space'?
- How may spatialization and diffusion be made musical?
- What are the important aspects of texture and gesture in digital music?

Digitizing Sound

This chapter examines the processes that take place inside the computer and therefore what it is that digital musicians actually *do*. It is necessarily rather technical, but does not go into any great depth regarding the mathematical and engineering aspects of digital signal processing (DSP), preferring to focus instead on its creative and musical consequences. All of digital music is fundamentally a form of digital signal processing, so these are very important concepts. There are further reading recommendations to the many excellent books on computer music. At all stages, examples are given from the repertoire and the creative projects are designed to take this rapidly into the practical area. Nevertheless, understanding the processes that take place inside the computer may be taken as core knowledge for a digital musician.

SAMPLING

At the heart of digital music is the sample. The word 'sampling' has come to refer to the process of digitizing recorded sound (we may sample an instrument, or the sound of a river, for example), but 'sample' is also a technical term to describe the smallest unit of digital audio. A computer encodes sound by transforming it into numerical data. The word 'digital' derives from counting on the fingers, or digits. In most digital systems, counting is done using binary numbers. Binary is simply a way of representing more complex numbers using only two digits: 1 and 0. The advantage of this method of counting is that it enables computers to translate 1s and 0s as 'on' or 'off' states at the machine level. Each 1 and 0 is called a binary digit, which contracts to 'bit', and a group of eight bits is called a 'byte' (by eight). There are several different ways of using binary counting to digitize sound, but the most common is called pulse code modulation, or PCM. This samples an analog sound at a given rate over time, the *sampling rate* or *sampling frequency*, with each sample containing a given number of digital values, the *bit depth*. When the samples are played back in the correct order at the correct speed, an aurally convincing simulation of the original sound will be heard. Figure 6.1 illustrates the process: the wavy line is an analog signal that varies over time (the x-axis) and the vertical bars are samples taken at a given rate.

It is important to understand that digital samples *contain no sound*. They are simply ways of representing sound so that it may be stored, processed and manipulated by the computer. They only become sounds when they are converted back into the analog domain through the loudspeaker. The human ear is analog: it registers vibrations in the air (or other medium). Acoustic instruments are analog: they physically vibrate, they embody sound. Traditional electronic media, such as tape or vinyl, are also analog, physically encoding the vibrations of sound into some medium. The process of digitization introduces a layer of abstraction that removes this physical quality. The computer itself emits little or no sound from its body, and in any case may be interchangeable with any other digital device.

This disembodiment is a defining characteristic of digital music. It has profound consequences for the way the music is made. Mapping of information to control systems

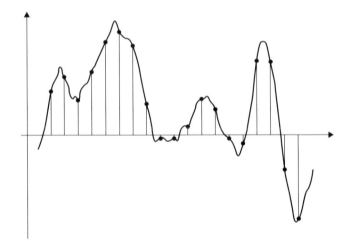

Figure 6.1 Digital representation of an analog time-series sampled at a fixed sample rate © Mike Toews

or playback systems becomes a distinctive feature of the musical process. Sampling an external sound is only ever an approximation to its natural state. Digitizing a natural sound may capture its detail in a highly effective way, opening it up for manipulation and transformation but, however fine-grained the sampling rate may be, there is always a sense of distance. Such issues of quality can generate whole aesthetics, such as the 'retro' 8-bit sound that is evocative of the early days of computer soundcards and still popular today.

The digital method of using numbers to encode sound is efficient because it is not subject to the same kinds of errors introduced by the physical properties of the analog medium. It is non-linear and, at least in theory, does not suffer degradation when identical copies are made (although a signal can sometimes be degraded at other stages in the process). This is the advantage of digital over analog. However, whether a sound comes from an external source (such as an instrument, voice or any other acoustic sound) or whether the sound input is a microphone or a cable (line), it will at some point have to be converted into digital form to be handled by a computer or other digital device, and the same applies in reverse at the other end of the chain.

A simple way to explore all the above ideas is to record an acoustic signal (a voice or musical instrument) with a good microphone plugged directly into the computer. By using software which allows for different settings of bit rate, sampling rate and resolution, the aural consequences of digitizing sound can be investigated. Setting the level deliberately high will also give the clipping effect. Digital audio, like film, is an illusion, because it consists only of a set of values which, when correctly decoded by the technology, translates into a sounding result. Of course, analog sound is also a kind of illusion, but its apparent reality derives from the nature of the medium onto which it is literally written. The underlying reality of digital audio is mathematics, whereas the underlying reality of analog audio is physics. This does not mean that the physical consequences of the digital manipulation of sound are any less, but the abstraction that sits at the heart of digital sound-processing also lies behind many attempts by instrument-makers and musicians to introduce more physicality and gesture into the act of performing digital music.

Fourier Transforms

Digitization is the basic process by which analog sound is encoded as digital audio, but sound organization and manipulation depends upon the computer's ability accurately to analyse the contents of a sound file. The most common method is called a *Fourier transform* (FT).[1] This is a digital representation of a sound in the time and frequency domains that reflects the detail of its changing spectrum to a level of accuracy that is limited by the processing power and speed of the computer. A good way to envisage an FT is to imagine a spreadsheet containing a number of rows and columns of cells. The rows represent narrow bands of harmonics, grouped by frequency range, and are called *bins*. The columns contain single digital samples. At a sample rate of 44,100 Hz (CD quality), this means each column lasts 1/44,100ths of a second. Each cell, therefore, contains a tiny amount of information about a sample and its constituent frequencies. In other words, there is a very small amount of energy in a cell.

Now, in order to analyse a sound for longer than the duration of one sample, it is necessary to increase the number of columns in the imaginary spreadsheet. This is called the *buffer size*, *window length* or *window size* and typically increases by a factor of two, thus: 512 samples, 1024, 2048, 4096, etc. Raising the number of rows in the imaginary spreadsheet can similarly increase the frequency resolution. This has the effect of narrowing the frequency range of each bin. The size of the window, therefore, gives the frequency resolution and the time resolution. The buffer size divided by the sample rate gives the duration of the buffer in milliseconds. The sample rate divided by the buffer size gives the frequency range of each bin.

In practice, there is a trade-off between these two resolutions. A bigger buffer gives more accurate pitch definition but less accurate time definition. A smaller buffer gives less accurate pitch definition and more accurate time definition (see Table 6.1).

Figures 6.2, 6.3 and 6.4 show three sonograms of the same sound, of 3 seconds' duration, with increasing window sizes. Time is shown along the x-axis, frequency up the y-axis. Notice how the bins become smaller.

Table 6.1 **Buffer sizes**

S/R	Window size time res (samp)	Window size time res (ms)	Bin width freq res (Hz)	
44100	32	0.73	1378.13	
44100	64	1.45	689.06	Fig. 6.1
44100	128	2.9	344.53	
44100	256	5.8	172.27	
44100	512	11.61	86.13	Fig. 6.2
44100	1024	23.22	43.07	
44100	2048	46.44	21.53	
44100	4096	92.88	10.77	Fig. 6.3
44100	8192	185.76	5.38	
44100	16384	371.52	2.69	
44100	32768	743.04	1.35	
		1000 ÷ (sample rate ÷ time res (samp))	sample rate ÷ time res (samp)	

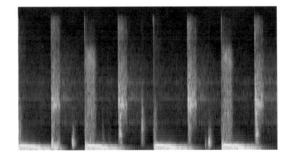

Figure 6.2 Sonogram – window size: 64 © Peter Batchelor

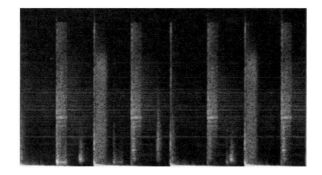

Figure 6.3 Sonogram – window size: 256 © Peter Batchelor

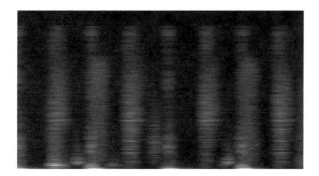

Figure 6.4 Sonogram – window size: 1024 © Peter Batchelor

An FT therefore, analyses the sound into a continuous spectrum of its constituent harmonics. It does this by calculating the frequency, amplitude and phase of the various sine waves within the given time frame. Because the amount of data produced by this process is large and the number of calculations per second can be prohibitively great, an algorithm[2] has been developed to enable FTs to be calculated quickly. This is called a fast Fourier transform, or FFT, and is the most common form of digitally processed sound. Input to an FFT is usually given an envelope whose shape can be chosen by the user. There are several of these window shapes, of which the best are: Hamming, Hanning and Blackman.[3]

Why is understanding such complex digital analysis so important? Because it provides the means by which musicians may shape and control their sound, which is one of the main goals. A thorough knowledge of the way digital sound is created, handled and manipulated is an essential skill. Furthermore, this knowledge and understanding will suggest creative possibilities. Consider the following example to illustrate the point.

The kind of errors thrown up in the timing processes of D to A conversion may be called *glitches*. However, a glitch is also just a fault in a system, such as an unwanted electrical pulse or a programming error. The idea could be extended to the surface noise on an LP, for example, or the accidental sound made by touching the tip of a jack plug before connecting it to an instrument. In the late 1990s, various artists and musicians became interested in these unwanted sounds and began using them, mainly in place of percussion. The result has been a burgeoning 'glitch' music genre, which operates on the margins of the techno scene. A survey of the Mille Plateaux record label's 'Clicks and Cuts' series will give an idea of the possibilities opened up by these artists. The best among them know what they are doing, just as surely as the best violinist knows how to get a good sound from the violin. These are not just arbitrary uses of digital artefacts: the digital musician combines engineering skills with artistic innovation.

FFT is not the only way to manipulate the spectral content of a sound. In the past decade or so, an alternative called the *wavelet transform* has begun to appear. These transforms parallel Heisenberg's Uncertainty Principle, which states that the momentum and position of a moving particle cannot be known simultaneously.[4] Whereas the FT works fine for stationary signals, that is to say, it renders the time and frequency information necessary for the spectrum of a sound to be understood discretely, as though it happened once and remained unchanged, the wavelet transform attempts to perform the same function for sounds whose spectra *vary over time*. Since Heisenberg's Uncertainty Principle excludes the possibility of complete knowledge of this, the Continuous Wavelet Transform (CWT) just gives as good a resolution as possible. The finer the resolution, the more computation required, with the result that the quality of CWT implementations, such as pitch-shifters and time-stretchers, in commercial software packages is variable.

PROJECT 18

Project 18 (Elementary): FFT Processing

Introduction

Digital sound processing might appear to transform a sound in a particular way (altering the pitch, slowing down, etc.), but this is merely the aural consequence of the production of a *new collection of data.* Any digital process can produce strange or unwanted artefacts, sounds that do not contribute to the aural impression the process is designed to create. In most cases, good software means that this is not a problem. This project, however, positively explores the creative possibilities that endless repetitions of a process can produce.

The Project

Take a recorded sound and apply an effect (timestretch, reverb, pitch shift, distortion, anything) repeating the effect over and over again until the sound is nothing like the original sound. Retain a copy of each step in the process. Now listen back to the sounds one at a time in reverse order.

Notes

Notice how the process diverges further and further from how it might be imagined to sound. Rather than going deeper 'inside' the sound, the process is in fact generating a *new* sound. Ask each time: What is heard? What does it mean? What is its source?

> **RECOMMENDED LISTENING**
>
> ▶ Oval (1994) *Systemisch* [CD] Mille Plateaux, 90718750065926.
>   Pioneering band that worked with damaged audio products and mutilated CDs to create glitch music.
>
> ▶ Various Artists. (2000–present) *Clicks and Cuts* series [CD]. Mille Plateaux.
>   The definitive series of glitch recordings.

FILE FORMATS

Once a sound has been analysed by the computer, it may be manipulated and transformed. However, the sheer quantity of data in a typical audio file can be prohibitively high. In order to maintain an aurally convincing illusion while being readable by software and, where necessary, reducing the size of the file, the audio data is normally organized into a specific format. These file formats generally use some kind of compression, which comes in two forms: lossless and lossy.

Lossless compression does not sacrifice any audio information but still manages to reduce the amount of data in the raw file. Typical lossless file formats include .wav (wave-form audio format) on the PC, and .aiff (audio interchange file format) on the Mac.

A well-known example of lossy compression is the mp3, or, to give it its full title, MPEG audio layer 3, format. MPEG stands for 'Moving Pictures Experts Group', which is the body charged with setting standards for the encoding of audio and video. Mp3 is typical of lossy compression formats, in that it discards musical information that may be regarded as less important or even irrelevant to the listener, such as very quiet material simultaneous with or immediately following very loud material.

Lossy compression formats use various types of encryption, which produce generally better sounding results as the number of kilobits per second (kbps) is increased. For mp3 encoding, 128 kbps is generally considered the lowest rate to produce good quality, but this is a matter of opinion and will vary according to the music that is being encoded and the ears of the individual listener. Other examples of lossy compression include the successors to mp3, WMA (windows audio media), AAC (advanced audio compression) used by Apple for its iTunes and iPod products, and Ogg Vorbis, which is an open, patent-free compression.

Project 19 (Elementary): File Formats

Introduction

This project is quite easy to achieve, but is a very useful way to understand the musical implications of different audio file formats. Musicians can tend to accept what the computer presents to the ear as a standard, but in fact there is considerable variation between file formats, often depending on the type of music that is encoded. Even lossless formats can exhibit certain audible characteristics, depending on the sample rate and bit rate.

The Project

Choose some music containing a wide range of contrasting dynamic (loud and soft) levels and sounds. Now use a software package to save the file in various formats and vary the settings to achieve different quality levels. Listen carefully and comparatively to the results. It might be a good idea to try this with several different examples. The aim is to try to hear what has changed, what has been lost, and what has been emphasized. An extension of this project is to create some music which is designed specifically for a certain file format.

Notes

In an mp3 culture, certain kinds of music adapt better to the file format. This project will quickly establish what those might be and why that is the case. This has implications for music that does not work so well in that format. Formats will change and music will adapt, but one interesting question to explore is whether the arrival of lossy compression formats has changed musical culture, particularly with reference to the kind of *music* that is made?

FURTHER READING

- Watkinson, J., *The Art of Digital Audio*, Oxford: Focal Press, 2001.
  A standard work on the subject written from a technical perspective which sets out the primary information for musical applications as well.

REPRESENTING

The preceding discussion looked at the way computers represent sound to themselves. However, the way in which digital music is represented to *us*, the users, is somewhat different and no less fundamental to our understanding. There are many forms of representation, from visualizations to code, from text files to metadata or keywords. Analysis of these may develop complex representations, leading to musical information retrieval systems and search possibilities by pattern-matching (rhythmic, pitch, melodic, spectrum, etc.), automated playlist-building, music recognition and so on. However, the most common form of representation is through a visual display on an interface. Such representations are often modelled on traditional electronic displays, but exploit the processing capabilities of the computer to deliver enriched information.

Wave-form Diagrams

The basic representation of a sound is the *wave-form diagram*. Figure 6.5 is a simple flat wave-form diagram of a pure sine wave, a single harmonic, oscillating at a given amplitude and phase.[5] The lack of any additional harmonics means that the wave form is smooth and regular, and the resulting sound is extremely pure. The second image represents exactly the same sine wave but shows the harmonic spectrum, which in this case consists, predictably, of a single peak at the relevant frequency.

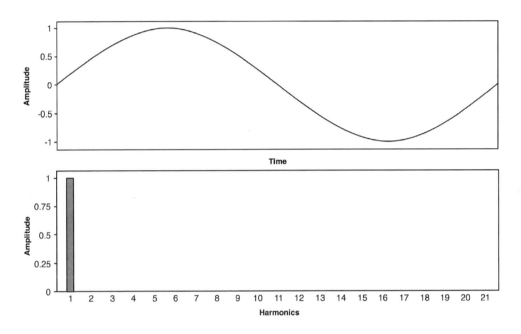

Figure 6.5 Sine wave © Peter Batchelor

A more complex wave-form diagram, such as the one shown in Figure 6.6, gives a summary of the harmonic activity in a sound, resulting in a single line which uses a process called 'spectral averaging' to convey a certain amount of information about (among other things) periodicity, or lack of it. This is useful for getting a general impression of the timbral character and, especially, for identifying pitch, but what is needed for a more sophisticated understanding is detailed information about all the harmonics and their complex relationships over time; in other words, the spectrum. There are a number of solutions to this, but the most commonly encountered is the spectrogram (also sometimes called a sonogram).

Spectrograms

Spectrograms are easy to produce digitally and provide ready information about the spectrum of any sound. Some software enables audible spectrograms, so that the user may listen to an individual harmonic. A typical spectrogram represents time along the x-axis and frequency along the y-axis, but the most important and distinctive feature is the amplitude of the various harmonics, which are usually shown as striations of varying depths or

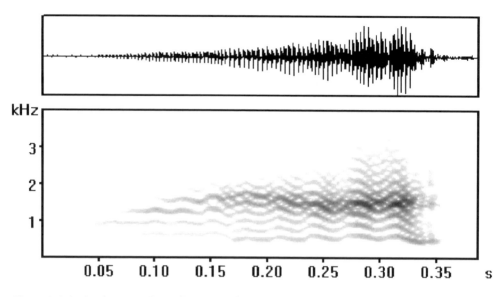

Figure 6.6 A simple wave-form diagram and a two-dimensional spectrogram of a frog call ©
    Raimund Specht, Avisoft Bioacoustics

intensity. These may be colour (rather like a weather map)[6] or monochrome, but in general the more dense or intense the striation, the stronger that particular harmonic will be in the spectrum. Figure 6.7 shows a two-dimensional (2D) spectrogram of a piano playing a note, followed by another a fifth above. The harmonic series may be clearly seen.

Figure 6.8 shows a 3D spectrogram of a sound showing the amplitude of each of its harmonics and their changing relationships over time, represented by the individual

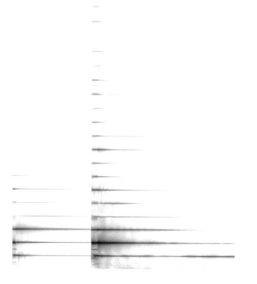

Figure 6.7 Spectrogram of piano notes © Peter Batchelor

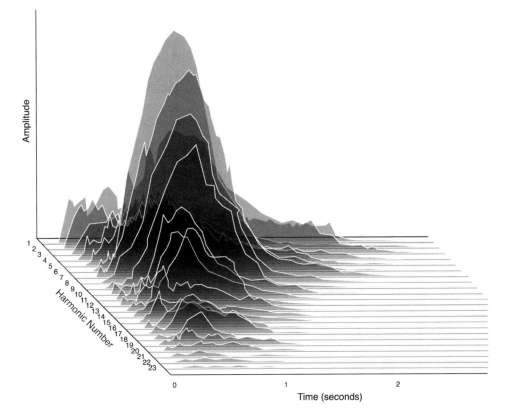

Figure 6.8 Three-dimensional spectrogram © Peter Batchelor

envelopes. Notice that the characteristics of the attack and decay of the sounds are as clear as the central continuant. This is a great advantage of spectrograms, whereas the conventional wave-form diagram is most useful in the continuant only. The perception of timbre is often located during the attack stage. There have been many psychoacoustical experiments to show that listeners cannot distinguish one musical instrument from another; for example, if the attack is removed and only the continuant is heard.

Figure 6.9 shows a 2D spectrogram of the spoken word 'sound', showing frequency information represented vertically and time horizontally. Notice the higher frequencies are most dense during the sibilant 's' sound, whereas lower frequencies predominate during the rounded 'ound'.

SYNTHESIZING

The grandfather of digital synthesis, Max Mathews, observed that it is '*very hard*' to create new timbres we hear as interesting, powerful and beautiful'. Whereas recording a sample has the advantage that the process captures the extraneous aspects, the 'dirt' of the sound, a synthetic sound created from within the computer has a certain 'cleanliness'. The extent to which this may be attractive or valuable is an aesthetic matter. We seem to have an innate tendency to prize sounds that come from nature and much effort is

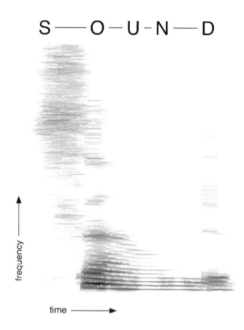

devoted in digital music to giving synthetic sounds that same 'natural' quality. On the other hand, a sampled sound is in the end identical to a synthesized sound, inasmuch as it consists of samples. Processing a sample may remove all trace of its natural origins, creating something that *sounds* synthetic. Does this reduce its capacity to be 'interesting, powerful and beautfiul'? And does this mean that a purely synthesized sound may *never* be 'interesting, powerful and beauutiful'?

INFORMATION: *SINUSOIDS*

The sine wave, or *sinusoid*, is most useful in synthesis, since it can readily be isolated or generated using electronic or digital equipment. However, synthesis does not normally restrict itself to pure sine waves but uses more complex variants, such as:

- *square waves* comprising the odd numbered harmonics of a fundamental
- *triangle waves* consisting of a fundamental frequency, with odd-numbered harmonics (these roll off in amplitude more quickly than in a square wave, producing a smoother sound)
- *sawtooth* waves, which normally ramp upwards over time, then sharply drop, although there are some which ramp downwards over time then sharply rise.

Notice how in Figures 6.10, 6.11 and 6.12 the name of the wave form derives from its visual representation rather than from its sound. Already, even with such simple waves, the representation has become the way in which the sound is understood.

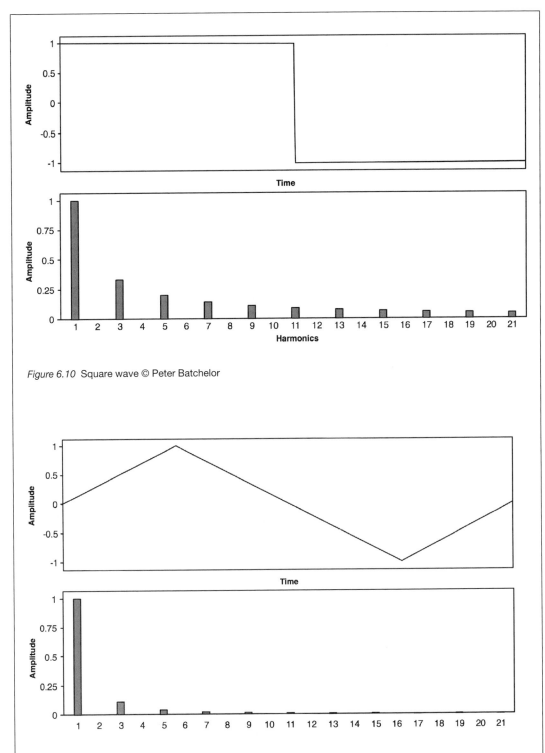

Figure 6.10 Square wave © Peter Batchelor

Figure 6.11 Triangle wave © Peter Batchelor

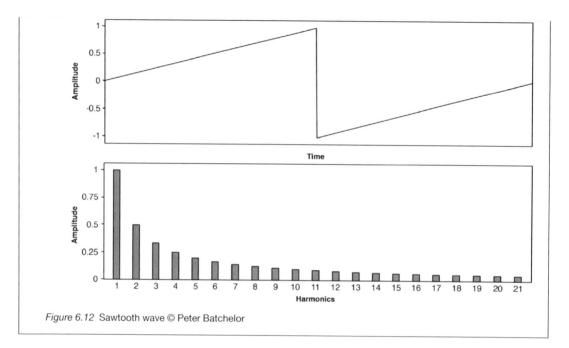

Figure 6.12 Sawtooth wave © Peter Batchelor

Most synthesis relies upon the analytical capabilities of computers described earlier to produce effective results. The creation of ever better algorithms for the many types of synthesizing process has preoccupied musicians and scientists since the 1950s. The earliest examples had their roots in traditional electronic processes, such as *additive* and *subtractive* synthesis. In additive synthesis, sine tones are combined and built up to create new sounds, whereas in subtractive synthesis filters are applied to a source in order to sculpt similarly new sounds. Both processes may readily be performed in the digital domain, and many digital synthesizers self-consciously set out to emulate their earlier analog counterparts, often seeking to capture the 'warmth' and unpredictability of those instruments.

Frequency Modulation, or *FM*, synthesis was introduced in 1967–1968 by John Chowning at Stanford University, and essentially consisted of using one sinusoid to modulate another, thereby creating more complex spectra. This technique formed the basic constituent of many of the most successful digital synthesizers, such as the Yamaha DX7, which was released in 1983. The modulation technique has applications beyond FM synthesis itself, and often forms the basis of creative experimentation in synthesis. For example, Phase Modulation exploits the fact that the rate at which the phase of a wave changes is the same as the frequency expressed in cycles per second. New variants of the FM algorithm have been introduced, including time-varying parameters and feedback. It remains a fertile area for digital synthesis.

Wavetable synthesis is another approach that builds upon the analytical capabilities of FTs. By storing complex wave forms in tables they may be reused at any point in the process of synthesis and in any order. The FT analyses the components of a wave form by identifying the sinusoids and their relative strengths within frequency bands in a single cycle. The resulting wave form is stored and made available for subsequent looking up. The various types of table include: *transient* wavetables that capture the evolution of harmonics in a sound over time; *formant* wavetables that reflect harmonic changes; *wave sequence* wavetables that have changeable harmonic content; and *speech* wavetables.

Physical modelling is a form of synthesis that attempts to create realistic approximations to acoustic sound. In many cases, this means the simulation of musical instruments. As computer technology has improved in speed and performance, so physical models have become increasingly available to digital musicians. Much of the music that is heard in broadcast media today is an amalgamation of sampled sounds and physically modelled synthesized sound. The techniques for physical modelling include: analytical approaches that directly transform acoustic information into digital data; 'mass-spring' models in which each element of a complex sound may be broken down into pairs of masses and forces (each force acting upon the sound-mass at a given moment); modal synthesis that analyses modes of vibration; and waveguide synthesis, which uses techniques similar to those described above to model sound waves.

The creative applications of physical modelling are many and varied. The boundaries between 'real' and 'unreal' may be blurred by creating imaginary instruments that perform feats of which no real instrument would be capable (e.g., a 'bionic' voice that can sing continuously across all registers) or impossible acts of virtuosity. Careful blending of synthesized, sampled and acoustic sounds may considerably expand the musical palette available to a composer or performer. Integration with artificial intelligence may offer yet more possibilities, with the real prospect of synthetic performers interacting convincingly with live human performers. Yet, these are techniques in formation that have yet to evolve to their full potential.

Whereas FTs operate in the frequency domain, it is also possible to synthesize sound through the time domain. The chopping up of a sound into small segments is called *brassage*, and is a common editing technique in digital music. *Granular synthesis* takes this idea to an extreme. Each grain is an extremely brief, barely audible event, lasting typically between one thousandth and one tenth of a second and sounding like a tiny, faint, click. Despite its brevity, this sound event contains the conventional features: a wave form and an amplitude envelope. By combining many thousands of such grains, a larger, more extensive, sound may be made. In the illustration of a single grain (Figure 6.13), the upper sine wave is high frequency and the lower is low frequency, but both have the same duration.

Grains normally last less than 50 milliseconds and cannot be perceptually subdivided into smaller units. The characteristics of the wave forms of the individual grains affect the texture of a resulting sound when they are combined. The timbre of the outcome also depends upon grain size and the frequency of the resynthesis. Furthermore, these tiny waves can acquire the characteristics of the much larger waves: they can be fixed within the grain, or vary over time; they can be simple sine waves or samples of recorded sound or they can have several elements combined.

Granular synthesis, then, is based upon enveloped grains in high densities of hundreds or thousands per second, often formed into *streams* or *clouds*. Streams contain grains following one another at regular intervals but with tiny delays between them. A good analogy for this process would be the relationship between individual hits in a continuous drum roll. The *density* of grains in a stream will appear to generate metrical rhythms up to a frequency of about twenty grains per second and continuous pitches beyond that. This emergence of pitch from rhythm is a fundamental idea in a great deal of electronic music,[7] and granular synthesis is an excellent way to understand the principles.

The perception of pitch in a granular stream, for example, will depend on a set of complex interactions between the frequency of wave forms, the grain envelopes and the grain densities. The synchronous nature of the grain *stream* allows these elements to be

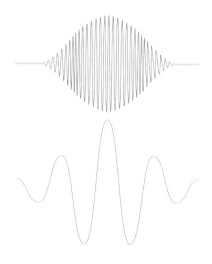

Figure 6.13 Image of two sine-wave grains © Gareth Howell

modified predictably over time. In the *cloud* model, however, the grains are randomly or chaotically distributed in time. Here, the density, duration, wave-form characteristics, amplitude envelopes and frequency bands may vary within the overall duration of the cloud. Granular time-stretching is an example of a technique that can integrate manipulation of both the spatial and timbral aspects of a sound, thus going beyond either time or spectrum-based processes alone.

Project 20 (Elementary): Analysis-Synthesis

Introduction

This will require some sound analysis/processing software that allows detailed study of a sound's spectrum, wave form, fundamental frequencies and partial contents, preferably through a visualization.

The Project

Record or download a guitar sample (a single note or a chord will do). Using appropriate software, find the frequencies of all the partials in the sound. Then create a synthesized version of the sound by adding sine tones of those frequencies together.

Does the synthesized version sound the same as the original sample? If not, why not?

Observe the spectrogram of the original sample closely. What can be heard 'inside' the sound? What are the relative strengths and weaknesses of the various partials? How are they shaped through time?

Notes

This useful exercise can be performed with a variety of original sounds. With practice it is possible to become very good at 'hearing' a spectrogram.

PROJECT 20

RECOMMENDED LISTENING

▶ Barry Truax (1986) *Riverrun* [CD] Wergo, 2017-50.
Classic work using granular synthesis to create a sound environment in which stasis and flux, solidity and movement co-exist in a dynamic balance.

▶ Max Mathews (1961) *Bicycle Built for Two (Daisy) Arrangement* [CD]. Computer Music Currents 13, Wergo 20332.
One of the most famous examples of early digital synthesis, in this case an uncanny voice.

▶ Eliane Radigue (1998) *Trilogie de la Mort* [CD] Experimental Intermedia, XI 119.
Extraordinary work influenced by Tibetan Buddhism. Radigue devoted herself to finding unique sounds exclusively using a single synthesizer, the ARP 2500 modular system.

FURTHER READING

■ Collins, N., *Introduction to Computer Music*, Chichester: Wiley, 2010.
The most recent of the recommended general introductions in this section. Has a strong technical basis, but also some relevant chapters on musical applications.

■ Dodge, C. and Jerse, T., *Computer Music: Synthesis, Composition, and Performance*, London: Schirmer Books, 1997.
A thorough and pedagogically well laid out text that examines digital synthesis using Csound. Includes discussions of musical works.

■ Moore, F. R., *Elements of Computer Music*, Englewood Cliff, NJ: Prentice-Hall, 1990.
A standard text that covers all the main areas, and is particularly strong on algorithmic composition.

■ Roads, C., *The Computer Music Tutorial*, Cambridge, MA: MIT Press, 1996.
Very well written, and covers all the important aspects of the subject. Embeds the historical aspects particularly effectively.

PROCESSING

Sooner or later the digital musician will encounter the vast array of plug-ins and digital signal processing modules that go under the general heading of *digital audio effects*. These are the processes that offer a rich field for creative exploration. To give a comprehensive account of all these would take a very large volume indeed[8] and in any case would require a 'how-to' explanation that is beyond the scope of the present volume. However, it is not possible to discuss digital music-making without giving at least a brief summary of their most important features.

While increasingly complex algorithms allow digital technologies to produce highly sophisticated results, they are not always musically 'better' than their analog counterparts. They are just different. Consider, for example, the resampling of a signal at a different rate. This will produce an effect that resembles speeding up and slowing down a tape-recording: the pitch will get higher or lower as the duration gets shorter or longer. When this is done as a digital technique, the results can sound even stranger than the equivalent analog manipulation, because the digital sound is not simply a transposed version of the original sound, it is a *brand new sound*, with its own features and characteristics.

Digital processes may be loosely grouped into five overlapping types based on their field of operation: time domain processes; frequency domain processes; dynamics processes; spatial processes; and spectral processes. In fact, these divisions are not hard and fast, as we shall see. The following summary descriptions covers each of the main domains with some typical parameters and creative musical uses, and explores some processes which combine two or more domains.

Time Domain Processes

The basic editing techniques, such as cut (or copy)–and–paste, are so commonplace that it is probably difficult to think of them as time domain processes, but that is in fact what they are. It is possible to layer many, many tracks and to fine-tune their relative positions in time to an extreme degree (i.e., one sample). 'Cut-and-paste' itself has become synonymous with a digital aesthetic based on sampled materials and rapid editing techniques. For the digital composer, this raises issues of quality. To take one very common example: it is usually considered desirable to make 'clean edits' that avoid clicks at the beginning or end, harsh entrances or cut-offs, abrupt changes in ambience and so on. In many instances, these would be cited as examples of bad technique. Yet there can be situations in which the reverse is the case, and 'dirty edits' are precisely what is wanted. The challenge for the composer is to convey the aesthetic idea convincingly enough that it is obvious to the listener that these are intentional 'lapses'.

One way to tidy up edits and remove unwanted clicks and pops is to make creative use of *fades*. The fade-in and fade-out gesture is common enough in recorded music and may be exploited over short and long time spans, or as a gesture within a musical passage. Cross-fades are a key element of editing, mixing and live performance, especially where beat-matching is part of the music. Handling cross-fade curves is something of an art in its own right, and whole instruments have been developed to enable this in live situations.

Most time domain processes derive from a fundamental musical problem: how to *extend*. Music is a process of extension and elaboration of sonic material over time, so it follows that a music based in sampled or synthesized sound will have to find ways of extending those sounds, even when they are formed into musical patterns. One very familiar technique for doing this is *looping*, which may be applied at the level of a single sound (e.g., by looping the sustain segment of the wave form) or at the level of a musical phrase or pattern. Variation applied to looped material may then build musical interest over time. Large quantities of music have emanated from these apparently simple processes which fulfil the listeners' requirements of repetition and variation.

Delays operate by storing the audio in a buffer for a certain amount of time then outputting it once again. A typical set of parameters for delays therefore includes: delay time (usually in milliseconds), feedback in terms of the percentage of amplitude, and decay time. Typical delay effects include *chorusing* (which mixes together many delayed copies to create thickening), *flanging* (combines the signal with variably delayed copies of itself), *vibrato* (wobbles the read pointer in a delay line, creating a 'human' effect), and *echoes* such as 'ping-pong' or 'slapback' (the kind of delay heard on classic rock and roll records).

At its most extreme durations, digital delay can be used to structure whole compositions, something which the computer has enabled with ever increasing buffer sizes. Delays may be synced to the tempo of the music, or may deliberately avoid that. They may also be 'ducked' to control levels relative to the music, or may be treated by filters to create rich effects.

One time domain process that is particularly useful in digital music making is *time-stretching*. This has a history going back to the 1950s and the 'Phonogène' of Pierre Schaeffer, a modified tape deck that altered the speed of passage of tape past several heads that sum the output to deliver a continuous sound. There are several ways in which to perform a time-stretch. One of the most common uses a *phase vocoder*, which breaks the sound down into short chunks, applies some processing and then typically recombines the FFT with the resulting chunks in some way. This has other further uses such as time-frequency filtering, which enables control of the gain for each frequency band, *dispersion*, which blurs a sound over time in the manner of the latency encountered in networks, *mutation* between two sounds, and *robotization*.

Time-stretch is traditionally used to correct small errors in timing that mean that the duration of samples in, say, electronic dance music, do not fit to the rigid beat. Parameters will typically include input and output length expressed in seconds or samples and, in many software packages, ways of 'locking' the stretch to the beats per minute or time signature of a song. Time-stretch may also be applied in time-varying ways in some packages, which gives even greater flexibility. It is worth bearing in mind that a time-stretch will generate a new sound that might perceptually resemble the original sound, but might also begin to introduce unexpected artefacts, particularly in the longer stretches. These may also be creatively exploited.

Frequency Domain Processes

An FFT enables the conversion of time domain information into the frequency domain. In other words, we can capture and represent the all the frequencies (and their relative amplitudes) that comprise the spectrum of a given sound. Processes may then be applied in the frequency domain.

A typical example is *EQ*, or Equalization. Both analog and digital EQ are designed to make the final recorded sound *equal* to the original source, by correcting inadequacies of both equipment and the recording environment. However, it can also be a highly creative tool when used skilfully. EQ adjusts the quality of a given sound by attenuating or boosting certain parts of the audio spectrum or bands of frequencies.

Two well-known equalizers are the *parametric* and the *graphic*. The parametric equalizer adjusts the *gain* (output level), *bandwidth* (frequency range) and *Q* (the width) of a frequency envelope[9] around a centre frequency. The graphic equalizer normally has fixed frequency and Q values. A four-band graphic equalizer, for example, might comprise two central band-pass filters, each of which is assigned to a particular range of frequencies, and one 'lo' and one 'hi' shelf filter. Shelving allows frequencies up to a shelf point to be adjusted and leaves those above (or below) unchanged. In some equalizers, the shelf point is specified by the user and is called a shelf because the areas being cut or boosted are fairly flat. These shelves vary in accuracy and usually have a *slope* either side of the shelf point. Parametric equalizers have controls which can be tuned to the desired frequency ranges and levels, and adjustable Q. They are therefore much more precise than graphic equalizers, but also harder to control.

EQ is really just a type of filtering. Filters of various kinds are found throughout digital audio, and their operations correspond fairly well to their analog counterparts, which tends to make understanding them relatively easy. A digital filter applies various processes to the samples which pass through it. A 'low-pass' filter, for example, allows low frequencies to pass through, but blocks high frequencies, whereas a 'high-pass' filter does the reverse, and a 'bandpass' filter allows through frequencies within a given band. Digital filters are often specified in terms of their permitted variations in frequency response, and can achieve a level of performance which far exceeds what is even theoretically possible with analog filters. For example, a low-pass filter that blocks a 1001Hz signal but allows through a 999Hz signal can be achieved. Such minute differences are not possible with analog filters.

A more complex filter is called a *comb filter*. This adds a slightly delayed version of a signal to itself, and it is called a comb filter because its frequency response wave form looks like a series of spikes. Comb filtering is really a corrective device, using *phase cancellation*[10] to avoid unwanted phenomena, but it is also useful for creating echo effects. The effect of an echoing cylinder, for example, can be created readily using this method. Here we start to see ways in which the time and frequency domains may be combined.[11]

Similar comments may be made about *pitch-shifting*, which transposes a sound by a fixed interval or even by time-varying intervals. This process may be allowed to affect the timbre of the sound as well as the pitch, or its timbral characteristics may be retained at the new pitch. The well-known, and rather controversial, auto-tune plugin is an example of a pitch-shifter that is used to correct errors in vocal intonation. Typical controls will allow adjustments by octaves, semitones or cents. Pitch-shifting will repay experimentation, and it is possible to create some extraordinary and new sounds by using this tool in ways not necessarily envisaged by its maker. Whole music genres, such as 'grindcore', in which the vocals are lowered by pitch-shifting, have arisen from this kind of experimentation.

PROJECT 21

Project 21 (Elementary): Reverse EQ

Introduction

This creative studio technique can produce some surprisingly useful musical results. It can even be undertaken in real time as part of a performance.

The Project

Take a sound with a clear decay and reverse it. Now apply EQ and other filters to modify the reversed sound until it becomes musically interesting. Finally re-reverse the sound to discover a new timbre.

Notes

This technique can be repeated and adapted for both composition and performance. There is even a conceptual aspect: imagining the reversed sound and the re-reversed sound.

Dynamics Processes

Dynamics processes relate to amplitude and often have their roots in electronic music. They are the basis, for example, of traditional guitar effects such as fuzz and distortion. However, it is important to note that digital distortion has its own peculiar characteristics, which are a normally undesirable clipping of the sound and artefacts that do not at all resemble the overdriven qualities of traditional distortion.

Modulation typically uses a sine wave to modify aspects of a signal, such as the amplitude, frequency and phase. A classic use for this technique is to create wah-wah and tremolo effects in the amplitude domain, or vibrato and flanging in phase modulations. The use of modulation in digital instruments, often controlled by wheels or joysticks, is so familiar as to have become somewhat musically clichéd today. So, for example, the tremolo effect that was intended to give a 'human' quality to a sound is now recognizably 'electronic', as are the 'clean' sounds of FM synthesis. Classic effects such as *ring modulation*, which multiplies the amplitude of two signals, and outputs the resulting sum and difference together (omitting the original signal), or the rotary loudspeaker effect, are very well known. This still leaves room for creative exploration, particularly when interacting with other effects such as delays and filters.

Enhancers and *exciters* work by adding harmonics and inharmonics into a sound. They are good for cleaning up old recordings by separating out noise, and in the simulation of analog components such as valves. They also are used to emulate analog processors such as: *limiters*, which adjust high peaks in a signal; *compressors* and *expanders*, which reduce or expand the dynamic range of a signal; *noise gates*, which prevent a peak signal's passage (usually with a fade-in/fade-out of the gain) and which may be used rhythmically to control the level of one signal via the dynamics of another; and *de-essers*, which essentially control filters on specific frequency bands associated with the sibilant sounds in speech.

Effective manipulation of compression, for example, has been a feature of digital dance music, in which *sidechains* are used to determine when a given process should begin. Clever use of these techniques maintains the compression of the overall mix and delivers that 'fat' sound that is so essential to the genre. This is an example of how creative exploration of tools that are intended for one use (error correction, in this case) may lead to another less expected application. The potential in this approach is considerable, and the digital musician in search of an original sound would do well to avoid the more clichéd uses of these effects and exploit more unpredictable results.

Spatial Processes

The most basic spatial process is *panning*, which emulates the behaviour of loudspeakers by adjusting the intensity of the signal between them. Sound trajectories, or looming, and well-known characteristics of sound in motion such as the *Döppler effect* will also be handled by these processes.

Reverberation simulates the effect of the environment on a sound source and its perception by a listener. Correlating reverb to space is a staple of sound-image work too, where any dislocation between the reverberant properties of the depicted space and the heard space can be particularly confusing for the viewer.

A typical reverberation plugin will include parameters for panorama, distance and space. Manipulating spatial effects is a mix of art and science and mastery of this technique can take years. You can expect to find detailed settings for *early reflections*, *predelay* (time between the direct signal and the start of the reverb), *reverb time* (the larger the space, the longer the reverb time), *reverb damping* (these are EQs applied to particular frequency ranges over time to enhance the illusion of more or less reflective surfaces) and *reverb EQ* (applies EQ to the entire reverb, or just the reverberation part).

Many reverberation plugins are in fact combinations of comb and allpass filters, or networks of feedback delay. Spectral processes such as *convolution* have arrived relatively recently as a reverberation technique, allowing the superimposition of the resonant properties of any given space onto a source signal. Reverberation can also be a by-product of granular synthesis, so the stretched bell sounds in *Basilica* (1992) by Barry Truax, for example, create an enlarged sense of the acoustic space of a church. This can be used in a concert situation to extend the space of the concert hall or in a non-concert situation to create a virtual space.

Spectral Processes

Spectral processing is an extension and combination of the time and frequency domain processes described above. It offers a range of creative possibilities, from blurring to emerging, from granulation to harmonization, from tracing to weaving, and many of the familiar effects available through other processes: pitch shift, chorus, comb filters and so on. Special effects include a 'gender change' voice which moves seamlessly from male to female, or instant vocal harmonization. Since they operate in the spectrum, the range of potential parameters is vast and new modules are being created very rapidly in the software development community.

Spectral morphing creates a seamless transition between two sounds by analysing their spectra and applying time-varying processes. These processes may include *interpolation* (where data from one file is inserted between data from the other) and *concatenation* (where the two sets of spectral data are combined in various ways). Often the most interesting part of a morphing process is the 'in-between' phase, and this can be further extracted and reprocessed.

Cross-synthesis or *vocoding* in which the timbre of one signal is used to modify another, traditionally that of the voice applied to an instrument, hence 'voice coder'. The pitch of the first sound is preserved, but its spectral shape is altered by the second.

De-noising selectively adjusts the levels of certain aspects of a spectrum over time, allowing for both 'cleaning up' of sounds and more unusual uses that exploit the effect creatively.

Formant changing replaces the spectral envelope of a sound with a warped version of another (as in the classic 'Donald Duck' voice effect).

Impulse Response filtering captures the response to a very short signal. The simplest form of such a filter is called a Finite Impulse Response (FIR) filter, in which 'taps' are taken from successive samples, which are then multiplied by a coefficient (a multiplicative factor) and the results are added together to form the output of the filter. This is called 'finite' because there are a fixed number of taps.

An Infinite Impulse Response (IIR) filter, by contrast, allows feedback between the output and the input, which can create some long-lasting results, including growth or decay over time. This is particularly useful for effects such as reverberation. Where the impulse-response of a physical space may be recorded by, for example, firing a gun or bursting a balloon, the IIR filter may be used to model the same digitally.

Creative uses of such filters includes *convolution*, which combines two soundfiles – the input and an impulse response – by multiplying their spectra together to produce a new sound file. Frequencies that are common to both sound files will tend to be reinforced and resonate together. The filter will try to match bin content across the two spectra. Where there is a match, the data is preserved. Where there is no match, it is discarded (or, strictly, multiplied by 0). Amongst other things, this enables the application of the reverberant properties of resonance to FFT windows over time and thus the superimposition of the reverberant characteristics of one sound upon another.

The creative implications of this technique are considerable. Convolution incorporates both the microsound (frequency-time) domain and the spatial domain, allowing for integration of timbre and space in processing. This goes well beyond merely adding a convincing reverb to a sound or track (which it does as well). The EARS site lists the following possibilities: 'spectral and rhythmic hybriding, reverberation and echo, spatial simulation and positioning, excitation/resonance modelling, attack and time smearing.'[12] To these may be added the more musical aspects of evocation and recontextualization.

In conclusion, we may observe that the transformation of sound is a highly important aspect of creating digital music. In a large composition, these sound transformations themselves may become a key formal or structural element of the overall drama of the work, by producing sonic images that form the basis of the musical argument. In Trevor Wishart's piece *Red Bird* (1973–1977), for example, the transformation from vocal sounds to other sounds was the starting-point for the form of the whole composition.[13]

Project 22 (Elementary): Sonic Morph

Introduction

Morphing is more usually found in animation, video and photography, where software enables one image to morph with another. In digital audio, a morph is a more sophisticated version of a cross-fade, in which the content of the two soundfiles is actually intermingled during the intermediate stage. This project, however, concentrates on the perceptual, rather than the technical aspects of a sound morph.

The Project

Take two recorded sounds, such as a hi-hat hit and a snare drum. Using any available tools (pitch shifting, time stretching, etc.) operate on *one* of the sound files only until it sounds as nearly as possible like the other. This may involve repeating the sound numerous times. Then do the same with the other sound file.

Notes

This is a fairly laborious exercise, and morphing software can perform what would be probably a more effective and smoother morph between the two files readily enough without all the effort. So why undertake the task? Because the aural awareness and understanding of the acoustic content of the sound it will produce will be invaluable. There will also be a spin-off benefit in understanding the time-based processes. Ask the following questions: Is there an obvious point in time at which the character of the sound changes? Can this point be moved? Is the point the same for other people?

PROJECT 22

FURTHER READING

■ Pellman, S., *An Introduction to the Creation of Electroacoustic Music*, Belmont: Wadsworth Publishing Company, 1994.
Aims to be accessible to students relatively inexperienced with electronic musical technology, while also sufficiently detailed for technical and musical achievement. Furthermore, it stresses the notion that, despite all the attention given to technique, the principal goal is musical expression.

■ Miranda, E., *Computer Sound Design: Synthesis Techniques and Programming*, London: Focal, 2002.
Covers most of the recent developments in digital synthesis and sound design techniques, including artificial intelligence and evolutionary computing.

■ Wishart, T., *Audible Design*, York: Orpheus the Pantomime Press, 1994.
Designed to complement the more philosophical *On Sonic Art*. This examines sound transformation techniques, with an illustrative accompanying recording.

RECOMMENDED LISTENING

▶ Trevor Wishart (1992) *Red Bird* [CD] October Music, 001.

▶ Larry Polansky (1991) *51 Melodies* [CD] Artifact, 02.
Computer-composed work for two electric guitars and optional rhythm section, or any two melody instruments.

▶ Amon Tobin (2011) *ISAM* [CD] NinjaTune, ZEN168.
Highly sculpted electronica album with sonic morphing at its core.

Discussion Questions

• What makes a digital sound 'interesting, powerful and beautiful' (Max Mathews)?

• What are the musical benefits and disadvantages of digitization?

• What does it mean to 'go inside' a sound? To what extent does digitization really enable this?

• Do file formats matter?

• What is bad technique in digital music?

CHAPTER 7

Creating Music

THE COMPOSER

One of the biggest changes in music in the past thirty years or so has been in the role of the composer. To be the originator in Western classical music traditionally implies a hierarchy and one that is consolidated by copyright laws. This hierarchy is based on the idea that the composer is a figure of ultimate authority, underpinned by an assumption that the composer's ears are somehow better than those of a musician. The new technologies have challenged this hierarchy. First, they have placed all the tools for composing within reach: it is easy to create music. Second, they have enabled a degree of interaction with the music that can blur the distinction between the originator and the consumer. People can instantly remix, mash up, or otherwise recreate music. Third, they have transformed the act of performance into (potentially) an act of composition. People can record as they perform and make identical copies, which never degrade in quality. The separation that has grown up between composers and musicians is breaking down. The musician may be as much of an originator as the composer. In certain circumstances, the audience can become the originator.

For many artists, the word 'composer' itself is problematic, conjuring up an image of a lone heroic genius or some historical character in a powdered wig. These artists do not call what they do 'composition', yet they are engaged in an activity which would undoubtedly be classed as such by most experts in the field, and they do it often with excellent results. The same issue arises in the case of sound designers and sonic artists, where the resistance to any kind of musical overtone to what is being done leads to a kind of horror at the idea of being classed as a 'composer'. The 'dots' composers, writing in the traditional way, would probably agree with that distinction. But the evidence tends to contradict them both.

'Composition' means, simply and literally, *putting things together*. The word crops up in contexts other than music, of course, including science, literature, even chess.[1] A musical composer, then, is simply someone who puts sounds together. The more conventional idea that a composer must write music notation and that others should be able to reproduce a given work in performance does not go far enough to cover electro-acoustic music, for example. To stretch the point, an improvising performer is also engaged in acts of instant composition. The education system complicates things further, by insisting that all students of both 'music' and 'music technology' engage in something called 'composition' which involves the origination of music. Today's musician is, to a great extent, a product of these developments. The digital musician is a composer.

Now, there is no reason to *insist* on someone who creatively puts sounds together using technology being called a 'composer' if neither the sonic artists (or whatever we call them) nor the 'real' composers want that. Except that, and it is a big point, there *is* a reason why traditional composers have evolved in the way they have: they understand composition. At the very least, the composers have something to teach the rest of us about composition. The study of existing music will always repay with dividends the effort expended, even if the music comes from a tradition that seems completely alien.

The major point here is that there is a blurring of roles in recent music-making and that a vastly increased number of people are today undertaking an activity that involves originating or combining sounds, often with musical intention or result. For the digital musician, engaged in such activity, developing a knowledge and understanding of composition may be regarded as highly beneficial, if not essential.

So, composition involves putting together sonic content so that it takes on some form or other. The new technologies make this easy, but the fact that it *can* be done does not mean it *should* be done. There has to be a reason to compose, especially if the composition is to be good. There has to be an intention behind the result. And the composer has to be able to judge the result when measured against the intention. The question now is no longer *whether* we can compose, nor even *what* to compose, but *why* compose?

WHY COMPOSE?

One approach to this question is first to identify the purpose of the music, or (to answer a question with a question) what is the music *for*? We are no longer under the illusion that there is an objective purpose that can be ascribed to music, other than that which we ascribe. What are some of those purposes? If the brief is commercial, then more often than not the function of the music will be clearly defined (usually by someone else). However, not all music is commercial music. In fact, some would-be commercial music can turn out *not* to be commercial, and vice versa! But the purposes of music can extend far beyond the question of a commercial brief. Here are some musings on the question: what is music for?

- to explore and expand human experience
- to awaken sensitivity to the divine
- to mark something out as special
- to facilitate social bonding
- to exercise the choice of being creative
- to extol, support, encourage
- to provide therapy
- to engage in a battle for supreme intellectual achievement
- to evolve the human race and its social systems
- to provoke questioning of the existing social order
- to enact freedom
- to calm the mind
- to provide emotional catharsis
- to encourage people to shop
- to encourage people to march, celebrate, worship, kill
- to encourage bodily health
- to avoid thought
- to seek answers to questions
- to better understand oneself
- to demonstrate to others how great you are
- to pursue a fascination
- to preserve a sonic environment
- to tell stories
- to avoid telling stories
- to pass the time
- to make a statement about self and/or group identity
- to irritate the neighbours
- to torture
- to induce ecstasy
- to pass a class
- to entertain the family
- to woo
- to build one's career
- to appear clever
- to give theorists something to talk about
- to make one feel [*fill in blank*]
- to experience pleasure or provide pleasure
- 'inner necessity'
- just because.[2]

What each of these has in common is an assumption that music is active, that it has a capacity to *do* or *say* something. In every sense, the music has an effect or a voice and, for many people, music has a *meaning*.

Academic discussions often focus upon an ancient debate about musical meaning. One camp argues that music resembles a language, with clear grammar and syntax and that, therefore, it is possible to ascribe meanings to, and even tell stories in, sound. The opposing camp argues that, in fact, music is 'absolute', that is to say, it has no meaning over and above the sounds that you hear and, as the composer Stravinsky famously, and provocatively, said it: 'is incapable of expressing anything but itself'.[3] The debate becomes particularly heated when the subject of the way in which music expresses *emotions* arises.

Most people would agree that music can express, or at least *seems* to express, emotions. However, there is general disagreement about what those emotions may be in a particular case. Listeners' emotional states vary, and the responses they make also vary. A piece that seems sad to one audience may be amusing to another. There is nothing inherently *in the music* that makes this so, but, then again, without the music there would presumably be no such feeling at all.

This has implications for the composer or musician. Let's suppose you feel angry, and you want to create some music to express that anger. First, it is hard to create music when gripped by a powerful emotion such as anger. When you try it, the emotion itself gets in the way of the rational thought needed to organize materials and equipment, to structure and give form to the music. You may know what it is to feel anger, but what you want to do is to create some music *that evokes that feeling.* That is a very different statement, but it will probably be far more successful as an approach to achieving the expressive goal.

You may start to draw upon music's evocative power by exploring the ways in which anger may be expressed musically in your culture. At first, perhaps, you might think of loud, clashing, jarring material, which seems to draw a direct parallel with the emotion you felt. A more subtle approach might in fact avoid the obviously loud, clashing music in favour of a more 'internalized', 'tense', almost psychological evocation of anger. Whatever solution you adopt, the sheer compositional craft involved will tend to make the musical depiction of anger distanced, reflective. In other words, the expression of emotion in music is to a certain extent a matter of technique. This does not necessarily mean it lacks feeling, or is in some way 'cold and calculated'.

Musical expression depends a great deal upon *context.* To take some material that is 'sad' and place it in some new context it does not necessarily mean that the quality of sadness will also have transferred to the new situation. Since a great deal of contemporary music uses such recontextualization, it is important to understand that any material, in any context, will have a relationship with its new context and its old context. The listeners' perceptions of this relationship will depend partly upon their knowledge of the two contexts and partly upon their abilities to deduce from the aural evidence. The fact that a composer knows both the origins and the destinations of recontextualized material does not guarantee that the listeners will share that understanding.

This can be extended to the question of intention and result. It is an unfortunate fact that whatever meanings you *intend* to communicate with your sounds, there is no guarantee that the listener will actually understand. Some recent research conducted by Robert Weale into the intention and reception of electro-acoustic music[4] tests this idea by playing various groups of listeners pieces of music with and without titles and additional information. Although there was some convergence in reaction, there were also differences in audience understanding *even when they had access to the composer's intentions.* Music as self-expression, then, seems, at best, an inaccurate weapon.

Despite this, the creation of music fulfils a need for such expression, and it is no accident that certain composers and musicians seem to communicate their ideas better than others. In some cases, this happens in spite of the composer. Stravinsky remarked, 'I was the vessel through which *Le Sacre du Printemps* passed.' On other occasions, the emotional involvement of the composer in his or her own music seems integral to its success (Beethoven is an obvious example).

There is no single answer to the question 'Why compose?' Each person should find his or her own reasons. There are plenty of reasons why *not* to compose, of which the most pressing is the sheer quantity of existing music. And yet, the desire to find a voice as an artist is so strong that many people feel impelled to do so. The wonderful thing about the new technologies is that they have enabled so many to produce good results and often with relatively little formal musical training or in unusual circumstances.

Project 23 (Intermediate): Inspiration Box

Introduction

This is a creative exercise in inspiration and meaning. It is designed for at least two partici-pants and can produce powerful results.

The Project

Assemble a box containing several objects that offer inspiration. These may include sound-ing objects or recordings, but also evocative or personal items such as photographs, writ-ings, in fact anything at all that has some meaning.

   Pass the box to another person who will create a piece of digital music inspired by what it contains. The personal meanings may be revealed before or after the music is com-pleted by prior agreement.

Notes

It is important that this project is undertaken seriously and with respect and open-minded-ness on all sides.

PROJECT 23

THE COMPOSITIONAL PROCESS

The computer has brought facility to the process of composition. Composing digital music is easy, and complex operations that could have taken weeks, months, or even years, to complete in the past using electronic or paper-based media may now be run very quickly. Furthermore, digital composition has opened up a new set of techniques that may have some things in common with previous practice, but were nevertheless impossible without the number-crunching capabilities of a computer. This facility does not necessarily mean that the quality of music has improved. Questions of aesthetic judgement will be considered in detail in Part III of this book. For now, let us simply remark that *any* sound has an aesthetic dimension, and that digital music-making is a two-part process of production and consumption.

Digital composition works with two kinds of sounds: those originating from a non-digital source such as a recording or a live feed, and those sounds generated by a system, such as in digital synthesis. A great deal of time and effort has been spent over the years in trying to lessen the distinction between these two. So, physical modelling techniques are used to digitally synthesize a convincing acoustic instrument, and sampled recordings are digitally processed to reveal sounds that do not resemble anything heard in the acoustic domain. However, it is important to bear in mind as a general principle that in digital music *all sounds are fundamentally the same*: collections of data encoded in binary form.

Digital composition, therefore, begins as a set of decisions taken by the musician or by the software about the datasets they are manipulating. These decisions may be conditioned by many factors, but will be profoundly influenced by the unifying properties of the digitization process. This process is by no means neutral in itself. Binary encoding is subject to various constraints and much variability. In particular, file formats dictate the way the resulting musical information may be perceived and handled. Different software packages will process data in different ways that are often not obvious to the user. Despite the enormous range of possibilities available to the digital composer, there is still a sense in which complete control of sonic materials remains out of reach.

The process of digital composition consists of a 'feedback loop' of creation and critical reflection. The process is completed by a release, either in the form of a publication or, more simply, in a 'letting go' of the resulting material. At that point, the composer's own judgements may become rather irrelevant, as audiences and wider critical opinions form their own views of the work. Even in digital composition where the aesthetic intention is to remove the human element from the creation of the work as far as possible, it is important to bear in mind that this represents a creative decision in its own right and still influences both the outcome and the way it is received.

FURTHER READING

- Miranda, E. R., *Composing Music with Computers*, Oxford: Focal Press, 2001.
  Focuses on the role of the computer as a generative tool for music composition. Miranda introduces a number of computer music composition techniques ranging from probabilities, formal grammars and fractals, to genetic algorithms, cellular automata and neural computation.

- Norman, K., *Sounding Art: Eight Literary Excursions through Electronic Media*, London: Ashgate, 2004.
  Eight extended literary compositions about the digital compositional process, whose structure, language and visual appearance are carefully constructed to amplify their theme – whether it be microsound or acousmatic art, electro-acoustic or radiophonic music, plunderphonics, turntables or noise.

- Roads, C. (ed.) *Composers and the Computer*, Madison, WI: A-R Editions, 2004.
  A collection of nine interviews with leading composers of computer music.

AURAL IMAGINATION

The role of the imagination has been somewhat transformed by digital technologies. The emergence of an aural culture, working directly with sound itself, has had certain consequences. One advantage of the notation-based system was that it forced composers in particular, but also musicians in general, to develop an aural imagination, often referred to as the 'inner ear'. This is the ability to hear accurately in the mind, without reference to any actual sound, a skill that is called *audiation*. Often, it would be combined with score-reading, such that a conductor, for example, would be able to 'read' a score off the page, hearing the music with the inner ear in the same way that one might read a book without speaking (or hearing spoken) the words.

The aural imagination has great creative potential, allowing musical forms and structures to be shaped by the individual before committing them to actual sound. It can also operate simultaneously with music-making, allowing the musician to imagine other ways to develop or manipulate the material as they do so. It is a means of experimentation, of creative play. To what extent should this be retained as part of the 'hands-on', concrete, way of working encouraged by the new technologies?

Sculpture provides an interesting parallel to illustrate this problem. A sculptor may begin by seeing a pattern in nature or by observing an aspect of human existence. Or they may set out to make a reproduction of an existing object. Whatever their purpose, sculptors will often use their materials to make something that resembles their imagination. In doing so, they might reveal to the rest of us something not seen before, some truth. More often than not, there will be a single material, such as stone or wood. Sometimes, what is revealed is the inherent properties of the material itself, which once again connects with the imagination: within this we might find *this*.

Project 24 (Intermediate): Sunset

Introduction

This project aims to encourage an awakening of the aural imagination. The most important part, therefore, is the early exercise, rather than the finished piece, hence the 'intermediate' tag. Nevertheless, if seen through to its ultimate conclusion, this could become quite a substantial work.

The Project

Watch a sunset. You will need to set aside a couple of hours or more to do this properly. You should watch from the moment at which the sun hits the horizon, to the point at which all trace of its colour has gone from the sky.

Now try to imagine how a sunset would *sound*. What are the main features? How do the elements of a sunset translate into sound? And, most importantly, how do the feelings the sunset produced in *you* translate into sound? How do you convey the impression created? Make written or aural notes to help you if necessary.

Now, create a piece that reproduces as nearly as possible what you have imagined. Observe and note the gaps between what you have imagined and the finished result. Have

PROJECT 24

other people listen to the piece, without telling them what the piece is about. Do they *get* it? Try again with a title ('Sunset' is the obvious one), or more information. Does that change things?

Finally, get hold of some video footage of a sunset and attempt the same exercise but with the addition of the visual imagery. What has changed? Is the imagination liberated or constrained by the visuals? Can anything be done to improve the imaginative experience?

Notes

The addition of the final phase takes this beyond a traditional composition exercise inspired by nature and into a more mediated, cinematic treatment. However, the first parts of the project are very important. This is not simply music to accompany a video. Instead, the music is the dominant element.

The project will probably take two or three weeks to realize if a satisfactory final piece is to arise.

Time passing, a sense of awe and mystery, the power of nature, are good sources of inspiration for an artist of any description.

FURTHER READING

■ Godøy, R. I. and Jørgensen, H. (eds), *Musical Imagery*, Lisse: Swets and Zeitlinger, 2001.
An edited collection of papers which explore our mental capacity for imagining sound in the absence of a directly audible sound source, meaning that we can recall and re-experience or even invent new musical sound through our 'inner ear'.

■ Théberge, P., *Any Sound You Can Imagine*, Middletown, CT: Wesleyan University Press, 1997.
Argues that digital synthesizers, samplers and sequencers in studio production and in the home have caused musicians to rely increasingly on manufacturers for both the instruments themselves as well as the very sounds and musical patterns that they use to make music.

INTENTION AND RESULT

In the creation of any work, there is an *intention* to create and a finished *result* of the act of creation. The imagination is most active in the gap between intention and result. It could be said that this is where the *art* resides.

Even in a situation where the computer is the composer, or an algorithm has been created which follows its own course regardless of human intervention, the initial intention to create such a musical situation must be there. The key to making good digital composition lies in the ability to adapt mentally to the nature of the work itself. In other words, it is no good condemning an algorithmic piece for showing a lack of freedom from constraints or an improvisation for lacking sufficient pre-planning, any more than it is fair to criticize a lion for not being a tiger. The work should be evaluated on its own terms.

The crucial elements of the critical reflection phase of the composition process therefore focus on the mapping of intention to result. The ability to self-evaluate, to criticize one's own compositional work, is an important skill. There may be situations where indifference to the outcome of the work is part of the creative project itself, but this kind of situation needs considerable conceptual and artistic maturity to succeed. In general, the composer or artist will have some idea of what they want to achieve and some sense of whether they have achieved it. Evidence of compositional ability will be provided by the following four elements:

1   *Technical Skill.* An evident ability to handle the equipment is a prerequisite of a successful piece. Any sign of a shortcoming in this respect will reduce the effectiveness of the work.

2   *Decision-making.* The choices made in the creation of the piece tell the listener much about the intention of the artist. Sometimes, success is measured more by what is *not* done than by what *is* done. A bad decision will be one that contradicts the perceived intention of the work. Manipulating this perceived intention through the decisions made is the sign of consummate critical judgement.

3   *Creativity.* Creativity is a broad and multifaceted concept.[5] At its simplest level, any action that produces a result, in any sphere, is to some extent 'creative'. But the creation of good music implies something more: the generation of new ideas, the presence of some original thought; in other words, *inventiveness*.

4   *Artistic Purpose.* Even though, as has been said, the piece of music is inevitably the result of some kind of intention, there is nothing that reduces the effectiveness of a work more than purposelessness. Nor can purpose be easily introduced into something that has none. To be purposeful is not necessarily to be 'useful'. Art for art's sake can be purpose enough. The purposefulness of a piece is not linked to its function in the world but rather to its sense of its own right to exist. This comes from a combination of aesthetic or artistic intention with effective organization of the materials. There should be purpose in the craft of composition as well as in the ideas that lie behind them. As before, this does not mean that a work cannot deliberately explore 'purposelessness' as an idea. That would be its purpose.

FREEDOM AND CONSTRAINT

Musical creation may begin with freedom or may be highly constrained. It would be a mistake to assume that a free approach leads to freer composition. In fact, constraints can often be highly liberating. Adopting a deliberately restricted process or pattern can trigger ideas and inspiration and is usually a good way to start to make music. Having said that, there is nothing inherently wrong with a free approach, except that it can be difficult to do *anything* if all possibilities are open to the musician. In practice, most people end up submitting to self-imposed constraints, even if these are fairly underdeveloped (e.g., genre conventions or personal taste).

Some typical examples of constraints might include:

- material constraints, where restrictions are placed upon the quantity or nature of the sonic materials
- process-based constraints, where the musical process itself unfolds according to rules (e.g., algorithmic music)
- compositional constraints, placing constraints on the act of composition itself (e.g., making music in a particular *style* or using a particular technique for a particular purpose).

When working with constraint, it is important to bear in mind that the constraint itself is not the piece. An example from history will help to illustrate the point here.

In 1952, the composer Pierre Boulez published *Structures 1* for two pianos. This was an example of extreme compositional constraint. Every element of the piece (intervals, rhythms, dynamics, etc.) was subject to mathematical rules in which the individual units (notes, durations, dynamic markings, etc.) were ordered into series. The result, often called 'integral serialism', was a work that exhibits a startling apparent randomness in its surface, while being so tightly constrained behind the scenes as to lack much evidence of the composer's hand at work.

At the same time, John Cage was composing a work for piano, also trying to remove evidence of the composer's hand but with a radically different compositional constraint. *Music of Changes* (1951) was created using chance procedures, in this case coin tosses, to decide the ordering of the musical elements. As Cage's fellow composer Earle Brown put it, Cage was 'beginning to consciously deal with the "given" material and, to varying degrees, liberate them from the inherited, functional aspects of control'.[6]

These two works were created very differently, yet the result is, to the ear, surprisingly similar. In fact, hearing one another's work made both composers reconsider their compositional approaches. Boulez gradually moved away from integral serialism, and Cage's chance procedures became more sophisticated and somewhat deterministic. Neither constraint has survived as a common working practice in music, and neither *Music of Changes* nor *Structures 1* finds a regular place on concert programmes.

This strange convergence of two extremely different, yet rigorously applied, constraints was a key moment in the evolution of music in the twentieth century. What they have in common is an obsession with control, either seeking to apply it thoroughly (in the case of Boulez) or to reject it utterly (in the case of Cage). What seems to have emerged is a realization that, in applying their constraints so vigorously, the result was *musically* indistinct. For both composers, the solution was subsequently to address musical questions, where appropriate, at the expense of the constraints.

The message for the digital musician from this anecdote is: work with a constraint, by all means, but do not let it override the music. If the constraint produces unmusical outcomes, either change it, or ignore it, but do not fall back on the 'system made me do it' excuse. Of course, the word 'unmusical' itself implies a subjective judgement, which refers back to the criteria described earlier.

Project 25 (Advanced): Sudoku

Introduction

Algorithms are sets of rules that produce a finished state. Using algorithms to make music has a long history which has expanded to include stochastic and chaotic, formal and linguistic, generative and quasi-neurological algorithms. The purpose of this project is not necessarily to create new algorithms or to investigate this field, but rather to understand the relationship between the musician, the computer and the algorithm. The popular puzzle Sudoku provides a useful tool for this purpose. Sudoku may be found in many newspapers, puzzle books or on the web. The rules are simple: fill the 9 × 9 grid so that each column, each row, and each of the nine 3 × 3 boxes contains the digits from 1 to 9.

The Project:

Make three digital musical versions of a Sudoku puzzle:

1   Computer-controlled.
2   'User'-controlled (where the user is someone other than the person making this project).
3   Composer/performer-controlled.

The numbers may map to any parameter of the music (sounds, rhythms, intensities, etc.).

5	3			7				
6			1	9	5			
	9	8					6	
8				6				3
4			8		3			1
7				2				6
	6					2	8	
			4	1	9			5
				8			7	9

5	3	4	6	7	8	9	1	2
6	7	2	1	9	5	3	4	8
1	9	8	3	4	2	5	6	7
8	5	9	7	6	1	4	2	3
4	2	6	8	5	3	7	9	1
7	1	3	9	2	4	8	5	6
9	6	1	5	3	7	2	8	4
2	8	7	4	1	9	6	3	5
3	4	5	2	8	6	1	7	9

Figure 7.1   A typical Sudoku puzzle and its solution

Notes

Mapping decisions are significant here. The computer-controlled version is straightforward to execute, but how can the results be made musically interesting? Giving the user control may require some kind of training, if they are to complete the puzzle successfully. Is it the solution, the original, or the processes involved in solving the puzzle that is being mapped? If this is to be performed by the composer, to what extent (if at all) can the algorithm be used to reflect compositional intentions?

FURTHER READING

- Cope, D., *The Algorithmic Composer*, Madison, WI: A-R Editions, 2000.
  Covers the background and fundamentals of the subject, and introduces Cope's own work including the ALICE (Algorithmically Integrated Composing Environment) project.

- Nattiez, J.-J. (ed.), *The Boulez–Cage Correspondence*, Cambridge: Cambridge University Press, 1993.
  Reveals the extent of the similarities and differences between Pierre Boulez and John Cage.

ORIGINALITY AND STYLE

Another key aspect of the compositional process concerns notions of originality and style. Who is the originator of a sample-based piece? The person who recorded the samples? The person who wrote the software that processes them? The person who diffuses the sound that results? Or is it, in fact, the person who takes all the decisions about these elements: the digital musician. The person who produces a recording, or creates the soundtrack for a computer game or makes a sound installation is a composer. Adaptive computer-game music pieces, or interactive sound installations, are not fixed objects in the manner of a notated score, and even a CD may be diffused by taking the stereo content and allocating it to multiple channels. What seems so fixed, so certain, is, in fact, highly mutable. The 'repeatability' of a 'performance' is by no means guaranteed. It is even a myth that a digital recording always sounds the same. In the hand of a good sound diffuser or performer, it *never* sounds the same.

The question of originality is, thus, a starting point for composition. To put it simply: to what extent should the composer use models or 'borrow' from other artists? Most music derives in some way or another from other music. However innovative a compositional idea or approach may be, it is practically certain that there will be some artistic connection with something already heard or known. This is not to deny the possibility of originality but simply to suggest that no music exists in a vacuum. For many young composers, the development and acquisition of technique is, in itself, sufficiently demanding, without having to create an entirely new musical language for themselves from the outset.

A traditional approach to this problem is to 'pastiche' known music. This crops up both in classical training (where stylistic exercises are commonplace) and band situations (in the form of the 'cover' song), but also a lot of multimedia and interdisciplinary work. Most Hollywood film music, for example, is almost entirely pastiche, generally of late nineteenth- and early twentieth-century classical orchestral music. Games soundtracks, too, can often call for film-like pastiche. Good pastiche of this kind is difficult to achieve and normally requires a traditional training.

There is a less clearly established set of values regarding pastiche work available to the digital musician, because both the media and the musical forms that arise from them are so new. The sample-based culture is pervasive. Where the techniques are deployed in a recognizable sub-culture or genre, then a clear knowledge of the conventions of that culture are obviously required. But it is usually the case that the individual musician has to go beyond those conventions if they are to succeed in that culture.

The early stages of personal musical development may well involve pastiche work and, as the abilities improve, so the distinctive content in the work will evolve. Where the music itself is more experimental or less obviously genre-based, then pastiche may be less relevant. Either way, the practice of pastiche can be valuable to further an understanding of both compositional process and artistic intention, but it should be used with caution. If the goal is musical innovation, then over-reliance on pastiche work will get in the way. Having compositional models in mind is *not* the same as pastiche. This is the difference between showing a musical influence and simply aping somebody else's practice.

Musical style is often linked to genre classification as it implies the use of a certain basic 'language'. Reggae style, for example, seems quite different from country music, so at first glance this appears to be fairly uncontroversial. However, style has increasingly become linked to the need to pigeonhole musicians for commercial purposes. The musician John Zorn wrote:

> Jazz. Punk. Dada. Beat. These words and their longer cousins, the ism-family (surrealism, postmodernism, abstract expressionism, minimalism), are used to commodify and commercialize an artist's complex personal vision. This terminology is not about understanding. It never has been. It's about money. Once a group of artists, writers, or musicians has been packaged together under such a banner, it is not only easier for work to be marketed – it also becomes easier for the audience to 'buy it' and for the critic to respond with prepackaged opinions.[7]

It is clear from this that the self-conscious adoption of a musical style by a composer is risky if an individual voice or a 'complex personal vision' is the goal. However, it is equally very difficult, in fact impossible, to produce music that has *no* style. Once again, the use of critical reflection and judgement will be the guide for the digital musician. The important thing, when creating music, is the *music itself*, which will develop its own style. In the modern world, this may be influenced by just about anything, regardless of the maker's geographical location or personal background, so sensitivity, integrity and awareness are fundamental.

FURTHER READING

■ Cope, D., *Virtual Music: Computer Synthesis of Musical Style*, Cambridge, MA: The MIT Press, 2001.
Virtual Music is about artificial creativity. Focusing on the author's Experiments in Musical Intelligence computer music composing program, the author and a distinguished group of experts discuss many of the issues surrounding the program, including artificial intelligence, music cognition and aesthetics.

■ Zorn, J., *Arcana: Musicians on Music*, New York: Granary Books, 2000.
Several collections of writings by many musicians about the process of making music. Raw at times, but fascinating and insightful.

Project 26 (Advanced): Pastiche

Introduction

Pastiche composition has a long history as an academic exercise. In fact, most of the famous classical composers used pastiche as a way of teaching and learning. In the post-war years in Western music, it fell out of use to a certain extent, because the goal of modern music was to be original or new. Pastiche was felt to be risky, because it seemed to imply a willingness to accept orthodoxies.

Perhaps, in the digital world of endless reproduction, the time has come to re-evaluate pastiche. The aim will be not only to understand technique, but also style, aesthetic and process. Short of actually sampling the original, it is highly unlikely that the pastiche will come close to its model in detail, so the chances of discovering something new along the way are quite high. At the very least, the pasticher will learn about the technology and how it could be handled.

The Project

Try to reproduce a chosen digital piece. Mimic its sounds and processes.

Notes

This exercise succeeds with pieces that are noise-based and/or with lots of effects and processing. Some pieces that seem to work well are: 'Meta-abuse' from *Making Orange Things* by Venetian Snares; 'Glitch' from *Amber* by Autechre; and '#15' from *Selected Ambient Works Vol. II* by Aphex Twin. However, the aesthetic qualities of these tracks may not be to everyone's taste. It is important that the pastiche exercise should be valued and seen as worthwhile, so the choice of music should be individual.

FORM AND STRUCTURE

Imagine a single sound. Its form will consist of the duration of the sound and the totality of what takes place within that duration. The content will be divisible into various elements, such as pitch, spectrum, rhythm, etc. The same may be said of an entire musical composition. In his book *Fundamentals of Musical Composition*, Arnold Schoenberg describes this interrelationship as *organization*.

Used in the aesthetic sense, form means that a piece is *organized*; that is, that it consists of elements functioning like those of a living *organism*. Without organization, music would be an amorphous mass, as unintelligible as an essay without punctuation, or as disconnected as a conversation which leaps purposelessly from one subject to another.[8]

The 'form' of a piece of music is not the same as its 'structure'. The structure of a piece (e.g., the intro–verse–chorus–verse–chorus structure of many songs) is really a skeleton, while its form is like an entire body. Just as any two persons are different even though their skeletons are alike, so any two songs may have the same structure, but their form and content will be dissimilar. The assumptions that underpin these statements are collectively called 'formalism'. This implies that some kind of system may be used to organize music and that form is the sum total of a piece of music and the relationships of all its parts.

The organization of music may take a 'top-down' or 'bottom-up' approach to form and structure. A top-down approach would see the composition as a large-scale, or macro-structure (possibly subdivided into various sections) waiting to be filled with content, whereas the bottom-up approach will start from a sound or collection of sounds and try to evolve a larger-scale structure from them. In practice, composition is normally a combination of these two approaches. The composer's job is to develop form and content together so that they relate to one another successfully. The criteria for judgement described elsewhere in this book will determine to what extent success has been achieved.

In digital sound organization, form and structure normally derive in some way from the editing process, in which the sounds are ordered into a desired sequence. The technology allows not just for linear sequencing (as in tape editing), but for non-linear and multi-tracked edits, or *montages*.[9] The structure of the resulting music is often called its 'architecture', a classical concept which has reappeared many times throughout history, most famously in Johann Wolfgang von Goethe's remark 'I call architecture frozen music.'[10] Sequencing, textures, and patterns therefore often provide the building blocks of structure and the content of forms in such architecture.

As in all music, repetition and variation provide the basic ways in which a listener might orientate themselves within a piece, but in digital music the repetitions are often timbral and the variations come from sound manipulations. Musical *gesture* becomes an important device, not simply in terms of the physical motions of a performer, but within the sound organization itself, as a way of moving on, of growing, developing and progressing *towards* something. This gesture will be the result of some *cause*, or perceived to be the consequence of some event or impulse. This provides the basic chain by which a musical 'argument' may be developed or a form evolved.[11]

Composers have explored both highly structured and highly chaotic approaches to creating music using computers. To give one influential example, Iannis Xenakis used a strict mathematical approach to make stochastic music consisting of randomly generated elements. Stochasticism uses probability theory to model ways in which the individual elements within an extremely dense texture might behave. The paths of individual birds in a large flock weaving across the sky, or the many individual calls that make up the song of cicadas in a summer field, provide natural parallels. The complexity of these calculations were best suited to a computer, and, after some early orchestral pieces such as *Pithoprakta* (1956), which attempted to deliver stochastic music via traditional means, Xenakis moved on to computer-based composition. By 1979, he had devised a computer system called UPIC,[12] which could translate graphical images into musical results. Xenakis had originally trained as an architect, so some of his drawings, which he called 'arborescences', resembled both organic forms and architectural structures. Their many curves and lines translated into musical elements, such as pitches or melodic contours, which in turn contributed to the larger gestures that formed the architectural structures of the composition as a whole. The UPIC page from *Mycènes-Alpha* (*Mycenae-Alpha*) (1978) shown in Figure 7.2 lasts approximately one minute.

The range of possible approaches to structure is vast. For example, the spatial dimension can become a *structuring principle* of the music by developing within the composition in ways which are distinctly perceptible by the listener. Alternatively, the spatial distribution of sounds could be imposed as a structure in itself, independent of the actual sonic content of the music.

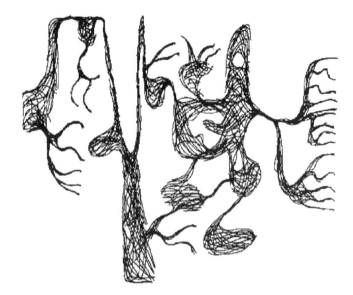

Figure 7.2   Iannis Xenakis, UPIC page from *Mycenae-Alpha* (1978) © Iannis Xenakis

The key importance of a structuring principle is to engage the listener in a meaningful discourse which leads to some kind of perception of organization. Sometimes, an extremely clear, even rigid, structure is the best means to achieve this, sometimes more 'organic' structures work well. Certain genres have given structures which represent a significant constraint for the composer. Working within these constraints can be beneficial for discipline and technical development. However, when approaching a free composition, some early decisions about structuring principles are normally necessary.

The best such pieces are those which convey a sense of an evolving argument or journey. Here, the structuring principle is based upon the idea that musical gestures can be developed beyond the point where they are simply a succession of more or less impressive effects. From the listeners' viewpoint, the question will always be '*Why* has such-and-such an event taken place?' The extent to which they can answer that question satisfactorily will determine the perceived success of the structuring principle that underlies the music.

A key formal aspect concerns the creation of a sense of movement through time. In traditional composition this is achieved by phrasing, which is the shaping of smaller musical ideas into coherent, sentence-like, sequences. A group of phrases may then go on to form a larger structure, such as a melody, and so on. There is a link here to the duration of human breath and the structures of human speech. It is surprising how often this is still applicable, even in musical situations where the content is not pitch-based. Every sound has its natural life span, and tends to 'breathe'. With machines, it is perfectly possible to work against this, and musical structures can be (and have been) devised to avoid an obvious sense of phrasing. But the absence or presence of a sense of motion through time is always a distinguishing compositional element.

Motion through time is a feature of 'closed-form' works, that is to say, works which are complete. Works in 'open' form are perpetually incomplete. This implies an ongoing experimental approach: one in which the *process* of creating the music, rather than the finished product, is important. This may have particular resonance in the age of digital music because, as Nicholas Negroponte points out: 'in the digital nothing is ever finished'.[13] Open form can seem more consistent with the handling of sound through time as a continuous data stream, which can be edited or modified in any way.

There are historical precedents for this in traditional music composition, with discontinuous forms of endless variation or mosaic-like constructions. A classic and very extreme example is *Vexations*, composed for piano in 1892 by Erik Satie, in which the same short musical idea is repeated 840 times. The piece can last around twenty-four hours, depending on how fast you play it. (Satie's directions are somewhat unclear.) Listening to (and performing) this piece is really an 'open form' experience, despite the repetition, because human memory changes over such a long time span.

More recently, open form has come to refer to 'mobile' works in which the ordering of sections or events within sections is left up to the performer. This concept is still best understood in relation to concert works that have a clear beginning and ending. Even so, the computer makes available a vastly expanded range of possibilities within open form, indeed it may be seen as a 'natural' device for the creation of a music that relies on variable re-orderings of material at all structural levels of a composition. This becomes even more the case in networked music, where aesthetic goals and technical constraints combine to make open form both most desirable and prevalent.

Glimmer (2004) by Jason Freeman is a typical example of an open form digital piece. Each member of the audience is given a battery-operated light stick which may be turned on and off at random. The computer analyses the on/off signals emanating from the audience and sends instructions to members of the orchestra to play musical material that is also computer generated. The result is therefore highly unpredictable. Another example, this time involving networked music, was the soundtrack by Erik Belgum for the *PHON:E:ME* project (1999), a sound poetry piece that exploited errors and glitches in the *RealPlayer* web application and constantly re-organized itself in unpredictable ways.

There is a strong temptation to assume that this kind of music has no particular direction, or is arbitrary in its 'goal-orientation', but, in practice, there is often, paradoxically, *more* of a sense of motion through time. The absence of a clear start and end point risks losing the attention of the listener, so the composer must ensure sufficient dramatic interest. The lack of opportunity in open form for musical development has become a central focus for certain types of computer composition which use evolutionary algorithms and other methods to simulate developmental processes.

To adopt open form can therefore be a risky strategy. There is the potential of losing musical identity, or the attention of the listener, and a possible surrender to the technology or the process involved. Nevertheless, as an experimental approach, or under the right situations, open form can produce worthwhile results. One interesting example was Peter M. Traub's *bits and pieces* (1999), which is

> a continuous composition that gets its source sounds from the web. Every morning a special search process looks for web pages with links to sound files. If links are found, the sound files are downloaded. The day's 'catch' is then used to create the pieces in 'bits and pieces' for the next 24 hours.[14]

This piece seems to succeed because the musical outcome maps the intention so well, and it fits with and reflects upon its context.

Project 27 (Advanced): Open-form Work

Introduction

This is a composition project that is designed to explore the organization of sound through time. A controlled spatial dimension may also be introduced if desired. The emphasis is on originality of concept and effectiveness of realization.

The Project

Create an original open-form composition for performance by musicians other than your-self. The work must involve digital technologies that are indispensable to its realization. However, other technologies may be used and non-digital instruments may be added.

The work should be time-limited to between 5 and 10 minutes, but it is acceptable to present part of a longer-term structure as a realization of the project.

At some point in the creative process, you should give the work a title and write a short programme note explaining the artistic and technical concept.

This is a collaborative project. It should involve other musicians, who may be experienced performers or novices or even members of an audience. The work must be practicable and capable of being realized – a theoretical outline or an imaginary composition is not acceptable!

Notes

The first step is to consider what is meant by 'open-form' and to be clear in your own mind how you will fulfil that brief.

Ask yourself the following questions: How will the musicians or participants interact with what you provide? To what extent will the technology make choices? What is the scale of the organization? At what level will the composition be 'open' – the macro (i.e., the whole piece, or large sections) or the micro (smaller sections, patterns, even single events or sub-events)? Will your 'hand' be evident in the result, or will the use of the computer remove the composer's presence? What are the aesthetic consequences of that decision?

Next, you have to work on the technological system for the realization of the project. This may involve using existing software or having to write your own. Either way, bear in mind the role of the participants at all times – whatever you produce must be usable. The work may be web-based or an installation or designed for a concert presentation. This platform decision will also be crucial to the nature of the finished piece. Will some form of notation be required? How will you communicate the instructions for operation of the system to the musicians?

Finally, you should allow plenty of time for rehearsal. View each session as an opportunity to critically evaluate the results. What can be done to refine and develop your composition? Remember that, even when the computer is making all the decisions, you still have a role. If your decision is to allow the computer to decide, that is a signficant compositional decision in itself. What are the musical consequences of such a decision? Why does it matter?

This project should take several weeks to complete and should culminate in a final performance or presentation.

FURTHER READING

- Dack, J., *'Open' Forms and the Computer in Music, Arts, Technologies, Toward a Critical Approach*, Paris: L'Harmattan, 2004, pp. 401–412.
  Analyses the place of the computer in terms of the realization of open form in electro-acoustic works from a historical, compositional and performance perspective.

- Eco, U., *The Open Work*, Cambridge, MA: Harvard University Press, 1989.
  A collection of essays exploring work that requires many different readings and which 'characteristically consist of unplanned or physically incomplete structural units'. Examples include musical compositions by Stockhausen and Berio.

- Emmerson, S., *The Language of Electroacoustic Music*, London: Macmillan, 1986.
  The central section on 'materials and language' looks at the types of materials available to composers and the way in which the internal structure of the sound can have implications for the overall structure of a piece.

- Thorington, H., 'Breaking Out: the trip back', *Contemporary Music Review*, 24:6, 2005, 445–458.
  Focuses on open composition and the challenges of internet-based musical interaction, including asynchronous time, lag and technical glitches, the advent of mobile devices and wireless networks and the migration of computing out of the desktop computer into the physical world, and the resulting changes in musical experience.

- Xenakis, I., *Formalized Music: Thought and Mathematics in Composition*, Stuyvesant, NY: Pendragon Press, 1992.
  First published in 1971, this is an essential text for understanding Xenakis' work, but also has a much wider relevance to the development of certain key ideas in computer music.

MOODS AND MODALITIES

The words 'mode' and 'mood' are closely related, and the modality of a piece of music has traditionally been linked to its spiritual or emotional effects. Where tonal music has a 'key' which may change during a composition, modal music is defined by a set of relationships or intervals that make up the mode and often relates to a fixed element such as a drone. The modal tradition in Europe was superseded by tonality in the seventeenth century but has seen quite a revival in the past century. A great deal of popular music, particularly rock and pitch-based electronic dance music, is modal in a traditional sense. This partly derives from playing techniques, because modal patterns tend to fit neatly under the fingers on the guitar, and limited keyboard skills will often result in a white-notes-only playing style. White notes form the pitch sets of the so-called 'church modes'. However, modality is more than just a collection of pitch sets. A mode is essentially a repetition of patterns, which may be intervals, but might also be rhythms, or resonances.

A central concern of music composed with new technology is how a sound may be extended. This, as has been suggested already, involves analysing and modifying the spectrum. Any sound, apart from pure noise, will have an inherent modality, because its spectrum will contain some dominant pitches, a certain resonance, even repeating rhythms. Very short sounds, such as clicks or glitches, acquire a clear pitch when stretched. Extending sounds and their spectral characteristics will therefore tend to create a magnified modality. One of the case study artists, John Richards, calls this 'Sonic Magnification'.[15]

There are also various performance modalities, which have become compositional techniques in themselves. Apart from the drone (which may be a persistent rhythm instead of a pitch), performance techniques based on call and response, such as hocket (interpolation of individual sounds by different performers which, when combined, make up whole phrases) and antiphony (alternation between two blocks of sound, often spatially separated) are not only common in (early) modal music but also in music played through loudspeaker systems.

It is surprising how relevant these ideas of modality can prove to be, even in entirely noise-based music. Often a key compositional decision is whether to include an element that 'binds together' the whole piece. This, then, tends to function as a drone. Musical excitement and interest is often generated by listener perception of the relationships between the various sonic elements, which add up to a 'mood' picture. Performance techniques involving hocket and antiphony can often be the most musically engaging. Acousmatic music can sometimes exhibit a quite startling modality.

Project 28 (Advanced): Night Piece

Introduction

The night-piece, or 'nocturne' is a classical form. This is something that can either be absorbed into the artist's aesthetic for this project, or ignored. Some typical examples include the 'night music' that appears in several works by Béla Bartók or, before that, Frédéric Chopin's collection of nocturnes for solo piano. What these works have in common is a poetic *evocation* of night.

The Project

Start by making a list of all the things you associate with night. These do not necessarily have to involve sound. Now start to think about creating mood and atmosphere, about resonance and silence, about presence and sound, about imagination and reality. Fix upon a duration for the piece. Finally, create a piece that evokes night.

Notes

Night is a particularly good time for listening. It is generally quieter than daytime, and the absence of light means that the ear is heightened. For this project, 'night life' does not mean parties and clubs, but rather the sounds of the night (which might include distant music) that bring it to life.

PROJECT 28

Discussion Questions

- Why do you compose music?

- What is your compositional process?

- Does your music have a narrative or a concept, or is it 'just' music? How does that affect the way you work?

- How do you make artistic decisions?

- What is original about your work?

- What do you understand by the word 'form' in relation to music? And 'structure'?

- Is music capable of expressing emotion? If so, what else can it express? If not, why not? Does any of this change in digital music? How?

CHAPTER 8

Instruments and Media

MUSICIANS AND THEIR INSTRUMENTS

The instrument they play traditionally defines musicians. A person is called a guitarist, or a pianist, or a sitar-player, before they are called a musician. A musician's instrument is usually considered to be an indispensable part of their musical identity and practice. In technology-based music, however, where the computer and other technological equipment is the means by which a musician performs, it is much more difficult to identify an instrument as such. Research conducted in 2006 by Thor Magnusson and Enrike Hurtado Mendieta highlights this problem.[1] Through more than 200 musicians' responses to a questionnaire, they were able to identify the following attitudes to digital and acoustic instruments (see Table 8.1).

The authors observe that for many people a crucial difference is the need to 'mould oneself' to an acoustic instrument, whereas a digital instrument can be created to suit the needs of the user. However, the mutability and lack of limitations of software can also be a weakness, because its short lifetime discourages the achievement of mastery. Technical problems such as latency (the delay between an action and the system's response) were also seen as problematic, but probably the most vexed issue was 'arbitrary mapping', or

Table 8.1 Musicians' attitudes to acoustic and digital instruments

Acoustic – Positive	Acoustic – Negative
Tactile feedback	Lacking in range
Limitations inspiring	No editing out of mistakes
Traditions and legacy	No memory or intelligence
Musician reaches depth	Prone to cliché playing
Instrument becomes second nature	Too much tradition/history
Each instrument is unique	No experimentation in design
No latency	Inflexible – no dialogue
Easier to express mood	No microtonality or tunings
Extrovert state when playing	No inharmonic spectra

Digital – Positive	Digital – Negative
Free from musical traditions	Lacking in substance
Experimental – explorative	No legacy or continuation
Any sound and any interface	No haptic feedback
Designed for specific needs	Lacking social conventions
Freedom in mapping	Latency frequently a problem
Automation, intelligence	Disembodied experience
Good for composing with	Slave to the historical/acoustic
Easier to get into	Imitation of the acoustic
Not as limited as tonal music	Introvert state when playing

the fact that 'there are no "natural" mappings between the exertion of bodily energy and the resulting sound in digital music'. One consequence of this is a difficulty in disengaging the brain and becoming 'one with the physical embodiment of performing'.[2]

In digital music, there are no fixed instruments, despite the efforts of manufacturers to convince the buying public otherwise There is only *bricolage*, or instruments constructed from a range of available software and media. Digital musicians are always responsible for building their own instruments, in some cases from pre-assembled components and in some cases from scratch. Even a choice to use, say, a single synthesizer, is not a simple one. All synthesizers contain a myriad of possibilities within their apparently uniform construction. The preset sounds are just the tip of the iceberg. The choices digital musicians make, and their ability to handle what results, will do much to define both the aesthetic of music and their musical expertise. Some areas of musical practice positively embrace this bricolage, even to the extent of deliberately suppressing the digital aspects, while others hide it beneath a technological veneer.

ORGANOLOGY

The study of musical-instrument technology is called *organology*. Up until fairly recently, to study music technology was in fact to study organology. Modern organology was first laid out by Curt Sachs in an influential text of 1913: the *Real-Lexicon der Musikinstrumente*. In 1914, he and Erich Moritz von Hornbostel developed this further with a classification system for musical instruments known as the Hornbostel-Sachs system. Although there have been changes and modifications to this system over the years, it remains the standard way of classifying musical instruments. They are grouped as follows:

1   *Idiophones*, which produce sound by self-supporting vibration (e.g., the marimba, and the xylophone, although metal idiophones are generally called metallophones).
2   *Membranophones*, which produce sound by a vibrating membrane (typically drums).
3   *Chordophones*, which produce sound by vibrating strings (violin, guitar, etc.).
4   *Aerophones*, which produce sound by vibrating volume of air (pipe organs, flutes, and so on).

Electrophones were added later. These are instruments such as theremins, which produce sound by electronic means.

A virtual instrument, capable of producing any sound and controlled by any means plainly resists organological classification. Conventional instruments that are technologically extended in some way might be easier to classify, but what value would this classification offer, given the likely mutability of the sound that results from the extension? And what about all those controllers – joysticks, light beams, sensor pads, motion trackers and the rest – that do not produce a sound in themselves but are essential to the music?

The point here is not to dismiss organology, which is in itself an important discipline, but to describe the vagueness and diversity of the situation that confronts the digital musician. To play a musical instrument, of whatever kind, will always be beneficial to a musician but, for the digital musician, there is no need to pursue this to a particularly high level of skill unless the emerging pattern of musical enquiry demands it. However, it is often the case in practice that digital musicians are also good instrumentalists.

PROJECT 29

Project 29 (Advanced): Infra-Instrument

Introduction

In a paper entitled 'Not Hyper, Not Meta, Not Cyber but Infra-Instruments', given at the 2005 NIME (New Interfaces for Musical Expression) conference in Vancouver, Canada, John Bowers and Philip Archer criticized recent developments in instrument making, arguing that all the 'hyper' and 'meta' instruments extend the capabilities of existing instruments with a view to increasing the virtuosity and complexity of the music made. The same is true of virtual instruments, but often replacing the hand gesture with some kind of controller or motion-tracking device.

They identify a different kind of instrument, called an 'infra-instrument', which 'engenders relatively simple musics' and is 'restricted in its virtuosity and expressivity', but is 'nonetheless aesthetically engaging and technically intriguing for all that'. They offer a number of examples. This project uses a couple of those.

The Project

Make, and perform on, an infra-instrument. Do this by using materials that are 'partway to instrumenthood' but do not make them into a recognized instrument. For example: a guitar is made of wood and metal and, possibly, nylon. An infra-guitar would use those materials, but would not be a guitar. (Sounding materials might include: wood, metal, string, water, stone, skin, plastic, glass, etc.)

Notes

Bowers and Archer's own instructions include the following additional notes that may be helpful in realizing this project:

Take an Instrument and Make it less. Break an existing instrument (irreversible procedures) or restrict its operation and/or how one interacts with it (reversible procedures).

Build an Instrument but Include Obvious Mistakes. Like selecting fresh vegetables as the material for construction.

Take Something Non-Instrumental and Find the Instrument Within. A DTMF phone dialer can be regarded as an infra-synthesizer, a Geiger counter as infra-percussion, and so forth.

Find Infra-Instruments Readymade. In contrast to the above, here we have in mind instruments which already are infra in status, at least in the minds of aesthetic snobs. This would include many musical toys or musical boxes and other 'amusements'.

EXTENDED ACOUSTIC INSTRUMENTS

Each musical instrument requires a different technique, its own set of skills. It can help to have a working knowledge of as many of these as possible. But there are two instruments (or types of instrument) that *all* musicians would be well advised to know, to at least a moderate degree. The first is the voice. Vocal music is fundamental to music itself. The phrases and shapes of music, including music where there is no vocal component, may usually be traced back to speech, to articulation, to acoustic communication, or to singing. Not everybody is blessed with a good singing voice, but it is important to explore vocal capabilities even so. This can take the form of readings, of speaking (in a controlled way), of chanting, of ululating (howling or wailing), of droning on a single note, of singing either alone or in choirs. It need not be done in public, but it should be done.

After the voice, a working knowledge of *percussion* instruments will be a great advantage. Percussion includes such an array of pitched instruments (xylophones, vibraphones, tubular bells, timpani and so on) and unpitched instruments (drums, cymbals, tam-tams, woodblocks, etc.) that it still offers a superb resource for discovering and creating sounds. The basic techniques for many of these instruments are relatively simple, although, to be sure, it is possible to develop extraordinary virtuosity on even the simplest percussion instrument. Ensemble percussion work is probably the best musical training available, since it engages both the intellectual and visceral organs of the human body in a way that surpasses other instruments. A wealth of research into music therapy has revealed the health benefits of banging a drum, and in all probability it satisfies some deeply buried human instinct.[3] Beyond the voice and percussion, it is very much a matter of personal choice to what extent time is spent pursuing the study of an instrument: the time will not be wasted.

Project 30 (Elementary): Sound Byte for Voice or Percussion

Introduction

This is a combination of sonic analysis and creative work. The object is to investigate the properties of the chosen sounds. The process will lead to a better understanding of how the voice or percussion instrumental sounds are formed, and how digital processes might be successfully applied to them.

The Project

Create a 20–30 second sound byte based on vocal or percussion sounds, demonstrating how elements of vocal sound can be 'taken apart'. Use any digital processing tools available to you, such as filtering, transposition and stretching.

Notes

The word 'demonstrating' is important here. This is not so much a compositional piece as a technical exercise. However, the 'demonstration' is likely to be better understood if it makes musical sense too.

If playing a conventional instrument proves musically fruitful, then it is possible to extend the capabilities of that instrument into the digital domain. This is a massively growing area of musical practice. However, it is also somewhat problematic, because the sheer quantity and variety of solutions available is bewildering and, more often than not, each of these solutions is unique. The best way forward is to make no attempt to survey the entire scene but to select an approach that appeals and work to develop within that.

The Massachusetts Institute of Technology's *hyperinstruments* draw on existing musical techniques, but extend the playing actions such as touch and motion using sensors. The hyperviolin (see Figure 8.1) is a typical example of such *gesture mapping*.

The audio output from the electronic strings and the movements of the enhanced violin bow provide the raw material for real-time timbre and synthesis techniques, which analyse parameters such as pitch, loudness, brightness and spectrum. The controller here is as close as possible to the conventional instrument controller (a bow, in this case).

A different approach that does not alter the physical characteristics of

Figure 8.1   The hyperviolin (Tod Machover, Tristan Jehan, Diana Young) © MIT Media Lab

the instrument itself, but processes the sound it makes, has been adopted by many artists. Kaffe Matthews, for example, has extended her violin using LiSa (Live Sampling) software from STEIM (Studio for Electro-Instrument Music) in the Netherlands. STEIM 'promotes the idea that Touch is crucial in communicating with the new electronic performance art technologies' and that 'the intelligence of the body, for example: the knowledge of the fingers or lips, is considered musically as important as the "brain-knowledge"'.[4] LiSa allocates a large chunk of memory to certain 'zoned' functions, such as various forms of playback, recording, reading, saving and copying data, all in real time. So the controller in this case is computer software, physically external to the instrument itself.

Another approach is to invent a new instrument that exploits the capabilities of the controller, rather than the other way around. There are hundreds of such new interfaces for musical expression (NIME),[5] apparently limited only by the imagination of the inventors. One example is the 'Tooka', an intimate instrument that uses two-person breath control (and some push buttons) to influence the music (Figure 8.2). Air pressure and flow, speed and direction, are mapped onto musical information (mainly pitch, in this case).

The whole area of extended acoustic instruments and new digital musical instruments is flourishing. This is where the culture of the digital musician is most active, not surprisingly given the earlier statements about bricolage. Even with fairly rudimentary equipment it is possible to adapt and create new instruments, by modifying a live feed or, more ambitiously, finding ways to map gestures onto sounds.

Linda Kaastra & Sachiyo Takahashi - "You and Me"

Figure 8.2   The Tooka (Sidney Fels, Florian Vogt) © Sidney Fels

FURTHER READING

- Miranda, E. and Wanderley, M., *New Digital Musical Instruments: Control and Interaction Beyond the Keyboard*, Middleton, WI: A-R Editions, 2004.
  Surveys the field, with a particular interest in gestural control and mapping, sensors and controllers, artificial intelligence and intelligent musical instruments.

- Battier, M. and Wanderley, M., *Trends In Gestural Control of Music*, Paris: IRCAM, Centre Georges Pompidou, 2000.
  The published results of a round-table discussion on gestural control.

SOFTWARE INSTRUMENTS

The computer removes the need to use anything other than itself. Software instruments can be built which will do all the things (and more) that can be done by physical instruments. Here, the controller is simply the mouse or keyboard, or sometimes a joystick, graphics tablet or trackball device. The concept of a virtual instrument is already well established in commercial software, and emulation packages provide a graphical interface that gives the illusion of handling physical electronic equipment.

Modular software is currently setting the standard for software instrument-building. The advantage of these systems over more familiar commercial packages is that they are entirely user-designed. Many of the prepackaged software instruments presume some particular kind of musical outcome (often electronic dance music) and do their best to facilitate that. For the digital musician experimenting with software instrument-building, the possibility of realizing an original idea is preferable. A typical environment includes MIDI, control, user interface and timing objects on top of which hundreds of objects can be built (generally called *patches*). Users of this kind of software have gathered together into online communities to share patches and discuss their use. This picture is replicated for other kinds of software and is a very effective way for musicians to communicate with one another.

There are many kinds of performance involving software instruments running on a laptop. One such is sometimes referred to as *electronica*. The origins of this term are unclear, but in the 1990s it came to refer to electronic dance music, and more recently that definition has widened to include more experimental electronic music. The cheapness and portability of laptop equipment have made this area of music an emergent and thriving cultural activity, based largely in clubs. It has even become something like a competitive sport. Figure 8.3 shows the electronica musician Quantazelle performing in fancy dress at *The Thunderdome Matches*, a 'battle' of musicians, in a club in Chicago in 2003. The audience played its part in the voting process, and innovation was a key element in judging the winners.

Software instruments have become very accessible in recent years, particularly as a new generation of applications for smart phones and tablets have come onto the market. The proliferation of possibilities and flexibility of control

Figure 8.3   Quantazelle, performing in 2003 © Quantaze.

offered by these devices gets close to the ideal of an instrument that is both highly intuitive to use and limitless in its capabilities and potential for expression. Touch, motion, breath, voice, keyboard, data flow and numerous other controllers may be embodied within a single handheld instrument that is networked and capable of considerable processing power such as might be required for evolutionary algorithms or artificial intelligence. This all represents a further extension of the facility introduced by the computer and is subject to the same comments as were made earlier. But the attractiveness of these devices and the vibrancy of the creative scene that uses them makes the development of software instruments an activity that occupies the time and attention of a very large number of digital musicians.

Project 31 (Elementary): Restricted Instruments

Introduction

These instruments can be built on computer or using a sampler. There is no attempt here to prescribe the interactivity, so that is very much a matter of free invention. In some cases, a controller that reflects the sonic materials used may well be appropriate.

The Project

Make a restricted instrument from a single sound source. Devise performances on the instrument to show as much variation and virtuosity as possible.

Notes

The instrument should reflect the acoustic properties of its sources in all its aspects. The challenge in this project is to make musical interest from very limited materials, so no additional processing or effects may be added. Working with a highly restricted palette like this can be a very effective way of developing the craft of digital sound manipulation.

PROJECT 31

FURTHER READING

- Jordà, S., 'Multi-user Instruments: Models, Examples and Promises', *Proceedings of the 2005 International Conference on New Interfaces for Musical Expression* (NIME05), Vancouver, Canada, 2005, pp. 23–26.

- Collins, N. and D'Escriváin, J. (eds), *The Cambridge Companion to Electronic Music*, Cambridge: Cambridge University Press, 2007.
  Includes discussions of electronica, interactivity and network music.

MIDI

MIDI also allows instruments to control one another. Thus there are: MIDI keyboards, wind instruments, guitars, drums, violins and the rest, which can all be programmed to trigger any kind of sampled sound (so a MIDI guitar can produce saxophone notes, for example). However, the content of the MIDI data stream can also be controlled by any varying modifiers, including: modulation and pitch bend wheels, sustain pedals, sliders, faders, switches, ribbon controllers, pots, in short anything that is capable of altering the parameters of a signal, usually in real time. These controllers may stand alone, or be fitted on, or plugged into, an instrument, depending on the manufacturer's specification. There are a total of 128 virtual MIDI ports available which can be assigned particular functions. Each port can transmit or receive messages which also carry one of sixteen channel identities. This channel information allows many instruments, or different parts of a multi-timbral instrument, to be controlled simultaneously through a single cable connection.

INFORMATION: SOME TYPICAL MIDI SET-UPS

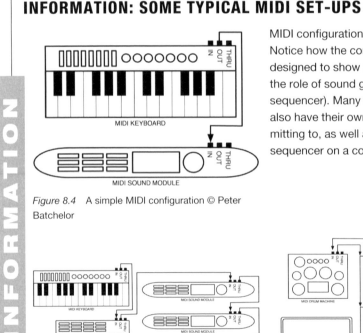

MIDI configurations can become quite complex. Notice how the configuration in Figure 8.6 is designed to show the computer performing the role of sound generator *and* controller (e.g., sequencer). Many (if not most) MIDI controllers also have their own sounds, so may be transmitting to, as well as receiving from, the MIDI sequencer on a computer.

Figure 8.4   A simple MIDI configuration © Peter Batchelor

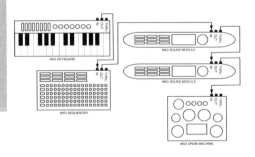

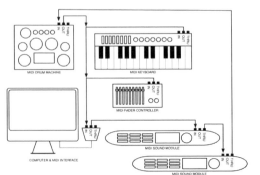

Figure 8.5   A MIDI configuration without computer © Peter Batchelor

Figure 8.6   A MIDI configuration with computer © Peter Batchelor

Alongside the channel information, a MIDI message may contain: note-on, note-off, pitch-bend, program change, aftertouch, channel pressure, system-related messages and continuous controller messages. In the interests of achieving a predictable outcome, there has been general agreement amongst manufacturers about which controller performs which function, but in practice these are often assigned differently under different circumstances. Computer-based MIDI sequencers take advantage of all this by enabling various kinds of MIDI data input from various kinds of devices, and often act as central controller for all aspects of the performance.

MIDI is also found as a control device for various studio machines, where it is called MMC (Midi Machine Control), and for lighting effects, pyrotechnics and other aspects of staging, where it is called MSC (Midi Show Control). These give some idea of the protocol's versatility and it seems likely that it will survive for many years to come.

MIDI has been somewhat controversial from a musical point of view. By contriving to give the illusion that digital music may behave in an analogous way to acoustic music, instrument manufacturers have created a set of expectations that is normally dashed by the experience of General MIDI, whose sounds are poor relations of their 'real' counterparts. It is all too common to hear MIDI-based compositions that clearly aspire to the status of instrumental music, but which sound quite impoverished. Music notation packages have resulted in a tendency to 'dots' composition that fails to appreciate the requirements of acoustic instruments and performers. The MIDI output is all too often accepted as a substitute for the actual sounds of a live instrument, often with unplayable results.

This is not to say that General MIDI sounds may never be used successfully, or that music notation packages are a bad idea. As in any sphere of music, it is the skill and knowledge of the musician that will realize the potential of the instrument. Digital musicians must be aware of what MIDI is and how it functions if they are to extract the best results. It remains a standard musical communications protocol and may of course be used to trigger and deliver *any* sounds. What is required is an ability to think appropriately about the sounds in question and to come up with ways to use MIDI that exploit its features to musical ends.

FURTHER READING

- Hill, B., *Midi for Musicians*, Chicago: A Cappella, 1994.
  Explains the musical uses of MIDI hardware and software, describes MIDI components and how they are connected, includes a shopping guide for keyboards and other components, and much more.

- Rumsey, F., *Midi Systems and Control*, Oxford: Focal Press, 1994.
  Provides comprehensive coverage of every aspect of MIDI. The second edition includes more examples of real implementations, more diagrams and the whole book has been rewritten to include a far greater practical element.

SOUND SOURCES

In whatever kind of musical situation the digital musicians may find themselves, the question of sound sources is bound to arise. A sound source could be a recording, a live sound, an acoustic instrument, a synthesizer, the human body, etc. In fact, *any* sounding object can be a sound source, but there must *be* a sound source. The choice of sound source, as much as what is done to it during performance, defines the music. Some musicians take an inclusive approach, assembling as many sound sources as possible and offering the maximum range of choices at a given moment. Others are more exclusive, preferring to work with a limited set of sounds for a certain situation. Where the work is being done within a known musical genre, the exclusive approach tends to predominate. There are fixed requirements for genre work, although the digital musician will always try to innovate even within the confines of genre practice. In other, perhaps more experimental, situations, a freer approach to sound sources will work best.

The idea of integrity is sometimes bound up in how sound sources are found or made. In an acousmatic music concert, for example, to use a sound downloaded from the Internet in preference to a sound you have recorded yourself could be seen to be lacking integrity. In a club gig, on the other hand, the idea of being over-fussy about recording your own sound sources may well be less important. Integrity here is often more to do with how you handle software.

The digital musician will constantly seek to explore the sonic properties of objects and spaces. Some kind of structured approach to, or self-devised classification system for, sound sources will probably be used as the sheer quantity of data increases, because it can become very hard to keep track of things. This is especially true once editing and processing the sounds begins. Documentation, backing up and systematic labelling are very important, in short: a database of sonic material stored on computer is usually created. In many software packages, the computer will automatically do a great deal of that work.

This is a distinguishing feature of the digital musician. Whereas a musician might work to extract good or interesting sounds from their instrument, the digital musician begins from a position of having unlimited sound sources. The processes of critical judgement, of cultural awareness, of musical intuition, may lead to a significant whittling away of extraneous material but, in theory, the digital musician *could* make any sound in any way and in any context. These sounds are then combined in such a way, or using such techniques, as to form an instrument. This new instrument resists easy classification and may even exist only for the duration of a performance.

HARDWARE HACKING

The phrase 'hardware hacking', with its overtones of computer hacking, indicates that this is a practice that is deeply informed by the digital world, even if its primary materials (mostly electronic devices) are not digital. It is closely allied to 'circuit-bending', which creatively adapts low power devices such as children's toys by re-soldering components in the electronic circuitry. Hardware hackers perform similar operations, modifying or 'modding' technology with a view to reinstating the physical element into electronic music. As Nic Collins explains:

> Computers are wonderful, don't get me wrong, but the usual interface – an ASCII keyboard and a mouse – is awkward, and makes the act of performing a pretty indirect activity – like trying to hug a baby in an incubator. 'Alternative controllers' (such as those made by STEIM and Buchla) are a step in the right direction, but sometimes it's nice to reach out and touch a sound.[6]

The most famous pioneer of circuit-bending, Rheed Ghazala, writing on his 'anti-theory' website, expresses his position as a way of overcoming aesthetic boundaries through self-taught acts of discovery:

> Circuit-bending creates 'naturalistic' music. It views sound as fluid sculpture, and persuades listeners to rise above the rudiments of the organized sounds we've become familiar with as 'music.' It exists more as an emotional construct rather than a danceable solution. Many people are realizing that beat music can be boring, and that more abstract sonic sculpture can be mesmerizing. This is an intense forward leap in consciousness. Bent circuits are too musical to be ignored, and have forced themselves upon a music-sensitive species. Boundaries will be bent.[7]

The unpredictable and even political aspects of hardware hacking are part of its appeal. There is an aesthetic dimension to this practice that sets itself against the slickness of the computer and its operations. The case study artist John Richards has developed an approach (and an ensemble) that he calls 'Dirty Electronics', which makes explicit how these activities may be seen in relation to digital music:

> The idea of dirty electronics is very much an extension of and closely allied to the practice of live electronics, where shared experiences face-to-face, ritual, gesture, touch, social interaction and the exploration of human interface are paramount.[8]

Hardware hacking moves away from the core activity of digital music and back towards a physical instrument that seems not so very different from earlier electronic or even acoustic instruments, but it does so from a very different perspective. The creative exploration of technologies, the idea of bricolage, and the questioning nature of the aesthetic, will resonate with the digital musician.

For those engaging in hardware hacking, a health and safety warning is always advisable. Powered devices are inherently dangerous and no modifications should be undertaken without a full understanding of the risks involved. Working with battery-powered devices will greatly reduce any potential dangers, but not eliminate them completely. At this point it may be expected that a practical project would be provided, but on this occasion the author would refer you to the recommended further readings, which have plenty of examples.

FURTHER READING

■ Collins, N., *Handmade Electronic Music: The Art of Hardware Hacking*, New York: Routledge, 2006.
Teaches practical circuitry; basic electronic principles; a brief history of twentieth-century electronic devices; how to work with all kinds of analogue circuitry and sounds; how to create your own cheap and practical instruments.

■ Ghazala, R., *Circuitbending: Build Your Own Alien Instruments (ExtremeTech)*, Chichester: Wiley, 2005.
Teaches both the theory and practice of circuit-bending and reveals a few tricks of the trade.

■ Richards, J. 'Getting the Hands Dirty', *Leonardo Music Journal*, 18, 2008, 25–31.
An academic discussion of dirty electronics and its musical and aesthetic implications.

MULTIMEDIA

Multimedia is pretty much the nature of media today. What was once remarkable – the integration of the arts into a single experience – is nowadays relatively normal. Most mediated experiences are in fact multimedia experiences. As Randall Packer and Ken Jordan put it:

> Multimedia is emerging as the defining medium of the 21st century. The World Wide Web, CD-ROMs, virtual reality arcade games, and interactive installations only hint at the forms of multimedia to come.[9]

The reality of multimedia is in some ways a realization of the vision of opera composer Richard Wagner: the *gesamtkunstwerk* or 'total work of art'. Writing in 1849, he stated:

> Not one rich faculty of the separate arts will remain unused in the United Artwork of the Future: in *it* will each attain its first complete appraisement.[10]

Multimedia, then, is simply any form of media that combines different forms of content, such as text, audio, still images, animation, video and so on, often with an interactive dimension. In theory this includes film and television, although in practice the word tends to get used in relation to more hybrid art forms. Since multimedia is so prevalent, there is an assumption throughout this book that the digital musician will work in that context very frequently and therefore many of the points that are made will apply equally well to multimedia as to audio–only situations. However, there are a number of issues that need to be borne in mind from the musical perspective.

It is rare nowadays to have an experience that is purely auditory. Even music players, which used to leave the listeners free to look at whatever they will, now offer visualizers or waveform diagrams. Music is often experienced in the context of video, indeed the commercial music industry is essentially a multimedia industry. Nor is art music unaffected, with a profusion of audiovisual and installation work that offers at least as much to the eye as to the ear. All this richness has consequences for music. It is surprising how often digital musicians have to fight for the importance of sound and music in a culture that is predominantly visual. As a maker of music, this is a very practical issue which confronts you on a daily basis. To what extent should the music be used merely to accompany or enhance the visual or textual content? Of course, there is no fixed answer to this question, and there may be many situations in which sound and music will most appropriately play a subordinate role. But just because this is the way things usually are does not mean this is the way things always should be.

In his influential book *Audio-Vision: Sound on Screen*, Michel Chion argues for an equality of sound and image, because the two exist in a state of co-dependency, the one affecting the other. Sound and music represent 'added value' in film, and are also thoroughly integrated through the voice (communication) and the contextual information provided by the soundtrack. Music itself, he says, has two modes: *empathetic* (in which it follows the rhythms, tone, and emotion of the scene) or *anempathetic* (in which it proceeds without reference to the scene). This egalitarian approach may be extended into all forms of work which combine image and sound. 'Music' and 'sound' are indissoluble. The *timing* of multimedia works has an inherently musical dimension. None of this will be surprising to digital musicians who are already familiar with the idea of organizing sound as musical expression. There are, however, certain peculiarities of particular situations which will provide the basis of the discussion in the rest of this chapter.

FURTHER READING

- Chion, M., *Audio-Vision: Sound on Screen*, New York: Columbia UP, 1994.
  Argues that sound in film qualitatively produces a new form of perception: we don't see images and hear sounds as separate channels, we audio-view a trans-sensory whole.

- Packer, R. and Jordan, K., *Multimedia: From Wagner to Virtual Reality*, New York: Norton, 2003.
  A collection of articles that tell the untold history of the multimedia revolution, showing how the interfaces, links and interactivity we all take for granted today grew out of a series of collaborations between the arts and the sciences.

FIXED MEDIA

The term 'fixed media' derives from a technical description of certain devices such as hard drives that are fixed within the computer, as opposed to removable devices. In digital music, and digital art in general, it has come to refer to any work that is fundamentally unchanged between performances so, typically, stored on a digital device and played back unvaryingly for a prescribed duration. This is distinct from 'real-time' elements such as live performance or time-varying digital processes. There may nevertheless be an interpretative layer, such as in sound diffusion. There are also many examples of hybrid works that comprise fixed media and live elements. Fixed media obviously includes not just audio-only composition, but also multimedia and audiovisual work. In its most familiar musical form, however, it is a concert piece that has a clear start and end point, and is commonly played back through loudspeakers, and it is this version that will mainly concern us in this section.

There is an implicit assumption in fixed media composition that the work will be unchanging on each occasion. Digital storage and playback seems to exaggerate this idea, with its extreme precision and lack of degradation. In practice, of course, this is far from the case. The stored sounds may be the same, but the listening situation will always be different. Even a classic acousmatic concert, with its darkened theatre and arrays of loudspeakers, will vary enormously depending on many factors: the configuration of the diffusion system; the make and positioning of the loudspeakers; the acoustic features of the venue; the presence of the audience; the decisions of the diffuser; and so on. Achieving precise effects, such as specific localizations of sounds, may well present a range of challenges. A 'sweet spot' for listening, for example, which may be available in the studio may not be so easy to find in the concert situation. Multimedia composition is even more variable, with typically less control available over the listening situation of users on the web or computer.

A first consideration in creating music for fixed media, therefore, must be the listening experience. Is the work designed to be reproducible in general situations or is it written with a specific venue or system in mind? How does this affect the overall aesthetic intention and, consequently, what are the most appropriate tools and techniques to realize the piece?

INTERACTIVE MUSIC

'Interactivity' is an important term but is also still the subject of much debate as to its precise meaning. Human communication is a traditional example of interactivity, but in the field of media, the term refers to human–computer interaction or human–human interaction that is mediated by digital technology. A word processor might possibly be called interactive, since it involves the user in an interaction with the computer, whereas machine-level processes that do not respond to human input are not interactive. The level of interactivity on offer in a word processor, however, is fairly limited, compared to that in a fully formed virtual environment. In such an environment, the human may move through and interact with objects, just as in the physical world. This means that the sound design has to take account of head movement, echoes and reverberations and the sonic properties of spaces and objects in general. It also has to process this information in real time.

Performance interaction can be between musician and technology, musician and other musicians and even between technology and technology. All, in some senses, represent aspects of being 'live'. That is to say, the extent of the musicianship will be the perceived success or otherwise of the interactions as they take place during a given time span. Technical questions can often dominate proceedings on these occasions, and they mainly concern the nature of the controllers. In theory, *anything* may be used as a controller: sound, gesture, touch, pressure, brainwaves, weather, data flow, motion and so on. It is simply a question of finding ways to translate these into digital data. In practice, this means that there is a vast array of more or less 'home-grown' interactive devices. An interactive device is anything that enables some form of communication between components, at least one of which can produce sound.

Haptic devices use touch, whereas *kinesthetic* systems use motion, but the two are closely related. In both cases, sensors register changes in state and convey information to the controller. The human body's motion through a space may be tracked by cameras and captured by a computer system. The resulting data stream outputs parameter messages that affect some aspect of the sound. A reciprocal relationship can also exist, where acoustic data is recorded and analysed to identify some characteristics, which then affect either the extended instrument or the nature of the sonic feedback. There comes a point in this process when the person who is triggering or influencing the sound *becomes* the musician. This person does not have to be a musician, or even be aware that they have become a musician! If well handled, the change in role can be attractively imperceptible. Whichever type of controller is used, the main technical challenges concern the design and build of the controller itself and how it maps its information onto sound. The musical success of the controller will often hinge upon these two elements.

A standard solution is to create a patch to map the human input onto some kind of sound-producing unit, often using MIDI as a trigger or to control parametric information. The computer will usually interpret the input in some way, often that relates the perceived expression inherent in a given gesture to some musical correlation (for example, a slowly raised hand might produce a sound that slowly rises in pitch, or gets louder). The decisions of the programmer of the controller, therefore, play a major role in determining the eventual outcome, so a mastery of at least some aspects of programming are more or less essential to success in this field.

In his interactive installations *MAP1* and *MAP2* (Figure 8.7), Garth Paine creates a space in which human movement controls sound synthesis. Using motion-sensing software, the mass, dynamic and direction of movement within predefined independent regions controls a real-time granular synthesis program to enable the user to manipulate sounds. The experience of figuring out and controlling the music through gesture and motion in space seems to reunite a form of dance and music. As Garth Paine puts it:

> The work explores the interaction between human movement and the creation of music. It attempts to create an environment in which people can consider the impact they make on their immediate environment and the causal loops that exist between behaviour and quality of environment. Personal aesthetic leads to decisions about preferential behaviour patterns and in turn preferential environment – one conditions the other.[11]

Where performance interaction is human–human, more traditional elements of musicianship apply. Good communication, sympathetic listening, timing are all key factors. The importance of visual cues should not be underestimated. There is a tendency for digital musicians to hide, behind equipment, in the dark, from one another. On some occasions, the performance aesthetic demands this, but it is more often a result of poor performance skills. Finally, and in many ways most importantly, in a live situation, communication with the audience is a musical skill, which must be learnt. Knowing how to dramatize, to have stage presence, to signal the end of a piece, to be seen to respond, are all aspects of

Figure 8.7   Users exploring *Map2* by Garth Paine © Garth Paine

musicianship that have more to do with theatre than with sound production, but any great live musical performer will have these abilities.

In many cases, the form of interactive music is *non-linear*. Of course, the listener hears all music as linear in the sense that there is a succession of audio events passing through time, but from a compositional point of view there is a world of difference between writing a fixed, linear piece that has a beginning, middle and end, and writing non-linear music in which material is accessed using some kind of digital procedure that orders events or samples in a different way each time the music is experienced. Music for computer games, for example, is typically organized using event-driven software that follows the hierarchical, tree-like structure of the game's database. Gamers may even create original soundtracks and, indeed, whole movies (machinima) by ignoring the objectives of the game itself and using the games engine creatively. At this point, the difference between the composer, the performer and the audience becomes so blurred as to be meaningless.

Non-linear composition is typically driven by 'if … then …' coding, or looping and branching. Here, the drama of the piece is more to do with the way the listener or user interacts with the material than with any formal structuring. This is sometimes called *adaptive* music, because it has to adapt in real time to a user's changing position in a given narrative or space. However, the kind of 'Adaptive Music' first coined by Christopher Yavelow in 1997 works slightly differently. As he describes it:

> adaptive music … relies on a continual feedback loop consisting of a user or users evaluating music generated by seed material provided by themselves (or itself generated). The software incorporates their preferences (opinions, tastes) into subsequent compositions by adapting the models it uses to compose in the future based upon this user feedback. Adaptive Music models are collections of compositional methods, rules, and constraints. The entire learning process allows the software to continually move closer to the ideal composition for an individual or collective group of users.[12]

This leads on to another question facing the digital musician: by what *agency* is the music to be made? If the answer is just an algorithm, then we are talking about a virtual agent. If the answer is through human interaction, then the virtual and the physical are combined. In either case, interactivity will operate at some level and the nature of its realization will be a distinctive component of the work's success.

FURTHER READING

- Collins, K., *Game Sound: An Introduction to the History, Theory, and Practice of Video Game Music and Sound Design*, Cambridge, MA: The MIT Press, 2008.
  A distinguishing feature of video games is their interactivity, and sound plays an important role in this: a player's actions can trigger dialogue, sound effects, ambient sound, and music. This book introduces readers to the many complex aspects of game audio, from its development in early games to theoretical discussions of immersion and realism.

- Rowe, R., *Interactive Music Systems: Machine Listening and Composing*, Cambridge, MA: The MIT Press, 1992.
  Provides a survey and evaluation of computer programs that can analyse and compose music in live performance.

- Winkler, T., *Composing Interactive Music*, Cambridge, MA: MIT Press, 2001.
  Essentially a tutorial in the use of *Max/MSP* for composing interactive music.

LIVE PERFORMERS

Case study artist Sophy Smith tells an interesting story about her collaborative work with dance:

> In one of my pieces with Motionhouse Dance Theatre, *Driven* (2007), there is a solo dance section, which became known as 'The Cleaner'. The character begins by mopping the word 'help' into a soapy floor and the choreography becomes more and more emotionally charged throughout. The choreographer and I discussed the section over the phone and I created the soundtrack, which I sent back for them to try out. Whilst it was a successful piece of music on its own, the soundtrack did not work with the choreography and 'flattened' the movement. So I started again, but next time the soundtrack made the movement seem overly dramatic. Over a fortnight I created six 4-minute pieces, each one different to the last in an attempt to find a good fit, but with no success. In the end, the problem was worked through with a practical solution. I packed the laptop, keyboard and speakers into the car, drove to the rehearsal studio and set-up there. This meant that I could try out ideas immediately to see what worked and what didn't, and within a couple of days, had created the finished piece. The portability of the digital tools I was using meant that I was able to move my creative space to where I could work best, allowing me to be flexible and responsive to the needs of the project.[13]

This anecdote raises a number of important questions to consider when writing for all kinds of live performers. Notice how the first problem was essentially aesthetic: the soundtrack 'flattened' the movement. In any collaborative situation, there will be more than one perception of the aesthetic impact of a piece of music. A basic question therefore, is: to what extent do you open your creative space to other people? Too much 'give' runs the risk of damaging your personal aesthetic or style. On the other hand, too little compromise might ruin the finished piece. In a collaboration, knowing when and how to insist on something is the defining feature of the creative process. In some instances, leaving room for interpretation by others can be a good way forwards. In others, being precise and exacting about what is required from the performers will be best.

In this case, Sophy was writing for a specific group of performers that she knew well. Even so, there was much disagreement about what 'worked'. When writing for unknown performers, the music has to be rather robust if it is to withstand the variations in realization or interpretation and retain your intention. 'Robust' here means that both aesthetic qualities and practical requirements need to be very clear and open to interpretation only to the extent that that is the intention of the work. The preferences of the performers, their likes and dislikes, will tend to dominate proceedings in any live situation.

The performance venue and the creative environment are also crucial. As Sophy's story illustrates, the physical relocation of her studio, its portability, was the key to eventual success. By turning the rehearsal venue into a creative music studio, and by being physically present, she was able to become 'flexible and responsive' in a way that was not possible from a remote location. All venues have characteristics and any performer will exploit those characteristics. It is therefore necessary when working with a specific venue to conceptualize the work in that situation. Think about the physical and acoustic constraints. How is the audience seated? Where do the performers stand or sit? Is movement possible or appropriate? Are there ways of creatively exploiting the space, or dramatizing the performance so that it enhances the music? What is the loudspeaker set-up and where are the musicians located? How will the physicality of the performance affect the experience of the work? What are the appropriate modes of delivery? How much performance gesture will be included? How is visual imagery integrated into the performance, if at all, and what are the technical requirements for that?

Of course, every set of answers to these questions will be unique to the occasion and the venue. Live music takes place in the moment. People change, and venues change. Simon Emmerson identifies two fundamental spaces, the *local* and the environmental *field*:

> *Local* controls and functions seek to extend (but not to break) the perceived relation of human performer action to sounding result.

> *Field* functions create a context, a landscape or an environment within which *local* activity may be found.[14]

There is a tendency for composers to write at the local level and rely on other factors, such as amplification, to carry their intentions into the field. However, amplification of a local gesture does not mean that the same gesture will map satisfactorily onto the field. The context has changed, which changes the meaning of the gesture. This is not only a matter of physical space: any local sound that loses contact with the gesture that produces it may be subject to the same dislocation. Emmerson makes the point that club spaces are essentially monaural, placing the listener inside the local, and personal stereo space is flattened by excluding the normal directional information that arrives at the ear.[15] Studio working will produce a sense of localization which is removed from the live perform-ance field, so only regular practical experience will make these ideas fully meaningful.

Composition that combines acoustic instruments with digital sound raises its own particular questions, both of performance gesture and of auditory experience. The major challenge is to avoid an inappropriate separation of acoustic and digital sound worlds. This is extremely difficult, because the embodiment of the performer's activities do not necessarily match the disembodied processes of the computer. Many solutions to this problem have been tried, such as feeding signals from contact microphones attached to the instrument or having the performer's gestures trigger sounds in a meaningful way. Alternatively, fixed media digital materials may be placed alongside the instrumental sounds, with more or less synchronization depending on the musical aesthetic, and blend and contact achieved at the acoustic level through matched harmonicity or rhythmic relationships or unifying any of the other parameters of digital music. Once again, the challenge for such compositions is how to overcome the discrepancy between the local and the field. In this case, the instrumental sounds will behave quite differently in a space from the studio-recorded, loudspeaker-mediated, electro-acoustic material.

FURTHER READING

- Emmerson, S., *Living Electronic Music*, Aldershot: Ashgate, 2007.
  Explores issues of 'live' performance in the age of the laptop, examining both the practical apsects and the underlying theories and concepts.

Project 32 (Advanced): ... From Scratch

Introduction

This project is designed to strip away previous ideas of 'musicianship', in order to re-evaluate the sounding properties of objects, how they may be made into instruments, how playing techniques might be developed and how music may be created as a result. It is not necessarily a 'digital' project as such, but its value to anybody working in a digital context should quickly become apparent, especially through its ability to awaken the ears. It is potentially a long-term project lasting several weeks and can work well with small or very large groups.

The Project

Participants find objects with interesting sonic properties to develop into a performance machine. Participants will develop new performance techniques using these objects, avoiding using their existing technical skills – the project is 'from scratch'.

PROJECT 32

1   *Find sonic objects*. Analyse the sonic properties of the objects. Can they be modified or tuned? Does an object have obvious musical potential? How can it combine with other objects?

2   *Research other people's uses of similar objects*. Is there a history of musical use of such an object? Are there any obvious musical or aesthetic associations? How have other people used and developed similar objects?

3   *Make an instrument*. How can the object be turned into an instrument? What are the best ways to exploit its sonic potential? How can it be made playable? Can it be combined with other objects to form a single instrument?

4   *Develop a performance technique*. What are the performance issues? Is it possible to become a virtuoso on this new instrument?

5   *Create some original music*. Will this instrument work best solo or in an ensemble? What kind of music would work best for the instrument? Is there any similar music which can be used as a model? Is the music notated or non-notated?

6   *Give a performance*. How best to present this music to an audience? How much rehearsal is required? What would be an appropriate performance mode?

Notes

This is a beneficial project for any group of musicians, but the particular importance for the 'digital musician' lies in the experimental approach, the sonic exploration and the removal of anything that resembles familiar technique. Computers may be used at every stage for analysis, research, planning, structuring, recording and even in performance, so there may be some obviously 'digital' component, but this is not essential.

Discussion Questions

• What would an ideal musical instrument look like? How would it function?

• To what extent have gesture-based devices such as tablets and active game controllers changed digital music?

• What are the consequences of removing physical gestures from the act of playing an instrument?

• What you understand by the term 'interactive'? How may this be applied in music?

• Are the sounds created on the fly when playing a computer game really musical? If not, why not? If so, how so?

• How do you compose digital music from live performers? What are the issues and strategies?

CHAPTER 9

Performing and Musicianship

Music is a form of social communication; musical performance is a site of social intercourse, and a form of social dialogue … In surviving oral cultures, the relation between musical senders and musical receivers is much more fluid and symbiotic than in modern Western society. The anthropological evidence is unequivocal. There are no composers in such societies set apart from other musicians in a separate caste, and music is far from an exclusive activity of specialized performers.
—(Chanan, 1994)[1]

THE PERFORMER

Performing and creating are practically indivisible activities for the digital musician. There is a historical basis for this. 'Performance Art', which has its own origins in the

Happenings of the 1960s, successfully removed the work of art from an object in a gallery to an action in a particular space at a particular time. Much early experimentation with music technology was allied to similar experiments with performance ritual. Nowadays, performance need not even involve human performers. An installation can be performative, and an artificial intelligence may also perform. Locations may be physical or virtual, and time may not be fixed. Certain types of movies may be interactively performed rather than just 'shown', and gaming too offers performance opportunities. A good example is 'machinima' (machine cinema), in which people use game platforms to create original theatre featuring the avatars, or virtual characters, and settings of a computer game, without adherence to the goals of the game itself. Once again, the creator, the performer and the audience constantly shift roles.

At some point in history, music education decided to separate performing and creating. The conservatoires and other mainstream performing-arts institutions generally place more emphasis on creative *interpretation* than original creation. Composition is a specialist option, and the creators (composers, in this case) are not necessarily expected to perform. The classical system of notated music, supported by pedagogy and academic research, has reinforced the specialization. However, the fact that the two activities are presented in different chapters in this book should not be understood as supporting their separation but rather as a matter of convenience for the organization of certain ideas.

The role of the performer has changed almost as much as the composer. We may even speak of a 'digital performer'. This phrase implies a new performance mode, which is more than just a traditional concert performance executed on digital instruments. A pianist playing piano music on a digital piano is not really a digital performer. If the same pianist were to process or manipulate the sound of the piano in some way, then digital performance starts to appear. There are a number of distinctly different activities in which this new performer might engage, such as sound diffusion or networked performance.

PERFORMANCE SITUATIONS

Live performance is always physically (as well as culturally) *situated*. Musicians in general should do more to take control of the performance situation, which in practice means handling the sound diffusion. It is all too often assumed that the sound system for a concert is set up and controlled purely by engineers or technicians who would not themselves be classified as musicians. Given the level of control these people exercise over the sound heard by the audience, this is a rather astonishing attitude. In fact, sound diffusion is, or rather *can be*, just as musical an activity as playing the piano. It is certainly a form of musical interpretation. Digital musicians cannot place themselves at the mercy of sound engineers if they are to achieve an original sound. It is essential that they (the musicians) master sound diffusion techniques to at least a basic level.

One of the performance challenges facing sound diffusers is the extent to which the audience can perceive what the performer is doing. The action of sliding faders on a mixing desk is quite uninformative compared to, say, the action of depressing a piano key. This becomes especially true when the fader motion controls parameters other than volume level, which it often does in live diffusion situations. The motion of sounds through space, the application of effects and processes, the grouping and assigning of a stereo source to various channels in a multichannel set-up may all be contained within a tiny hand motion which is, more often than not, invisible to the audience. For acousmatic situations, where the ideal is to remove visual distraction, this can be desirable, but in less refined circumstances it can lead to misunderstanding about the role of the diffuser.

The next major performance challenge, consequently, is the way in which musical gesture is interpreted through diffusion. There is an active debate about this. The premise is that the same types of gestures that are present in the shaping of the material that makes up electro-acoustic music should be reflected in its diffusion. Where sound is ascribed to channels and motion between channels is already built into a composition, there is apparently little need to actively 'interpret' the result. The assumption is that the set-up itself will perform the diffusion. However, in reality this is often not the case. A stereo piece played back over stereo speakers in a large concert hall will often lose the stereo image because of the size and reverberant characteristics of the space. A multichannel set-up is the solution, at which point the choices made during the diffusion become key performance decisions.

To be absolutely clear, then, sound diffusion is a *musical*, rather than a purely technical, activity. The diffusion should aim to reveal the formal nature of a work, its underlying structures as well as its local detail. The piece must be thoroughly rehearsed in advance of a performance and account taken of the characteristics of the space and set-up. Musical questions such as the rate at which diffusion changes take place and the kind of spatial motion that is introduced should be decided upon.

FURTHER READING

- Chanan, M., *Musica Practica: Social Practices of Western Music from Gregorian Chant to Post Modernism*, London: Verso, 1994.
  A historical investigation into the social practice of Western music which advances an alternative approach to that of established musicology. Chanan sketches out an unwritten history of musical instruments as technology, from Tutankhamen's trumpets to the piano, the ancient Greek water organ to the digital synthesizer. The book concludes with reflections on the rise of modernism and the dissolution of the European tradition in a sea of postmodernism and 'world music'.

- Goldberg, R. L., *Performance Art: From Futurism to the Present*, London: Thames and Hudson, 1979, 2001.
  Explores the extensive history of this hybrid form of performance. Analyses artists as varied as the Dadaists, Laurie Anderson, John Cage, Cindy Sherman, Mariko Mori, Paul McCarthy, Matthew Barney, Karen Finley, Forced Entertainment and Desperate Optimists.

- White, P., *Live Sound (Performing Musicians)*, New York: Sanctuary, 2005.
  This is a practical guide to equipment and sound for small- to medium-sized gigs. It covers everything from choosing PA equipment to selecting the right type of microphone and finding your way around a typical live sound mixer.

- Wyatt, S. et al., *Investigative Studies on Sound Diffusion/Projection at the University of Illinois: A Report on An Explorative Collaboration*, University of Illinois, 2005.
  An interesting short study of some of the main issues in sound diffusion.

NETWORKED PERFORMANCE

Figure 9.1 shows (left to right) Leaf Tine, Susan St John and case study artist Synthia Payne in 2005, engaged in a networked performance entitled *Lubricious Transfer*, a telematic collaboration between New York University and University of California, Santa Cruz. The show was directed by Ted Warburton and instigated by Dr John Gilbert. Synthia comments:

> That photo represents so much to me. It truly was a dream come true as I had been thinking about being able to play live music online with other people for about five years, and I was and still am an avid participant.[2]

There are five main types of networked performance or telematic music:

1   Music that uses the network to connect physical spaces or instruments.
2   Music that is created or performed in virtual environments, or uses virtual instruments.
3   Music that translates into sound aspects of *the network itself.*
4   Music that uses the Internet to enable collaborative composition or performance.
5   Music that is delivered via the Internet, with varying degrees of user inter-activity.

A typical situation might have a group of musicians sharing control of the parameters of a given sound file or collection of sound files. Modular software enables each individual to interact with the sound files in various ways while simultaneously communicating with one another. If the musicians are physically present in the same space, visual,

Figure 9.1   Lubricious Transfer (l-r Leaf Tine, Susan St John, Synthia Payne) © Jim Mackenzie/UC Santa Cruz

verbal and textual clues may be exchanged, but the idea can be extended to remotely located musicians too. Telepresence is a relatively under explored aspect of this kind of music.

There are various kinds of network used in music, ranging from small local area networks (LANs) to wide area networks (WANs) that connect towns, cities and countries. The 'Internet' is a network of networks and is never used in its entirety, but 'net music' and 'Internet music' are terms that encompass music made on all kinds of network. The majority of such networks comprise nodes that are physically connected by cable, but, of course, there are also wireless networks and satellite networks, of which the best known are the mobile phone networks. All of these may be used in music-making.

The technical constraints that confront the musician on the network mainly relate to *latency* and *loss*. Latency is the amount of time required for a signal to traverse the network, and loss of data is partly a consequence of the bandwidth which, in networking terms, is the capacity or data rate of a link. To illustrate the scale of the challenge these create for music, consider this quotation from an article by Álvaro Barbosa:

> For the human ear to perceive two sounds as simultaneous, the sounds should not be displaced in time more than 20 msec, which means that for mutual awareness to be supported in a bilateral performance, the maximum threshold would be around 40 msec (the time it would take a performer to perceive a second performer's reaction to his or her action). It should be noted that the perception of two different sounds performed simultaneously is strongly dependent on sound characteristics (timbre, pitch and loudness), musical style and other types of feedback such as visual or physical stimuli. Nevertheless, a 20-msec threshold should be adequate. If we consider the smallest possible peer-to-peer connection between two opposite points on the planet, we have an approximate distance of 20,004.5 km (half the distance of earth's perimeter: 40,009 km). Even with data transfer at the speed of light (approximately 300,000 km per sec) and unlimited bandwidth, bidirectional latency would reach approximately 133.4 msec, which is much higher than the tolerable threshold.[3]

Since unlimited bandwidth is a pipe dream, this problem is considerably magnified in many musical situations, and solutions usually concentrate on ways of accommodating the limitations of the network itself. Even quite small LANs can exhibit significant latency.

Network architecture is a vast study in its own right, but the two types of network that crop up repeatedly in relation to music are the traditional client/server network and peer-to-peer (p2p) networks. In the former, the server generally runs intensive software (e.g., databases, email and so on) and the client usually consists of an interface that can request data from the server. P2p networks operate rather differently, each connected machine sharing its computing power and data with the others on the network, without using a central server.

Where interactivity in network music is the goal, various solutions have been developed using different programming languages. Here are a few examples: *JSyn*[4] ('Java Synthesis') uses the Java programming language to allow users to develop interactive applications such as synthesizers, audio playback routines and effects–processing algo-rithms; *Jade*,[5] on the other hand, takes a modular approach based on Max/MSP to allow multiple users to analyse, generate and process audio and video; *NinJam* is an active com-munity of networked musicians based on a software architecture that uses a distributed clock to share delayed streams, thus avoiding latency issues; and *jackTrip* is a hardware solution developed by David Willyard and Chris Chafe (Stanford CCRMA) that is increasingly being used in many telematic performances.

In recent years, making music in virtual worlds has become widespread, partly as a result of online gaming. The virtual worlds themselves are essentially object-oriented programming environments enriched with multimedia capability. These allow the users to build their own environment, to interact with other users, to create objects and so on. A virtual world is, therefore, made by its inhabitants according to their own imagina-tions, and in several such worlds musical communities are developing formed entirely of virtual musicians. They build virtual instruments, which they sell or barter, and they perform virtual concerts or have virtual jam sessions.

Such new media represent more than just a technical development. They contain a fundamental cultural shift too. Now that non-linear music and network performance are a practical reality, numerous home-grown technical solutions to musical and multimedia problems are springing up. The digital musician may well contribute to these. It is not enough to use new media to disseminate music that could be heard equally well another

---

PROJECT 33

Project 33 (Advanced): Ping–Hack–Rom–Seed

Introduction

There are many ways to create a networked ensemble. A quick search of the web, using a string such as 'networked music performance', will bring up many examples. This project is aimed at getting the musicians to think about the philosophical and aesthetic aspects of networked performance, rather than providing a 'how-to' manual for putting one together.

The Project

Create a networked ensemble of at least three members. Give the ensemble a 'digital' name, either: 'ping' or 'hack' or 'rom' or 'seed'. Now try to create music that lives up to or evokes the name of the ensemble.

Notes

These names seem to imply things: a different kind of repertoire, perhaps, or a different approach to music technology. Some immediate thoughts:

- ping – communications ('pinging' another machine), signs, insignificance
- hack – coding, programming, manipulating the materials of others
- rom – processing, memory, data mining
- seed – evolution, growth, development.

FURTHER READING

■ Bailey, A., *Network Technology for Digital Audio*, Oxford: Focal Press, 2001.
Highly technical study of all aspects of network technology for audio.

■ Gaye, L., Holmquist, L. E., Behrendt, F. and Tanaka, A., 'Mobile Music Technology:
Report on Emerging Community', *Proceedings of the 2006 Conference on New
Interfaces for Musical Expression* (NIME-06), 2006, pp. 22–25.
Examines the field of mobile music at the intersection of ubiquitous computing,
portable audio technology and new instruments.

■ Jordà, S., 'FMOL: Toward User-Friendly, Sophisticated New Musical Instruments',
Computer Music Journal, 26:3, 2002, 23–39.
Describes F@ust Music OnLine, an attempt to create a new, integrated online
instrument.

■ Weinberg, G., 'Local Performance Networks: musical interdependency through
gestures and controllers', *Organized Sound*, 10:3, 2005, 255–266.
Discusses four novel local musical networks that use gesture controllers.

way. Rather, the digital musician will seek to unlock the creative potential in networks, in multimedia, in sound design, sonic art and music.

PERFORMANCE SCORES

Performance scores may comprise a set of written instructions combined with some imagery, or a diffusion score for fixed media work. Diffusion scores may range from the highly technical to the lyrically interpretative, as may be seen in the following examples. Scott Wyatt's score (see Figure 9.2) shows time running vertically up the page and the eight channels, arranged in three stereo pairs plus two single channels for front and back centre speakers, are given vertically. Wyatt explains:

> Black graphic shapes indicate the amplitude contour information for each chan-
> nel, the thicker the shape, the higher the amplitude and vice versa. Comments are
> often written in the vertical margins to alert the projectionist to specific cues or
> types of articulation.[6]

Claude Schryer's diffusion score for Francis Dhomont's *Chiaroscuro* (1987), on the other hand, shows time running from left to right across the page and gives almost no detailed information about the activities in the loudspeakers, preferring instead to use its imagery to evoke the character and gesture of the music itself (Figure 9.3).

Once again, these scores give only partial information about the ways in which a piece may be realized, and often give little or no clue to how it may actually *sound*. The computer file is the only full representation.

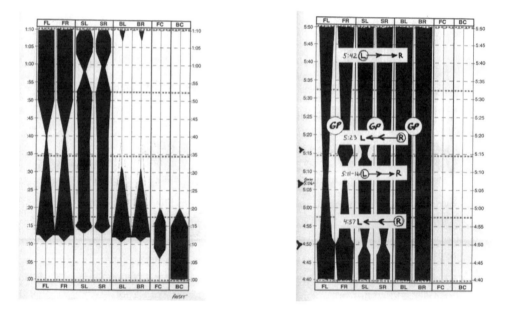

Figure 9.2   Two pages from the diffusion score for *Aftermath* (2005) © Scott A. Wyatt

03m30

04m30

05m30

Figure 9.3   Excerpt from Claude Schryer's diffusion score for Francis Dhomont's *Chiaroscuro* (1987) © Claude Schryer

BEING LIVE

Whatever the situation, a common tendency these days is for the digital musician to work solo, whether diffusing sound or originating sound, or playing 'instruments' or a laptop. This is a reflection of both the developments in technology, which allow individual control of the sound, and the desire of the digital musician to produce an original sound. It is therefore understandable, but it is nevertheless potentially problematic.

One thing that has changed in digital performance is the notion of 'liveness'. In acoustic music, it is normally clear what is live and what is not. The human performer, sharing a space with the listener and making sound at that moment is performing live. There are some acceptable extensions to this concept: an offstage choir, an electronic relay from another building, even a simultaneous broadcast but, in general, being 'live' means *synchronous* musical activity.

For the digital performer, the situation is not always so straightforward. Performance across a network, sound installations, automated or algorithmic work, interactive music, may all be to some degree not synchronized, or *asynchronous*. Real-time performance is a network ideal, but is not always achievable, so the network latency becomes the equivalent to the resonant characteristics of a given space. Just as the synchronous musician must allow for acoustic delay, or reverberation, in a space (e.g., a church), the asynchronous musician must take into account the latency of the network.

In a sound installation, the human performer need not actually be simultaneously present with the audience for the performance to take place: a virtual presence may suffice. In some kinds of algorithmic music, as we have seen, the user *becomes* the performer, but unawares, using materials created in advance by another musician. In many such cases, the user is practically unaware of their role as performer.

For the digital musician to develop skills, it is very important to engage in collective performance activities as well as solo work. Eye contact, visual cues, verbal and non-verbal communication during performance are all musically important, but there is a

Figure 9.4   Kaffe Matthews performing live © Kevin Altamirano Zubiría

larger ethical issue too: people *should* learn to work together. Physical gestures do more than simply ensure synchronization between performers. They are part of the social exchange of performance.

Despite the importance of the technology and the development of interactive media, the human musician must develop in a human way. It may seem an obvious thing to say, but a human being is not the same as a machine. Artificial intelligence (AI) has developed considerably over the past few decades, but the average chicken is still far more intelligent than any robot. AI tends to focus on behaviours rather than the independent workings of the mind which, of course, are still little understood.

A fair proportion of AI is still mainly rooted in a branch of psychological research called 'behaviourism', which ignores mental states in order to enable an objective study only of people's behaviour. The computer scientist Alan Turing was responsible for creating tests to identify the differences between man and machine, to establish the moment at which artificial intelligence and human intelligence would no longer be distinguishable. In terms of behaviourism, we are already close to (or past) this point. However, despite their remarkable achievements, few AI scientists would claim to have replicated the human mind. Humans are more complicated than behaviourism would suggest.

So, the human performer must be at ease with the technology but must also be at ease with other humans who use technology. The latter is the greater challenge. Technology can extend human attributes, but an automaton still lacks a will of its own, it has no real freedom of choice. The human musician must make decisions, make choices, even if those choices are merely to initiate an algorithmic process. This implies a lack of indifference to the sounding result; in other words, *musicality*. The extent to which a performance is successful, therefore, is the result of a balance between the conceptual and the practical aspects, between right and left hemispheres of the brain. Virtuosity in performance comes from the audience's perception of this balance. Thus, we can admire the choices made by a DJ, the decisions made by a sound diffuser, the understanding shown by a multimedia artist. We trace the path made by these decisions through a field of possibilities. We appreciate the technical skill, the aural awareness and even the cultural knowledge that is shown in performance.

FURTHER READING

■ Landy, L., *Experimental Music Notebooks*, Newark, NJ: Harwood Academic, 1995. This text describes a workshop approach for those who have trouble finding a way into the appreciation of experimental music. It enables teachers to create circumstances for music experimentation for the classroom, as well as in other, sometimes unusual contexts.

■ Small, C., *Musicking*, Middletown, CT: Wesleyan University Press, 1998. Asserts that music is not a thing, but rather an activity. 'Musicking' is a verb that encompasses all musical activity from composing to performing to listening to a personal stereo to singing in the shower. Small demonstrates how musicking forms a ritual through which all the participants explore and celebrate the relationships that constitute their social identity.

IMPROVISATION

At some point in the history of Western classical music, improvisation was downgraded to the level of a frivolous activity. Somehow, just 'making it up as you go along' was deemed to be in no way equivalent to the more elevated activity of producing works that were fixed by notation. This is strange, because many of the great composers of history were in fact leading improvisers. Beethoven, for example, was famous in his time as an improvising pianist, and several of his compositions are, in fact, written out improvisations. The same goes for Liszt. It is only church organists who seem to have retained improvisational skills. Many classical orchestral musicians asked to improvise today would find it immensely difficult to do so.

This is not the case in most other musical traditions. In much non-Western music, for example the Indian *raga*, improvisation is still part of the required skills of a successful musician. Jazz, of course, has also retained improvisation as a key element of performance. Here, the improvisation generally relates to a harmonic framework (the 'changes'), over which the improviser may develop melodic or rhythmic ideas. In practice, these tend to be built from motivic elements: short phrases containing characteristic melodic shapes, intervallic sequences or rhythmic patterns. In this respect, jazz improvisation resembles Indian *raga* or, indeed, Western classical music. What is distinctive is that it takes place in 'real time'.

Free improvisation is probably the form of improvisation that is the most useful to the digital musician. Free improvisation is somewhat different from 'free jazz', which sets about removing the harmonic skeletons and familiar phrases of jazz in the interests of finding novel forms of expression. Free improvisation begins by trying to remove *all* traces of style or idiom from the music. In the words of its greatest theorist and practitioner, Derek Bailey, it is 'playing without memory'.[7] This can be extremely difficult to achieve in practice, but it is often a good starting point for musical creativity and works particularly well in technology-based performance, where a certain indifference to the cultural implications of the material can sometimes be an advantage.

What does quickly happen in free improvisation sessions is that the participants become aware of and responsive to the other members of the group. In fact, free improvisation is not really 'free' at all. It is highly constrained by the rules of social intercourse, rather than musical convention. For the digital musician to develop as a musician, interaction with other musicians is essential. If that interaction is to be just a question of finding other people to realize a single creative vision, then the interaction is limited. It is also unnecessary to use more than one person in the production of music. So, improvisation and, in particular, free improvisation, can open up dialogue and develop musical practice in unexpected and innovative ways.

This kind of improvisation can be useful in many different situations, particularly for developing a collaborative approach to music-making. Many rock bands use a similar process in the recording studio, just 'messing about' and collectively agreeing upon what does and does not 'work'. A more structured approach might have the musicians take individual responsibility for a particular aspect of the music by mutual agreement. So Musician 1 might handle the beat, Musician 2 the dynamics, Musician 3 the mix or texture, and so on.

Another useful approach that emphasizes the drama of improvisation is to use a verbal score as a structure. There are a few examples of verbal scores, which deliberately set themselves up as structures for improvisation.[8] It is easy enough, however, to make one up. The advantage of a pre-agreed structure is that all the participants understand the relationships between the musical elements and 'characters', and the overall shape and process of the performance is to some extent predictable. Adopting a constraint-based approach to an improvisation can further develop this. Perhaps individuals are limited to a fixed number of sounds, a particular set of cues, a single effect, and so on. There may be even more rigidly imposed constraints about timing or level. Constraints in perform-ance, paradoxically, do not necessarily mean a lack of freedom.

Project 34 (Advanced): Improvisation Ensemble

Introduction

There are many ways to approach improvisation, but the main thing to bear in mind in the context of this book is that it is not helpful to allow improvisers simply to demonstrate their technical prowess on a given instrument or with the computer. In fact, there can be a positive advantage in having only limited technique on the given instrument. Vir-tuoso improvising is not about showing-off, but rather about collective understanding and collaboration.

The Project

Form an ensemble that does nothing but improvise. The ensemble must have more than three members.

Notes

The important thing is to develop aural awareness to the point of being able to make only meaningful sounds in the improvisation. It is acceptable to make no sound at all. A highly constrained improvisation might allow each musician only three sounds, which have to be carefully chosen and timed. Often, improvising in the dark can help to focus the ear. One exercise is to try to imitate a sound, passing it around the room 'Chinese whispers'-style. Another is to try to make the *opposite* sound each time (so a high, loud, long sound would be followed by a low, quiet, short one).

It is normally a good idea to time-limit an improvisation until the group has gotten to know one another to the point that they can 'feel' when to stop. Starting and finish-ing are often key moments in any ensemble improvisation, and various solutions will be found to what constitutes an appropriate ending. A 'riff' can sometimes be the death of a good improvisation, because it tends to encourage a 'jam-session' mentality, lead-ing to an abandonment of careful listening. On the other hand, a well-constructed and careful use of repetition at the right time can be very successful. The key to a good improvisation is the right mix of repetition and variation. This is probably true of music in general.

PROJECT 34

FURTHER READING

- Bailey, D., *Improvisation: Its Nature and Practice in Music*, New York: Da Capo Press, 1993.
  First published in 1980. It was the first book to deal with the nature of improvisation in all its forms: Indian music, flamenco, baroque, organ music, rock, jazz, contemporary and free music. Includes interviews with John Zorn, Jerry Garcia, Steve Howe, Steve Lacy, Lionel Salter, Earle Brown, Paco Pea, Max Roach, Evan Parker and Ronnie Scott Bailey.

- Dean, R., *Hyperimprovisation: Computer Interactive Sound Improvisation*, Middleton, WI: A-R Editions, 2003.
  Looks at computer interactions in improvisation.

- Lewis, G. E., 'Too Many Notes: Computers, Complexity and Culture in "Voyager"', *Leonardo Music Journal*, 10, 2000, 33–39.
  Discusses the computer music composition, *Voyager*, which employs a computer-driven, interactive 'virtual improvising orchestra' that analyses an improviser's performance in real time, generating both complex responses to the musician's playing and independent behaviour arising from the program's own internal processes.

LIVE CODING

Live coding is a kind of improvisation that may also be one of the purest forms of digital music. Live coding is 'the art of programming a computer under concert conditions'[9] In other words, a live coder will write and edit the code that produces digital music in real time in front of an audience.[10] As a musical practice, live coding is currently in its infancy and has sparked some controversy, mainly because of its abstraction from the more familiar physical aspects of performance. There is animated discussion among live coders about the best way to present this activity in a concert situation in order to avoid audience disaffection or to show the coding process and its effects upon what is heard. Live coders seem generally agreed that invisible typing is not a particularly engaging activity from an audience perspective. Most solutions therefore involve some kind of multimedia presentation or overhead display. Figure 9.5 shows one such set-up, created for an on-the-fly performance by Ge Wang and Perry R. Cook.[11]

It is also possible to use a more physical interface than just the computer keyboard. Amy Alexander's VJ tool *The Thingee* is a dance mat laid out with symbols,[12] and Dave Griffiths' *Betablocker* relies on joystick control.[13] Even the physical movements of the live coder at the computer may be readable as an input.

Live coding generally uses modular sections of code which can be edited separately. The coding needs to be concise, so that rapid changes can be made, and it needs to allow for precise synchronization. In other words, the system has to be both flexible and manageable. TOPLAP[14] lists more than a dozen such systems on its website. In a recent article on the subject, the live coder Nick Collins draws a parallel between learning live-coding technique and the practice regimes of the nineteenth-century composer–pianists.

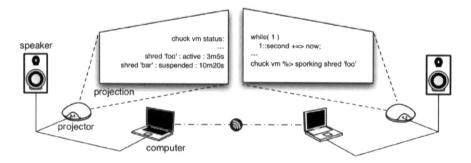

Figure 9.5   On-the-fly aesthetic © Ge Wang

He lists several exercises, including 'isolation exercises' such as algorithm composition and sound synthesis, and 'connectivity exercises' such as layering, mixing, enveloping and reacting to other code. TOPLAP have even suggested a system of 'grades' analogous to the traditional performance grades in music.

Live coding appeals to both musicians with programming skills and programmers with musical leanings. As a result, a number of competitive events and a sub-culture of live coders has grown up at the intersection of the two disciplines. Live-coding 'battles' are quite frequent, in which the artists challenge one another in various ways, such as: 'root wars', in which the hackers try to undermine each other's systems or to occupy areas of spectral information; or a 'Tetris challenge', in which each player presents the next with a chunk of code to use. A more cooperative activity is the combined rework-ing of code, sometimes using a tag team of coders, or in a laptop 'jam' session. It looks as though live coding could become a virtuosic activity in the right hands, but Collins is keen to downplay any arrogance at this early stage of its development:

> Right now, I think live coders are equivalent to potentially talented 11 year olds.
> Give us seven years of intensive practice and come to one of our gigs in 2014. …
> We currently have no master teachers to guide us, and must risk the possibility of
> ineffective practice whilst enjoying the sense of open discovery.[15]

FURTHER READING

■ Collins, N., McLean, A. and Rohrhuber, J., 'Live Coding in Laptop Performance', *Organized Sound*, 8:3, 2003, 321–330.

■ Cook, P. R. and Wang, G., 'On-the-Fly Programming: Using Code as an Expres-sive Musical Instrument', *Proceedings of the 2004 International Conference on New Interfaces for Musical Expression (NIME)*, 2004, pp. 138–143.

■ McCartney, J., 'Rethinking the Computer Music Programming Language: Super-Collider', *Computer Music Journal*, 26:4, 2002, 61–68.

■ Wang, G. and Cook, P. R., 'ChucK: A Concurrent, On-the-fly Audio Programming Language', *Proceedings of International Computer Music Conference*, 2003, pp. 219–226.

MUSICIANSHIP

Technical skills, aural awareness and cultural knowledge are all things that distinguish the digital musician, but they are not the things that make him or her a *musician*. A non-musician may equally well be computer literate, aurally aware and culturally knowledgeable. Here we reach a crucial part of this book, for if there is to be such a thing as a digital musician, who is distinct from other musicians, then it follows that their musical abilities will be substantially different yet identifiably 'musical'. What are the *musical* skills required to be a digital musician? Traditionally, these are summed up by the word 'musicianship'.

Musicianship is commonly understood to refer to the set of skills and artistry required to perform, listen to, or compose music. Good musicianship makes evident through the act of performance, or listening, or composition the extent to which a person is in possession of this knowledge. Virtuosity is achieved when good musicianship is surpassed, but not sacrificed. There is an argument which says that the term should not be used at all in the digital domain, since it is purely traditional and therefore irrelevant. On the other hand, digital technologies have had a considerable impact on all aspects of music-making, including instrumental music. There is clearly a need to summarize the diversity, complexity and variability of skills required by those making sonic art, digital music, or whatever we choose to call it. 'Digital musicianship' may seem like a fairly weak term, but in this context it is probably the best we have. If music is organized sound, then digital music is sound that it is organized digitally, and the people who undertake this activity may be called 'digital musicians' who therefore exhibit a distinctive musicianship.

Musicianship is distinct from musicality, which is a more innate condition of being sensitive to, or talented in, music. Broadly speaking, musicianship is something that is learned and is objectively measurable, whereas musicality is something that is felt and is more subjectively evaluated. It might be assumed that good musicianship requires good musicality, but it is not always so. A criticism often made of otherwise excellent musicians is that, while their musicianship may be fine, their performances lack musicality. By contrast, someone with no musicianship at all (e.g., a dancer) may nevertheless display musicality. But good musicianship can do much to release musicality, and the highest musicianship will make a performance seem deeply musical.

Musicianship in the digital age has been affected by two main factors: the impact of new technologies on human musicians, and the rapid development of machine musicianship. These have a reciprocal relationship, as Robert Rowe observes:

> Computer programs designed to implement any of [the musicianship] skills – that is, to make sense of what is heard, perform music expressively, or compose convincing pieces – can similarly benefit from a musician's fundamental level of musicianship.[16]

An artificially intelligent musician is called a *live agent*, and there are many different types in existence. All of them are modelled in some way on human musicians, often using generative algorithms to introduce an element of creativity into their performances. The live agent has to be able to contribute meaningfully to any musical situation which presents huge challenges for programmers and engineers. As Nicholas Collins points out:

> The social roles of musicians are an important part of different musical settings, from full democratic participation to particular lead and subsidiary roles … This full social participation, as an equal human participant, shows exactly how the musical AI problem turns into the full AI challenge.[17]

Since machine musicianship grapples with essentially the same issues as human musicianship (and often quite traditional musicianship at that), the following discussion will focus on the human musician, on the understanding that working with live agents may form part of the skillset of a digital musician.

The elements of digital musicianship may be summarized under the following headings, which at first glance look quite familiar from traditional musicianship. It is in the detail and content of these that the nature of the change may be found:

- technical mastery
- critical judgement
- aural skills
- musical literacy
- ensemble abilities
- creativity.

As was discussed in Part I, an individual's musical background should be no obstacle to acquiring these skills. Every previous experience will contribute to their development. On the other hand, the difference between digital musicianship and other forms is quite profound and a significant change in thinking and practice will be required, so to become expert requires a certain open-mindedness and willingness to embrace new ideas. In some cases, this will involve abandoning some long-cherished ideas and replacing them with something quite new. This is nothing to fear and in fact should be welcomed when it occurs, because it provides an opportunity to experiment and discover new approaches and ways of working.

Technical Mastery

The first essential ability is an understanding of the technology that is used. This is somewhat different from the understanding of the piano shown by a pianist, for example. The required bricolage approach will mean that a digital musician will often explore new technologies. In all probability, he or she will have a fascination with the market for second-hand equipment and will want to keep pace with new developments as they arise. This does not necessarily mean a rejection of old technology. In fact, innovative and unique music can be made just as well with old equipment as with new. To give one example, valves gave way to transistors back in the early days of radio, but recently people have realized that a valve can produce an attractively 'warm' sound in a way that a transistor cannot, and so valves are back. Music technology now is often digital, but not exclusively so.

Whatever configuration of hardware and software is chosen affects the character of the music. Linearity or non-linearity of form and content, the degree of interactivity between humans and virtual agents, the sound qualities of the result, will all be dependent upon these choices. In general, what is wanted from the equipment is responsiveness and controllability. The interface is, therefore, crucial, and interfaces exist between human and computer, between computer and computer, between analog and digital equipment, and even, in a performance situation, between performers and audience. Key decisions have to be made early on, therefore, about the types of interface to be used, about synchronization and about how those map onto the sounds that will be produced.

These are all performative decisions, equivalent in significance and musical qualities to the traditional 'tone' that an instrumentalist might produce from their instrument. In other words, the technological set-up is not just a way of making an 'instrument' upon which to perform, it is integral to the nature of the sound that is produced, to the distinctive sound that makes the digital musician into the performer, to the musicianship itself. The musician's ability to handle the interface, or the controller, is a powerful indicator of the level of technological understanding.

Loudspeakers and microphones are basic elements of digital music, so an understanding of these is essential, as is a thorough knowledge of the digitization process. Being able to identify, gather or create sound sources of good quality is another important ingredient. The quality of sound is crucial to establishing a sense of musical ability, which is not to say that the sounds should always be the best possible quality, but rather that decisions about sound quality will always affect the result.

Programming skills, in the sense of being able to write source code in a programming language, are not absolutely essential, yet are in fact practised by all musicians working with digital technology through the software that is used. Depending on the design of this software and its interface the extent of user programming skills required will be more or less evident. In any event, an understanding of the principles behind algorithms and software architecture is important, and it seems likely that, sooner or later, the digital musician will feel impelled to write some code.

Critical Judgement

This will be the major focus of Part III of this book, so this section will restrict itself to the observation that *uncritical acceptance of the output of the computer or algorithm is bad musicianship*. The 'feedback loop' of the creative process described earlier should be practised at all times. An understanding of the physical and technical aspects of musical performance is not the only significant factor in musicianship. The ability to critically reflect is key to improving both creativity and musicality. The goal of the digital musician is to develop a 'sound', in much the same way as a traditional instrumentalist. In many cases, it is the setting and refining of musical goals over many performances and the process of learning from experience that enables this development.[18]

Such reflective practice is a circular activity: the musician will listen to a sound that is made, make another sound that in some way addresses the 'problem' posed by the first sound, then listen to that sound and so on. This process can take place almost instantly (in real time) or after some delay. It is a dialogue between the musician and the musical material he or she creates. The idea of reflective practice was first described by Donald Schön in his book *The Reflective Practitioner* (1983), in which he declared that: 'the knowledge inherent in practice is to be understood as artful doing'.[19] He identified two forms of reflective practice: reflection-in-action and reflection-on-action. Reflection-in-action is swift – thinking on your feet:

> The practitioner allows himself to experience surprise, puzzlement, or confusion in a situation which he finds uncertain or unique. He reflects on the phenomenon before him, and on the prior understandings which have been implicit in his behaviour. He carries out an experiment which serves to generate both a new understanding of the phenomenon and a change in the situation.[20]

Reflection on action takes place after the event, and in a musical context may be greatly helped by recording. Its purpose is to explore why and what was done. It may take the form of a private diary or log, or it may involve discussion with fellow performers or listeners. This process helps to build up a repertoire of ideas and actions upon which to draw on future occasions.

Critical reflection is relevant to any performer, but to the digital musician for whom creativity is so centrally important, it is indispensable. It is only through a reasonably objective appraisal of what is created that development and progress can be made.

Aural Skills

This includes aural awareness, that was extensively discussed in Part I, so requires little further elaboration here other than to emphasize once again its supreme importance in both musical and non-musical situations. The aural skill set retains a number of the characteristics of previous musical systems, except that now it includes *any* sound, focuses on spectrum and transformation, reduced listening and contextual sensitivity. Active listening is essential and should be underpinned by a knowledge of acoustics and psychoacoustics. An understanding of harmonics and inharmonicity is also necessary.

Musical Literacy

The nature of musical literacy has changed considerably. In classical music, the phrase traditionally refers to an ability to read five-line staff notation. However, in digital music, this notation system has been largely superseded. Traditional music notation is really a set of instructions to performers, to make certain sounds at certain times. It works very well for a certain kind of music-making, but is generally inadequate to describe the full range of activities and sounds in digital music. What has emerged in its place is an assortment of notations, from textual instructions and computer code, to spectrograms, pictograms, and various audio, diffusion and performance scores.

The fact that the traditional music score has become an object of study, a 'readable' substitute for the act of music-making, is a by-product of the evolution of, variously, academic (i.e., conservatoires, universities, etc.) and commercial (i.e., music publishers) interests. The consequences have been profound. Christopher Small recounts[21] the story that the composer Brahms turned down an invitation to attend a performance of Mozart's *Don Giovanni* because he would rather stay at home and read the score. The implication is that a performance of a piece of music is a poor substitute for the 'object' that is represented in the score (and in the inner ear). Performance becomes reduction by definition. This inversion of the natural order of things seems to go against the 'sculptural' approach of sonic manipulation driven by aural awareness. The supreme elements here are the sounds themselves, not any notated representation, let alone any instructions to the performers.

Digital musical literacy therefore equates to a computer literacy, but also to *transliteracy*, which has been defined by Sue Thomas as follows:

Transliteracy is a new term derived from the verb 'to transliterate', meaning to write or print a letter or word using the closest corresponding letters of a different alphabet or language. Today we extend the act of transliteration and apply it to the increasingly wide range of communication platforms and tools at our disposal. From early signing and orality through handwriting, print, TV and film to networked digital media, the concept of transliteracy provides a cohesion of communication modes relevant to reading, writing, interpretation and interaction.[22]

This term is equally relevant to music as to any other medium. The ability to 'read' *across* a range of software and tools, media and platforms and creative and performance situations is crucial. The digital musician must be able to adapt rapidly and comfortably to an increasingly varied world. This transliteracy might even, under the right circumstances, include an ability to read conventional music notation, in order to be ready for those situations in which the digital musician encounters other musicians who have that kind of literacy. In addition, there may be situations in which the production of some kind of 'score', be it graphical or textual, technical or conventionally musical, becomes necessary. The essence of transliteracy is that there are many musical situations in which various forms of 'notation' may be used and for which the digital musician should be prepared on a need-to-know basis.

Ensemble Abilities

Good ensemble is one feature of traditional musicianship which is hard to translate into a digital context, especially in networked music where the musicians may be physically separated. When working with others, being able to listen and respond appropriately, to balance one's contribution, to synchronize effectively, to blend or stand out as required, are all important skills. Visual cues remain effective, although they may be digitally mediated in some way. When working alone, there is still the relationship with the audience to consider. Digital music performance can be alienating for an audience which has little to look at and limited comprehension of what is actually taking place. How may the musician communicate effectively and convey a sense of togetherness (which might even involve reinforcing the sense of alienation in some aesthetics)? This is a challenge for any digital musician, and the way it is handled will say much about the musicianship.

Creativity

The ability to be creative with technology is the essence of digital musicianship.

Virtuosity

A virtuoso digital musician is one who demonstrates consummate abilities in handling technologies and interactions and is both musically transliterate and capable of advanced reflective practice. A virtuoso is able to both originate and develop successful musical materials and forms. A virtuoso will be someone whose evident accomplishment in these areas is so impressive as to leave no one in any doubt as to their expertise. Creativity and innovation will be the hallmarks of their virtuosity.

Project 35 (Intermediate): Visual Score

Introduction

Around the turn of the twentieth century a number of leading painters began developing an abstract art that drew heavily on music. The Blue Rider group, *Der Blaue Reiter*, included Arnold Schoenberg and Wassily Kandinsky (1866–1944), who began to paint *Improvisations* and *Compositions* during the years immediately preceding the First World War. Kandinsky was inspired by Theosophy and other spiritual ideas to create work that aspired to the condition of music. He also experienced synaesthesia, in which the senses become confused, by 'hearing' specific sounds when seeing certain colours or shapes (yellow as the note 'C' played on a trumpet, for example). Many other artists and composers explored these ideas, for example, Alexander Skryabin (1872–1915) whose *Prometheus: The Poem of Fire* (1910) included a part for 'light organ', which was intended to bathe the concert hall in colour from electric lights corresponding to the changing tonality of the music.

The Project

Make a musical realization and performance of a painting or drawing by Wassily Kandinsky. The image can be interpreted in any way.

Notes

This project should be carefully planned and not done as an improvisation. There are various aspects of the painting to consider: line, point, shape, colour, motion. These can be mapped in various ways to musical parameters. The overall aesthetic may also be captured, along with the dynamism of the composition.

The following book may be useful for this project: Maur, K. v., (1999) *The Sound of Painting*, Munich: Prestel-Verlag.

FURTHER READING

■ Rowe, R., *Machine Musicianship*, Cambridge, MA: MIT Press, 2001.
Explores the technology of implementing musical processes such as segmentation, pattern processing, and interactive improvisation in computer programs, and shows how the resulting applications can be used to accomplish tasks ranging from the solution of simple musical problems to the live performance of interactive compositions and the design of musically responsive installations and websites.

■ Schön, D. A., *The Reflective Practitioner: How Professionals Think in Action*, London: Temple Smith, 1983.
Examines five professions – engineering, architecture, management, psychotherapy and town planning – to show how professionals really go about solving problems. Finds that the process is as much one of improvisation as of acquired learning.

■   Webster, P. and Williams, D., *Experiencing Music Technology: Software, Data, and Hardware*, Boston: Wadsworth, 1999.
Examines the uses of music technology in an educational situation.

Discussion Questions

- How does digital technology change your approach to performing?

- What is meant by the term 'repertoire' in digital music?

- How may digital musicianship be assessed?

- What is a live presence?

- What would an *authentic* sound diffusion performance be like?

PART III

Knowing

CHAPTER 10

Cultural Context

Whatever becomes information, anyone can now store and reproduce, repackage and refashion to their own purposes without anyone's permission, without payment, and largely without detection. Hence the expanding domain of information threatens the principle of private property … The results can be heard in the cacophony and confusion of contemporary music, which the recent introduction of synthesizers and samples has only increased. On the one hand, the technification of music has distorted the process of listening and damaged our hearing. On the other, it increasingly throws everything back into the arena, as the ease of reproduction allows the circulation of music to escape the control of the market and discover new forms. In short, the old hierarchies of aesthetic taste and judgment may have broken down, but music continues to breathe and to live according to its own immanent criteria.
—(Chanan, 1994)[1]

Michael Chanan was writing in 1994, just as the Internet began to take shape and the digital culture to form. The living and breathing music he predicted still finds its most vivid expression in performance situations, where many of his threats to private property pass through the momentary forms of samplings and borrowings, of mash-ups and remixes, of nods and homages, cut and paste. However, thanks to these technological developments, the 'immanent criteria' of today's music seem once again to have become those of the community.

The phrase 'cultural context' refers to the culture that surrounds the individual. A hundred years ago, this would have been conditioned to a great extent by geographical location. When Paul Gauguin relocated to Tahiti, he deliberately changed his cultural context, intoxicated by the 'exotic' world beyond Europe. This had an effect not just upon him as a person, but on the art he produced, as is clear from the painting on the cover of this book. But the 'cultural context' is not just one's immediate *physical* surroundings: it also refers to literature, art, social interaction, science and all other forms of human activity. Gauguin's initial ideas about Tahiti came largely from the writings of Europeans.

All artists, including musicians, make work that is to some extent a product of their cultural context. What has changed in recent years is the level of access to cultures beyond what may be thought to be 'one's own'. A knowledge of the cultural world around is therefore an important attribute for the digital musician. Given the sheer quantity of cultural activity, acquiring this 'cultural knowledge' is easy to find but difficult to absorb. To 'move into the unknown' can be both challenging and intimidating, and requires considerable curiosity and engagement.

FURTHER READING

- Ayers, M. (ed.), *Cybersounds: Essays on Virtual Music Culture*, New York: Peter Lang, 2006.
  A collection of essays that examine the cultural aspects of internet music.

- Berman, M., *The Reenchantment of the World*, New York: Cornell University Press, 1981.
  A critique of the dominance of scientific thinking in Western culture.

- Bull, M. and Back, L., *The Auditory Culture Reader*, Oxford: Berg, 2003.
  An overview of the role of sound and music in culture, including much discussion of digital sound.

- Drobnick, J. (ed.), *Aural Cultures*, New York: YYZ Books, 2004.
  An essay collection that examines sound in art and contemporary culture. The authors come from a wide variety of backgrounds, including communication, anthropology, art history, film studies and philosophy.

- Holtzman, S. R., *Digital Mantras: The Languages of Abstract and Virtual Worlds*, Cambridge, MA: The MIT Press, 1994.
  A philosophical examination of the role of computers in creativity.

- Jacobson, L. (ed.), *Cyberarts: Exploring Art and Technology*, San Francisco: Miller Freeman, 1992.
  A collection of essays covering topics as diverse as multimedia, interactive toys and entertainment, holography, 3D sound and music, techno-aesthetics and much more.

■ LaBelle, B., *Background Noise: Perspectives on Sound Art*, New York: Continuum, 2006.
   A historical study of sound art.

■ McLuhan, M., *The Global Village: Transformations in World Life and Media in the 21st Century*, New York: Oxford University Press, 1989.
   Extends the visionary early work of Marshall McLuhan, by application to today's worldwide, integrated electronic network.

■ Rheingold, H., *The Virtual Community*, Cambridge, MA: MIT Press, 1993, 2000.
   An early study of the social and political aspects of social networks.

■ Rheingold, H., *Smart Mobs: The Next Social Revolution*, New York: Basic Books, 2002.
   A discussion of the convergence of pop culture, cutting-edge technology, and social activism through mobile devices.

DIGITAL CULTURE

The cultural context for today's musician is very different from anything previously known. Digital technologies have not only made other cultures and their products more readily available, but they have also presented and represented them in a different way. Our sense of cultural value has changed, as has our sense of ourselves. This affects music as much as anything else.

If we want to hear Tuvan throat singing, or play a virtual bamboo xylophone, or examine a score by a contemporary composer, or buy and sell music technologies, we can readily do so with a decent broadband connection.[2] Each action takes a roughly equivalent amount of effort on our part. The only prerequisite is that we have to *want* to do those things in the first place.

But the influence of the new media goes far beyond a collection of interesting websites. Music itself is culturally present in a way that has never before been the case. Almost every cultural experience there is, from watching TV to shopping, from having a meal in a restaurant to going to the movies, comes gift-wrapped in music. Then, we can further configure our musical landscape with personal stereos, mp3 players, CDs, and the rest. We might even go to a concert now and then. Never has there been so much music.

Our listening choices have become markers of our personal and social attitudes. Music as lifestyle, or music expressing a tribal or communal identity, is commonplace. To be found listening to the right sort of music can become a badge of honour, and an entire industry exists to support and exploit this view. So we are consumers of music, and the industry supplies huge quantities of the stuff, targeted with an ever-greater precision.

This has all had an effect on classical music, where audience attitudes have been transformed by CDs and digital downloads. The challenge for a live concert today is to offer an experience that exceeds what can be had, in comfort, at home. At some recent classical music concerts, the audience has been invited to purchase a CD of what they just heard as they leave the concert hall. The message is clear: you *heard* the music, now *buy* it and take it home.

In pop music this situation is often reversed. People attend a concert having become very familiar with the recording. The familiarity means that they are generally seeking some kind of added value from the live version, which nevertheless must match the quality of the recording. The most successful live acts are the ones whose performance skills are up to the task, and who manage to avoid the obvious trap of over-long repetition of familiar patterns.

In either scenario, the influence of digital sound recording and manipulation techniques is strong. The perfectibility of the musical performance, the availability and transferability of the sound data, the slickness and style of the finished product, are all things that have a cultural impact, which is not to diminish the importance of the 'liveness' of the live concert. That is what makes it distinctive, unique and worth attending. The orchestra sounds quite different live to a recording, and to actually witness a pop concert, surrounded by many thousands of fellow fans, is a thrilling experience. The point here is that the consumption of music stored in a digital format now greatly exceeds the consumption of live music. Since the digital form sounds so acceptable, this is a trend that seems set to continue.

FURTHER READING

- Cook, N., *Music, Imagination and Culture*, Oxford: Clarendon, 1992.
  Drawing on psychological and philosophical materials as well as the analysis of specific musical examples, Cook defines the difference between music theory and aesthetic criticism, and affirms the importance of the 'ordinary listener' in musical culture.

- Emmerson, S. (ed.), *Music, Electronic Media and Culture*, Aldershot: Ashgate, 2000.
  All kinds of sounds are now brought into the remit of composition, enabling the music of others to be sampled (or plundered), including that of unwitting musicians from non-Western cultures. This sound world may appear contradictory – stimulating and invigorating as well as exploitative and destructive. This book addresses some of the issues now posed by the brave new world of music produced with technology.

- Frith, S. (ed.), *On Record*, New York: Routledge, 1990.
  Classic sociological analyses of 'deviance' and rebellion; studies of technology; subcultural and feminist readings, semiotic and musicological essays and close readings of stars, bands and the fans themselves by Adorno, Barthes and other well-known contributors.

- Gere, C., *Digital Culture*, London: Reaktion, 2002.
  A historical survey that covers the era of cybernetics, the digital avant-garde and counter-culture, and 'digital resistances'.

Project 36 (Intermediate): I Hate …

Introduction

'Music appreciation' has traditionally been taught by enthusiasts who are keen to awaken listeners to the marvellous features of the work they love. They have often done this very well. In extreme cases (such as Leonard Bernstein, whose passionate advocacy of Gustav Mahler rescued his music from relative obscurity), this has had far-reaching effects on the evolution of music itself. However, this project has a somewhat different purpose: to help understand individual taste.

The Project

Find some music you hate. Listen to it over and over again. Try to understand exactly why you hate it. Write down your reasons. Do you get to like it better the more you listen, or does your hatred increase? Why? Is the problem in the music itself, or is there some other factor? When you can't take it any more, listen to something you love as a reward!

Notes

This may seem like torture, but it is a way of reaching self-knowledge and aural awareness. The ability to articulate what you are *not* is a good way to understand what you *are*. A deliberate attempt to reach this understanding can also produce surprising results. You may even find out you like things you thought you did not, and vice versa.

THE THINKING MUSICIAN

So where does all this leave digital musicians? Given the cultural landscape they inhabit, and given that they are intent on going beyond known musical practices, they *need* cultural knowledge. This knowledge will enable a greater understanding of cultural identity, and therefore *integrity*. Without integrity, the digital musician is in danger of drowning in a sea of information, being swamped by a mud of culture, being lost in a forest of musics. The sense of identity begins with a search for certainties. Some certainties have acquired exceptional prominence in the digital age.

The first certainty is *change*. It is guaranteed that today's technologies, and the skills associated with them, will rapidly become obsolete. So it is very important to be adaptable and open to new possibilities. Integrity means developing or creating something that is unique to the individual, but not necessarily clinging to that thing in the face of a changing world. It also means having the skill and judgement to know when to move on, when to develop, when to diversify, and to what extent.

The second certainty is *diversity*. Wherever one may 'be', musically speaking, at a given moment, there is always something somewhere else, something different, and even something unknown. Awareness and embracing of this diversity is vital. The philosopher Ludwig Wittgenstein suggested that a door might be defined by pointing to everything in the universe that is *not* a door. This might seem a laborious way to go about such an apparently simple task, but it can be advantageous to know what you are *not*, before deciding what you *are*.

The third certainty is a *context*. Whatever music is made will to some extent relate to the other things (not necessarily music) that surround it. The context for music now is multi-disciplinary, because music is very often heard alongside other forms, whether they are visual, textual, or performative. It could be argued that music has *always* been this way, since the ritual of live performance is a kind of theatre in itself, but since the advent of recorded sound the live element has been capable of almost complete suppression. And the context for music is not simply 'musical', or even 'artistic', but social.

The defining qualities of the digital musician, therefore, are: *open-mindedness* and *cultural curiosity*. In short, he or she should be a *thinking musician*, who overcomes the less forgiving aspects of digital technologies through an awareness of other musics, an ability to listen critically and to form judgements based on more than instant reactions, historical knowledge and a sense of future possibilities, in particular where these concern developments in electronic music and technologies.

Equally important is knowledge and awareness of developments and practices in other art forms, especially the visual and text-based arts. It is not enough to be *only* a musician, unable to converse with fellow artists or ordinary people about anything other than music. While to specialize is a likely consequence of audio manipulation techniques, this does not mean that it is beneficial to ignore developments elsewhere in the digital world. Ignorant musicians will be unsuccessful musicians in a culture that naturally and wholeheartedly embraces multimedia.

All this cultural knowledge therefore has a direct and practical application. You might be the best musician in the world, but if nobody knows of your existence, you might as well not be a musician at all. In order to advertise and promote your work, to disseminate and diffuse your practice, you will need an understanding of *networking*, including Internet and virtual interaction, and a knowledge of your own culture, as well as the music industry, its management and working practices.

FURTHER READING

■ Cope, D., *New Directions in Music*, Long Grove: Waveland Press, 2000.
A very thorough examination of the philosophies and techniques of the mid- to late twentieth-century's avant-garde composers. Contains extensive analysis of improvisation, indeterminancy, and other departures from tradition.

■ Eno, B., *A Year With Swollen Appendices*, London: Faber & Faber, 1996.
A year in the life and creative thinking of Brian Eno.

■ Toop, D., *Ocean of Sound: Aether Talk, Ambient Sound and Imaginary Worlds*, London: Serpents Tail, 1995, 2001.
Explores the evolution of a culture absorbed in perfume, light and ambient sound, from Erik Satie to the Velvet Undergound; Miles Davis to Jimi Hendrix.

EMERGENCE

There is a paradox at the heart of this notion of a 'digital culture'. At its most fundamental level (that is, binary mathematics) the computer *lacks a context* whereas 'culture' is
all about context. The juxtaposition of the two words is therefore an extreme expression of an apparent opposition between mathematical and organic realities. Yet the two
somehow seem connected enough that the phrase 'digital culture' has resonance and
meaning.

In *The Language of New Media*, Lev Manovich identifies five principles which underlie a digitized culture:

- *numerical representation* (digital code), which allows programmability
- *modularity*, by which objects may be combined with other objects without losing
  their independent identity
- *automation*, by which the computer replaces certain types of human activity
- *variability*, in which numerous different variations can be generated, often automatically, from single originals (such as a database)
- *transcoding*, the process by which media is turned into computer data.[3]

Manovich makes a distinction between the 'cultural layer' and the 'computer layer'. In
musical terms, this would be the difference between, for example, a song and the computer processes that are used in the creation of the song.

For the digital musician, there is an indissoluble relationship between these two
layers. Whether one is working to produce a CD or DVD, giving a live concert or
making an installation, making music on the Internet or for a computer game, the computer layer has a profound effect on the cultural layer, and vice versa. However, music
and musicians tend to flow best when the means of production present little apparent
obstacle in practice to musical expression. It is increasingly the case that digital technology is so widely used, so unremarkable, that the fact that it is digital goes unnoticed.
This is true of many consumer goods, such as fridges, cars and televisions, where a
computer of some description is the heart of the machine. In music, too, digital technologies may be integrated with non-digital technologies, so that a seamless transition
between, say, an obviously 'digital' and a clearly 'acoustic' sound can be heard on a
CD, or played on a computer. In fact, both the digital and the acoustic sounds are
really digital; it is just that the digitization of acoustic sound is so commonplace that it
seems natural.[4]

This is an evolving state of affairs, and its effects vary a great deal depending on the
context. It may best be described as *emergent*. This is the technical term for work that
is not entirely pre-designed by an artist or composer, but rather involves the conscious
use of the shifting boundaries between the consumer and the maker. This label applies
to many aspects of the digital culture and seems to encapsulate both the technological
advances and the cultural changes that accompany them. Nowhere is this more consistently the case than in networking and communications technologies, and for the digital
musician the ongoing emergence of internet music is probably the most significant cultural development of recent times.

FURTHER READING

- Kuhn, T. S., *The Structure of Scientific Revolutions*, Chicago: University of Chicago Press, 1996.
  A classic text, first published in 1962, that proposed an episodic (rather than linear) model of scientific evolution and introduced the idea of paradigm shift as the way in which new ideas emerge.

- Manovich, L., *The Language of New Media*, Cambridge, MA: MIT Press, 2001.
  Uses concepts from film theory, art history, literary theory, and computer science to present a coherent theory of new and emerging media.

- Pratt, V., *Thinking Machines: The Evolution of Artificial Intelligence*, Oxford: Basil Blackwell, 1987.
  Examines the history of the efforts of scientists to develop a machine able to think like a human being.

CULTURAL DIVERSITY

This is an age of unprecedented access to the music of other cultures. The efforts of ethnomusicologists,[5] 'world music' scholars and enthusiasts, and talented musicians who have been prepared to face the rigours of travel, have opened up these possibilities. But even more significant than these has been first the availability of good quality recordings, and then, more recently, the Internet. In 1889, Claude Debussy was amazed to hear folk music from Indo-China at the Exposition Universelle in Paris. By 1999, it was possible to find whole online communities devoted to particular forms of folk music whose members had not necessarily even heard *live* versions of the music they gathered to explore. As the Internet continues to evolve, there is even talk of an ethnomusicology of cyberspace.

It can be a dangerous thing for a musician to adopt the musical language of a foreign culture without sufficient understanding. It is also strictly impossible, because many of the folk musics are the result of centuries of cultural, even familial, evolution that is difficult to penetrate. At one end of the scale, therefore, lies *cultural imperialism*, which is the wholesale and unthinking 'lifting' of someone else's culture to suit one's own ends, while at the other end lies *cultural tourism*, where the culture itself is pre-packaged for the benefit of the outsider, often distorting its essential character in the process. Avoiding these two pitfalls is difficult. The goal is not so much to become a completely different musician, as to establish a creative discourse with these other cultures, to learn from them and to absorb their influence.

Listening to, reading about and, indeed, playing other musics will have the benefit of opening up the ears to new possibilities. Through trying to engage seriously with other traditions and ideas, the digital musician may achieve a more profound understanding of the ways in which music may be structured or may function socially or culturally. These 'other' musics need not necessarily come from the other side of the world. They might in fact be examples of different musical practices within the musician's own culture.

The point is that they present the musician with something unfamiliar, something new. They will all be examples of subcultures, in the sense that they are defined and particular areas within the broader culture called 'music'.

They may contain identifiably common elements, resonances with known music, revelatory ideas about musical practice, insights into the purpose and effects of music, and some practical ways in which these might be an influence. To illustrate these points, the following discussions examine three examples which are sufficiently well known to offer ready access to Western musicians, but are also sufficiently distinct to raise some important and interesting questions about digital music. They come with a word of warning: there is no way that a few paragraphs in a book of this size can do justice to the richness and complexity of these cultural traditions. The point of the discussions is merely to illustrate some of the potential benefits to the digital musician of looking at the music of other cultures. Each discussion concludes with some illustrative examples of how these traditions have been developed in digital music.

Gamelan

The traditional music of Java, Bali and a few other Indonesian islands seems to have absorbed early influences from India, China and even Europe, and then evolved from about the ninth century AD into a distinctive music all of its own. The Western world first became aware of this music in the nineteenth century, and it has had an influence on many composers and musicians ever since.

There is some difference in practice between Java and Bali, deriving from the fourteenth century split of the two islands into Islamic Java and Hindu Bali. This resulted in a highly developed practice that occupied a unique position in both societies. Gamelans are often used to support shadow plays, puppet theatre and significant religious and social occasions. But the gamelan also forms a central part of village life, with the musicians often gathering after work to play. Everywhere you go in Java and Bali, gamelan music can be heard.

In the Western world, it is usual for musicians to specialize on a single instrument. Some musicians may play more than one but, with a few exceptions, would not normally do so during a single performance. It is also not necessary generally for the individual musician in an ensemble performance to understand the entire composition being played and their role in relation to the other musicians, other than on an occasional, local basis. Gamelan is quite different, because all the musicians in a gamelan orchestra are, in theory, capable of playing any of the instruments. This is in turn because all the musicians understand how the composition is structured, and what part each instrument has to play. Gamelan music is not improvised, yet has been described as a 'negotiation between musicians'.[6]

A typical gamelan orchestra consists mostly of percussion instruments, traditionally made from a single lump of bronze. The instruments are regarded as sacred: it is not permissible to step over them or move them without offering up a prayer, or apologizing. The instruments have onomatopoeic names that resemble the sounds they make. The *Gong Ageng* ('gong' is in fact a Javanese word) is the largest instrument. Once struck, the gong is never damped. The *Bonang* are pot-shaped gongs, mounted in trays. They are often detuned slightly from one another, so that when they play their characteristic interlocking patterns, a shimmering effect is produced. They are never damped. The

Kethuk are small, damped gongs. These produce a frog-like sound, which delineates the structure of the composition. The *Saron* are metal xylophones. The player damps the preceding note with one hand while playing the next note with the other, producing a smooth, seamless, melodic line.

Every gamelan instrument is duplicated: one with a five-note tuning system, and one with a seven-note tuning system. The five-note system, called *slendro*, is in fact an equal temperament system, but the division of the octave into five obviously means that the intervals between each step are relatively wide. *Pelog*, on the other hand, is an unevenly tuned system, with some intervals being very close together, and others spread wide apart. In fact, each gamelan has its own unique sound, because the tunings are always slightly different, based on the resonant properties of the instruments. Thus a *slendro* gamelan will have five roughly equal steps to the octave.

Even with a limited number of notes per octave, gamelan tunes are highly selective about which notes are used, restricting themselves sometimes to only three or four, with an occasional colouristic extra note added to accentuate the contours of the melody. It is also not unusual for the same tune to be played successively in the two tuning systems. It is still reckoned to be the same tune, even though the tuning makes it sound quite different. The reason for this is that it has the same shape and number sequence (all gamlan music is played by memory using a system of numbers) and the structure remains the same.

Every gamelan composition is built around the central melody called the *balungan* (skeleton), which is played in unison by the mid-range instruments such as sarons. All the other instruments either decorate this melody, or delineate its structure. All the musicians in a gamelan performance know the melody, and know the way in which their particular instrument may treat the melody. Gamelan music is highly structured, with various gong strokes dividing up phrases into (usually) groups of 4, 8, 16, etc. A drummer leads the orchestra, and gives cues for changes of tempo. One of the most exciting things in gamelan music is the way in which the whole ensemble speeds up and slows down together. The interlocking patterns played by the smaller instruments change as the tempo reaches its highest speed. The effect is of shifting gradually to a new plateau.

If you play gamelan (and playing it is even more fun than listening to it), then you quickly learn to hear those around you very accurately. You listen for the drum cues, you move in time with your neighbour, and at all times you keep the *balungan* in mind. You experience a sense of the whole piece, and of your role within it. This sense of wholeness also comes through when just listening. The music emerges from the initial big gong hit, and dies away back into a gong hit at the end. The music changes speed, and contains amazingly fast and intricate motion within it, but it does not appear to *go* anywhere. Despite all the activity, it is static, and a result is that attention shifts to the overall timbre of the sound, the tuning of the instruments, the attacks of the various hits.

There have been many examples of electronic and digital musicians who have absorbed the influence of gamelan by using similar structuring and techniques, either with actual gamelan instruments or applied to a variety of sonic objects. Some fairly recent examples include: Wendy Carlos's album *Beauty in the Beast*, which combines gamelan and Western orchestral sounds (amongst other things); Ensemble Robot, which has combined a gamelan orchestra with new technologies in pieces such as *Heavy Metal* (2006) by Christine Southworth,[7] for Balinese gamelan *Gong Kebyar*, guitar, violin, bass, lyricon and robotic instruments; and even works which do not contain the actual sounds of gamelan, but are imbued with its spirit, such as the performance pieces of

Augustinus Kus Windananto (aka Jompet), whose *Glorified* pieces from 2001, or the more recent *Ultraoutput* project, use the human body as a trigger for a 'gamelan' of mechanical and electronic sound.

Indian Classical Music

To achieve a full understanding of Indian classical music would probably take a lifetime, or more. There is tremendous variety, from Hindustani music in the North to Carnatic music in the South, and other types in between. What all the music has in common is a highly developed theoretical system based on an extreme refinement of the ear, and a religious purpose that variously worships the Hindu gods in all their manifestations. Whereas it is quite easy to learn to play gamelan music, it is less likely that a Western musician will play Indian classical music, because of the prohibitive length of time it takes to absorb both its musical and its devotional aspects. Even to play the drone, the simplest element, requires considerable technique.

At the heart of the music is the *raga*. This is a single melody, but it is also a collection of pitches and gestures, of intonations and inflections, of musical rules and shared cultural understandings. Each element of the *raga* and each *raga* itself is highly expressive and detailed, although it is hard to define in words precisely what the expression may be. *Ragas* may be performed on specific days or at specific occasions, even at appropriate times of the day.

A *raga* must contain at least five notes, of which one is the *Sa*, the tonic, or the 1:1, and another must be either the fourth or fifth. A *raga* is characterized by the pattern of ascent and descent (*aroha-avaroha*) from the low to the high *Sa*, a pattern which may well omit certain notes in either direction, or flatten or sharpen notes. These small variations in pitch or interval are called *sruti*, and allow much of the expressive abilities of the performer to come through. In addition to the tuning, the way in which a note is approached and left, whether by a slide or a step, and the ways in which certain notes are emphasized or weakened, gives much of the character to a particular performance. The musician will often work with small groups of note patterns, forming distinctive shapes and patterns within the overall melody of the *raga*, thus allowing performances to last half an hour or more.

The *raga* may be accompanied by rhythmic patterns played on *tabla*. The rhythmic patterns are called *tala* and are no less precise and structured than the *ragas* themselves. Time is divided up into a fixed number of counts, which then repeat in cyclical fashion, as in the following patterns: dadra (3 + 3); rupak (3 + 2 + 2); kaharva (4 + 4); jhaptal (2 + 3 + 2 + 3); ektal and chautal (2 + 2 + 2 + 2 + 2 + 2); dhamar (5 + 2 + 3 + 4); dipchandi (3 + 4 + 3 + 4); addha tintal/sitarkhani (4 + 4 + 4 + 4). Rhythmic variations are introduced as the tempo changes, so the playing may get faster and faster, producing some very rapid hand motions. The patterns are memorized using vocal syllables, which may actually be spoken by the musician during the performance, and quite often a pattern will be repeated three times in succession to bring a *raga* to a close.

The melodic aspects of the *raga* may be sung, or played on instruments such as the well-known *sitar* but also a host of other plucked and bowed string instruments, wind instruments and keyboards. In a typical performance, the *raga* emerges freely and gradually in an opening section called the *alap* or *alapana*. A faster section follows, with the entry of the *tabla*, and generally the music becomes faster and tighter. There will be ornamentations and interactions between the main soloist and the percussionist. The performance may well end with a restatement of the main *raga* theme itself, but it should always be remembered that *ragas* are dynamic and the forms are not precisely fixed. The word *raga* means 'colour', and the essence of the *raga* is a colouristic expression of emotion.

The influence of Indian classical music on Western music has been lasting and profound, from Ravi Shankar's famous performances with The Beatles, especially George Harrison, in the 1960s and 1970s, to jazz artists such as Miles Davis and John McLaughlin, and experimentalists such as La Monte Young and Terry Riley. Indian film music and popular forms such as bhangra have retained some links with the classical tradition, and this comes through even in their fusion with genres such as hip-hop.

Given the emphasis placed upon the *instrument* and its traditions in Indian classical music, it is no surprise to find that, beyond the use of drones, samples and perhaps rhythmic patterns, digital music has had to grapple with some difficult challenges to absorb the finer nuances of the music but, even so, attempts have been made. In 2003, a live collaborative music performance entitled 'GigaPop Ritual'[8] took place simultaneously at McGill University in Canada and Princeton in the USA, based on two *ragas:* Raga Jog and Jai Jai Vanti. The performers were linked via a bi-directional high-speed network and the instruments included an *eDholak* (electronic Dholak), an *RBow* (a violin bow extended with motion sensors), and a *DigitalDoo* (an electronically extended digeridoo), alongside conventional instruments such as sitar and tabla.

In his essay 'Bézier Spline Modeling of Pitch-continuous Melodic Expression and Ornamentation',[9] Bret Battey describes a technique he has devised for 'analysis and computer rendering of melodies such as those found in Indian classical music, in which subtle control of the continuum between scale steps is fundamental to expression'. He has subsequently used this technique in a number of works, including his audiovision piece from 2005, *Autarkeia Aggregatum*. As he succinctly puts it: 'I spend my life trying to make my computer sing.'[10]

West African Drumming

Rhythmic patterns are mathematical subdivisions of time. This makes them fairly easy to create using digital equipment, and much of the abundant cross-fertilization between different types of rhythm-based music from around the world has been greatly facilitated by this fact. More or less any non-Western percussion-based music will therefore be of interest to the digital musician. West African drumming is here chosen partly because it has particular social characteristics, and partly because its influence is still being explored in many educational establishments, and by many musicians. Of special interest is the extent to which a very local tradition, with considerable meaning to a specific group, is capable of making a transition to a wider public without losing its significance.

West African drumming, like Indian *raga*, is a form of music that is usually performed on special occasions and for specific functions. The drummers form a circle and play a variety of drums made from animal skins stretched over hollowed-out logs. The drums may have various pitches, depending upon their size and head tension, or even contain more than one pitch in a single drum. The 'talking drum' has leather thongs connecting a skin at either end. When the drummer squeezes the thongs, the resulting change in tension 'bends' the pitch of the drum, which is played with an L-shaped stick. In addition to the drums, a variety of bells, rattles and whistles are used, along with a chesty, rasping singing voice that makes much of swooping, glissando sounds. Vocal lines are often sung by more than one singer, harmonizing in parallel intervals such as thirds and sixths.

The drum music is constructed from many overlapping rhythmic patterns, set against a constant timeline laid down by bells. A master drummer will also improvise solos over the top of the patterns, and will generally lead the ensemble. This kind of music exists in various forms in the West African countries of Senegal, Gambia, Guinea Bissau, Guinea, Sierra Leone, Liberia, Ivory Coast, Ghana, Togo, Benin, Nigeria and Cameroon, and inland to Burkina Faso and parts of Mali, Niger and Chad. However, the regional variations are enormous, and rhythmic patterns that are common in one country, or region, or even village, may be unknown elsewhere in West Africa.

The attraction of this music beyond the region may be exemplified by the surge in popularity of the *jembe*, or *djembe*, ever since the world tours of *Les Ballets Africains* (led by Fodeba Keita of Guinea) in the 1950s. The djembe offers several different tones, including a deep bass note made by striking the centre, a slap made by slapping the rim, and a tone note, also made at the rim. Using only these sounds, very complicated and yet rhythmically precise patterns can be achieved, which when combined produce thrilling polyrhythms. Because the drum rhythms are literally understood to 'talk', and what they say is peculiar to a small, localized community, the assembly of larger regional, national, or even 'West African' ensembles for a European audience has led to some curious combinations of apparently unrelated rhythmic patterns.

Djembe music has quickly spread across the world. A quick internet search on the word will reveal large resources and a thriving culture devoted to all aspects of the music. To take part in a djembe ensemble can be a thrilling experience: apart from the sheer excitement and energy of the music, the structuring of the patterns and the way they interconnect is highly intriguing. For the digital musician, what may be learnt from this is the importance of communal or social interaction. Rhythmic ensemble work like this is an excellent way to quickly achieve mutual understanding amongst a group of musicians. The connection with dancing, and physical motion generally, is an important reminder of the physicality of performance, given that digital music can often require little or no performance motion. Also, the social context for the music can be very different from the formality of a Western concert hall.

The influence of West African drumming on music created with new technologies is probably best exemplified by the work of Steve Reich, whose most recent multimedia and digital pieces still show evidence of the pattern-based processes he first exploited following time spent studying with a master drummer in Ghana in the early 1970s. He explains:

> I became aware of African music via a composers' conference that was held in 1962 in Ojai, California, when I was still a student of [Luciano] Berio's at Mills College. ... Although I had heard African music before – I'd heard records, I knew that it swung, I knew you made it with drums, I knew it was very rhythmic – I hadn't the faintest idea of how it was made; how it was put together.[11]

The most immediate influence of the drumming techniques was on his 90-minute work for percussion ensemble with female voices and piccolo, *Drumming* (1970–71). However, this instrumental piece is itself an example of a synthesis of technology-based processes with drumming techniques, because of the inclusion of 'phasing', discovered by Reich in the mid-1960s, when he played two tape loops simultaneously and used varispeed gradually to adjust their synchronization. Applying this technique to instrumental music enabled a variation on traditional drumming which lacked none of its rigour and fascination. Although he rarely uses phasing as a technique today, Reich has continued to draw upon his studies of West African drumming. Digital works such as *The Cave* (1993/2003), for amplified voices and ensemble, use the rhythms and inflections of speech to generate musical patterns and melodies that overlay video images, in an echo of the 'talking drum' tradition.

Another digital musician who has worked in West Africa is Lukas Ligeti, whose *Beta Foley* ensemble includes performers from the Republic of Guinea, Ivory Coast and Burkina Faso. The band works with many conventional African instruments, including *wassamba*, *kora*, *balafon* and *djembé*, along with computer and an assortment of MIDI controllers. Ligeti describes the purpose of his first visit to Africa thus:

> I felt that an interesting premise for this voyage would be for me not to attempt to play African music, and not to ask the African musicians to play in a European style, but to construct a 'third plane' on which we could meet and interact, exploring the creative possibilities of musical electronics.[12]

FURTHER READING

- Brinner, B., *Knowing Music, Making Music: Javanese Gamelan and the Theory of Musical Competence and Interaction*, Chicago: University Of Chicago Press, 1995.
  How do musicians know what they know? Using the intricate collaborative structure of gamelan – Javanese ensemble music – as a point of departure, *Knowing Music, Making Music* lays the foundation for a comprehensive theory of musical competence and interaction.

- Charry, E., *Mande Music: Traditional and Modern Music of the Maninka and Mandinka of Western Africa*, Chicago: University of Chicago Press, 2000.
  Eric Charry offers the most comprehensive source available on one of Africa's richest and most sophisticated music cultures.

- Chib, S. K. S., *Companion to North Indian Classical Music*, Delhi: Munshiram Manoharlal, 2004.
  This book gives intelligible and straightforward information about the various ragas of Hindustani music along with historical background.

- Greene, P. and Porcello, T. (eds), *Wired for Sound: Engineering and Technologies in Sonic Cultures*, Middletown, CT: Wesleyan University Press, 2005.
  This collection of eleven essays employs primarily ethnographical, but also historical and psychological, approaches to examine a range of new, technology-intensive musics and musical practices such as: fusions of Indian film-song rhythms, heavy metal, and gamelan in Jakarta; urban Nepali pop which juxtaposes heavy metal, Tibetan Buddhist ritual chant, rap and Himalayan folksongs; collaborations

between Australian aboriginals and sound engineers; the production of 'heaviness' in heavy metal music; and the production of the 'Austin sound'.

■ Nettl, B., *The Study of Ethnomusicology: Thirty-One Issues and Concepts*, Illinois: University of Illinois Press, 2005.

This book looks at the field of ethnomusicology as a field of research. Nettl selects thirty-one concepts and issues that have been the subjects of continuing debate by ethnomusicologists, and he adds four entirely new chapters and thoroughly updates the text to reflect new developments and concerns in the field.

■ Pesch. L., *South Indian Classical Music*, Oxford: Oxford University Press, 1999. This provides an overview of the historical and cultural contexts of the music, its instruments, composers, leading practitioners and schools.

■ Pickvance, R., *A Gamelan Manual: A Player's Guide to the Central Javanese Gamelan*, London: Jaman Mas Books, 2006. This is a comprehensive description of the performance practice of the central Javanese gamelan.

■ Shelemay, K. K., *Ethnomusicology: History, Definitions, and Scope: A Core Collection of Scholarly Articles*, New York: Routledge, 1992.

This anthology of twenty-five scholarly articles offers a broad historical overview of the history, definition and scope of ethnomusicology. The essays range from early summaries of the field's subject matter and state of research to later, comprehensive discussions spanning the discipline at large, its intellectual history and future prospects.

■ Small, C., *Music of the Common Tongue: Survival and Celebration in African American Music*, London: Calder, 1987. In clear and elegant prose, Small argues that by any reasonable reckoning of the function of music in human life, the African-American tradition, that which stems from the collision between African and European ways of doing music which occurred in the Americas and the Caribbean during and after slavery, is the major Western music of the twentieth century.

■ Stone, R. M., *The Garland Handbook of African Music*, New York: Routledge, 1999, 2008. A collection of essays that offer detailed, regional studies of the different musical cultures of Africa and examine the ways in which music helps to define the identity of this particular area.

CULTURAL TRANSLATIONS

This section looks at some representative digital works that have drawn substantially on the music of cultures other than the composer's own. They are all examples of how to absorb the lessons from other musics, while retaining one's own creative identity.

The major questions to be asked while listening to these pieces are: To what extent do Western and non-Western musical cultures become apparent during these pieces? What are their major features? Is the translation from one culture to another successful? How do these pieces reflect their non-Western models? Does the composer/musician's own voice come through and how does this happen?

Bret Battey (2005) *Autarkeia Aggregatum*

This is an audiovision piece which may be experienced online at http://www.mti.dmu.ac.uk/~bbattey/Gallery/autark.html (the piece should be experienced full screen and was created in HD video 720p (1280 × 720). Quicktime Pro 7 playback is usually adequate).

The piece is deeply influenced by a year spent in India (2001–2002) during which Battey studied Hindustani classical music, and his ongoing practice of Buddhist Vipassana meditation. The title derives from the philosopher Leibniz's theory of fundamental particles of reality (*monads*). *Autarkeia* is Greek for self-sufficiency, and *aggregatum* is Latin for joined, or aggregated.

The visual component comprises continuous movement and transformation of over 11,000 points. Similarly, the audio emphasizes ebb and flow between different states, minimizing hard edges and events. The music was composed using Common Lisp Music (by Bill Shotstaedt) and Common Music (by Rick Taube), and Battey's own Pitch Curve Analysis and Composition toolkit (PICACS). The tool makes mathematical models of glissandi such as those found in classical Indian vocal performances, enables editing of those models, and renders them as synthesized sound. The music is also influenced by Western electro-acoustic art music, and spectromorpholoigcal gesture in particular.

The visual effects method initially used the Java programming environment Processing (by Ben Fry and Casey Reas). The algorithm was then translated into a plug-in for Apple's Motion 2 video effects software.

Notice how the music in the opening section centres on certain pitches which resemble drones, with microtonal glides leading towards them. The sweeps from 3' 25" onwards vaguely resemble the characteristic sound of the sitar, without in any sense being a copy or sample of that sound. An extended melody in *raga* style begins at 4' 37" leading to a climactic sweep from about 5' 50" onwards. There is a powerful evocation of vocal content and spatialization from 8' 09" in which the multitude of dots seem to resemble torches held aloft in a large cave. The piece ends on a single pitch.

This is music that has thoroughly absorbed its traditional influences from another culture, and yet remains an example of highly inventive digital art.

Wendy Carlos (1986) 'Poem for Bali' from *Beauty in the Beast*

This album is available on CD: East Street Digital ESD 81552.

'Poem for Bali' is a piece in ten sections that move through both *pelog* and *slendro* tunings and culminates in having a gamelan accompanied by Western orchestra, which would be impossible in real life, but is achieved by '[cheating] equal temperament toward the pelog scale and the pelog toward equal temperament'.[13] The music is at times very close to its models and at other times 'an impressionistic canvas of moods amenable to this magical island'. The digital technology allows a level of control over tuning systems, speed of performance and textures that would be impossible in live performance. Yet the music manages to retain a sense of performance, partly because of the inclusion of sections of dance music (section four is a Barong dance, for example), but mainly because of the composer's sensitivity to the pacing, feel and musicality of gamelan.

This is music that treats the computer and samples as a means to recreate an acoustic instrument, or collection of instruments, but at the same time expands their capabilities beyond what is possible in the real world. The form and structure are also quite conventional, with clearly defined sections emerging from one another in ways that mimic gamelan practice. At times, the music resembles environmental sounds, as in the transitional episode from 4' 00" to 4' 30". Gamelan music is usually played outdoors and recordings often have background sounds of weather or frogs which seem to blend with the music itself. Here, the environmental atmosphere is created musically, as is the sense of layering and distance in the alternations between solo instruments and full ensemble. But the primary musical component is melodic: just as gamelan music is structured around the *balungan*, so this has a skeletal melody that holds together all the episodes. Particular intervals from this melody recur as thematic devices, also drawing attention to the tuning system. Carlos manages to convey the sense of human performance, despite the fact that this is a sequenced album. Yet, transitional episodes, such as the strange rising sweeps at 15' 01" to 15' 20", constantly pull the listener back into the world of computer music. This is not Balinese music but, as the title says, music *for* Bali.

In the rest of the album, Carlos goes on to explore other approaches to tuning systems, and influences from other parts of the world (Bhutan, Tibet, Africa, Bulgaria and so on). The strength of these cultural translations lie both in her technique and in the conceptual unity, governed by a discerning ear, that the album possesses.

John Hassell/Brian Eno (1980) *Fourth World, Vol. I – Possible Musics*

This may be found on CD: Editions EG Records B000003S2B.

This is a quietly influential album that has progressed many of the developments in world music, as well as representing another departure within the canon of Brian Eno's 'ambient' music. The album features Jon Hassell's trumpet, but so digitally processed that its sound is barely recognizable as a trumpet on any of the tracks. The main processes are filtered delay and echo.

Hassell wrote about this album: 'Fourth World music is a unified primitive/futuristic sound combining features of world ethnic styles with advanced electronic techniques.' He drew on his training in Indian classical music with Prandit Pran Nath to shape melodic and textural contours in a vocal style. At the same time, the form of the tracks is typical of ambient music, with slowly repetitive looping, a generally quiet and smooth sound, a harmonious surface, and a layering of material that emphasizes clarity. Notice how there are never more than four simultaneous layers, making it possible to follow each layer simultaneously and for the ear to move rapidly between them.

Two tracks are particularly interesting as examples of cultural translation. 'Delta Rain Dream' features some vocal droning mixed with synthesized sounds that emphasize the overtones and the harmonic series. This is overlaid on some low conga drum patterns, reminiscent of the music of Burundi. The trumpet performs a slow, repeating melodic phrase that is highly processed to give a very breathy, almost chordal, sound. 'Griot' uses handclapped rhythmic patterns very reminiscent of West African music. The title is a reference to the wandering musician/storytellers called *griots*, who have sung traditional stories in western Africa for centuries. Here the trumpet delivers animal-like cries and an occasional high drone to complement the lower pulsed droning in the rhythm track.

Both pieces have the same basic form: the repetitive, ambient, material appears slowly at first, then the trumpet contributes its solo material, then the track dies away. As with all Eno's ambient music, there is an implication that the track could go on much longer, even for hours, with no particular start and stop point. However, this is also a characteristic of both Indian and African music, which emphasizes timelessness by lacking clear goal-orientation. Even so, there are peaks and troughs within the music which maintain interest. The electronic presence is maintained throughout and successfully translates the apparent sources into the digital domain.

Alejandro Viñao (1991) *Chant d'Ailleurs*

There are three *Chants* on the CD 'Hildegard's Dream', Musidisc MU 244942, in which the human voice is taken on a journey through an imaginary culture. Viñao sums up the nature of the cultural transformation in the sleeve notes:

> I imagined this culture as one which had developed technology in spite of having remained rural. This improbability accounts for the ritualistic and at times monodic nature of the singing, coupled to a computer part which seeks not to harmonize or orchestrate the songs but rather to extend the phrasing and timbre of the voice beyond its natural acoustic means. … I based the invented singing style on the traditions of different Eastern music and in particular on one Mongolian folk tune which I specially like for its beautiful use of melisma and glottal vibrato.[14]

The music also emanates from the Western electronic tradition, showing the influence of Berio and other composers who have treated the voice, such as Stockhausen. The piece focuses in particular on ornamentation, beginning with some cries that resemble animal sounds, that develop into more melodic phrases broken up by what appears to be ritual chanting. Despite all the digital treatments, the composition never loses touch with vocal production. All the phrases are short, within a single breath span. At times, the music seems to imply an ensemble of singers, at others it reverts to a single voice. The constantly repeated gesture of building towards a climactic point, usually with intervals fanning out in both directions, towards high and low, keeps the sense of forward momentum and urgency. Something is being communicated here, but it is hard to say exactly what that might be, which is exactly the kind of cultural ambiguity the composer intends. Here the cultural translation leads us into the unknown, away from a familiar music towards something that only the computer can produce. We are constantly being led to a 'different' place.

Project 37 (Intermediate): Cultural Translation

Introduction

This project encourages both the study and the understanding of the music of another culture, and the development of digital musical techniques that deepen that understanding. It is an exercise, but may well lead on to more profound works.

The Project

Study the music of a culture that is unfamiliar to you. Using only synthetic means (no recorded samples, no live instruments) attempt to recreate a short section of that music.

Notes

As well as the challenge of generating appropriate sounds, which may be derived from existing synthesized sources or may be synthesized entirely from scratch, there are also musical questions of structure, rhythm, tuning and so on to consider. What do you learn by this process? How does it reveal your own cultural approach to music?

PROJECT 37

Discussion Questions

- What does the phrase 'digital culture' mean?

- What is 'post-digital' and why is it important?

- How has globalization affected our understanding of other cultures? And how has it affected those cultures themselves?

CHAPTER 11

Critical Engagement

Critical engagement arises from a study of the cultural context for music and from a personal desire to engage with it in an informed and intelligent way. In order to achieve successful critical engagement, the digital musician therefore needs to be culturally aware and keen to develop. He or she will deploy some of the techniques and ideas that emerge from the fields of philosophy, critical theory and cultural studies.

The phrase 'cultural studies' describes a broad mixture of investigations into the meaning and practices of everyday life. It is a hybrid discipline that has come to under-pin much theorizing in universities and colleges, combining aspects of social sciences, anthropology, philosophy, art history, media studies and other areas. It has a background in radical thought, and often focuses on issues of race, gender, ideology and class. 'Critical theory' similarly emerges from social science, but also overlaps with literary criticism. Some of the early figures of critical theory, such as Walter Benjamin (1892–1940), Theodor Adorno (1903–1969) and Roland Barthes (1915–1980) addressed both music and technology in their writings.

CRITICAL THEORY

This began in the 1930s as an activity that aimed to change society through critique. Many of the early critical theorists were dissident Marxists, and the Frankfurt School, in particular, set out to establish a theoretical basis for potential revolutionary action. Later on, critical theory became more linked to aesthetics, and literary criticism in particular. In the 1960s, the critical theorist Jürgen Habermas (b. 1929) redefined the social theo-retical approach to include self-reflection and psychoanalysis as emancipatory forces for the individual. He described an idealized 'communicative action' through which people freely exchange intentions and beliefs.

Meanwhile, literary criticism was also expanding to incorporate some of the radical social aspects of critical theory. In particular, there was an ever-increasing focus upon language. Issues of text and meaning became fundamental to the humanities and, once again, psychoanalysis was admitted, to the point that the literary side also became predominantly concerned with communication. Both sides of critical theory were interested in processes and in particular the way in which culture emerges or happens. This extended to a study of cultural artefacts (objects) and phenomena. The latter study is called *phenomenology*, which is a branch of philosophy that examines the appearances of things and the way we experience them.

Many recent advances in critical theory have come from a critique of, or reaction against, earlier critical theories. These reactions have taken various forms, ranging from accusations of elitism (after all, who are these people to assume that they can make a better world with their 'critical theories'?) to a reassertion of the thing the critical theorists themselves reacted against: logical positivism. This philosophy asserts that only mathematical, scientific or logical statements can contain truths, so the dependence of critical theory upon language and interpretation makes it meaningless.

Given the complexity and heat of the arguments, it can sometimes be difficult to see the point of engaging at all with these ideas. There are two main reasons why it is worth the effort: first, the theories (whether or not we agree with them) do succeed in identifying certain cultural tendencies and phenomena and, second, in doing so they help us come to an understanding about our own activities and productions. There are several key themes and a number of important texts in critical theory that are directly relevant to music. The key themes include broad cultural ideas such as modernism and postmodernism, structuralism and deconstruction, and, ultimately, the business of forming critical judgements about music itself.

FURTHER READING

- Barthes, R., *Image, Music, Text*, London: Fontana, 1977.
  A classic collection of highly influential essays, including 'Introduction to the Structural Analysis of Narrative' and 'The Death of the Author'.

- Heidegger, M., 'The Question Concerning Technology', in *Martin Heidegger: Basic Writings*, London: Routledge, 1953/1978.
  'We shall never experience our relationship to the essence of technology so long as we merely conceive and push forward the technological, put up with it, or evade it. Everywhere we remain unfree and chained to technology, whether we passionately affirm or deny it.'

- Lechte, J., *Fifty Key Contemporary Thinkers*, London: Routledge, 1994.
  Short summaries of the ideas of the most influential thinkers through structuralism, semiotics, modernity and postmodernity.

MODERNISM AND POSTMODERNISM

It is much easier to draw lines through history than it is to do make sense of the cultural scene today. It is always hard to see what is immediately significant, to 'see the wood for the trees'. History conveniently sifts out what it deems to be relatively unimportant. Critical theorists have created the labels 'modernism' and 'postmodernism' to describe certain broad trends in Western culture of the past one hundred years or so. These can be very helpful towards reaching an understanding of today's digital culture but – a word of warning – it is also possible to become seriously lost when applying them.

Modernism, as the name implies, describes a culture that believes in progress, in newness. Although it is mostly a historical term, there are many who argue that modernism is still a part of contemporary culture. The modernist impulse seems to have arisen first towards the end of the nineteenth century, but the event that gave it such a strong impetus was the First World War (1914–1918). The war exposed the cultural values of the nineteenth century as a failure, with a variety of consequences. For some, the only solution was political. The most striking example of this was the Russian revolution. For others, particularly those in the arts, it meant the development of radical, forward-looking movements, such as Futurism, which aggressively rejected the past. This tendency was given further impetus by the Second World War, after which some artists even sought to remove evidence of their own hand in their work, seeking instead to create music using less subjective laws, such as those of mathematics or chance.

It is hard to encapsulate the modernist vision in a few sentences, but at its most intense it seems to seek a core emotional truth, uncorrupted by irrelevant cultural information. An essay called 'Purism', written in 1924 by the modernist architect Le Corbusier and the painter Amédée Ozenfant, sums up this quite extreme idea as follows: if you show a billiard ball to a native of Papua New Guinea who has never encountered any other human beings beyond his own village, he will not understand that it is a *billiard* ball. He will, on the other hand, understand the form of a *sphere* (even if he has another name for it). The writers called the sphere a *primary form*, and its function as a billiard ball a *secondary cultural association*. Modernism, broadly speaking, emphasizes primary forms at the expense of secondary cultural associations.

One of the most influential writers and thinkers about modernist music was Theodor Adorno (1903–1969). In his book *The Philosophy of Modern Music* (1949), he made a critique of mass or popular culture, arguing that it manipulates people by offering them an illusion of choice in a process he called *pseudo-individualization*. He described 'cultural industries' that feed the needs created and satisfied by capitalism, and contrasted these with the 'true needs' of freedom, creativity or genuine happiness. In musical terms, this led to a comparison between the composers Igor Stravinsky and Arnold Schoenberg, with the latter emerging clearly as a standard-bearer for modernism. Interestingly, both composers ended up in Hollywood: Stravinsky through choice, Schoenberg as a fugitive from Nazi Germany. While neither composer achieved commercial success in the film industry (both tried),[1] Stravinsky was generally happy and successful in tinsel-town, whereas Schoenberg loathed the place.

Post-modernism, or postmodernism (as it is generally written), is a reaction to and development from modernism. In many ways it represents a rehabilitation of, and glorying in, the 'secondary cultural associations' of Le Corbusier and Ozenfant's essay. The characteristics of postmodernism are eclecticism, digression, collage, pastiche, irony, in short a move away from a simple line of historical progression that modernists often called the Grand Narrative. Postmodernism is highly diverse, and suggests that individuals first *construct* their knowledge of the world, and then, in order to make a critique, *deconstruct* it again. Postmodernism asserts that no single global explanation of human behaviour is credible, and that technology leads to *reproduction*, rather than the modernist *production*. The leading postmodern theorist Jean-François Lyotard describes the social consequences of postmodernism in *The Postmodern Condition* (1979), declaring that all previous, unified conceptions of society as an organic whole, or a system, or even (as in Marx) as opposing classes, have lost credibility. In postmodernist thinking there is no possibility of an ultimate truth, and the digital age has brought about a state of ever-increasing complexity.

In music, postmodernism does not take on any one particular style or technique; rather, it is just the condition of things *after* modernism. Postmodern music may include more or less any type of music and resists hierarchies, especially those based on notions of 'high' and 'low' art. The music may contain traits of *bricolage* (do-it-yourself), and *polystylism* (multiple styles in a single work), and involve *recontextualization* (presenting familiar material in a different context), but it need not *necessarily* do any of these. The main quality is a cultural *knowingness*, a cultural awareness; in short, cultural knowledge. It is hard to resist the idea that we live in a postmodern age.

One useful text in the study of postmodernism in music is *Image, Music, Text* (1977) by Roland Barthes. This includes the seminal essay 'The Death of the Author', in which he states:

> The text is a tissue of quotations drawn from the innumerable centres of culture. ... [It] is made of multiple writings, drawn from many cultures and entering into mutual relations of dialogue, parody, contestation, but there is one place where this multiplicity is focused and that place is the reader, not, as was hitherto said, the author. The reader is the space on which all the quotations that make up a writing are inscribed without any of them being lost; a text's unity lies not in its origin but in its destination.[2]

The 'listener' may be substituted for the 'reader' here. The word 'text' is used by Barthes to refer to any kind of cultural artefact, not just literature. The phrase 'innumerable centres of culture' suggests a highly fragmented picture, one in which there is no single culture but instead many different cultures or subcultures.

A subculture is a set of people with a distinct set of behaviour or beliefs that recognizably sets them apart from the larger culture. Where this is in opposition to the dominant culture, it would be called a counterculture. There are many aspects of the digital music scene, which suggest that people place themselves within particular subcultures. Musically speaking, these would be defined by styles and techniques, but this is only part of the story, because lifestyle concerns are also a defining characteristic of subcultures.

FURTHER READING

■ Adorno, T., *The Philosophy of Modern Music*, Continuum International, 2003, new edn.
In this study of the aesthetics of twentieth-century classical music, Adorno revolutionized music theory through an analysis of two composers he saw as polar opposites: Arnold Schoenberg and Igor Stravinsky.

■ Gablik, S., *Has Modernism Failed?* London: Thames & Hudson, 1984.
Although mostly concerned with visual art, the arguments in this book are relevant to all art-forms. Gablik describes a consumer culture in which the central ideas of modernism have largely broken down.

■ Kittler, F. A., *Gramophone, Film, Typewriter*, Stanford, CA: Stanford University Press, 1999.
A historical study of the emergence of new technologies and the critical and philosophical ideas that accompanied them.

■ Lyotard, J-F., *The Postmodern Condition*, Minneapolis: Minnesota University Press, 1979.
Examines science, technology, and the arts, the significance of technocracy, and the way the flow of information is controlled in the Western world.

STRUCTURALISM AND DECONSTRUCTION

Structuralism, like most critical theory, has a history that goes back to the nineteenth century. However, the aspect that has made a significant impact upon today's music arose during the 1960s and afterwards. Structuralism focuses on the way in which structures influence human behaviour. The structures themselves may be social, cultural, linguistic, or mental. They are layered upon the deeper elements that make up language, literature and so on. In other words, structures are conventions of meaning or patterns of relationships. Structuralism 'reads' these structures just as one would read a text, literally deciphering them for evidence of the underlying elements. An important part of this process is called *semiology*, or the study of 'signs'. A sign is anything that is used to stand for something else. Codes, such as literary or cultural codes, give a context to these signs. According to Gérard Genette (b. 1930), structuralism is:

> a study of the cultural construction or identification of meaning according to the relations of signs that constitute the meaning-spectrum of the culture.[3]

Structuralism successfully opened up whole areas, such as anthropology, that were previously unavailable to cultural studies. However, debate continues to rage about the merits of structuralism in relation to literary criticism. The application of the linguistic theories of Ferdinand de Saussure (1857–1913) and the anthropological discoveries of Claude Lévi-Strauss (b. 1908) to narrative, in particular, has led to the argument that a text can only be said to be truly new if it creates a new structure, as opposed to new characters or new style. Since most stories are structurally derived from a handful of archetypal narratives or myths, it follows that the text is to be seen merely as the function of a system. The structures may be universal and timeless and it is they, rather than the individual, that produce the meaning.

An important tool of structuralism is *deconstruction*. This is a very difficult term to define succinctly, but according to the leading writer Jacques Derrida (1930–2004), it is not a destruction, but rather a kind of analytical reading. It employs a questioning of the apparent essences of a text, by finding elements *within the text itself* that seem to differ from its own intentions, thus laying bare a different meaning. As such, it has become a popular way of describing the process of dismantling someone or something by exposing their inherent weaknesses, or just what makes them up. A great deal of artistic product of the past fifty years or so purports to 'deconstruct' meaning, convention, the artist, society, or the work of art itself.

Derrida himself moved structuralism into a new phase, usually called post-structuralism, which reappraised some of its key assumptions. Post-structural thought says that the underlying structures are *themselves* the products of culture. In particular, it asserts that the author's intentions are secondary to the meanings perceived by the reader. Barthes described a 'metalanguage', or high-order language that is used to explain language. One result of these developments is that post-structural theories themselves are very hard to read and to understand.

One philosopher whose work fits into this school and who has had a considerable influence on developments in music (and other performance arts) was Gilles Deleuze (1925–1995). His book *A Thousand Plateaus* (1980), written with the economist Félix Guattari, describes a vision of the world that is modelled on a *rhizome*. This is a term from botany, which describes a network of interconnected tubers (such as a lawn). Deleuze suggests that in the rhizome, theories and research are connected in such a way as to allow for multiple, non-hierarchical entry and exit points. Knowledge is transferred in a manner similar to horizontal gene transfer, in which an organism transmits genetic information to another cell that is not its offspring. Although Deleuze does not mention the Internet, the description of the rhizome seems uncannily similar to the way in which cyberspace operates today.

Many of the ideas of structuralism and deconstruction have found their way into the writings of artists, critics and media theorists. A good example was Marshall McLuhan (1911–1980), whose famous statement 'the medium is the message', discussed in his book *Understanding Media: The Extensions of Man*, became the basis for much subsequent media theory. Fundamental to his thinking at this point was the idea that percept is more important than concept; in other words, that the experience itself takes preference over its subsequent rationalization. Another key concept was the 'global village', a vision of a future in which society would be organized through 'electronic interdependence', when new media would replace the visual with the aural or the oral. As McLuhan put it: 'The future masters of technology will have to be light-hearted and intelligent. The machine easily masters the grim and the dumb.'

Jacques Attali (b. 1943) is even more direct about the social role of music. In *Noise: The Political Economy of Music*, he theorizes that 'the only thing common to all music is that it gives structure to noise' and that 'our musical process of structuring noise is also our political process for structuring community.' He declares: 'Music runs parallel to human society, is structured like it, and changes when it does.'[4]

For Attali, the way in which music is made in today's society is fundamentally self-deceiving, because modern distribution techniques 'contribute to the establishment of a system of eavesdropping and social surveillance'.[5] Attali was writing before the download culture began, and uses Muzak as an example to illustrate his point, but his words still have considerable relevance:

> What is called music today is too often only a disguise for the monologue of power. However, and this is the supreme irony of it all, never before have musicians tried so hard to communicate with their audience, and never before has that communication been so deceiving. Music now seems hardly more than a somewhat clumsy excuse for the self-glorification of musicians and the growth of a new industrial sector. Still, it is an activity that is essential for knowledge and social relations.[6]

FURTHER READING

■ Attali, J., *Noise: The Political Economy of Music*, Minneapolis: University of Minnesota Press, 1985.
   Examines the commodification of music and its value in predicting social change.

■ Barthes, R., *The Responsibility of Forms: Critical Essays on Music, Art and Representation*, California: University of California Press, 1991.
   Some rich essays on aspects of the visible and the audible, including the idea of the 'grain' of the voice.

■ Buchanan, I. and Swiboda, M. (eds), *Deleuze and Music*, Edinburgh: Edinburgh University Press, 2004.
   Explores the presence of music in Deleuze's work, including the musical relevance of the notion of the rhizome.

■ Deleuze, G. and Guattari, F., *Mille Plateaux (A Thousand Plateaux)*, London: Continuum International, 1980.
   'A plateau is always in the middle, not at the beginning or the end. A rhizome is made of plateaus. Gregory Bateson uses the word "plateau" to designate something very special: a continuous, self-vibrating region of intensities whose development avoids any orientation towards a culmination point or external end.'

■ Kamuf, P. (ed.), *A Derrida Reader: Between the Blinds*, New York: Columbia University Press, 1991.
   A collection of essays offering an accessible introduction to the work of the great theorist of deconstruction.

■ McLuhan, M., *Understanding Media: The Extensions of Man*, New York: Mentor, 1964.
   A discussion of mass media, introducing concepts such as 'the global village' and 'the medium is the message'.

Project 38 (Advanced): Creative Deconstruction

Introduction

The aim of this project is to use deconstruction as a creative tool to enhance an under-standing of critical theory and produce a musical outcome.

The Project

First, take any piece of modern popular music (preferably with a clearly digital origin) and attempt to deconstruct it. This is a 'paper' exercise in identifying and understanding the aesthetic and meaningful content of the piece. This may include or ignore any associated video. Isolate the various musical gestures and lines. Do their instrumentation, musical style, means of production, context, and so on, imply any particular idea? Are there any underlying structures in them that draw upon pre-existing models? What are these? What is their significance?

Next, having performed this analysis, try to rework some of the musical ideas to present them in a new way that reveals what you have discovered in the first step. You might wish to recontextualize, recompose, or re-orchestrate some of the material. Particular gestures may be extended or reduced exaggerated or diminished. Remember, the purpose of the exercise is not to destroy, but rather to reveal the original. What does your new composi-tion 'say' about the source?

Notes

Derrida famously said: 'there is nothing outside the text', by which he meant that everything you can say about a text (or a piece of music) is itself a text, subject to the same underlying structures as the original text itself. The idea of this project is to examine the truth of that statement. The piece of music produced at the end, therefore, is a new 'text' that reveals aspects of the original text (or song, in this case).

The project will involve a painstaking process of editing and reworking, and cannot be done in a hurry. There will be a temptation, seizing on the word 'deconstruction', to adopt an anarchic, or even mocking, approach to the original. But this is not simply an exercise in chopping something to bits!

Finally, it should be noted that the prime material will undoubtedly be subject to copy-right laws, and so your finished piece should be for private consumption only. People who have undertaken similar projects in the past and have then broadcast the results have fallen foul of the law.

PROJECT 38

SOME NOTES ABOUT SEMIOTICS

The 'semiotics' of a piece of music refers to the distinctive and recognizable *signs* that contribute to its behaviours and stylistic attributes, within a given musical culture or subculture. Semiotics has been applied successfully to the analysis of both classical and popular music. In his *Introductory Notes to the Semiotics of Music*, Philip Tagg comments:

> [We need to discover] which sounds mean what to whom and in which context.
> And this, obviously, is a semiotic matter. That is why [this text] is devoted to (a)
> basic semiotic terminology, (b) a definition of 'music' and 'musical structures', (c) a
> sign typology of music, (d) how music can be studied semiotically without knowing
> what a diminished seventh is.[7]

Tagg's exhaustive analysis of the theme tune for the television series *Kojak* demonstrates
a thorough application of these ideas.

Despite its potential, semiotics has so far been relatively under-used in the analysis of
digital, electronic or electro-acoustic music. Nevertheless, there have been attempts, of
which probably the most influential has been that of Jean-Jacques Nattiez, who defines
analysis as a 'metalanguage' applied to a musical fact. This metalanguage adopts different
types of discourse in its examination of the object, in this case a piece of music with all its
many variables. Analysis adopts a methodology to make a 'semiological interrogation' of
the music. Nattiez devotes an entire chapter of *Music and Discourse: Towards a Semiology
of Music* to a discussion of the 'sound-object' (after Schaeffer), in which he identifies its
neutral, poietic and *esthesic* levels. 'Poietic' refers to that which underpins the making of a
work: the deliberations or intentions that lie behind it; the operations on its materials;
its production. The 'esthesic' is the enjoyment, contemplation, or indeed analysis of the
experience of a work. He concludes:

> On the neutral level, it would be easy enough to identify and describe the sound-
> objects that make up these works, to describe the laws governing their succession
> and their integration into various syntactic arrangements, on various levels. We
> would then, from this *arrested* description of the material, *proceed to extract* those
> constituent traits that account for a sense of continuity within the succession of
> isolated moments that make up the work. But this essentially esthesic explanation
> (we perceive a 'sense of continuity') will never be possible unless one first
> has access to a material description of the work; that is to an analysis of its
> neutral level.[8]

The 'neutral level' presumably equates to a 'scientific' analysis of the sounds themselves,
which raises a problem of distinction between the understanding and organization of
sound. This breaking-down of the process of analysis into two distinct levels is reminiscent of structuralism.

Since digital music, as we have seen in previous chapters, is often built from
sound materials removed to a greater or lesser extent from their original sources,
and recontextualized within a new musical framework, it seems likely that the study
of its semiotics will increase. Indeed, the extent to which semiotic theory has been
absorbed into and understood by the wider culture is already a part of the collective ability to 'decode' music. Popular music may offer the clearest examples of this
literacy, but electro-acoustic music also is full of signs that are readily understood by
audiences.

FURTHER READING

- Chandler, D., *Semiotics: The Basics*, New York: Routledge, 2002.
  A clear and concise introduction to the key concepts of semiotics in accessible and jargon-free language.

- Nattiez, J-J., *Music and Discourse: Towards a Semiology of Music*, Princeton: Princeton University Press, 1990.
  Asks some fundamental questions, such as 'what is a musical work?' and 'what constitutes music?', and proposes a global theory for the interpretation of specific pieces.

- Monelle, R., *Linguistics and Semiotics in Music*, Chur, Switzerland: Harwood Academic Publishers, 1992.
  Describes the application of analytical approaches from linguistics and semiotics to music.

- Tagg, P., *Kojak: 50 Seconds of Television Music*, New York State: Mass Media Music Scholars' Press, 2000.
  A highly detailed semiological analysis of a TV theme tune.

MUSICOLOGY

Musicology, or the study of music, has been affected by critical theory, modernism, postmodernism and all the other developments described in this chapter. It has also been as profoundly changed by the arrival of computers as any other academic discipline in what is often now called the 'digital humanities'. The capacity that computers afford to represent and store music in a variety of ways and to apply analytical and critical processes has facilitated many new developments in the field.

At the same time, the scope of musicology has significantly expanded. Whereas it traditionally tended to restrict itself to historical accounts and note-by-note analyses of classical music, in recent years there has been an increasing interest in exploring the meaning and significance of music in social and cultural terms. One of the leaders of this 'new musicology', Susan McClary, has described music as:

> a medium that participates in social formation by influencing the ways we perceive our feelings, our bodies, our desires, our very subjectivities – even if it does so surreptitiously, without most of us knowing how. It is too important a cultural force to be shrouded by mystified notions of Romantic transcendence.[9]

This has led to increasingly abundant studies of popular and folk musics, in short every aspect of musical life, often from a sociological, anthroplogical, or cultural analytical standpoint.

The musicology of digital music itself has opened up some new fields of investigation or has given new impetus to previously known areas. Sound, its organization, categorization, structuring, synthesis and analysis has proved fertile territory for musicology, taking it beyond previous studies based on notes. The practice of sound art, novel types of performance and interactivity have grown into musicological fields in their own right, as has the study of new instruments and expanded organology discussed in previous chapters. Multimedia and sound design for film, television and computer games is generally considered to be part of media studies, but has also spilled over into musicology. There is a recurring question in musicology as to whether music that is not made as art is worthy of study. Whereas commercial and popular music now sits comfortably within the musicological field of vision, such apparently incidental products as the soundtrack to a computer game, for example, present more of a challenge. Nevertheless, there is an emerging interest in this area whose frame of reference is becoming increasingly musicological in nature.

Computer music itself, and particularly the applications of artificial intelligence and computer-generated music of all descriptions, has an established musicology with a history stretching back to the earliest music programming languages. This musicology sometimes owes much to traditional models and at other times has some novel features. The presence of so many computer scientists and engineers in the field tends to introduce a quantitative methodology into the study of the musical outputs that is unusual compared to the more qualitative approach of most musicology.

The study of notation has been altered in many ways by the arrival of computers, which have introduced not just an expanded palette of standardized symbols of traditional notation, but have also generated their own forms of notation, that have been discussed earlier in this book. Likewise, archiving has undergone a transformation, with vast digitized collections becoming available and searchable in a host of new ways. The archiving of digital music itself is a highly important branch of musicology which presents particular challenges as the technology evolves and the sheer quantity of music grows exponentially. It is surprising how unstable digital music collections can be. Reading a hard disk from a fifteen-year-old computer may in fact be impossible today.

FURTHER READING

■ Hooper, G., *The Discourse of Musicology*, Aldershot: Ashgate, 2006.
  Considers issues central to recent debates about the nature and direction of contemporary musicology, including its relevance and legitimacy.

■ Landy, L., 'Reviewing the Musicology of Electroacoustic Music', *Organised Sound*, 4:1, 1999, 61–70.
  Surveys the field and seeks to identify areas for future development.

■ Manning, P., *Electronic and Computer Music*, Oxford: Oxford University Press, 2004.
  Probably the most authoritative musicological account of the subject.

■ McClary, S., *Feminine Endings: Music, Gender, and Sexuality*, Minneapolis: University of Minnesota Press, 1991.
  A text that successfully mixes cultural criticism with traditional musicology.

AESTHETICS

Aesthetics is a discipline in philosophy that considers questions of beauty, taste and cultural value. The word has also come to be used loosely to describe the general character a work of art or an artist. We may speak of something or someone 'having an aesthetic', which seems rather more substantial than 'style' or 'character'. Perhaps this is a nod back to the Aesthetic movement of the nineteenth century, led by artists such as Oscar Wilde, who reacted against the sentimental and moralizing art of the time by emphasizing an appreciation of sensual beauty in their work. Despite the large amount of theoretical writing in the field before and since, it is their practical adoption of aesthetics as a cause that has left a lasting impression on the popular mind.

Contemporary thinking on Aesthetics has developed much more slowly than the art it contemplates. The field is still underpinned by thoughts and writings from the eighteenth century and even before. These are epitomized by two important philosophers, whose approaches will be recognized as still having considerable relevance. It would not be an overstatement to say that these two still represent the opposite poles of opinion on the subject.

In 1757, the philosopher David Hume (1711–1756) published an essay entitled 'On the Standard of Taste'. Hume began by outlining a sceptical position that will be very familiar to the reader: the beauty of something is equal to the sensation of pleasure it gives. On this basis, all judgements of artistic products seem to be worth exactly the same, because anybody's opinion of anything is equal. Nobody is ever wrong about anything in art or music.

This view has the merit of being quite simple and very radical. It also gives total power to everybody in the business of making critical judgements. Hume, however, while stating that evaluative responses are neither true nor false, accepted that common sense dictates that some judgements are better than others; otherwise there would not be general agreement about good and bad works of art. He went on to outline five factors that enable people to improve their critical judgement-making: 'strong sense, united to delicate sentiment, improved by practice, perfected by comparison, and cleared of all prejudice'. He did point out, however, that the ability to make critical judgements are not simply a matter of training or education, but there are natural differences between people and their tastes, and there are certain unavoidable preferences due to a person's age (generational differences) and culture (cultural preferences).

On the face of it, there seems to be little to dispute in Hume's argument, and indeed the Humean view of critical judgement is the one that generally prevails in culture today. However, there is one significant omission in his theory, which boils down to the clichéd question: is beauty only in the eye of the beholder or (in music) the ear of the listener? By making an individual's critical judgements and taste the decisive factor, standards or no standards, Hume seemed to refute the idea that something can be beautiful *in itself*. This was entirely in keeping with his general philosophical position, so it took another philosopher, Immanuel Kant (1724–1804), to explore the opposing idea.

In his book *Critique of Judgement* (1790), Kant put forward a series of complex arguments that defend a notion of *inherent beauty*. Kant's view was that something may be beautiful in itself, and human perception must develop to unlock that beauty. The sensation of aesthetic taste, or pleasure, is ideally the result of a free play of imagination and understanding that judges an object based on its form rather than its purpose. These judgements must be both *universal* and *necessary* if we are to care about the beauty of, say, a sunset. 'Common sense', therefore, was interpreted literally by Kant as a universal sensing (rather than understanding) of things. Critical judgements may relate to human cognition, but the object being critically judged can be beautiful a priori (before everything else, including human perception). For Kant, a work of art becomes universally pleasing when it allows room for reflective judgement or, as he famously said, when it shows 'purposiveness without a purpose'.

Kant's position is much more complicated than Hume's, but one of its key points is that it allows for *transcendence*. The beauty of something is not necessarily dependent upon our appreciation, and is not subject to something as arbitrary as taste. Kant discusses 'the sublime', which he says is something that seems to overwhelm us, that we cannot get our heads around, such as a violent storm or a very large building. In Kant's view, it is not really the storm or the building that is sublime, but rather the sense of scale we get from the ideas of absolute totality or absolute freedom that they seem to embody. However big the building may be, we know it is small compared to absolute totality; however powerful the storm, it is weak compared to absolute freedom. Thus, in Kant's view, we should aim to base our judgements literally *in* the common sense. This is a skill that needs cultivation, and which may also be moral. Beauty may also be a sign of moral goodness. In Kant's philosophy (unlike Hume's) there is room for a faith in God.

Although there was much refinement of these two basic positions in the next two centuries, it was not until John Dewey wrote his important text *Art as Experience* that a radically new idea about aesthetics appeared. Dewey criticized earlier philosophy on the basis that it only considered works of art and, in general, high art, as *objects*. Dewey argued that aesthetics should consider the entire *process* of art, which consists of not just a single object, but rather an experience with potentially life-changing characteristics. Dewey stated:

> An experience is a product, one might almost say by-product, of continuous and cumulative interaction of an organic self with the world. There is no other foundation upon which aesthetic theory and criticism can build.[10]

By reuniting art with life in this way, Dewey emphasized its social dimension and introduced ethics into the aesthetic debate. For him, the quality of culture's aesthetics was a measure of its civilization. Art is not a spontaneous expression, but the product of lengthy reflection and observation that culminates in the clarification of a work. It cannot be separated from other experiences in life. Isolating art from science leads to an incoherent society, he argued. Art can have a social value by bringing people together and improving communication.

As the twentieth century evolved, aesthetics became intertwined with critical theory and cultural studies, resulting in both modernist and postmodernist theories. The modern tendency took its cue from science and from analytic philosophy. One leading modernist aesthetician, Monroe Beardsley has argued that neither the intentions of an artist nor the reactions of the receiver can have any logical relevance to the three ways of critically appraising a work: descriptive, interpretative, and evaluative.

> Judging a poem is like judging a pudding or a machine. One demands that it work. It is only because an artifact works that we infer the intention of the artificer ... A poem can *be* only through its *meaning* ... yet it *is*, simply *is*, in the sense that we have no excuse for inquiring what part is intended or meant.[11]

This removal of intention and reception opened up the possibility of an empirical aesthetics based on experimental and scientific evidence. So, for example, building on Gustav Fechner's *Vorschule der Aesthetik* (1876), Daniel Berlyne developed a disinterested approach in the 1970s that became known as *experimental aesthetics*. This used psychology and biology combined in an interdisciplinary way to examine people's responses to art, expressed through both verbal and non-verbal means. Berlyne observed the 'arousal potential' of a piece of music through variables such as novelty, complexity, meaning and intensity. He concluded (amongst many other things) that people prefer music with a medium degree of arousal potential and dislike music with either a very high or very low arousal potential.[12]

Postmodern Aesthetics has tended to react against such scientific analysis of art and our reactions to it, instead re-asserting the importance of sensuality over meaning, energy over intellect. Revisiting Freud, Jean-François Lyotard described the *figural* as emanating from the unconscious (like the 'id'), as opposed to the *discursive* (ego), which is concerned with questions of interpretation. He saw modernist aesthetics as essentially discursive: an ever-increasing attempt to intellectualize, codify and repress the 'libidinal energies' which give rise to art. In a figural area such as art, he contended, no single interpretation can ever succeed in accurately comprehending what is taking place. Thus, Lyotard ends up rehabilitating Kant's idea of the sublime: 'It is in the aesthetic of the sublime that modern art … finds its impetus and the logic of avant-gardes finds its axioms.'[13]

There have been some attempts to develop a purely digital aesthetics, as opposed to an application of general aesthetic theories to the digital domain. The German computer scientist and artist Jürgen Schmidhuber, for example, has elaborated an aesthetic theory based on low complexity. He postulates:

> Among several patterns classified as 'comparable' by some subjective observer, the subjectively most beautiful is the one with the simplest (shortest) description, given the observer's particular method for encoding and memorizing it.[14]

In other words, a digital work will be perceived as beautiful if it looks (or sounds) 'right' and, at the same time, the algorithm that has produced it is extremely short. Both these properties must be perceptible by the viewer. Such ideas are rooted in cybernetics, information theory and artifical intelligence, all of which have developed an aesthetic dimension.

Cybernetics studies goal-oriented systems of control and regulation in humans, nature and technology. An important figure in the post-war development of the field was Norbert Wiener (1894–1964), whose studies of feedback and noise within such systems inspired great interest from many different quarters, including the US government, that subsequently invested very large amounts of money in the Defense Advanced Research Projects Agency (DARPA) to continue the work. The research at DARPA developed both military and civilian applications of cybernetics, including the first Internet.

Modelling social, economic, or biological systems using digital technology also appealed to artists, and a cybernetic aesthetics evolved naturally alongside this practical work. Central to this aesthetics was the presence of technology and a change in the relationship between the spectator/listener and the work itself. Roy Ascott, for example, saw the computer as an 'intelligence amplifier': 'The computer may be linked to an artwork and the artwork may in some sense *be* a computer.'[15]

In an influential essay from 1964 entitled 'Behaviourist Art and the Cybernetic Vision', he articulated the new aesthetics as one on which technology and experience combined to make the artwork fully interactive:

> The dominant feature of art of the past was the wish to transmit a clearly defined message to the spectator, as a more or less passive receptor, from the artist, as a unique and highly individualized source. This deterministic aesthetic was centred upon the structuring, or 'composition,' of *facts*, of concepts of the *essence* of things, encapsulated in a factually correct visual field. Modern art, by contrast, is concerned to initiate *events*, and with the forming of concepts of *existence*. The vision of art has shifted from the field of objects to the field of behaviour … A feedback loop is established, so that the evolution of the artwork/experience is governed by the intimate involvement of the spectator.[16]

Cybernetics overlapped with information theory, which focused on the ways in which information is quantified in digital systems. Initiated by Claude Shannon (1916–2001) with a paper published in 1948, the field rapidly expanded to cover not just digital information but also physics, ecology, economics and so on. Information theory was most concerned with increasing the efficiency of systems by understanding their limitations (its applications have included compression formats such as zip files and mp3). Information aesthetics has therefore concerned itself with the *meaning* of data, and hence often with complexity. Interactions across networks, large repositories of artefacts or texts, organizational relationships, and many other enormous bodies of information may be captured and visualized by computers in ways which are both interactive and aesthetically peculiar to the digital world.

Both cybernetics and information theory envisaged that computers would have a significant capacity to extend human abilities. At a conference in Dartmouth in 1956, Alan Newell and Herbert Simon predicted that it would not be long before a computer was world chess champion, would theorize psychology, prove mathematical theorems and compose music that had aesthetic value. This pronouncement launched Artificial Intelligence as a discipline, although the ideas were hardly new in themselves. Computers today do compose music that has aesthetic value. One interesting question is: does that value amount to a separate digital aesthetic, or are the products of computer composition to be judged only in traditional aesthetic terms?

Both cybernetic and information aesthetics point out that the human brain can only process discrete bits of information transmitted via the senses at a rate of about 16 bits per second and short-term memory only operates for about 10 seconds, meaning that the amount of information in any artwork that may readily be assimilated at any one moment is in the region of 160 bits.[17] This limitation of the human machine may be exceeded by a computer, which introduces the possibility of a genuinely digital aesthetics.

Despite these developments, it is surprising to what extent the ideas of Kant, Hume and Dewey still dominate aesthetics. Social media, with its 'like' buttons, and recommendations based on tracking people's habits, and notions of 'the wisdom of crowds', seems to be reinvigorating a Humean approach to critical judgement that is rooted in 'common' sense. At the same time, Kantian ideas of truth, beauty and the sublime still permeate concert halls and art galleries, with their elevation of the work to a kind of sacred status, adored by thousands. Cybernetic aesthetics, with its emphasis on interaction, by contrast sees the work of digital art as something in which the user is immersed, in the manner of Dewey's life experience. Digital technology has apparently not advanced the aesthetic debate very much.

Project 39 (Intermediate): Aesthetic Experiment

Introduction

There are many different ways in which to approach the question of aesthetics, ranging from the scientific to the philosophical. This project proposes a very limited experiment with the aim of introducing some of the key ideas and introducing a methodology that may well be unfamiliar to musicians. The project relies on the willing participation of several other people.

The Project

The idea is to test the aesthetic properties of sounds under experimental conditions.

- Step 1. Make a small collection of three to five short sounds that have some strong meaning or association for you. Assemble an equal-sized collection of sounds that have no such meaning.
- Step 2. Devise a questionnaire (this may be online) that examines the aesthetic properties of the sounds. Questions may cover: like and dislike, evocative power, meaning or association, emotional response, sonic characteristics, musical qualities and so on. The questionnaire should use a Likert scale. In this system, you should make a simple statement about the sounds and the participant should be invited to indicate:

  1. Strongly disagree
  2. Disagree
  3. Neither agree nor disagree
  4. Agree
  5. Strongly agree.

So, for example, a question may look like this:

  a. this sound is pleasing to the ear
     Strongly disagree | Disagree | Neither agree nor disagree | Agree | Strongly agree

The participant will indicate one of the answers. This process should be repeated for all questions against all sounds.

- Step 3. Analyse the results. A good way to do this is to produce a bar chart of the responses, then provide additional commentary where there is a result of particular interest.
- Step 4. Compare the analysis with your own personal responses. Are there any obvious differences? Why might they occur? Does this change the way you think abut the sounds?

Notes

This project may be extended to cover whole pieces of music. It is important when conducting this kind of research that the participants are anonymized and that they have agreed in advance to take part and allowed the resulting data to be used by you. Obtaining informed consent in writing is usually required for any such experiment on a large scale.

PROJECT 39

FURTHER READING

- Ascott, R., 'Behaviourist Art and the Cybernetic Vision', in Packer, R. and Jordan, K. (eds) *Multimedia. From Wagner to Virtual Reality*, New York: W. W. Norton & Company, 2002, pp. 104–120.
  Seminal essay on cybernetic aesthetics.

- Boisvert, R., *John Dewey: Rethinking Our Time*, New York: SUNY, 1998.
  A brief introduction to all aspects of Dewey's philosophy, including aesthetics.

- Graham, G., *Philosophy of the Arts: An Introduction to Aesthetics*, London: Routledge, 2005.
  An accessible introduction to the key ideas in the theory and philosophy of aesthetics.

- Meyer, L., *Music, the Arts and Ideas*, Chicago: University of Chicago Press, 1994.
  Discusses the criteria for judging works of art and music, and offers some predictions for the future which are then reviewed in a Postlude.

- Wenzel, C., *An Introduction to Kant's Aesthetics: Core Concepts and Problems*, New York: Blackwell, 2005.
  A clear introduction to Kant's *Critique of Judgement*.

CRITICAL JUDGEMENT

Aesthetic theories have had a considerable impact on the practical business of making critical judgements. For most people, such judgements will be formed in some way between the two poles of Kant and Hume. There are some situations where a *relativism* in forming judgements is useful, especially when ignorance, or a lack of cultural knowledge, might lead to sudden or rash verdicts; on the other hand, there are times when a sense of the beauty of something may come through *in spite of oneself*, where it is not possible to be sure of one's own taste. One thing is certain: simple 'I like it/I don't like it' judgements, while not wrong in themselves, are almost never enough. Mere 'instinctive' reactions have to be gone beyond in order to improve critical judgements.

It is very often the case, when creating music, that decisions are made without really understanding the reasons behind them. Indeed, it is generally seen as a virtue for a musician to be natural, for the music to flow through them. An ability to form critical judgements should not be allowed to interfere with such natural processes. One cannot spend all one's time pondering one's own decisions. To do so would rapidly lead to a drying-up of creativity.

On the other hand, digital music, more than analogue music, demands a constant stream of decision-making, from large-scale decisions about form and structure, to moment-by-moment decisions about the nature and shaping of sounds and processes. In live situations, these decisions may be made on the fly. It is possible to have the computer make most, or even all, the decisions, but such a move is of course a decision in itself. The resistance in the process of making digital music comes not from the physical properties of instruments, but rather from one's own intellectual struggle with the medium. To what extent may the technology take over? If uncritical acceptance of the output of the computer is bad musicianship, how may an artificial intelligence create good music? And how do we know what is good?

The answers to these questions are a matter for personal reflection. They will do much to inform and condition the aesthetic qualities of whatever you produce. In finding and developing your own 'voice', you will inevitably take decisions about the role and nature of the technology you use that will be defining. Such judgements will be critical, in both an aesthetic and an ontological sense (where 'ontological' means how things *are*). Often, these decisions, once taken, are subsequently forgotten about as creativity takes over. Critical judgements may feel instinctive or natural as a result. But it is always worth bearing in mind that something sounds 'right' for a reason, however obscure that may be, and that we construct meaning from our experience. Understanding that experience and the way we make choices will help to make better and more effective critical judgements.

The sheer diversity of postmodern and contemporary culture can be bewildering. It is difficult for an individual to locate himself or herself when things change so rapidly and newness is always present, where names have to be invented in order to describe things. The digital world is so messy and vague, teeming with information and data, to the point where even 'secondary cultural associations' are hard to pinpoint. One thing, however, is certain: sooner or later, a digital musician is going to have to exercise critical judgement, even if only to decide what *not* to absorb. In many senses, a musician is the sum of all the critical judgements he or she has ever made.

Project 40 (Elementary): Balloon Debate

Introduction

This project is a spin on an old favourite of debating societies: the balloon debate. In this format, each person is required to take on the defence of a chosen figure from history and defend their right to remain in an imaginary balloon which needs to jettison ballast. The person who remains after the rest have been voted out one by one is the winner.

The Project

Scenario: all of culture is to be destroyed, except for the one thing that is worth keeping. What is that one thing? Make a presentation to defend the choice. Trick answers which try to avoid the spirit of the project automatically fail. The 'thing' should be an artefact or a body of work, but not a land mass or a people.

Notes

This is a good way of understanding and articulating the idea of cultural value. The presentation will need to give clear reasons for the choice, from which a value system and set of critical judgements may be deduced. If done in a group situation, the subsequent voting can also be revealing of the collective set of shared values.

PROJECT 40

Discussion Questions

- How do you judge music?

- What is good music, and why?

- What is bad music, and why?

- What would be good examples of 'modernist' and 'postmodernist' music? Why?

- How do computer games soundtracks use semiotics?

- To what extent is the metaphor of the rhizome (Deleuze and Guattari) a useful way of describing digital music?

CHAPTER 12

Understanding Digital Music

DIGITAL MUSIC

In his book *Music, Society, Education*, the musicologist Christopher Small suggested that consumerism has led to music in the West (and increasingly in India, Indochina, Africa and everywhere else) becoming a *product* rather than a *process*. In the following passage, he discusses the effects of Western consumerism on traditional Balinese virtues of valuing the moment, collectivism and spontaneity. The same points may be made about African music too.

> I must emphasize again that since the end of the second world war these values have become severely eroded as western commercial values and consumerism take over; the change from artistic creation as a process involving the whole community to art as a commodity made for sale by a few professional artists has happened here, as throughout the non-European world, staggeringly quickly'.[1]

Small could not have foreseen the emergence of digital culture, nor the extent to which the 'erosion' to which he refers would itself become eroded. Today there is once again a community based culture, collective and spontaneous, sharing in artistic creation. The rise of a social Internet, which increasingly configures itself to suit the individual user, has enabled this development. Social media, blogs and wikis, user-groups and forums, mp3 sharing and individual playlists, in short: everything that personalizes cyberspace means that the consumer culture is increasingly morphing into an online culture. To be sure, commercialism is always present and the commodity merchants are always busy trying to figure out how to exploit the new digital culture. Meanwhile, people interact and share online, grouping around common interests and passions, around ideas and sounds. The major difference, of course, is that geographical location is no longer the defining characteristic of this community.

What is fascinating about the changes brought about by digital music is the extent to which, once again, we are building an aural tradition based on this communal understanding, on shared tools and practices, and to some extent on regional variation. It is true that there is a great deal of *production* and especially commercial production in digital music, but the 'product' itself is also seen as part of a process. In fact, the phrase 'music production' increasingly refers to the process of creating music, rather than a layer of polish applied to a finished artefact. Perhaps the digital musician is making a new kind of music, and the musical situation is once again coming to resemble the informal, process-based, communal activity of some parts of the non-Western world.

In order to apply the same kind of ethnomusicological approach that has already been used to consider *gamelan*, Indian classical music and African drumming in relation to digital music, some attempt to identify its key characteristics must be made. This is not easy, because the phrase 'digital music' covers such a potentially vast range of types, categories and genres that a purely musical system of classification rapidly becomes unworkable. A more fruitful way of approaching the problem might be to consider the role of the *musician*. This is a method that also fits well with the central theme of this book. By using a human-centred classification system, the vast and messy field of digital music may be organized into three broad types: audience or user-controlled music; computer-controlled music; and composer/performer-controlled music.

FURTHER READING

- Lysloff, R. and Gay, L. (eds), *Music and Technoculture*, Middletown, CT: Wesleyan University Press, 2003.
  A collection of essays that examine the relationship between technology and ethnomusicology.

- Small, C., *Music, Society, Education*, Middletown, CT: Wesleyan University Press, 1977.
  Examines the social implications of Western classical music.

- Taylor, T., *Strange Sounds: Music, Technology and Culture*, New York: Routledge, 2001.
  Examines the cultural embedding of sound technologies and how they convey meaning.

Project 41 (Elementary): Random Play

Introduction

Download culture has significantly changed the way we experience music. Whereas previously to jump tracks on an LP, or worse still a cassette, required some tricky physical manipulation, the CD has automated the 'random play'. Music can be heard in any order, even if that was never the intention of the artists. The mp3 player takes this one stage further, and allows all the tracks of an entire record collection to be randomly played. The results can be startling.

The Project

First, simply listen to a succession of completely unrelated (the more unrelated the better) tracks in a random order. Do any surprising connections emerge? Try it again.

Next, assemble a collection of short excerpts or sounds. Make each one under five seconds. Now randomly play these back a few times. Make sure there is no time gap between each track, so as to create a seamless composition.

Finally, try to repeat the second step using ever-shorter clips of music or sound. How short can they be before the musical sense is lost?

Notes

The final step will probably involve some editing work. This is a crude exercise and the editing can be done quite arbitrarily. The best effects are achieved when the 'jump-cuts' are violent or shocking.

PROJECT 41

Audience or User-Controlled Music

Here the person who receives the music may determine when it begins and ends and, to a greater or lesser extent, what happens in between. The musician (and possibly the computer) has a hand in creating prime content, and possibly in the context within which the music appears, but no more.

Musical attention in this category usually focuses on the nature and extent of the interaction. In computer games, for example, the sounds (whether obviously 'musical' or not) that accompany the action are capable of combination and recombination in many different ways. This is event-driven music, and is shaped by the user's decisions in the context of the game. The sounds are created so as to enable the user to seamlessly make a transition from one into another. This process can even be extended to user-made adaptive compositions in which the choices made in some way condition subsequent outcomes.

A different kind of user-control is encountered in sound installations, which may range from public sculptures, to interactive stands in museums or attractions, to art gallery pieces. Here the interaction is usually physical rather than virtual, and often the user's own actions will change the nature of the sonic activity. However, this might also include all kinds of ambient music designed to enhance a given location, including muzak. *Sound environments* are also relevant here, because once again the user is placed at the hub of the musical activity, usually with a decisive role. An immersive environment is a virtual reality in which the user can interact with objects and experience sounds within a digitally fabricated world. In the physical world, a soundscape may be created (such as through a soundwalk, as described earlier) which has its users interact meaningfully with the sounds around them.

What all these have in common is some degree of interactivity, which means that they tend to beg the question: who *is* the artist or, in the context of this book, who *is* the musician? If the users control their experience, then in a very real sense they become the composer and the performer in that situation, and the role of the originator of the prime material, which they are manipulating, is relatively diminished.

FURTHER READING

- Packer, R., 'Composing with Media: Zero in Time and Space', *Contemporary Music Review*, 24:6, 2005, 509–525.
  Describes the theory and creation of a sound installation: *The Pavilion*.

- Paine. G., 'Immersive Virtual Environments: A Social Perspective', *Journal of Electroacoustic Music*, 12, 1999, 24–26.
  Explores ways in which Paine's Immersive Virtual Environment (IVE) installations draw on and reflect attitudes and cultural predisposition within Australia.

Computer-controlled Music

Here both the listener/user and the musician are subject to some process that is undertaken by the computer. This is generally algorithmic music, since the computer must use rules to run the process. Algorithmic music has included systems based on: chance, randomness and stochasticism; number series, sets and fractals;[2] evolution, genetics and L-systems;[3] network information, statistics and magnetic fields; and so on. In fact, any organizational system may provide useful algorithms.[4] Some of these emerge from activities that would not normally be considered musical at all, such as *sonification* of data. In this practice, sounds replace visual information, typically as a way of monitoring or modelling scientific or medical information (the clicks emitted by a Geiger counter used to measure levels of radiation are an example of sonification). Yet, even such material may be treated in a musical way.

Such 'machine music' is often a product of an analytical process, so the computer can control things in such a way as to produce stylistically convincing results. There are numerous examples of machine music that produce pastiche composition, or can successfully accompany human musicians within a known genre. It is the way in which the algorithm is mapped onto musical information that distinguishes the sounding result.

Once again, this begs the question: *who* is the musician? Does the computer compose and perform the music, or does the person who programmed the computer take the credit? It is certainly possible to speak of a 'computer composition' and 'machine creativity'. This may be aesthetically desirable where the removal of the human hand is the artistic goal. However, no computer begins an algorithm of its own volition, so at some level there is some kind of human intention. The tendency for the human to erase him or herself from the creative process may be an aspect of a certain mistrust of the notion of a single authorial figure that is a defining characteristic of contemporary digital culture.

FURTHER READING

- Schwanauer, S. and Levitt, D. (eds), *Machine Models of Music*, Cambridge, MA: MIT Press, 1993.
  Brings together representative models ranging from Mozart's 'Musical Dice Game' to a classic article by Marvin Minsky to demonstrate the ways in which music can push the boundaries of traditional AI research and vice versa.

- Willcock, I., 'Composing without Composers', in Mahnkopf, C.-S., Cox, F. and Schurig, W. (eds) *Electronics in New Music*, Berlin: Wolke Verlag, 2007.
  Investigates machine composition.

Composer/Performer-Controlled Music

This is the largest category, because it includes the traditional mode of musical delivery and reception, and presents relatively few conceptual difficulties. Here the musician originates or produces the sound, and the listener/user simply receives the result. However, the size of the category does not make it more significant in the field of digital music, and it has some distinctive features. First, the role of the composer/performer has become substantially blurred, as has been mentioned before. Second, the assumption of passivity on the part of the listener is risky, because the many different ways of listening to digital music, from in-ear headphones to concert halls, can make this a more active process than might previously have been imagined. Third, the possibilities opened up by digital technologies have led in some instances to an unusual performance and listening state, as for example in the kind of loudspeaker orchestra situation found in some acousmatic music in which the sources of the sounds are not evident to the listener.

There are some overlaps between the three categories outlined above, but not so much as to destroy completely the distinctions between them. Consider, for example, the case of *radiophonics*: the experimental use of sound in radio. Here the listener does have ultimate on/off control and a great deal of flexibility in how they listen, but it is still the radiophonic artists who are really controlling the musical experience. The main point of these classifications is to show that a musician may have multiple and changing roles during a given musical experience, and that the consumers of music are not completely passive.

The lessons of gamelan, Indian classical music and African drumming can equally well be applied in digital music. There is now a new listening context for music, which may fluctuate from headphone-space to club-space, from concert hall to studio. What defines all these arenas is the extent to which the listener, the user, is in control. The user's playlist itself becomes a kind of digital composition. The DJ becomes a super-listener and a musician. The 'mash-up' and the remix constantly explore a plurality of unexpected associations. The studio engineer becomes the 'producer' who actually *makes* the music. Even in the classical concert hall, the audience expresses its preferences by its attendance, influencing the development of the music through its sheer economic will. Where all this leads is to increased user satisfaction through the creation and evolution of a multitude of *genres*.

Project 42 (Intermediate): Mood Music

Introduction

The idea of this project is to place the musical experience in the hands of the user. At its simplest, it can be realized by a 'point-and-click' method which enables the user to choose what to listen to and when. More elegant solutions involve a degree of animation and interactivity which will require some technical abilities in appropriate software and possibly hardware.

The Project

Devise a multimedia interface which allows users to configure the musical experience according to their mood. The music they hear may be original or otherwise, but the results of user choice should either create or respond to a mood state.

Notes

It is notoriously hard to be precise about mood, so part of the challenge in this project is to find a way to satisfy the majority of users, but without expecting that *everyone* will be convinced. Colour and shape may be useful elements of the interface design in order to help establish the mood in the user's mind.

FURTHER READING

■ Kahn, D. and Whitehead, G., *Wireless Imagination: Sound, Radio and the Avant-Garde*, Cambridge, MA: MIT Press, 1992.
Essays and historical documents relating to the development of audio and radiophonic art.

GENRE

'Genre' was a relatively little-used term until fairly recently. Music might be divided into 'classical' and 'popular', or 'jazz' and 'folk', but not much beyond that outside of the specialists. Music-lovers who knew 'folk' music, for example, might recognize a distinction between, say, Celtic and Gaelic music, but these terms in themselves would not necessarily constitute a genre but rather a *style* of music within the larger genre category of 'folk'.

Digital culture has brought about an explosion of genre, to the point where almost all digital music can be heard in relation to a known genre or be seen to have created a new genre. In electronic dance music, for example, new genres come and go so rapidly as to constitute the whims of fashion. At the technological level, this genre-multiplication has come about because of the possibility of adding digital 'tags' to sound files giving basic information that will enable future classification or 'sorting'. At a more cultural level, it may be seen as an example of postmodernism.

The approach to specific genres requires a warning bell. One of the fundamental requirements of the digital musician is to develop an original sound. Genre work is potentially limiting in that respect because genres generally involve conventions and traditions, even constraints. These can be very useful for initiating creative work, but if they dominate the musician too much then there is a danger of becoming merely a reproducer of other people's ideas. It is important for the digital musician to retain a creative originality, even if working within the confines of an established musical genre.

An extreme example will illustrate the point: *plunderphonics*. The name of the genre originated in 1985 from an essay and CD by John Oswald and refers to music stolen from existing, usually well-known, recordings and subjected to various modifications. There is a political dimension to this music, which attacks the hypocrisy surrounding copyright. The original 'Plunderphonic' album fell foul of various laws and its cover, depicting Michael Jackson as a naked white woman, landed Oswald in court. In his various essays and articles[5] he makes it clear that his work is by no means unique, citing examples from classical and contemporary popular music where composers and artists have openly 'lifted' other composers' music. The influence and practice of plunderphonics can be traced in the work of bands such as *Negativland*, turntablists like Christian Marclay, 'mashed-up' pop music, and even some works by contemporary classical composers. Plunderphonics could therefore be seen as a genre that accurately reflects the cut-and-paste culture of sampling and the Internet, and the technique itself offers many creative possibilities, as well as a considerable danger.

The question facing the digital musician is therefore: to what extent to adopt plunderphonics as a technique, given that others have already developed identifiable voices within that genre? This is a question that will be relevant in any genre. There is no fixed answer, but for the digital musician to retain integrity and to move from the known to the unknown will not allow for simple aping of the mannerisms of others. A technique will not in itself guarantee distinctive results; it is all a question of how it is used, what is done with it.

Consider the recent list of (just) electronic dance music genres in Table 12.1.[6]

Given that almost all these genres have arisen in the past decade, this will readily illustrate the complexity of the subject. This takes us well beyond the various dance-types in traditional dance halls, and beyond the various types of rock music too. The digital musician could become a kind of alchemist, combining elements from several of these, perhaps even to formulate a new genre. It is likely that none of these genres will remain particularly stable.

All the above-listed genres have something in common: they have arisen as a result of a collective agreement by the community they serve. It may be that there are certain

Table 12.1 Dance music genres

Ambient	Breakbeat	Downtempo/IDM	Hardcore	House	Industrial	Jungle/Drum and Bass	Techno	Trance
Dark Ambient	Electro	Balearic Beat	4-beat	Chicago House	EBM	Darkcore	Acid Techno	Psychedelic Trance/Goa trance
Illbient	Big Beat	Bleep	Bouncy Techno	2Step	Noise Music	Ragga	Detroit Techno/US Techno	Acid Trance
New Age	Breaks	Electroclash	Breakbeat Hardcore	Acid House	Old-school EBM	Drill and Bass	Electroclash	Vocal Trance
Psybient	Miami Bass	Electropop	Breakcore	Deep House	Futurepop	Jump-Up	Freetekno	Minimalist Trance
Ambient Dub	Brokenbeat	Laptronica	Digital Hardcore	Eurodance	Powernoise	Liquid Funk	Ghettotech	NU-NRG
Ambient Goa	Cut & Paste	Bitpop	Gabba	Ghetto House		Neurofunk	Minimal Techno/	Progressive Trance
							Glitch Techno	
Ambient House	Florida Breaks	Chiptune	Happy Hardcore	Freestyle House		Techstep	Nortec	
Lowercase (music)	Nu Skool Breaks	Minimal Electronica/Glitch	Hardcore Trance	Hi-NRG		Clownstep	Rave Music	

Progressive Breaks	Acid Jazz	Hardstyle	Funky House	Schranz
Turntablism	Nu Jazz	New Beat	Hip House	U.K. Techno
				Euro Techno
Grime	Trip Hop (aka The Bristol Sound)	Nu Style Gabber	Pumpin' House	
		Speedcore	Italo House	
		Terrorcore	Minimal House/ Microhouse	
			Garage	
			Hard House	
			French house	
			Progressive House/Tribal House	
			Tech House	
			Disco	
			Italo Disco	
			Spacesynth	

key individuals that are responsible for the distinctive musical characteristics of these genres (beats per minute, effects, activity level, etc.), but the genre has to be validated by a community who is willing to recognize it as distinct. There is then a platform for virtuosity within the genre. This is clear enough in dance music, but is also present in other forms of music. The makers are the consumers and the consumers are the makers. This is true for 'art' music just as much as 'popular' music.

This ongoing exchange between the makers and the consumers, the musicians and their audience, the artists and the non–artists, is the sign of an active musical community. Christopher Small need not have worried: process has not been replaced by product. The forming of ideas remains an integral aspect of music creation, and the commodification of music will continue both to provide a useful entry point for the interested listener and to lag behind the changes and developments that make music such a vibrant and life–enhancing activity. In that respect, at least, digital music is no different than the best music from the past.

RECOMMENDED LISTENING

This selected listening list introduces some leading digital works that are hard to classify. It includes works by two of the case study artists: Oswald Berthold (Farmer's Manual) and Kaffe Matthews.

All the works seem to be located in a genre, and yet push beyond the limits of that genre. The main questions to ask are not so much 'what genre is this?' as 'what are the defining characteristics of this music?' and 'what is its context?'

- ▶ Autechre *Chiastic Slide* [CD] Warp, 49.
- ▶ David Behrman *Leapday Night* [CD] Lovely Music, LCD1042.
- ▶ Kim Cascone *Parasites* [CD] anechoic media, a001.
- ▶ Richard Chartier *Of Surfaces* [CD] LINE, 008.
- ▶ Farmer's Manual *Explorers_We* [CD] Or, SQUISH04.
- ▶ Bernhard Günther *Un Peu de Neige Salie* [CD] Trente Oiseaux, TOCSE01.
- ▶ Ryoji Ikeda *0°C* [CD] Touch, TO:30.
- ▶ Phil Jeck *Vinyl Coda I-III* [CD] Intermedium, INTER 002
- ▶ Christian Marclay *More Encores* [CD] Recommended, RER CM1.
- ▶ Kaffe Matthews *ebb + flow* Annette Works [CD] AWCD0005-6.
- ▶ Merzbow *Merzbox Sampler* [CD] Extreme, XLTD 003.
- ▶ Negativland *These Guys Are From England and Who Gives A Shit* [CD] Seeland, 0021.
- ▶ John Oswald *69 Plunderphonics 96* [CD] Seeland, 515.
- ▶ Steve Roden *Four Possible Landscapes* [CD] Trente Oiseaux, TOC00.
- ▶ Scanner *Lauwarm Instrumentals* [CD] Sulphur, SULCD002.
- ▶ Squarepusher *Feed Me Weird Things* [CD] Rephlex, CAT037CD.

Project 43 (Advanced): Digital Minimalism

Introduction

This is a project with a strong research element and a possible performative or compositional outcome. It could, however, equally well form the basis of an essay or seminar presentation.

The Project

Investigate and research musical 'minimalism'. To what extent does it relate to minimalism in the other arts and architecture? And to what extent is it evident in digital music? Extend the research by making and/or performing a piece of digital minimalist music.

Notes

Suggested reading:
Baker, K., *Minimalism: Art of Circumstance*, London: Abbeville Press, 1988.
Batchelor, D., *Minimalism*, London: Tate Gallery Publishing, 1997.
Battock, G. (ed.), *Minimal Art: A Critical Anthology*, London: Studio Vista, 1969.
Griffiths, P., *A Guide to Electronic Music*, London: Thames and Hudson, 1979.
Mertens, W., *American Minimal Music*, London: Kahn and Averill, 1983.
Meyer, J. (ed.), *Minimalism*, New York: Phaidon Press, 2000.
Nyman, M., *Experimental Music: Cage and Beyond*, Cambridge: Cambridge University Press, 1999.
Potter, K., *Four Musical Minimalists*, Cambridge: Cambridge University Press, 2000.
Prendergast, M., *The Ambient Century: From Mahler to Trance – The Evolution of Sound in the Electronic Age*, London: Bloomsbury Publishing, 2000.
Salzman, E., *Twentieth-Century Music: An Introduction*, New York: Prentice-Hall, 1974.

Suggested listening:
Gavin Bryars (1975) *Jesus' Blood Never Failed Me Yet* [CD] Point Music 438–823–2.
CHIC (1979) *Good Times* [CD] Atlantic.
Brian Eno/ Harold Budd (1979) *Music for Airports #2: The Plateaux of Mirror* [CD] EG Records.
Philip Glass (1969) *Music in Similar Motion* [CD] Nonesuch.
Philip Glass (1983) *Koyaanisqatsi* [CD] Antilles/Island.
Bernhard Günter (1999) *univers/temporel/espoirs* [CD] Trente Oiseaux TOC991.
Tetsu Inoue (1994) *Ambiant Otaku* [CD] Fax.
Kraftwerk (1976) *TransEurope Express* [CD] EMI/Capitol.
Alvin Lucier (1992) *Music on a Long Thin Wire* [CD] Lovely, LCD1011.
Derrick May (1996) *Innovator* [CD] Transmat.
Mike Oldfield (1973) *Tubular Bells* [CD] Virgin.
Orbital (1993) 'Halcyon + on + on' on *Orbital 2* [CD] FFRR Records.
Steve Reich (1970) *Drumming* [CD] Deutsches Grammophon.
Steve Roden (2003) *three roots carved to look like stones* [CD] Sonaris. Terry Riley (1964) *In C* [CD] 20th Century Classical.
La Monte Young (1969) 'Excerpts from Map of 49's Dream The Two Systems of Eleven Sets of Galactic Intervals' on *OHM: The Early Gurus of Electronic Music: 1948–1980* [CD] Roslyn, New York: Ellipsis Arts.

PROJECT 43

NOTATION

The various forms of computer representation of sound have already been discussed. Such scientific representations do convey a large amount of useful information, but they also have drawbacks. From a musical point of view, they need to be decoded or 'read'. They have an inherent analytical quality which is excellent for understanding the detailed frequency content of a short sonic moment, for example, but less useful for revealing the musical function or context of that sound. A less accurate, but possibly more musical, way of representing sound, therefore, is the *pictogram*.

Pictography is a pictorial form of writing. Typical examples include hieroglyphs and cuneiform, a system of writing dating back to the Sumerian civilization around 3000 BC. Pictograms resemble the thing they represent (as opposed to ideograms, which convey ideas) and many early cuneiform symbols had a phonetic value; in other words, they represented a vocal sound. A pictogram in a digital–music context may therefore be defined as *any* symbol or image which represents a given sound or collection of sounds. Music notation is one form of pictogram, but it is usually inadequate for digital sound. However, there is no generally agreed set of pictograms that is used to represent sounds, so individuals or groups will often devise their own. Three concentric circles might represent the sound of a raindrop, for example, but so might a dot, or a tick, or any other appropriate symbol.

Despite this tendency to idiosyncrasy and imprecision, pictograms are actually often used in digital sound representation. They mainly appear in various kinds of 'aural score', in which graphical indications of sound location, musical gesture, frequency and amplitude content are useful for diffusion, synchronization or analysis. One special case is the 'evocative transcription', in which a graphic representation of sounds and music is created mostly for analytical purposes. These pictograms may be subjectively designed but are nevertheless often quite clear as to their sonic and musical meanings. One classic example from an aural score is given in Figure 12.1.

Artikulation is a tape piece composed in 1958 by György Ligeti. Rainer Wehinger made his aural score with reference to Ligeti's compositional notes. The full score is in colour (see the book website for an excerpt), and the various symbols relate to aspects of the music. The dots represent filtered (pitched) or unfiltered impulses; the combs

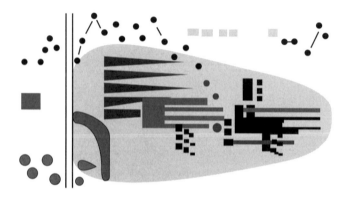

Figure 12.1 Excerpt from an 'aural score' by Rainer Wehinger of *Artikulation* (1958) by György Ligeti © Schotts Ltd

represent harmonic and sub-harmonic spectra; the thick lines and blocks are pitched sine tones (so the declining line near the start is a rapidly descending pitch); and the shaped background field indicates resonance. Time runs from left to right, and the higher the symbol on the page, the higher the pitch. Such aural scores are not reproducible in a performance situation, of course, so are not strictly 'scores' as the term is traditionally understood. They are rather more suitable as *evocative transcriptions*, which have great use in analysis of digital music, as will be discussed later. Annotated spectrograms and other digital representations also crop up in electro-acoustic music analysis.

ANALYSIS

The purpose of music analysis is to reveal how music works. In traditional notated music, the elements of harmony, melody, rhythm and so on, could be analysed with reference to a score. This led to an assumption that the methodologies of music analysis are abstract. In other words, it was considered acceptable to analyse the music divorced either from its social and political context, or from its effects on the listener. In fact, even traditional musical analysis usually made some effort to account for such apparently extra-musical aspects, but the way they were described was sometimes so impressionistic as to be useless as analysis.

This is one of the great challenges for analysis: how to go beyond the merely descriptive towards something that has some 'scientific' foundation. Both ethnomusicologists and analysts have consequently adopted many of the approaches outlined by critical theory. Various methods of music analysis have emerged, ranging from the structuralist (such as Lerdahl and Jackendoff's 'generative' attempts[7] to specify the linguistic structures that an informed listener hears in a piece of music), through to the anthropological (such as the work of John Blacking[8] and many others that attempt to analyse music in terms of its social function in world cultures). When analysing electronic and electro-acoustic music, however, some of these methods and approaches can become rather problematic. The tools that work for, say, tonal music or folk music are less satisfactory for analysing a music based on sounds or samples. Harmony, melody and rhythm are not necessarily the main constituents of this music. An analysis of a timbre presents specific difficulties that soon challenge the capabilities of the written word. A piece constructed from digitally processed water sounds lacks the note-to-note procedures that lend themselves well to a database-driven, structuralist approach. The social function of a musical language that is not obviously vernacular can be hard to articulate. The difficulties that are faced by analysts of this music therefore include establishing typologies of sound and standardized analytical terminologies and procedures, through to identifying common musical languages or sets of shared practices.

Techniques for analysing digital music are in their infancy. Just as the computer has expanded the language of the music itself, so it has made available new tools for analytical purposes. However, this is an emerging field, and there is no generally agreed analytical methodology, and the tools are in a state of continuous evolution. What follows is therefore an indicative survey of possible approaches, and some projects that will focus analytical thinking. It should always be borne in mind that any analysis of a piece of music is partial. What matters is the extent to which it offers insights and aids understanding of the music in question.

A *parametric* analysis tends to focus upon Nattiez's 'neutral level', in that it tells the reader what happens when, and perhaps how. The conventional musical mileposts of bars or measures, key changes and themes, are usually absent in digital music, so the best method is to give timings to indicate the locations of significant sonic events. However, it is important not to ignore the musical features of the work, so any sign of repetition or variation, modality or tonality, rhythmic structures or regular patterns, even phrases and melodies, should be indicated as an overlay on the timing graph.

Parametric analytical methods have included approaches based on Schaeffer's catalogues of sound-objects. In the *Traité des objets musicaux* (1966), he identifies morphologies (such as mass, timbre, harmony, dynamics, grain, allure, profile) and typologies that classify sounds by factors such as duration, variation, equilibrium and so on. *Typo-morphology* has formed the basis of subsequent approaches by analysts such as Denis Smalley and Stéphane Roy. Both these have developed extensive classification systems for sounds, with a view to creating listening analyses of electro-acoustic music. Simon Emmerson extends such listening analysis into a field of discourse, either aural (abstract musical) or mimetic (imitation of nature), within which music may express itself through a purely abstract syntax or an abstracted syntax derived from the materials themselves. He proposes the language grid provided in Table 12.2, which shows a range of possibilities, within which he convincingly places selected works from the electro-acoustic repertoire.[9]

The works selected as examples are as follows:

1. Milton Babbitt *Ensembles for Synthesizer*.
2. Jonathan Harvey *Mortuous Plango, Vivos Voco*.
3. Denis Smalley *Pentes*.
4. Luigi Nono *La Fabbrica Illuminata*.
5. Michael McNabb *Dreamsong*.
6. Bernard Parmegiani *Dedans-Dehors*.
7. Karlheinz Stockhausen *Telemusik*.
8. Trevor Wishart *Red Bird*.
9. Luc Ferrari *Presque Rien No. 1*.

The tools of parametric analysis may include many kinds of visualization, such as sonograms and spectrograms, diffusion and graphic scores, computer data files and other

Table 12.2   Simon Emmerson's 'Language Grid'

	I: Aural discourse dominant	II: Combination of aural and mimetic discourse	III: Mimetic discourse dominant
Abstract syntax	1	4	7
Combination of abstract and abstracted syntax	2	5	8
Abstracted syntax	3	6	9

|_____   MUSICAL DISCOURSE   ____|

multimedia representations. In recent years, some software explicitly designed for para-metric analysis has been made available, such as the *Acousmographe* (by the Groupe de Recherches Musicales) and *iAnalyse* by Pierre Couprie. No doubt many more such tools will become available as techniques improve.

Whereas a parametric analysis objectively describes what we perceive, a more sub-jective approach is an *affective* analysis. This focuses upon the way in which the music affects the listener, but also to some extent on the way in which it achieves that effect. This may be linked to the perceived intentions of the artist, or to the cultural context for the work. Such subjectivity does not inevitably produce vague, unscientific, infor-mation. A group affective analysis, in particular, can be revealing, as common reactions and threads are drawn out by a neutral figure (usually an educator). In some situations, this kind of analysis may be best deployed before the parametric analysis, in order to ensure the listeners' full attention is engaged by the work. The degree of interpretation will often depend upon the method used, whether a graphic score or a language-based description.

François Delalande is a leading exponent of this approach to analysis, using listening sessions to gather information about people's subjective experiences and understandings of the music. In his opinion, there can be no definitive analysis because of the subjec-tivity of the listening experience. He identifies three types of listening: *taxonomic*, in which listeners get an overall picture of a work and identify (and may attempt to memorize) contrasts and changes; *empathic*, in which people respond only to the feelings that the music produces in them; and *figurative*, in which the listener creates a personal set of images or metaphors that seem to represent something or tell a story in the music.[10]

A different approach is implied by a socio-cultural or anthroplogical analysis. Here the interest is not so much in the music itself, but rather in the social and cultural position it occupies. Once again, semiotics may be a useful tool, and also some of the methods of social science. A *quantitative* method uses empirical observation and mathematical or statistical information to support its hypotheses. This is probably a less practical (although not impossible) method for music analysis than the *qualitative* methods, which investigate the 'why' and the 'how' of decision-making. A qualitative analysis relies on case stud-ies supported by interviews and other data gathering, so it is important for any socio-cultural analysis to have access to this kind of information. A typical socio-cultural or anthropological analysis might explore, for example, why and how a particular musical genre arose from a particular group at a particular time.

Comparative analyses, which treat musical examples as cultural 'texts', can be help-ful. The aim is to compare and contrast two or more pieces of music. The first step is to identify the frame of reference for the comparison, which might be an idea or theme, a specific question or even a theory. Next, establish the grounds for the comparison by giving reasons for the choices. Now develop the argument by exploring the relation-ships between the two chosen pieces, indicating where they appear to complement or contradict one another. This can be presented as a separate discussion of the two works, or as a point-by-point comparison. Finally, some appropriate conclusions should be drawn. This method is a staple of literary criticism and forms the basis of many examina-tion questions and student essays in the humanities. However, the phrase also crops up in computer science, economics, and social science with a somewhat different meaning and often used for predicting the behaviour of a system.

Genetic analysis focuses on the compositional process and requires access to all the materials that were used in the creation of a work. Another approach is to look at the historical position of a work, its influence and effects on future composition. Perhaps a suitable word for this would be *entropic*, to borrow a technical term from the physical sciences to describe the way in which things proceed over time. This also requires considerable access to documentary evidence.

All these analytical approaches presume that the 'work' being analysed is a fixed entity that already exists in a completed state. This is by no means the only way to approach analysis, and the creative or making process itself contains an analytical element. *Practical* analysis therefore links directly to the notions of reflective practice, critical engagement and cultural content discussed earlier. Even the understanding, representation and processing of digital sound itself has a considerable analytical relevance, and the computer can be cautiously introduced as an analytical tool at any stage of the process. A spectrogram may be an 'analytical' representation of a sound, but it also needs to be decoded and the sound placed in a context if the analysis is to reveal anything very much about how the music works. Nevertheless, there is a perpetual loop between creation and analysis which is part of the musical process itself and may be captured in some form for analytical purposes.

Analysing interactive music in particular might take on a documentary form that enables such practical analysis. Computational records of the interactions between human and machine, or machine and machine, may be combined with multimedia capture of the same interactions, in order to build up a picture of the experience of the work. This may apply in artistically driven situations, but also in gameplay. The analysis of sound and music in computer games is an underdeveloped field, but it is clear that interactivity takes it beyond merely a question of a soundtrack in many cases. Since much interactive music is built in a modular way, obtaining the patches and relevant computer code may be regarded as a basic first step towards an analysis. The documentary records may then be used to demonstrate decision-making processes and choices made in the work. The extent to which those choices are based on aesthetic or cultural factors will provide another layer to the analysis.

FURTHER READING

- Delalande, F., 'Music Analysis and Reception Behaviours: *Sommeil* by Pierre Henry', *Journal of New Music Research*, 27:1–2, 1998, 13–66.

- Emmerson, S., 'Relation of Language to Materials', *The Language of Electroacoustic Music*, London: Macmillan, 1986, 17–39.

- Hugill, A., 'Towards an analysis of Papa Sangre, an audio-only game for the iPhone/iPad.' Available HTTP: http://www.orema.dmu.ac.uk (accessed 20 April 2012).

- Lerdahl, F. and Jackendoff, R., *A Generative Theory of Tonal Music*, Cambridge, MA, and London: MIT Press, 1983/1999.

EVOCATIVE TRANSCRIPTION

One excellent way to begin the process of analysis, which can incorporate all of the above approaches to some extent, is to make an Evocative Transcription. By creating a system of graphic symbols to represent the parameters of the music, analysts can both notate an 'aural score' and develop their listening skills and perceptions. Extending this into a Flash movie can further create a useful 'real-time' map of the work. The Evocative Transcription can also be useful evidence of analytical listening.

In traditional music, a *transcription* is a rewritten version of something previously heard in a different medium. One classic example is the piano transcription; very popular in the nineteenth century, when whole operas or symphonies would be reduced to a playable version for the home pianist. The composer Ferruccio Busoni who was a master of the technique of piano transcription, took this idea one step further and, in his seminal text of 1911, *Sketch for a New Aesthetic of Music*, suggested that notated music is itself the transcription of a musical idea: 'from the moment the pen touches the paper, the idea loses its original form'.

For Busoni, this was a loss, and his essay may in many ways be seen as a protest against the limitations of the musical language of his day, and even an anticipation of technological developments that were to follow. It is not necessary to follow Busoni all the way down this path in order to recognize that a transcription is not, and can never be, the same as what it transcribes, and yet contains sufficiently recognizable features to *evoke* the music in the mind of the listener.

The notation of digital music, particularly where it is based upon spectral information, can often be problematic, because the emphasis is upon the aural element. However, in order to develop the ear, it can be beneficial to attempt to transcribe what is heard into some form of visual (or even verbal) representation. This is not in order to use the result as a basis for a reconstruction of its model, but rather as an evocation, or a reference for understanding the content of what is heard.

The first step in making an Evocative Transcription of a chosen piece of electronic or electro-acoustic music is to devise a system of symbols. This is rather subjective, but might include a time and frequency line (possibly a graph), and a system of colours or shapes to indicate sound types, intensities, behaviours and so on. This can be done on paper, then extended into a digital format.

The next step is to make a paper evocative transcription, using the colours and shapes as described. The idea is to *evoke* the sounds of the music, rather than necessarily to represent them scientifically. At the same time, the transcription should accurately convey how the music works and aim to reveal something about its form and content.

Finally, and optionally, the image may be scanned into the computer, or animation software, such as Flash, may be used to create a movie that corresponds to the music. Notice that this is *not* the same process as creating a music video, although the results may be visually engaging.

The Evocative Transcription reveals to what extent, and how accurately, the transcriber has *heard*. Although such visualizations are not notations of music in the traditional sense, and certainly are no substitute for actual listening, their value lies in the extent to which they represent an act of conscious listening and reflection. The Flash version of this project makes explicit the similarities between, and limitations of, the process of digitizing sounds and images. The book website contains some excellent examples of evocative transcriptions made by students.

PROJECT 44

Project 44 (Advanced): Analysis Project

Introduction

This is a substantial and challenging project which is nonetheless simply stated. In all the options below, starting with an evocative transcription may be a useful first step. It is important, before commencing the project, to set some limits to the analysis. Decide on an approach and stick to that regardless of what may be missing in the final outcome. Remember, no analysis will ever be a complete explanation of a work.

The Project

Analyse a piece of digital music. Some possible works:

- Aphex Twin *Bucephalus Bouncing Ball* (Track 4 on *Come to Daddy*)
- Boards of Canada *Telephasic Workshop* (Track 4 on *Music has the right to children*)
- Francis Dhomont *Chambre d'enfants* (Track 1 on *Forêt Profonde*).

Of course, any work of your own choice will also be suitable.

Notes

Adopt one of the approaches to analysis described in this chapter. The process should begin with repeated listenings. Notetaking may be introduced at some point during this phase. Try to identify the key ideas, structures, contrasts, and any other features of particular interest.

   The course of the analysis from here will depend very much on the approach decided upon. It will always be useful to gather as much background information about the pieces as possible.

   To produce a really thorough analysis could take several weeks, and plenty of time should be allowed for reflection between sessions of work.

Discussion Questions

- What is the role of the human hand or presence in digital music? Does music that lacks this presence lose or gain something? What might that be?

- What are the advantages and disadvantages of genre classification of music?

- How might you go beyond genre?

- What is the purpose of analysing digital music?

- How would you analyse interactive music?

- Is there a 'neutral layer' (Nattiez) of digital music?

PART IV

Being

The Digital World

What I like about the Futurists is that they didn't just make groundbreaking art and music: they published recipe books and had Futurist dinners too![1]

THE DIGITAL MUSICIAN

A 'digital musician' is typically an amalgamation of performer, composer, engineer and informed listener, all to a certain extent. It is highly likely that each individual will have more skills in one of these areas than the others. The 'sound designer', the 'sonic artist' and the 'digital musician' have overlapping skill sets and, for the purposes of this book, are practically the same. As Ronald Herrema points out, what all these people share is 'an understanding of the manipulation of sound in time, how that relates to gesture and how it relates to drama, or the dramaturgy of the work'.[2]

A digital musician is conscious of the questions posed in the Preface to this book. The time has come to attempt some succinct answers to those questions. This is not easy, because there is no single answer that is good for everyone. The following are the author's own personal responses, based on what is written here. The readers will, it is hoped, make their own replies.

All this potential to make music, but what music?
The music that has your voice, which has been found with integrity, out of curiosity, and through awareness.

What is there to 'say'?
John Cage said 'there is nothing to say, and I am saying it'.[3] This neat paradox illustrates the central purpose of music, or of any art: to reveal the human condition. There's no need to get too hung up about this – what needs to be said will be said.

Why create music?
The reasons are many. However, the most successful musician will not be somebody who wants to make music, but somebody who has to make music.

And what about existing music? How to approach that?
With cultural awareness and critical engagement.

And which music to approach?
The music that is unknown.

And how do we know what is good?
By forming our own judgements, informed by the judgements of our peers.

The rest of this chapter considers the practical aspects of being a digital musician, from the changing workplace to career paths, from business to education, looking at the various ways in which a living may be made and the issues that confront anybody working in this way in the creative and cultural industries.

THE CHANGING WORKPLACE

Over the past few decades, the workplace for any musician involved with technology has changed, from a large fixed recording studio, through a miniaturized version of the fixed studio called the digital audio workstation (DAW), to a laptop studio that is 'on the move'. The fixed studios and the DAWs still exist, of course, and the laptop equivalent is often modelled to a greater or lesser extent on them. In the recording studio situation, the digital musician is normally confronted with the paradox of a glass barrier that separates the 'musicians' from the 'engineers'. There is often an assumption that the former neither understand the work of the latter, nor are allowed to get involved. However, the most creative and productive musical developments often start when this demarcation breaks down.

To explore this point a little further, consider the works of Glenn Gould (1932–1982), Frank Zappa (1940–1993) and Sir George Martin (b. 1926): three quite different artists who all saw the potential of the recording studio and devoted much, even nearly all, their careers to the use of the studio as a creative device.

Glenn Gould was a virtuoso concert pianist who gave up performing in 1964 because he preferred to work in the studio. He saw tape-editing as part of the creative process, and positively embraced the use of dubbing to produce effects that are not possible in live performance. The second of his two recordings of Bach's *Goldberg Variations*, made in 1981, was the first digital recording issued by CBS. There is much documentation by and about Gould, including several documentaries and a film: *Thirty Two Short Films about Glenn Gould* (1993, dir. Don McKellar). The Glenn Gould archive is also available online.[4]

Frank Zappa managed to fuse many different musical styles and idioms during his prolific career, including rock, jazz, R&B, doo-wop, disco, reggae, new wave, serial and electronic music. The methods he used, even in live performance, were based on an almost obsessive use of the recording studio, where he developed unique techniques with many pieces of equipment. These included 'xenochrony' or, literally, 'strange time', which used a collection of material (usually guitar solos) as a kind of database to be accessed and included anywhere on an album. Many writers have discussed Zappa's 'intertextuality' and his critical stance towards the 'culture industry',[5] and Zappa himself gives an entertaining account of his career in *The Real Frank Zappa Book* (co-written with Peter Occhiogrosso).

George Martin is often called 'the fifth Beatle', because his mastery of the recording studio was so crucial to the sound produced by the 'Fab Four' as they moved increasingly towards studio albums. He worked with a vast array of other artists too and may justly claim to be the most influential record producer of all time. There is so much documentation about his work that further discussion is largely unnecessary. However, at the time of writing, he (with his son Giles) has just issued 'Love', an experimental digital remix from original Beatles tapes.

The DAW represents a logical development from such studio creativity, by placing both the recording and editing tools in the hands of the digital musician and, in effect, making everyone a potential Glenn Gould, Frank Zappa or George Martin. This does not entirely remove the need for high-quality recording studios, however, because most DAWs do not have the kind of sound-isolated environments, monitoring set-ups and recording equipment needed to produce the best results. The laptop workstation embraces those very limitations, reinforced by ever-greater processing power, data-storage capability and accuracy, along with mobile connectivity. Audio quality and monitoring have improved, but also the limitations of the portable system have become a conditioning factor for the music itself.

There has been one very significant consequence for music-making from these changes to the workplace. The typical computer workstation is designed for the single user, often further isolated under a pair of headphones. The act of music-making becomes an act of production, with perhaps a CD or DVD, film or website as the outcome. This object may be passed on, once again, with only minimal social contact. If the musician in question does not engage in live performance, then he or she becomes an almost completely isolated figure. It should be stated and restated that *music is a social activity*. Isolation can be musically unhealthy, and the pervasive culture of individualism has a downside.

Another consequence has been for the notion of *repertoire*. Whereas in the past there were generally agreed bodies of repertoire which all musicians could share, the tendency of digital culture towards individualism is creating a situation where each musician invents their own. One of the major challenges facing the digital musician, then, is how to engage musically with others, including the public. Such engagements can take place live or across a network, but social and acoustic communication are crucial to their success. The new generation of social-networking tools on the Web have made it easier for digital musicians to connect with others, but these will never entirely substitute for face-to-face interaction.

Digital musicians will find themselves in a range of situations beyond the studio or workstation. Real-time music-making and studio production have expanded to include a range of new media and multimedia situations. The phrase 'real time' means that there is no significant time gap between the production of a sound and the listener's perception of it. So, a conventional live concert is real time, but so are many types of network performance and life-linked performance activities. The live concert situation covers a vast array of different activities ranging from laptop gigs to electro-acoustic music concerts, from working with traditional orchestras and ensembles to playing with bands or solo. The role of the digital musician may be different in these situations: here, as a performer originating sound; there, as a diffuser projecting sound into a space; here, as a DJ or turntablist; there, computer programming.

Musical performance does not have to be delivered in a traditional situation. In fact, many digital musicians prefer to avoid the conventions of a concert. Life-linked perform- ance, where there is a seamless transition between daily life and the performance activ- ity, has increased steadily since its early days in the 1960s. The use of mobile and Flash technologies, real-time sampling and soundscape composition, as well as the activities of bootleggers and plunderphonicists, hackers and net-artists, can create a situation where the distinction between the 'concert' and 'life' breaks down. Here, the digital musicians develop a reciprocal relationship with their cultural context. They become their own audience but, at the same time, the wider audience (the 'non-musicians') are drawn into the musical process to the extent that they can share in becoming musicians.

An interesting special case is *telepresence*, in which a live musician may interact with a virtual entity or in a remote environment. This gives the experience of being fully present at a live real-world location but remote from the actual physical location. Some- one experiencing telepresence would therefore be able to behave, and receive stimuli, as though at the remote site. This is an unusual (and currently fairly rare) musical situation that presents particular challenges and properties. To achieve good results through per- formance requires first what might be called 'action and agency' (audible and visual cues) and then 'choice and intention'; in other words, the psychological aspects of musical activity. There needs to be a human presence in the social area that is the auditorium.

What is intriguing about the role of the digital musician in the above situations is the extent to which it changes day by day and hour by hour, moving from a performative mode here to a compositional mode there, from originating creator to critical listener. This is especially evident in the context of *interart* such as music for theatre, dance, per- formance, interactive installations, video art and so on. The extent to which new media and new technologies appear in these contexts will determine to what extent the musi- cian draws upon the knowledge and skills discussed in this book, but it is clear that there is an increasingly subtle use of digital technologies in everything from virtual environ- ments to sound environments, from *son et lumière* to *cirques de soleil*.[6]

FURTHER READING

- Kac, E., *Telepresence, Biotelematics, Transgenic Art*, Maribor: KIBLA, 2000.
  A collection of essays about Eduardo Kac's work, which ranges from telepresence to transgenic art.

- Nisbett, A., *The Sound Studio: Audio Techniques for Radio, Television, Film and Recording*, Oxford: Focal Press, 2004.
  A classic and encyclopedic work on studio techniques.

- Rumsey, F., *The Audio Workstation Handbook*, Oxford: Focal Press, 1996.
  A thorough introduction to all technical aspects of the DAW.

CAREERS

Given the enormous range and diversity of these situations, it might be objected that we are in fact talking about several different types of musician, who work in one or other of these areas. It is certainly true that it is unlikely that a single individual will undertake work in *all* these situations in a lifetime. To develop a career, it is probably necessary to specialize to a certain degree. However, the digital musician who has acquired the skills outlined in this book *could* work in any of these situations, because the technology allows it and because there are certain musical abilities that are useful in all of them. In other words, the skills of a digital musician are transferable. The application of these skills in the development of a career is a skill in itself. The challenge facing digital musicians is to find a situation for their work, to exchange, to disseminate.

The hardest thing for a digital musician to decide is not what skills should be acquired but what *not* to learn. Given that the skill set draws upon so many different and well-established disciplines, it is always possible to go further into any one of them in order to specialize in a particular area. A theme that emerges, therefore, is the sheer number and variety of employment situations or careers. Here is a quick list of just *some* of them: programmer, music and effects for games, music and effects for cinema (location sound, ADR, Foley, sound effects, re-recording engineer, composer, session engineer, etc.), music and effects for industrial video, audio-loops designer, audio-effects designer, mobile phone ringtone designer, radio producer, studio engineer, record producer, mastering engineer, music-related retail sales, music software support, jingle writing, music-events producer, live-sound engineer, band member, session musician, arts administrator, self-promoted musician, internet-based microsales, record-label manager, talent scout, A&R (artist and repertoire) representative, acoustic designer, arts/sound museum/events coordinator, events/festivals technical support, PA system consulting and installation, DSP inventor, instrument inventor, writer for electronic music magazines, sound for web (commercial record sales samples, sound design for sites, interactive sound), bulk media reproduction, teaching, music therapy, new-age market (relaxation tapes, mind manipulation, etc.), Muzak, corporate sonic environments, multimedia development, busking, lawyer, music librarian, artist.

Most of these (and the list is by no means complete) have the capacity to offer either full-time or, more likely, part-time or temporary employment. Much of the work in digital music is freelance. Digital musicians, ready to respond to a variety of situations and demands, can transfer knowledge and skills from one arena to another. They are multi-faceted, and their skills can always be applied. But, as everybody knows, the job market changes as constantly as the rest of culture. To enter this market, therefore, requires a willingness to change and engage in different activities.

Many of the jobs are in emerging areas relating to new media. It is hard to predict exactly how these emerging areas will develop, so the skills and abilities outlined in this book may be regarded as basic prerequisites for most situations, but the need to specialize will also be important as the career develops and the culture changes. To give a simple example: thirty-five years ago the Internet did not exist, but now it is a fact of life. Those musicians who have adapted to the Internet are achieving a greater success than those who have not.

It is most likely that the digital musician will mix freelance work with performing, composition, perhaps some teaching, and other sources of income. Roughly half the time will be spent handling administration and business matters. This aspect of a career can be demanding and is essential, but must not be allowed to overshadow the creative work. Achieving a balance between these elements is the key to a successful career. Freelance work can be very rewarding but requires excellent time management and business skills, and ultimately lacks the stability of salaried work. Making a living as a performer is a commitment to an enormous amount of gigging and touring, and can be a difficult lifestyle at times. Managing fees and travel, organizing venues, technical specifications, sound checks, and all the rest, is probably more than one person can handle. Composition can pay dividends, but commissions come through personal recommendations more often than not, and so rely on good personal networking skills and, of course, high-quality music.

It is a good idea to get involved in a programme of workshops that are routinely offered in most cities. By participating in this experimental culture, important contacts and understanding may be gained. Workshops are generally a two-way process, and if well handled by the tutor can be genuinely empowering for participants. Establishing a free and open atmosphere, in which 'mistakes' do not matter, is a skill which workshop leaders must cultivate. The best way to learn this is by being a participant. In time, you may become a workshop leader yourself, which is excellent training for many teaching situations. Part-time or occasional work in universities and colleges may well present itself if this path is followed alongside a career as an artist. Teaching in schools, of course, requires appropriate qualifications. In fact, teaching in universities and colleges also tends to lead to academic qualifications, although real-world experience may well be a great help.

Once again, the challenge is to identify the fixed elements in a changing world. Industrial models are often invoked to describe the digital-music culture, such as: 'the music industry', 'the entertainments industry', 'the cultural industries' or 'the creative industries'. Where the work undertaken is purely commercial, these models can be useful, and the 'product' (whether music or musician) can be successful within that context. However, a more fluid approach is often needed, particularly where the work is either non-commercial or unclear in its industrial aim. There are porous boundaries between contexts, between subcultures, between industries. Music flows, and music's contexts change. The digital arts and technologies tend to blur into one another, and the people who work in those areas often have ill-defined roles. In fact, many successful digital musicians may never have set out to be musicians in the first place. They may have found themselves making sound or music by accident or default.

FURTHER READING

- Kusek, D. and Leonhard, G., *The Future of Music: Manifesto for the Digital Revolution*, Boston, MA: Berklee Press, 2005.
  A challenging look at the effects of the digital revolution on the music industry. Predicts 'a future in which music will be like water: ubiquitous and free-flowing.'

- Sound and Music (2011) *Artists' Toolkit*. http://www.soundandmusic.org/artist-area/artists-toolkit.
  A very useful collection of web resources that cover most aspects of life as a digital musician. Although aimed at the UK, much of its content is applicable in any country.

BUSINESS

In matters of business, there is little difference between being a 'digital' and a 'non-digital' musician. Good organization and time management are as crucial to the digital musician as to any other creative or performing person and form a significant aspect of any attempt at self-promotion. Musicians of all types live by their calendars and contacts. It is vital to have these in good order.

Financial management is also essential. You will need to be able to issue invoices and manage paying bills. Keeping a record of expenses, with receipts, will be necessary in most freelance situations involving external funding. Preparing tax returns is also a reality of life with certain unique features for a digital musician. Performance clothing, home studio equipment, software, and many more such items that are part of a professional life may be set against tax. However, collecting royalties and setting necessary expenses are complicated procedures that may well benefit from the assistance of an accountant.

Lawyers, too, are a good idea if moving into contractual negotiations with large companies. There are enough horror stories about musicians being exploited to make anyone think twice before entering a significant contractual negotiation without the support of a lawyer. However, they are not necessary for small-scale, day-to-day activities. Depending on the type of work that you do, you may wish to issue contracts. The range of contracts includes band agreements, performance agreements (basic and advanced), publishing agreements, sound contracting agreements and many more. Each has its own tax liability implications. There is much good free advice available online about contracts, but sooner or later it is likely that legal advice will be required – it's a matter of judgement.

Intellectual property rights, and copyright, are one of the main ways in which money may be made, so an understanding of the basic principles is important. However, this is a notoriously complex area so once again professional advice may become necessary at some point. The consequences of a mistake in this field can be severe, so it pays to get this right. The creator of a piece of music (i.e., the composer) owns the copyright provided it has been self-assigned. Writing 'copyright (or ©), name, date' on the work should be sufficient as an assignment, but some people take the precaution of mailing a copy to themselves and keeping it unopened for the date stamp, or depositing it in a secure vault. In many cases, the composer will assign copyright to a publisher, who then will own the work and license it for use under an agreement with the composer. Performers also have rights in their own performances, as do record companies in their own recordings. These are all a matter for contractual negotiation at the time of the creation of the work.

Royalties are normally collected through a performing rights society which licenses premises and venues. These royalties are then redistributed to rights holders on a complex formula basis. There are in fact many forms of rights, including: audiovisual rights (for multimedia); synchronization rights (for soundtracks); master use rights (for master recordings); grand rights (for dramatic works such as operas and musicals); public performance rights; and mechanical rights (issued on a fee-per-unit-sold basis). Copyright itself normally expires seventy years after the death of an artist. Using a work in any way without the permission of the rights holders is a breach of copyright and is against the law. Penalties for such misuse may be severe. Record companies in particular are extremely vigilant about such abuses.

Finally, there are moral rights, which are:

> what might happen if a license is granted and someone used the music in way that the composer doesn't like. A composer can say, first of all that he insists he is credited as the composer of the work whenever it is used with certain exceptions, such as if it's distorted or mutilated in a way that will damage the integrity of the work. A classic example is if permission is granted to use music in a film and it turns out that it's a pornographic film or that it promotes a product that the composer doesn't agree with like tobacco or alcohol. He might be able to evoke his moral rights in that situation.[7]

'Royalty free music' refers to music that may be used without royalties, but only in certain specified circumstances. It does *not* mean the music is generally free from royalties. Creative Commons offers a standardized alternative to traditional copyright licences, by allowing licensors to retain copyright while allowing others to copy, distribute and make some uses of their work. There are several varieties of Creative Commons licence,[8] all of which require credit being given to the licensor. A more anarchic venture is the Free Music Philosophy which, as its name implies, allows work to be freely copied, covered, or otherwise manipulated without copyright implications. This does not mean, however, that Free Music artists cannot charge money for their work.

The evolution of digital music rights has been famously tortuous and slow. Peer-to-peer file sharing (e.g., Napster) has largely given way to paid download services, such as Apple's iTunes, which are beginning to dominate a culture which has traditionally assumed that everything is free. Various forms of digital rights management software and encryptions have been deployed to try to prevent piracy and illegal copying. These have been the subject of much controversy, with objections ranging from the technical (incompatibilities between systems) to the political (infringements of civil liberties) to the philosophical (music needs to share freely in order to evolve). Advocates of a 'rip, mix, burn' culture are engaged in an ongoing battle with the traditional business models and practices of record companies and other commercial organizations. For some people, this *is* the culture that feeds creativity and this battleground contains the very essence of what it means to be a digital musician. 'Mash-up' is a practice that is enabled by digital technologies and is the modern mode.

Licensing authorities are responding to this by creating single online licences to cover all situations which require permissions, thus overcoming the convergence of technologies that encourages multiple copying. They are also increasingly working in an international way to provide global licensing and protection. At the same time, they are making efforts to seek out and prosecute illegal piracy. As more people become willing to pay for downloaded content, there will probably be a cultural change with regard to these issues. In the meantime, it should be pointed out that

> from a copyright perspective, the use of music on the internet is no different to any other so-called 'off-line' uses … In most cases, there are two 'copyrights' to be considered: the one in the musical work, song, composition or whatever, and the one in the sound recordings of the song, composition, etc.[9]

If this is always borne in mind, digital musicians should be confident of staying on the right side of the law.

Beyond all this, the business aspects of being a digital musician are largely a matter of deciding to what extent to deal with other professional services. Arts managers and agents exist and may, under certain circumstances, be useful, depending upon the kind of career that is being developed. Music publishers, too, where appropriate, will provide a degree of management and guidance. Insurance will be necessary at various points and, since premiums are often high for musicians, getting advice and 'shopping around' will be a wise move. Union membership may well offer assistance and protection in many respects. There are also various societies for musicians and self-organizing groups for mutual benefit.

On the whole, the digital musician is a self-managing entity and would be well advised to retain as much artistic control over his or her product as possible. It is generally not a good idea to grab a deal at any price. If there is sufficient interest in the work for one deal to be on offer, then often another, perhaps more favourable, deal may be found. There is an inevitable tension between the artistic and business aspects of any career. For some, working in a commercial way is anathema, for others it is the purpose of making music. Yet it is true to say that, whatever your motivation, business activities are an inevitable part of life as a musician, and it is usually best to embrace them wholeheartedly and not see them as an obstruction to creative work. Even if you are making music as a pastime rather than a profession, there is something to be said for adopting sound business practice. For music to gain ground as a respectable career, then all those who work in it should behave in a professional manner. This has not always been the case, and musicians as a group sometimes have quite a poor reputation. This leaves them all too often vulnerable to sharp practice, and is something that can only be changed by the community of musicians itself.

FURTHER READING

- Borg, B., *The Musician's Handbook: A Practical Guide to Understanding the Music Business*, 2008.
  Includes pricing and legal structures, lists of contacts, agents, and a range of practical information.

- Halloran, M., *The Musician's Business and Legal Guide*, Boston: Pearson, 1996.
  Written specifically for musicians by legal and business experts in the music industry, this text covers nearly all of the confusing business and legal situations musicians find themselves in on the way to and through a professional career.

- Schwartz, D. D. and Wilsey, D., *The Musician's Guide to Licensing Music: How to Get Your Music into Film, TV, Advertising, Digital Media & Beyond*, Hollywood: Billboard, 2008.
  Covers digital rights and licensing.

NETWORKING AND SELF-PROMOTION

Whatever the field of work, social networking and self-promotion are always essential if people are to be aware of a musician's name and abilities. This can be done in person or through third parties, through marketing or by reputation. The aim is to convince people of the value of the work, whether that is financial or artistic value. The digital musician, therefore, has a vested interest in avoiding contributing to activities that generally cheapen music, whether commercially or artistically. At the time of writing, the proliferation of cheap music (in both senses) is doing exactly that, and the service industries are becoming a major employer. If musicians are to avoid becoming only servants, then the digital musician needs to value both his or her skills and the work that he or she produces. This is not an argument against novel methods of dissemination but rather in favour of self-promotion. This sense of value *will* come across to a prospective client or employer.

There are certain situations where slick marketing techniques will produce results, but a far more important aspect of professionalism is the ability to be easy to work with and reliable. This is as much a question of interpersonal skills as musical abilities, is worth a thousand marketing campaigns and may be summarized by a common-sense statement: if other people find you a pleasure to work with, then they will call on you again. This skill is not easy to acquire, however. There will be many situations in which artistic goals contradict one another, or ideas and approaches fail to cohere. In a commercial situation, the client has bought the right to define and change the brief. In a non-commercial situation, individuals are free to define their own path but, even so, remember that everything a musician does will contribute towards their reputation. Word of mouth and contacts will get much further in any aspect of the music business than a slick image and an over-confident manner. Negotiating skills will also be essential, particularly when making artistic as well as the more obvious financial, contractual or professional decisions.

One unique aspect of all this for the digital musician is the need not only to know the market but also, to some extent, to *create* the market. Many of the skills they will bring to bear are unfamiliar to musicians, let alone to the non-musicians who often end up being clients or employers. This means that the musicians themselves will sometimes need to do some consciousness-raising about what it is that they do or bring. Many people in business will already have a notion that 'creativity' is valuable, but this will be quite unfocused. The musician will need to be ready to explain how digital creativity works and what makes it special. The level of detail in the explanation will be a judgement-call, because people vary in their ability to absorb either artistic or technical ideas, but at the same time it is important that the newness and uniqueness of the musician's activities comes across clearly. Doing so will be infectious, and the very presence of a digital musician will start to alter the surrounding culture. When people are meekly accepting clichés and well-worn formulae, it is the digital musician's job to show them the benefit of going beyond that and investing time, money and attention in interesting new areas.

The single most important aspect of networking and self-promotion for the digital musician is internet presence. This generally means building a website, but it can also mean rather more than that, so it needs to be considered separately. The Web is now the first port of call for anyone seeking information about anything. It is also the location for a great deal of cultural activity. The digital musician *must* have a website that is representative and accessible. It should include, as a bare minimum, a CV and biography, a portfolio of past and current work, some up-to-date news, links to other sites and contact information. It will also pay dividends to develop other forms of internet presence such as a blog or a personal web space where people can download the music, interact, make contact and so on. E-mail lists and online forums or discussion groups are also a good starting point, and the digital musician should join those which cover areas of interest. Some groups form around particular pieces of software, others around shared artistic or philosophical ideas. Such online communities form and dissolve rapidly, but what they all have in common is a shared and mutual interest on the part of their inhabitants.

The best way to become involved in an online community is to begin by 'lurking'; in other words, to become a member but say nothing for a while until the 'feel' of the group sinks in. However anonymous the characters may seem to be, there is always a real person behind the avatar or virtual character. People will often behave online in ways in which they would never behave in '3D'. This can make internet interaction quite different from real-world interaction. Speech, in particular, lacks a 'tone of voice', hence the pepperings of 'emoticons' (smiley faces, etc.) in online interaction. Remarks that are intended to be ironic or humorous can often be taken literally and give offence. Similar comments apply to online game playing and interaction in virtual worlds. Although the audio capability of these worlds is limited at the time of writing, it seems likely that it will improve. In some of the worlds, people build and sell or exchange virtual objects including musical instruments, give performances and concerts and design virtual environments. This can be a fertile situation for a digital musician, a different kind of 'real world'.

In the physical world, networking and promotion are usually done through collaboration and cooperation. It is a good idea to have some printed matter about yourself available for social situations: business cards, postcards, leaflets and so on. But collaboration goes beyond marketing and influences the work itself. Working with others is in fact a form of self-promotion, but not obviously advertised as such. Taking your work into venues, even as a solo artist, is a form of collaboration. You should take time to understand the venue and your position in its programme. Working with in-house staff around technical requirements and the acoustic characteristics of a space will do much to shape the performance or exhibition. This is even more true in non-traditional venues and site-specific work, which is an area of growth for digital music. The impact of a performance on the surrounding area, in terms of noise and health and safety issues, should always be considered in conjunction with the people who are staging the event. Relevant permissions and insurance may need to be obtained, risk should be thoroughly assessed and managed, and even something as apparently simple as power supply should not be taken for granted. Such practical matters might seem as though they have nothing to do with self-promotion, but in fact the way an individual deals with this will communicate very effectively to the very networks which might host future work.

From time to time, there will be opportunities to present about your work. Being able to talk clearly and authoritatively is a skill that requires considerable practice. However, its importance should not be underestimated, for it is the most effective form of self-promotion beyond the work itself. Finding the right language for the right situation is perhaps the most challenging aspect of this form of self-promotion. It pays to have a least two PowerPoint presentations available at any time on a laptop. These should be created with different audiences in mind and capable of rapid and easy editing. At the same time, you should be able to speak about your work without the support of any technology or musical examples. In either case, you should seek to convey the work's value, its context, its content, and your own creative identity as discussed earlier in this book. Just telling people how great you are tends to be counter-productive. On the other hand, being able to put across what drives you as an artist and musician can be inspirational. Being relatively inarticulate is not necessarily a disaster, provided the essence of the work is communicated effectively, but a confused, halting, or incoherent presentation can damage a career. It is always wise, therefore, to rehearse presentations with friends, colleagues and members of your peer group. It is this same group that, ultimately, will validate your position.

PROJECT 45

Project 45 (Intermediate): Pecha Kucha

Introduction

Pecha Kucha nights are now an established format for presentations in the creative industries. They began in 2003 in Tokyo, and were started by Astrid Klein and Mark Dytham of Klein Dytham Architecture as a way to attract customers to their nightclub. They now take place in many major cities around the world. The name derives from the Japanese for 'chit-chat'.

The Project

Up to fourteen presenters each give a slideshow of twenty images. Each slide is shown for 20 seconds, giving a total time of 6 minutes 40 seconds per presentation. Sounds may be included freely within the allotted time span. The presentations should focus upon a particular project or may be used as a summary of the presenter's work as a whole.

Notes

The advantage of the very tight timings is that presenters are obliged to be extremely focused. The format also allows for an uninterrupted flow of presentations, and Pecha Kucha nights normally develop a very convivial and energized atmosphere quite quickly. The range and diversity of the presentations can be both exciting and energizing, as well as informative.

FURTHER READING

- Kennedy, G., *Everything is Negotiable*, London: Cornerstone, 2010.
  First published in 1997, and recently updated for the third time, this is a book about business negotiation that has applications in all aspects of professional life.

- Kimpel, D., *Networking Strategies for the New Music Business*, Boston, MA: Artistpro, 2005.
  A guide to personal and professional networking techniques.

- Spellman, P., *The Self-Promoting Musician*, Boston, MA: Berklee Press, 2000.
  A guide to connecting you and your work with a public.

- Spellman, P., *The Musician's Internet*, Boston, MA: Berklee Press, 2002.
  Covers creating a website, online broadcasting, building a fan base and many other aspects of life online.

PRODUCTION AND PUBLISHING

Music production relies on software. To specify precisely *which* music software packages might be useful to the musician is futile, because the software market changes so rapidly. However, it is possible to identify generic types of music software, as follows:

- sound recording, editing and sequencing software
- processing applications (including plug-ins)
- software samplers
- virtual instruments
- synthesis software
- live-performance software
- notation software
- composition software
- analysis or representation software
- modular or build-it-yourself software.

Additions could be made to this list, in relation to new media, aural training and other less obviously musical applications, but the digital musician should know more than one example of each of the above. It is also highly advantageous to be able to work across platforms and, specifically, to have abilities in both the Windows and Mac operating systems. Knowledge of Linux and open-source systems and software may also be regarded as desirable.

Of course, software is always designed by somebody, and the nature of that design will often (although not always) be linked to a perceived commercial market. The digital musician will need to be aware that such software can try to steer musical content in a particular direction, even towards a specific genre or style. Sometimes music production is a matter of finding ways to achieve something original *in spite of* the software design. Everybody has favourite applications (usually the ones first learned), but in order to unlock the potential offered by a general understanding of computer music, the tendency to be driven by the design and interface of a particular piece of software must be overcome.

Unless the artist is very lucky indeed, the creative process will produce large quantities of discarded material along the way. This is by no means irrelevant to the final production, even if it is never heard. There can be confusion between process and product, even to the extent of regarding 'music production' as having a set of 'production values' which have nothing to do with creativity. This might derive from film, where the post-production phase is a separate part of the creative process. The contribution of George Martin's studio techniques and creativity to the *Sergeant Pepper's Lonely Hearts Club Band* album was as integral to the creative process as Paul's melodies, John's lyrics, George's guitar-playing and Ringo's drumming. Any musical 'product' is the result of a process, in which all the various elements have played a part.

Some composers produce a lot, some produce very little. This is unimportant unless it is *too* much or *too* little. But if musical integrity is to be the goal then, whatever the quantity of product, the creative process must be subject to some rigor, some set of value judgements. If fulfilling a commercial brief, then the client must be satisfied and the brief fulfilled to the highest standard. If working more freely, then the artistic imperatives of that particular project, of the musician's own beliefs, must be met. A compromise in these areas will result in a very short career. People are generally good at sniffing out a fraud.

In multimedia and new media, the music exists alongside other disciplines, such as text, graphics, animation and video. The digital musician might take a particular interest in audiovision, sound design, and text–sound work, which comes out of poetry. Music for film and television is a separate study in its own right but is plainly a fertile ground for the digital musician too. However, many films still tend to divide their soundtracks into 'music' and 'sound effects'. The great Hollywood film composers are musicians in the traditional sense, writing scores that mimic classical techniques. Not all film music is like this, and there are numerous examples of sound designers and Foley[10] artists, who have achieved extraordinary results, but, even so, it is a relatively rare thing to find a director who treats sound as music. The various new media are probably a more appropriate location for this kind of work.

The term 'new media' is generally taken to refer to various interactive and multimedia technologies that have arisen during the 1990s and since. This includes the Internet, computer games, portable technologies and interactive media in general. It is likely that the digital musician will be active in some or all of these. Certain new media such as computer games, interactive DVDs and online environments are rooted in concepts of virtual reality (VR). This may be defined as a computer simulation of an environment and is generally focused mainly on the visual domain. Sound is often used purely to reinforce the illusion of reality and so normally simulates the behaviour of sound in the physical world, often with only limited means. The processing and memory demands of the video stream frequently require a degraded sound quality (generally stereo, but often with low sampling rates and bit depths). However, a creative musician will always accept limitations when they occur and find ways to work within them. There are many examples of good music produced for new media, and this looks set to be the most expanding market in the immediate future.

Music publishing may be divided into two types: the publishing of paper scores or other materials; and the publishing of recordings and/or live broadcasts. The first type will generally be of much less concern to a digital musician than the second. In either case, a decision will have to be made about whether to self publish or to sign a contract with a publisher or record company. There are obvious advantages and disadvantages to both. To be 'signed' offers a ready-made network of support and context for your work as well as a sense of validation. In return you must surrender control over some or all aspects of your creativity and persona, as well as a slice of your income. To self-publish requires a considerable amount of effort as well as business acumen and administrative skill. The advantage is that you retain full control and rights over your work.

To self-publish requires the formation of a limited partnership or a limited company. Setting up a proper legally constituted organization is essential if rights, contracts, finances, and all the rest, are going to be properly handled. Registering with the bodies that control performance and broadcast rights is also necessary. This is not a trivial operation. Often a partnership deal with an independent record label will be preferable to creating one's own label, if such labours are to be completed relatively easily. There should be no illusions that working in this way is a route to making lots of money. The field is overcrowded and the world is full of self-publishing artists. The primary aim should be to break even and, most importantly, to fulfil your artistic objectives. Self-publishing will not be your sole source of income.

Digital distribution can be a very effective way of placing your work before large numbers of people. There are several online organizations that exist to distribute CDs and, more importantly, downloadable music, largely for the benefit of the members.

Such commercial operations should not entirely replace free sharing using social media, which has a promotional value in its own right. But if an income stream is being sought, then digital distribution is the way forwards. Distributors divide up into 'aggregators', which are in effect digital warehouses that hold licensed content, and 'widgets',[11] which are software applications that stream digital content to the user in a number of different ways. The nature of the contracts and benefits offered by such digital distributors varies enormously, and a great deal of research needs to be done into both the business aspects and the artistic qualities of a distributor before signing away any of your rights. Some distributors aim at a smaller, independent market, whereas others are clearly designed to try to achieve mass distribution. Distributing to major online stores such as Apple's iTunes is a claim made by many of the aggregators, which should be checked out with documentary evidence, as should the level of fees taken by the service.

Let's conclude this discussion with the following thoughts from Andrew Dubber, Reader in Music Industries Innovation at Birmingham City University:

> Ultimately, you don't have the right to make money from your online music – but you do have the opportunity. Money can be made to the degree that you create cultural meaning for people. And you make cultural meaning for people by connecting with them, being relevant, and allowing them to hear your music, share your music and live with your music.
>
> What you then sell them or charge them for is a question to start asking once they are willing to give you money – not as a barrier to entry for hearing your music in the first place. In other words, the question is not 'Should I give my music away?' or even 'How can I make money from my music?' but rather, 'How can I create an amazing amount of value for a significantly large number of people?'
>
> Answer that, and the other questions will more or less take care of themselves.'[12]

Project 46 (Advanced): Sonic Branding

Introduction

The ability to produce numerous versions of a single idea for a client is an indispensable skill in a commercial situation. Even if there are only slight variations between each version, the client must be offered a choice. This project is the aural equivalent of logo design and, despite its musical insignificance, may be the most lucrative activity ever undertaken by a digital musician.

The Project

Find a short video clip that could be suitable for a 'sonic brand'. Produce at least ten different audio clips to accompany the video. Make a presentation to a 'client' to sell the audio brand.

Notes

The following book may be useful for this project:

Jackson, D. L. (2003) *Sonic Branding: An Essential Guide to the Art and Science of Sonic Branding*, London: Palgrave Macmillan.

PROJECT 46

FURTHER READING

■ Cunningham, M., *Good Vibrations*, New York: Sanctuary, 1999.
An interesting history of record production.

■ Nardantonio, Dennis N., *Sound Studio Production Techniques*, Blue Ridge Summit, PA: Tab Books, 1990.
A technical guide to studio production.

■ Sobel, R. and Weismann, D., *Music Publishing: The Roadmap to Royalties*, New York: Taylor & Francis, 2008.
Covers legal and copyright issues, publishing agreements, digital publishing and many other aspects inclding the flow of money and control.

EDUCATION AND TRAINING

One major consequence of the emergence of the digital musician is a change in music education. There is almost a 'chicken–and–egg' relationship between the education system and the musicians it produces, because of the sudden rapid proliferation of 'music technology' as a subject at all levels. Of course, it is not necessary to have studied music academically *at all* in order to be a good and successful musician of whatever type. However, in the case of music technology, it can help enormously to have pursued some kind of course or training programme. Whereas, at one time, formal musical training was essential for a classical musician (and sometimes a handicap for a band musician), a digital musician will benefit from education in a wide range of areas, and not just 'music'.

Choosing the right course, whether a university degree or a technical qualification, can be challenging. It would be nice to think that all students have a clear set of goals and that courses exist that are tailored to them. In reality, however, the picture is much more fuzzy, and rightly so, because openness to new and unexpected directions is part of being a student. Nevertheless, it pays to research courses thoroughly before taking them, and to ask to what extent they seem to match your aspirations. Music, as a subject area, generally covers instrumental and historical music. Music Technology, as the name implies, is a cross disciplinary subject that sits somewhere between music and engineering, and so is a more natural home for digital music. There is a wide range of music technology courses, however, which tend to emphasize either the musical or the technological aspects. Despite the hybrid nature of the musicians described in this book, there are few courses that genuinely sit equally in between the two disciplines.

The differences between 'music' and 'music technology' curriculums do summarize the somewhat confused picture of education in this field. As Dr Matthew Adkins observed in a recent paper, there is a strong contrast between the two:

> On the one hand we have those from a traditional music background, who have had little use of technology (perhaps notation software) but are highly musically literate. On the other hand we see those from an unorthodox music background, with high technological literacy, but no notational skills.[13]

In addition to these observable tendencies are the financial constraints upon schools and colleges which have reduced instrumental tuition to a fraction of its former level and failed to equip classrooms or train teachers adequately in technology. This situation is changing, but it is quite common at present to find school pupils who have greater access to, and better understanding of, the technology than their teachers.

There is a general agreement among young people, at least, that a good knowledge of music technology is an essential part of contemporary musical life. The curriculum, on the other hand, struggles to keep pace with the rate of change. In universities, meanwhile, a large number of music-technology programmes have sprung up based largely upon the ideas and skill sets outlined in this book. These degree and sub-degree level courses may include the words 'creative' or 'sonic art' or even 'commercial' in their titles but, whatever their particular flavour, they are all fundamentally based on the same observable developments. The first-year programmes on these courses are frequently devised specifically to fill in the gaps in either musical or technological education that have appeared at school level.

For the digital musician, all this offers a great opportunity both to receive a varied and stimulating education and, to some extent, to set the agenda for the future. The education system is becoming increasingly flexible where music is concerned. This does not mean an outright and wholesale rejection of traditional skills and knowledge but rather an *opening up* of these to a wider, less restrictive, understanding than previously. Music technology as a subject area is in the process of maturing and will eventually find its own roots and produce its own flowers.

The very real and exciting prospect is that the digital musician can readily develop a unique voice. The new technologies have enabled people to create, to share and to develop together in ways that would have been unforeseeable thirty years ago. Education and practice are at last beginning to correspond more directly, and this trend will continue, to the point that a higher qualification will represent an enlivening and growth of the available set of possibilities. The final product of this process will be not 'digital musicians' as such, but musicians for whom the digital technologies are just as familiar as conventional acoustic music technologies. These remarkable individuals will be responsible for the growth of new forms and new musical experiences that will prove every bit as satisfying and rich as anything heard to date.

Discussion Questions

- How have changes to the workplace affected digital music-making?

- What career(s) would you choose, and why? How would you go about achieving that?

- Should digital music be free? If not, how should it be paid for? If so, how will artists make a living?

- What is the difference between 'music' and 'music technology' in education? Should they be closer or more divided?

- What social media do you use to promote your work? Why are those a good fit?

- Which is more important: making art, or making money? Why?

CHAPTER 14

Case Studies

Research Questions
Biographies
Interviews

RESEARCH QUESTIONS

An important part of the research behind this book consisted of many discussions and interviews with digital musicians of all types and at all stages of their careers. The aim of this research was to build up a picture of shared ideas and practices in digital music. The picture that emerged was, not surprisingly, very diverse, but some common themes could be detected and several key questions arose. In order to examine these questions further, several artists were selected as case studies. These were chosen from a range of backgrounds and each represents a different approach or way of working. There are representatives from the USA and Latin America, Europe and Scandinavia, Canada and Japan, from academia and the commercial world, from pure digital to mixed-media backgrounds. Many areas of music are represented, including popular and electro–acoustic, film and television, multimedia and installation work, networked music and new media, music for theatre and dance, laptop work and instrumental performance.

Each musician was asked to supply a short biography, a description of their creative use of technology, and answers to the following questions:

- What music do you make?
- Why do you make music?
- Is any of your sound-based work not 'music', as such?
- Do you consider yourself a performer, a composer, a technologist, an engineer, some combination of these or, indeed, something else?
- What is the cultural context for your work? Are you influenced by music in other cultures? And the other arts?
- What skills and attributes do you consider to be essential for you as a digital musician?
- Do you have any other useful or relevant things to say about being a digital musician today?

The answers echo a number of the key themes that have been explored in this book, sometimes from some unusual or particularly interesting angles. Musicians may not always be objective about their own work, but they can have a way of cutting to the heart of the matter that is illuminating.

What follows is an edited selection from the interviews, which draws out areas of remarkable similarity and difference, and points to some interesting avenues for further investigation. The complete interviews may be read on the book's website, along with creative projects contributed by the artists themselves. But first, let's meet each of the case studies in more detail.

BIOGRAPHIES

Oswald Berthold (OB)

enter world. awakening of the internal program. learned to play an instrument. formed a band. acquaintance with more instruments including electronic devices. left home. meet computer. short studies in music technology. meet internet. establishment of a studio and founding of a collective that lives until today. embed dance in an electronic music scene. playing concerts. start learn programming. playing more concerts. doing regular work in website construction. shifting interest to installations. picking up studies in computer science. still going. vacillate between art and science.

Nick Collins (NC)

Nicholas (Nick) Collins has indulged in both mathematics and instrumental composition in the past. His interests run the gamut of topics in electronic music, but particular specialisms include algorithmic composition, live electronica, machine listening and interactive music systems.

He was born near Oxford, grew up in Burntwood, Staffordshire, received a first degree in mathematics, a Master's in music technology, worked for Sony for a year on film SFX software, then became a programmer and part-time lecturer in London. Nick escaped to Cambridge to sort out a PhD, where he also learnt the dark art of writing in the third person about himself. He is now a lecturer in computer music at the University of Sussex.

Julio d'Escriván (JE)

I am a composer and creative music-technologist. I studied music traditionally, my instrument was the classical guitar, but I was interested in electronic music from very early on. Because of this I experimented with electric guitars, synths, recordings and tape delays in the late 1970s. I went to what is today Anglia Ruskin University where I studied composition with John Hopkins. Later, I studied composition for a year at Cambridge University (Trinity Hall) with Robin Holloway and then at City University London with Simon Emmerson and Robert Saxton where I took my PhD in Electroacoustic Composition in 1991.

I have worked as a composer of music for media since 1989 (it started as a way to fund my living expenses at the end of my PhD) but I have been a full-time academic only since 2005. I was also a consultant for Yamaha Research and Development in London, on sampling and synthesizer voicing projects between 1989 and 1991. Before I became an academic, I supported my more experimental sonic explorations by being a music producer for my own small company bitBongo Music. As such I have produced (written, directed session musicians, recorded, etc.) music for commercials, TV documentaries, TV and radio sound IDs and edited several CDs of popular music as well as scoring a few film soundtracks. I have also worked extensively for A&E (Arts and Entertainment) Latin-America, a US cable network that is part of the HBO group as an in-house composer. Since 1991, I have recorded music for a great variety of brands including Kraft, Pepsi, Gatorade, P&G, Nabisco and also for the Venezuelan banking industry.

Ambrose Field (AF)

Ambrose Field writes music which combines human performance and digital technology. He is a three-time award winner at the Prix Ars Electronica, Linz, with honorary mentions for digital music in 1997, 1998, 2006. Field's work crosses style and genre boundaries, and explores new territories resulting from an unusual cinematic approach to source material. BBC Radio 3 commented that Field's work is 'Music pushing against its boundaries and aspiring to the visual.'

His latest project, *Being Dufay*, is recorded on ECM and has achieved international critical acclaim. He has been a guest of studios as diverse as Recombinant Media Labs/ Apshodel to Hungarian National Radio, researching creative answers to new digital opportunities.

Rob Godman (RG)

Working as a composer, sound designer and programmer, Rob has a passionate interest in how sound behaves acoustically and has developed a number of techniques for controlling and building virtual spaces for use within live performance and installation. His fascination in the work of the Roman architect Vitruvius has led to frequent conference engagements and appearances on documentary TV shows.

An enthusiastic collaborator, Rob has worked on experimental and large-scale commercial music and sound design projects including the interactive installation *The DARK*. Other research and compositional interests include interactive audio (live and responsive), multi-speaker sound projection, programming, commercial expectations and industry requirements, collaborative methods and cross-arts. He is also a Reader in Music and Programme Leader for Composition at the University of Hertfordshire.

Chris Joseph (CJ)

I am a writer, artist and musician who works primarily with digital text, sound and image. My past projects include 'Inanimate Alice', a series of interactive multimedia stories, and 'The Breathing Wall', a digital novel that responds to the reader's breathing rate. I am editor of the post-Dada magazine and network 391.org, and a founding member of The 404, a group of digital and traditional artists exploring early modernism within new media.

Thor Magnusson (TM)

I studied music from a young age and was involved in various bands in Iceland until I moved out of the country in my early twenties. My academic background is philosophy, focusing on the philosophy of mind, language and aesthetics, but also on Indian philosophy. Through the philosophy of mind, I got interested in computing and AI. When I learned programming, it became obvious that a meta-machine like the computer is a fantastic tool for creating musical instruments and compositions, so I've spent over a decade now researching and creating digital instruments and algorithmic/generative music. I am the co-founder (with Enrike Hurtado Mendieta) of the ixi software project, which concentrates on experimenting with graphical user interfaces in musical software. We also have a label and regularly run workshops across Europe where we teach audiovisual software development for artists and designers. At the moment I teach at the University of Brighton and the University of Sussex and have a research fellowship with the Creative Systems Lab, concentrating on human–machine interaction and intelligent tools for musical production and playing.

Kaffe Matthews (KM)

Playing classical violin from the age of seven, singing badly in one band but getting further with bass and drums in the next, in 1985 I discovered electricity, listening and, with that, my current trajectory. Since then, acid house engineering, electrically reconstructing the violin, Distinction for a Master's in Music Technology, introducing and running a Performance Technology course at Dartington College of Arts, establishing label Annette Works and in 2009 launching the audio research lab, AudRey in London's East End. I also set up a collective wholefood shop and did a Zoology degree along the way.

Since 1990 I have been making and performing new electro-acoustic music worldwide with a variety of things and places such as violin, theremin, Scottish weather, desert stretched wires, NASA scientists, melting ice in Quebec and the BBC Scottish Symphony Orchestra. Currently I am researching 3D composition for outdoor enjoyment through Hammerhead sharks in Galapagos and sustainable vibratory interface design with *'music for bodies'*.

My 2004 collaboration *Weightless Animals* was awarded a BAFTA. I received a NESTA Dreamtime Fellowship in 2005 and an Award of Distinction, Prix Ars Electronica 2006 for the work *Sonic Bed_London*. In February 2006, I was made an Honorary Professor of Music, Shanghai Music Conservatory, China and in 2009, a patron of the Galapagos shark conservation society.

Randall Packer (RP)

Randall Packer is internationally recognized as a pioneering artist, composer, educator and scholar in the field of multimedia. His book and accompanying website, *Multimedia: From Wagner to Virtual Reality*, has been widely adopted as one of the leading educational texts in the field. He is concerned with the aesthetic, philosophical and socio-cultural impact of new media in an increasingly technological society.

In 1988, he founded Zakros InterArts and has since produced, directed and created critically acclaimed new-media performance, installation and net-specific works. Since moving to Washington, DC in 2000, his work has explored the critique of the role of the artist in society and politics. He founded the virtual government agency US Department of Art and Technology in 2001, which proposes and supports the idealized definition of the artist as one whose reflections, ideas, aesthetics, sensibilities and abilities can have significant and transformative impact on the world stage.

Pauline Oliveros (PO)

Pauline Oliveros (b. 1932) has influenced American music extensively in her career spanning more than sixty years as a composer, performer, author and philosopher. She pioneered the concept of Deep Listening, her practice based upon principles of improvisation, electronic music, ritual, teaching and meditation, designed to inspire both trained and untrained musicians to practise the art of listening and responding to environmental conditions in solo and ensemble situations. During the mid-1960s she served as the first director of the Tape Music Center at Mills College, aka Center for Contemporary Music followed by fourteen years as Professor of Music and three years as Director of the Center for Music Experiment at the University of California at San Diego. Since 2001 she has served as Distinguished Research Professor of Music in the Arts department at Rensselaer Polytechnic Institute (RPI) where she is engaged in research on a National Science Foundation Creative IT project. Her research interests include improvisation, special needs interfaces and telepresence teaching and performing. She also serves as Darius Milhaud Composer in Residence at Mills College doing telepresence teaching and she is Executive Director of Deep Listening Institute, Ltd where she leads projects in Deep Listening, Adaptive Use Interface. She is the recipient of the 2009 William Schuman Award from Columbia University for lifetime achievement.

Synthia Payne (SP)

Synthia Payne is an award-winning scholar and artist originally from Los Angeles, California. Her pioneering live Internet music shows occur on a global scale – literally musicians from all over the world playing together in real time. Synthia was Technical Director for John Gunther's multi-location telematic concert performance at CU Boulder's ATLAS theatre between participants from CU Boulder's Jazz Studies onsite, NYU's Steinhardt School and Korea's KAIST. And she was a featured vocalist and improviser in an online concert with the Stanford Laptop Orchestra. Synthia is adjunct faculty for the University of Denver's Digital Media Studies department, and is developing curriculum for classes in telematic arts collaboration. Synthia holds an MFA in Digital Arts and New Media, and a BA in Film and Digital Media with an electronic music minor, all from UC Santa Cruz.

Quantazelle (Q)

A self-proclaimed 'multi-hyphenate', Liz McLean Knight – the sole woman behind Quantazelle – is thoroughly immersed in technology, fashion, music and the often-surprising overlaps between. When attempting to circuit bend battery-powered music toys for an upcoming music performance, she discovered that electronic components can be turned into elegant jewelry and started an entire tech-fashion line called Zelle.

While devising a content-management system for her online experimental electronic music magazine, *Modsquare*, she learned various web-based programming languages and related technologies, having a head start from her one-time computer-science college major. With that knowledge she then started an online store, Fractalspin to sell not only her jewelry but also accessories and gear for the technologically sophisticated yet fashionably minded crowd.

Desiring to assist similar artists reach a greater audience as well as provide gear for electronic musicians, she started Subvariant – a record label and accessories company behind the well-received Electronic Musician's Emergency Adapter kit. As laptop-DJ Liz Revision, she selects both experimental ambient and glitchy techno in response to the aura of each night. As Quantazelle, she combines complex percussive programming, sonic innovation and engaging sound design together with an approachable melodic sensibility and often booty-shaking result.

John Richards (JR)

John Richards' work explores performing with self-made instruments and the creation of interactive environments. He performs regularly with electro-noise improvisers kREEPA and the post-punk group Sand (Soul Jazz Records), and he is actively involved in the performance of improvised music and community music projects. In 2002, his work with kREEPA helped initiate the OIK project at STEIM, Amsterdam that involved the hacking of commercially available hardware to create economic musical interfaces. He has worked with many leading improvisers and musicians in the field of live electronics and has performed extensively across the globe, predominantly in Europe, as well as Japan, Australia and the USA. He completed a doctorate in electro-acoustic composition at the University of York, UK, in 2002, and he is currently part of the Music, Technology and Innovation Research Centre at De Montfort University, Leicester, UK. Since 1990, he has also taught improvisation at Dartington International Summer School.

Sophy Smith (SS)

I am a classically trained musician (piano, French horn, singing), but I stopped orchestral performance when it was no longer necessary for my formal education. My undergraduate degree was in inter-arts and this cross/interdisciplinary approach to my work led me to complete an MA in contemporary performing arts. It was during this course that I began to write music. My undergraduate degree course had no music technology provision, and so my compositions were all for orchestral/vocal ensembles. This had a direct effect on my future compositional development and style, as I am essentially self-taught in all aspects of music technology. This lack of experience (and equipment!) resulted in my early music technology experiments involving any cheap lo-fi equipment I could access, and using it in any way I could find; for example, cheap 1980s sampling keyboards, electronic toys, tape recorders and four-track machines. When I began to work as a professional composer, my reliance on sound-based and sample-based work was too restricting for the different types and styles of music that I was being asked to write, and so I learned sequencing and editing software and techniques to widen my skills.

My professional work covers a wide range of work. I currently work as a professional composer, writing music mainly for dance and theatre companies as well as running my own live art company, Assault Events. The company creates original devised performance events as well as planning and delivering a range of specialist residencies. We also undertake research and consultancy projects for clients including the Creative Partnerships, regional arts organizations and local education authorities.

Atau Tanaka (AT)

Atau Tanaka is a Japanese/American composer and researcher. He bridges the fields of media art and experimental music, artistic and scientific research. His work seeks the continuing place of the artist in democratized digital forms. He creates sensor-based musical instruments, searching for the idiomatic voice in the interface. He composes for network systems, considering data transmission delay as the acoustic of the network. His works include solo and ensemble concert works and exhibition installations. His work in the 1990s with the trio Sensorband continues today in gestural sound-image perform-ance with Sensors_Sonics_Sights. He publishes theoretical writings and conducts funda-mental research at Sony CSL Paris to develop and document his socio-artistic approach. His work has been presented at Ars Electronica, SFMOMA, Eyebeam, La Villette, ICC, V2 and ZKM. He has received support from the Japan Foundation, the Fraunhofer Society, the Daniel Langlois Foundation and is mentor at NESTA.

Martyn Ware (MW)

Martyn Ware was a founding member of both The Human League and Heaven 17 and is one of the UK's most successful and in-demand producers. His work includes Terence Trent d'Arby's *Hardline* album and hits for Tina Turner and Marc Almond. Martyn has also worked extensively writing music for film, theatre, television and radio. His most recent venture is The Illustrious Company, formed with long-term collaborator Vince Clarke (of Erasure, Yazoo and Depeche Mode), which makes original music soundscapes often in visual contexts. They recently staged a series of events called The Future of Sound.

INTERVIEWS

What follows are edited responses by the case study artists to the various questions, anno-tated to draw out particular issues of similarity and difference, features of interest and relevant personal aspects. The compete interviews may be read on the website.

Please describe your creative use of technology, particularly digital technology

The strongest impression to emerge from the answers to this question was the extent to which technology is both inspirational in itself and provides a direct link to the sources of inspiration.

> My creative process is completely suffused with digital technologies. I use them for inspiration; to create text, images and sounds; to edit, program or otherwise manipulate those elements; to allow the reader/audience to respond to and

influence the work's ('interactivity'); to collaborate with other artists around the world; to publish, distribute and promote my work; and many other related uses between and besides. (CJ)

I have been interested in the use of interactive technology for musical expression. I perform with musical instruments built from sensor systems, create network music infrastructures, sound-image installations and participative mobile locative music experiences. (AT)

My use of technology is compositional, I am not interested in developing technological tools for others to use (although I am happy to share the few ones I make). I use digital technology to synthesize, record, manipulate and perform sound. In recent works I have used smartphones and video game controllers, which are now rather common in electronic music performance. At the moment of writing, I am creating a new work for video game player as performer (projecting the game progress to the audience) and an electro-acoustic ensemble that includes a laptop section and reacts to the game much in the spirit of silent film. (JE)

i am interested very generally in wave phenomena as they are evident in, or rather, constituent of all of nature's processes. sound then seems well suited for conveying information about the trajectories of these processes' variables, particularly as they unfold along time, be they external and tapped or simulations. this suggests a toolbox equipped with devices such as supercollider, octaver, and a good text editor, a lot of glue, utilities and scripts of diverse provenance and a box filled with I/O apparatus, sensors, soldering iron and such. (OB)

I am actively exploring: machine listening and interactive music systems (for example, works for piano and electronics, baroque instruments and electronics, computer systems supporting improvisation), computer-generated composition (including a series of 'infinite length pieces' in musical areas from nonstandard tuning systems to automatic electronic dance music), laptop performance (from live coding, to live audiovisuals). (NC)

Digital technology is a tool for creating sounds as well as putting them together, and having both these elements in one place means that I can work quickly and allows me to be much more flexible and effective. Digital technology is ideal as it allows me to quickly re-edit/and alter pieces of music, which is vital in the situation I compose in where I often compose in the rehearsal studio with the dancers/actors whilst they are devising. This allows the work to be a much more collaborative experience than it would if I had to keep going back to a large analogue studio or writing for instrumentalists who were not present. (SS)

I use all technology that I can get hold of. (TM)

All the artists take a creative approach to the particular software and hardware they use, with some favouring modular solutions such as Max/MSP or programming languages such as SuperCollider that encourage a 'self-built' approach to music-making.

I use programming languages like SuperCollider and MaxMSP/Jitter to structure the sequencing of the sound objects and give form to my musical ideas. I often work in a live-coding style with SuperCollider, this allows me to test complex ideas very quickly and to create interesting variations easily with minor changes to the code. In the end, I like leaving the music 'fixed', which often means that a similar sound process is applied in the same section of the music but with constrained randomness in selected aspects when the code is re-run in performance. This makes the most of variability but ensuring you can recognize the piece on a second hearing! (JE)

On the computer, I work most of the time in a programming language called SuperCollider, which is specifically designed for audio programming. My work with SuperCollider can be roughly divided into two areas: (a) building instruments that are designed for live improvisation and are therefore quite flexible, allowing for spontaneousness; (b) algorithmic compositions where I create software that generates music that is never the same when you listen to it. I always try to make software that supports working with acoustic instruments, hopefully creating a symbiotic relationship between the acoustic and the digital. (TM)

My work is based in performance and has incorporated nearly every form and genre of new media. Currently I am working with HD video and surround sound for an upcoming music theatre production. (RP)

I compose using an Apple Mac running Logic Pro, Pro Tools and Wave Burner. I use soft synths including Absynth and Sculpture. My music also uses a wide range of samples which I manipulate in Logic. I use the technology both as a palette where I can create and mix new sounds and as a canvas where I can compose the work. (SS)

I'm a Mac addict. I had one of the first Macs in the country in the 1980s. The Mac is central to just about everything we do, from composition through to soundscape assembly, through to 3D surround-sound convolution. We use a proprietary system that has been built with our advice by Paul Gillieron Acoustic Design which enables us to move things around in three dimensions and actually see where things should be in a wire-frame diagram. It can move up to sixteen different sound frames simultaneously at 25 frames per second. We also use Logic, an industry standard product, as a front-end. We also use Macs for all our business needs, designing websites, etc. And, although we are famous for using analogue synths, nowadays we use virtual instruments as well, so more or less everything we do is mediated through technology. (MW)

Self-devised instruments are also common, especially where digital technologies are combined with acoustic or analog technologies. John Richards, for example, describes his approach to instrument building as follows:

The Kreepback instrument [is] a modular environment of analogue DIY electronic devices, audio hardware and digital bits and pieces patched together to create a feedback labyrinth. The instrument's name is derived from my work with the group kREEPA and the idea that sound creeps back on itself. Since 2000, I have been developing the instrument and approaches towards performing with it. Some of the modified 'physical' objects tend to catch the 'eye'. However, as far as the ear is concerned, digital technology plays a big part. I have been hugely influenced on different levels by object-orientated programming languages. I initially conceived the feedback network of the Kreepback instrument using Max/MSP and the inputs and outputs of an audio interface. Despite being quite a different instrument to the one I currently use, the genesis of the instrument is here.

… In regards to specifically digital technology I currently use in performance, the Nord Micro Modular is used as a 'module' in the Kreepback instrument. The programming language of the Nord offers great flexibility, and its small size, robustness and control features make it a really powerful device to help coerce and steer the feedback produced by the other modules that make up the Kreepback instrument. For example, using a mixing desk as a matrix, I can use a low frequency oscillator (LFO) from the Nord to modulate some of the analogue signals. Within the digital domain of the Nord I also have created feedback labyrinths and networks that I control with MIDI: there are feedback loops within feedback loops within the overall instrument. Having worked with Max/MSP, programming the Nord was an extension of the same modular approach.

Finally, Quantazelle made this amusing observation:

What's great about computers is that they are amazing tools that allow you to completely stretch, distort, invent and reinvent sound like no other instrument. And, there's usually an 'undo' command. :-)

What music do you make?

The case study artists were mostly reluctant to describe their music in any way that would enable it to be 'pigeon-holed' into a particular genre or style. Some found this a difficult question to answer. The most common descriptor is 'electronic':

I make mostly electronic music. I am interested in stylistic crossovers between experimental electronica and classical, jazz, rock, pop and ethnic musics. (JE)

Music involving humans and technology. (AF)

Strangely, I found this a rather difficult question. I know what I don't do. (RG)

Electronic music in a wide range of styles, often with collaborating singers or musicians who are part of the 391.org network. (CJ)

I make experimental electronic music, but I use the word 'electronic' music only because to most people, the word 'electro-acoustic' means nothing. In fact, I make both electronic and electro-acoustic music. (KM)

Perhaps 'edgy experimental-yet-melodic electronic' or 'glitchy-yet-catchy instrumental electronic'. It continues to evolve as I do. (Q)

Improvisation features in several of the answers.

I mostly play with improvisation bands, using a mixture of acoustic instruments and electronics, but I also enjoy improvising with other electronic musicians which happens frequently in various club or festival settings. (TM)

Currently I improvise music with my Roland V accordion (all digital). I use my Expanded Instrument System (EIS) to process my instrument and spatialize the sounds. I also compose music for acoustic and electronic instruments and voices. (PO)

I make music with my voice and I play synthesizer keyboards mainly in collaborative improvisations with others, and most often taking place in real time online sessions with people from all over the world via Internets. (SP)

Most answers prefer to describe the music in terms of the medium for which it is created:

I make music as a function of the medium or infrastructure for which I am composing. I seek out the sonic voice of the chosen medium. (AT)

My collaborator, Vince Clarke from Erasure, and myself compose together, creating soundscapes for exhibitions, events, etc., etc. We also do Hollywood-quality sound design in three dimensions. So, the work we do ranges from 3-D 'narratives' that have nothing to do with traditional music, through to traditional music pieces that are rendered in three dimensions. (MW)

I mainly write music for dance and theatre companies for touring shows. This involves creating soundtracks of between 40 and 75 minutes in length, comprising of a number of shorter tracks. Usually, all these tracks are 'written through' so that the soundtrack is heard as a complete piece of music without gaps. The type of music I write depends on the movement/action that it works with, but includes orchestral pieces, sound-based work, vocal work and electronic dance music. I think I am more defined by my approach to composition through collaboration with other art forms rather than a particular style. (SS)

I also make generative music in the form of software, the latest piece in a collaboration with Runar Magnusson where we used field recordings from Iceland to create 'schizotopic' soundscapes where the pieces/locations are never the same. We intend to release the software so the user can generate an endless amount of music and share with others. (TM)

I've created a lot of collaborative works with other artists that might be described as 'installation'. I write concert-hall works for instruments and electronics where live performance and perception of 'liveness' is an integral part. Space [or acoustics] – in the widest sense of the word – is an important part of my work. (RG)

I used to create fixed products including 'impossible tape music illusions' but, more recently, have often concentrated on full time on live performance. The various facets of this include an audiovisual experimental electronica duo (live improvisation of mappings), designing systems for real-time interactive situations and competitive live coding battles. (NC)

Some of the case studies go into more detail about the music itself:

Although a lot of the music I have created has dense textures, complex rhythms and could be considered as 'loud', I am also interested in extreme contrasts, the use of silence and sparse musical landscapes. Similarly, the idea of contrast in my music is also explored through the relationship between the performer's involvement and non-involvement (total process) in performance. (JR) put extremely, it's not making music but rather transforming music. consider music as the continual evaluation of a vector valued function of multiple variables. whew. phenomenologically it's again a progression, one of parameterized sounding entities, elements that vary mostly microscopically, that recur among diversely different timescales, maybe slowly evolve. hums, hisses, buzzes, tonal drones, optionally and quasi periodically pulsed, also blips, squeaks, tweets, squirts, grunts and other more short lived creatures. (OB)

Why do you make music?

The answers to this question were clearly very personal and deserve to be quoted in full. Despite their variety, some common threads do emerge: a sense of compulsion, of absorption and of necessity. To put it simply: it is not a matter of *wanting* to make music, but rather a matter of *having* to make music, for whatever reason.

> i slipped into this, not noticing myself and now i can't find a way out. (OB)

> The answer to this would itself vary based on the work and the time of day. But here is a selection of responses:
>
> - to make social contact with people I'd be too shy to talk to, to assist communal forgetting of the everyday, for particular functions (a club event, promoting dancing) to undermine particular functions (deliberately awkward music disrupting dancing)
> - to create artefacts as a challenge to my own and other's intellectual and emotional states
> - to become lost (or transcendent, meditative?) in the flow of composition and performance. I can achieve such direct flow in more intellectual pursuits (though I also play piano in traditional musicianship and can become lost there in a motor memory assisted kind).
>
> I'll stop before your patience wears thin. (NC)

> I make music because I love it. It's one of the few things I am able to do that is a reward in itself. (JE)

> Firstly, for the audience. I'm not interesting in making music nobody is going to hear. Secondly, to explore, define, create and seek out new things. (AF)

> This is a question I often ask myself, and a difficult one to answer. The best answer I can give for now is that it is a kind of compulsion – a need that must be satisfied to remain happy and sane. I think part of the reason may be that when I make music I often feel completely absorbed in the process/moment, to an extent that comes more rarely when creating with other forms. I almost want to say that it is a more 'pure' form of creation, but maybe better would be to say that it is more immediate, and there is something in that immediacy that makes it a hugely enjoyable activity. (CJ)

> For me, music is an outlet of ideas and states of mind that I am dealing with. I get inspiration from everything I hear, see or read, and working with music in an environment like SuperCollider allows one to experiment from a very basic level. To

me, SuperCollider is an experimental laboratory of sound, a research tool, a work-shop for instrument building, a compositional environment and a musical instru-ment, all at the same time. Sound is an important part of my world, and research-ing and experimenting with sound and its physics is for me a meditative process of understanding the environment. For example, recording sound in nature gives me a richer and deeper 'presence' and 'experience' of the nature itself. It is as if the ears become hypersensitive. I imagine this is analogous to a painter painting nature or even a hunter that has to pick up signs from the natural environment in order to find the prey. (TM)

I don't know. I just know that that is what I have to do. But, if you want a story: in the mid-1980s, when I was in a band playing bass and drums, I went to West Africa for a couple of months. I lived with some drummers, and they taught me traditional rhythms on tam-tams, and, within that, I learnt very simple things about how the texture of the skin on your hand, and the shape of the hand, and the tight-ness of the drum skin and the shape of the drum, these tiny, tiny details, would change the sound of the drum when your hand hit the skin. The changing of that sound would alter the pattern and so completely alter the music and its meaning. Also, how the simple patterns, simple cells, interlocking with each other, would produce music of great complexity. I came back to Nottingham, where I was living at the time and had this epiphany – I just had to make music. Sound essentially is my medium. It's not emotional expression, or personal experience. I'm more of a channel. Overall, making music and using it is a continuously questioning journey that never stops which makes some sense of living. (KM)

I make music to expand my mind and because I enjoy it. (PO)

Because I can. (RP)

Tapping into a creative process is exhilarating and can be very satisfying. When I am creating music there is a connection between my deepest psyche and the waking world that helps me live well. I remember at a very young age thinking that making music was something I could do for my whole life without reservation. (SP)

I feel that I have a particularly unique audio perspective on creating music that's not dependent on any particular instrument, machine, plug-in or genre to make it sound like it came from me. I've participated in this Iron Chef of Music competition put on by the krac5ive label, but which has worldwide participation via the Internet and various 'nodes' (physical meet-ups) throughout the world. The idea is that they give you one audio sample, and two hours, and you can use any program or effect to create a track from that one sample, but you can't use any other instrument. I thought it was absolutely fascinating how everyone who participated took the same source material but used it in completely different ways. And I was able to recognize the ones that were produced by my friends, because it just *sounded like them*. Even though all of us who participated started from the same place with the same materi-als, we each produced something uniquely different. I sort of feel that way about what I do – I have a particular approach that sounds like me that you'll never hear anywhere else, even though there are people using the same software and plug-ins as I do. I feel as if I'm contributing something unique to all the available recorded electronic music. If I ever stumble across anyone who sounds like I want to sound, but doing it better, I'll just retire and subscribe to all their future albums. (Q)

I do not really have a rational answer to this question. Making music is part of my fabric as a human being and is something that has always been there. I have sometimes thought about how I might stop making music, but these thoughts have been fleeting. (JR)

I enjoy creating things from scratch – music is one of my outlets for doing this! I find it challenging and stimulating and hugely enjoyable. I do not write much music for its own sake but rather enjoy writing music for collaborative things (e.g., environments, events) in which music is one of a number of parts that go to make the whole. I can't remember choosing music – I just can't remember doing anything else! (SS)

I continue to make music because ideas continue to come, and I have been unsuccessful to stop making music despite efforts. (AT)

Because it's the only means I have of making a living. And for pleasure. I tolerate no interference with the creative process. I never have done, throughout my career as a musician and writer, composer and producer. One of the conditions of me working is that I can't deal with working by committee, particularly when composing. For that reason, we don't do much work with the advertising world, for instance. The presumption in that kind of world is that if they pay you enough money they have the right to interfere. I'd rather earn less money and provide a clean path towards resolution of a creative idea. And it's my life, and has been before I got signed as a professional musician, since about 1972 when I bought my first synthesizer and started playing with imaginary bands, with my mates in Sheffield. It makes me laugh when people talk about retirement, because I'll be doing this until the day I die, if I can. (MW)

Is any of your sound-based work not 'music', as such?

There was a clear split down the middle on this question, with six case study artists answering unequivocally 'yes', seven unequivocally 'no', and three being unclear either way. The 'no' replies were generally simple (some being one word answers, some a little more elaborate), for example:

No. I consider everything I make with sound to be music. (KM)

No. This is not a value judgement though, I simply don't make documentary forms of pieces, field recordings or sonifications. (AF)

Music that does not arise from the Western traditions of melody, harmony and rhythm but from sound orientation is often said to not be music. This is a misunderstanding of music arising from the sounds of 20th and 21st century life. For me both traditions are music. (PO)

Well I suppose my mother might say yes, but I don't think so. (Q)

I regard it all as music. Some people would say: 'that's not music'. It all has an artistic element. (MW)

Some of the 'yes' answers make a distinction between various forms of sound–art or sound design and music:

> Because of my personal history all my work with sound responds to a musical sensibility. Yet I would say that according to newer definitions of sonic art, music itself as we understand it historically may be better understood as a particular form of the arts of sound but not the only standard by which all work in sound is measured. (JE)

> This gets a little tricky but I think there is a distinction between music and sound art. I've created a few harsh noise pieces, and I like to do what might be considered acousmatic or musique concrete. I like to call it sound collage. (SP)

> Aside from the creation and manipulation of sounds as part of my multimedia works, many of my longer sound pieces would probably be better described as something other than music. What that something is, I wouldn't like to say. (CJ)

> Yes, some of my research is on the effects of sound on the mind or direct explorations of sound physics. I don't consider that necessarily 'music', and it changes according to contexts, so it's quite hard to answer this question really. (TM)

> I describe myself as a composer mainly although I'm very interested in the composition/sound-design crossover. I find it quite amusing how we get very messed up with these types of labels. 'Composer' seems to be about right for me – an organizer of sound. As an academic, I find myself researching areas that might not be considered music. (RG)

Oswald Berthold is the only case study artist positively to embrace the idea that he does not create music:

> most of it, yes. it appears to me i have arrived at this definition by searching for a local optimum in personal manoeuvring space. i enjoy a lot of music 'as such' but i enjoy in a very similar manner many more temporal structures occurring in my immediately perceptible surrounding and wonder about the imperceptible.

Do you consider yourself a performer, a composer, a technologist, an engineer, some combination of these or, indeed, something else?

This question prompted some lengthy answers, with the majority of the case study artists seeking once again to avoid defining themselves as any one thing in particular, preferring instead to be hybrids or to resist *any* categorization. Some were quite clear, however:

> I'm a composer, as most of my time is spent looking for new forms and structures, and creating the raw materials for pieces from scratch. (AF)

> I am a composer of media. (RP)

> Mostly a performer and composer. I don't really see myself primarily as a technologist, as first and foremost I write music, and the digital technology is my means for doing this. I definitely don't see myself as an engineer, probably as I have no formal training in this area. My music often drives my engineering-orientated

collaborators mad as my engineering is 'wrong'! In terms of engineering, I tend to experiment until I find what I like, rather than knowing what to look for. Really, I suppose, I see myself as a facilitator of sorts. (SS)

I am a composer who performs, an artist who uses digital technology as his canvas. (AT)

Good question. Nowadays, less of a performer, although during the 'Future of Sound' events I MC the whole thing, because I'm the most famous person involved and it's my baby anyway, so I can do what I want! I like public speaking now, whereas it used to horrify me. I've turned from a performer in the music sense to a performer in the didactic sense. Since I've had children (now aged eleven and nine), I've become much more interested in distributing the experience I've acquired over thirty years.

I think of myself more as a composer now, in the real sense of the word, than a writer. I'm a producer-composer. The skills I acquired as a producer were invaluable in terms of organizing the material required to get a message across, especially in the complex world of 3D sound and how that information is imparted to the observer.

I don't like the word 'technologist', but I have become fascinated by technology. Our 3D sound needs to be, or rather often is, accompanied by visual imagery. Interesting new forms come out of that collaboration. So I have become, of necessity, much more *au fait* with all the technologies that are out there to do with interaction, with digital manipulation of information, infomatics and new forms of coding that enable you to do things that weren't previously possible in combining digital visual generative work and sound. So, I've expanded my skills base to incorporate a lot more things. (MW)

Selections from the 'hybrid' answers will illustrate the complexity that this question can engender:

I'm probably a hybrid of most of these although I'm never sure what a technologist is. (RG)

clearly, all of the above and then some. maybe not quite a generalist but at least a student in many disciplines. (OB)

I've made the comparison before of nineteenth-century composer/pianists and twenty-first-century composer/programmers. People are an implicit and untangleable blend of characters and change as the context suits; so I can be any of the above, but certainly, happy to be labelled a digital musician where this might simply mean someone working at the cross-disciplinary juncture of these types. (NC)

After thinking about it for the last few years, I still consider myself a composer first but these days I also think of myself as a creative technologist. By this I mean that I am not interested in technology per se but in how it can be (mis)used for artistic purposes. (JE)

Any of these terms would fit some part of my practice, which is why I always have difficulty answering the question 'What do you do?' I tend now to describe myself as a writer and artist, which is sufficiently vague to cover and leave open all possibilities. (CJ)

All of these in addition to being an inventor. As with the term 'music', I don't find it productive to define myself (neither for myself nor others), so it depends on context what mask one might have to wear. In fact I prefer the term 'musician' as it is vague and meaningless enough. I consider everybody a musician, just of varied skills, practice and maturity. (TM)

I am a person who makes music through constant questing. …

I am a performer. I can get into showing off too, one of the reasons I no longer go on stage – I don't want audiences to get distracted by my prancing about rather than just listening.

I am a composer in different ways. I compose on the fly in live performances, improvising and working with software to create chance events to which I respond then and there. I also slowly make carefully constructed, thought-out pieces for dance and film. …

Part of the skill which I have been trying to acquire through practice with the live work is to ask: is this decision I am making now the best one? Is it right? (Whatever that means.) Is that interesting? Is this a decision that's worth making? Or should I actually not do what I think I should do? Of course, I begin with an idea, launch off, I'm playing and I have no idea what will come next, like life really. So sometimes it's great, and then slam, a disaster, and I have to deal with that. And all witnessed with an audience.

I'm not a technologist. I use digital technology as my instrument, my tool. I'm not an engineer either. But I got into what I do now because I went to work in a recording studio in the early days of acid house and discovered that you could use technology to make sound accessible as a material. At that point, I stopped making conventional tunes and began to play with what the machines might do, crashing and coming up with things I would never think of. That's where the collaboration began, and I began to feel that music-making was really possible. I also made the decision then not to be an engineer but to use the studio and its gadgets creatively. I wouldn't be doing all this if computers didn't exist. (KM)

Online musicians have to be able to set up their computer, get online, mix and perform all at the same time. I am an improviser first, but I am also listening for form and content in a way that constitutes real time composition. I am also engineering the Internet connection and the computer and audio equipment, and mixing. The simultaneity of one person performing all of those functions at once is perhaps unique. (SP)

I'd say all of those on some level. These days, I've toned down the actual 'performance' of my shows a bit (haven't worn a costume in forever, haven't done any costume changes or participated in any laptop cage matches in quite a while) and have just been focusing on the sonic experience that I create as a sound technologist in a live setting. Plus, just creating all the musical intricacies in one track requires a few days of such focused nerdery in front of my laptop that I kind of run out of time and energy to think about how I could make it more 'performative' in a live setting. (Q)

I have found it increasingly difficult to call myself a 'composer', although I am, at times, clearly composing. There is a lot of baggage with the term 'composer', some of which, I do not like. For example, the composer as someone that sits at the top of a musical hierarchy, the limited reference of the term in regard to Western culture, and the composer as something distinct from a musician. …

I am also a technologist, engineer, designer, programmer and artist. However, for cultural reasons I do not call myself any of these. To be, for example, a sculptor, you have to earn the right to be called this: have a studio and exhibitions, a commitment to sculpting. …

Furthermore, I feel very strongly that the distinctions associated traditionally between science and the arts are perfunctory. In the UK, for example, people study to become a Bachelor of Science or Arts. It is clear that many students do not fit into either of these categories. This is also true of the majority of digital musicians. (JR)

What is the cultural context for your work? Are you influenced by music in other cultures? And the other arts?

Several clear themes emerge from the answers to this question: the importance of non–Western musics; the influence of visual culture; the role of the Internet; and a general sense of eclecticism and wide-ranging and open-minded appreciation of many forms of music.

I'm definitely influenced by music from all around the world. I've always been very eclectic in my tastes, from way back before even I was involved in making music. I don't think 'ooh, I've just discovered music from Mali, or Tuvan open-throat singing'. Everything is music to me. I can't alter the context for my work. Everyone knows I'm an electronic musician. We've always tried to do electronics with soul, and that's what interests me, not just in musical terms but also in personal terms. I only work with people who approach what they do with soul, with a sense of humanity, of generosity and openness to new ideas. So the context for me is *innovation*, I think. I'm more interested in new forms than I am in perfecting existing forms. (MW)

I have lived in several countries in my life so feel no direct identity with one particular culture. I draw upon the different cultures of my background in ways that I could not have if I had not left them. Also, I believe that there is a culture of technology, as well as a culture that questions technology. My works sits at this intersection, ultimately embracing a visceral vision of digital sound. (AT)

I am influenced in some way or another by all music I hear, but I don't think that I am hugely influenced by any particular music in other cultures. I am influenced by any music that I like and find interesting – usually something that has an instant emotive hit! Some of my music does have different cultural nuances, but this is really because the sound itself reflects what I want to convey in the music for a particular scene or dance sequence. I am very influenced by the other arts as I have a very cross/interdisciplinary approach to my composition. This manifests itself in two ways, either in creating collaborative work with other disciplines or experimenting with different creative processes and concepts used in other art forms. If my music is influenced by anything, then it is a combination of my past experiences as an orchestral instrumentalist and vocalist and a desire to create music that will connect with people and that they will find interesting and enjoyable. (SS)

Culture of the Amateur. Although most of the people I play with are highly skilled in music, engineering, and technology, most of us don't make a living playing or engineering music. Probably most online musicians would love to play music full time, but few do. However, this avoids having to worry about financial or commercial gain from the music we play. There is a cultural context in academia as well because of the experimental nature of real time online collaboration. … My musical creativity resonates strongly with African tribal music, and with the Carnatic music of India. Language and poetry are also strong influences and when I am composing in real time I like to vocalize on nonsensical syllables that I develop into English words. I have done several projects that utilize video art, dance and theatre. A new interest is brain music and triggering sounds with brain waves. (SP)

My work has been performed in festivals ranging from Early Music Events in the Vienna Konzerthaus to hardcore Dance Music Festivals in the middle of rural Italy. I don't specifically locate my music in any cultural context. I do however bring a wide range of historical ideas into my compositional process. I am also influenced by my own past experiences. I think it is important as a world citizen to know about music from as many cultures as it is possible to find out about. I'm currently enjoying researching Pansori. However, I will not try and emulate Pansori in any of my pieces. Some of the structural decision making may inform how I approach a new work I'm engaged with, but that's about it. (AF)

My major musical influences would probably be post-war popular musics, principally rock, pop and electronic music; the classical music I played in orchestras when I was younger; and Dada. But there are a huge number of other influences that wax and wane. I am certainly influenced by the other arts and digital arts in particular. (CJ)

My work is influenced by social and political issues. I recently completed a political music theatre work entitled *A Season in Hell* a project of the virtual government agency I created shortly after 9/11, the US Department of Art and Technology. (RP)

About two years ago, I started to realize that I no longer wanted my work to be available just to those who already know about the kind of music I make; the largely young, male, white audiences who come to galleries, warehouses, basements, cellars and so on to enjoy shows. I think that experimental electronic music, if you can find a way into it, can be profoundly rewarding, even life-enhancing. It gives you a way of tuning in to what life is like through your ears, through listening. If you listen, rather than look all the time, it can transform your life. (KM)

1 white elitist western art music, sound art, sound hacking, slow code, media art + theory. 2 in no way directly. only through the filter of being published on recording media. 3 i draw inspiration from all over movies, literature, people, visual, sculptural,

electronic and/or performing arts, physics, biology, mathematics, electronic and hacker culture, (in ad-hoc order) and other unworldly terrain. generally i go with the notion of arts and sciences overlapping, a tendency to syn rather than sci. (OB)

I am interested by all musics, but am especially drawn to those of counter-cultures and experiments. Of course, from a Western perspective, sometimes the main-streams of other cultures can seem like subversive voices! All arts and sciences are good sources of human richness. In particular, I'm actively involved in multimo-dal art (audiovisuals). (NC)

My context is a mixed baggage of urban/world music popular idioms with a healthy dose of South American and Latin folklore, and other ethnic elements as well as high brow pretentious European concerns which I can afford to never take very seriously because I am not a European by birth. Like a lot of my contemporar-ies I am particularly sensitive to visuals and visual art-forms like cinema and video. I also practice photography and my music today is very dependent on it. (JE)

Strangely (again), I found this a rather difficult question. I've never felt a terribly strong sense of cultural identity. Am I part of an experimental and/or academic cul-ture? Hope not …, although I'm glad to say that the perception of such an identity/culture is now largely over generalized and frequently inaccurate. Travel is an impor-tant part of my life as an artist and having the opportunity to exchange ideas with other, not necessarily like-minded, people is crucial. It forces you to question your thoughts and ideas. I'm not conscious of exploring techniques from other cultures but suspect I do so subliminally (with particular relation to pace and time in time-based arts). I enjoy being slightly outside of my comfort zone and working with other artists and disciplines can make that happen. Collaborative working is fascinating. For the most part, my collaborations have been successful on an inter-personal level but I remember a hideous occasion when I felt I was being bled-dry of ideas so that the other artists could pilfer them. I like human beings for the most part and am fas-cinated in how we communicate (or don't) and relate (or don't!) with each other. (RG)

The cultural context of my work is a mixture of the cultures of experimental music and academia. I play regularly in various concerts and music festivals, but over the past years I have been working on my project – ixi audio – in an academic setting, and that has taken me to various academic conferences and festivals. I enjoy both worlds, although I think the most interesting stuff musically is happening outside the academic settings. As for music from other cultures, I have to admit being obsessed with Indian music (and philosophy), and this has had strong influence on my own musical practice. I studied music in India for a while, which was an enlightening experience. I'm also interested in various African musical cultures, such as those of western Africa – Mali and Morocco in particular. (TM)

I grew up in Houston Texas listening to the sounds of nature and of music lessons given by my mother and grandmother. I started playing the accordion when I was nine years old. I played other instruments in school musical organizations. I was always attracted to sounds and music that was new to me or unfamiliar. I became exposed to world music via Henry Cowell's radio programs and Radio KPFA in Berkeley California. Music broadcasts of all kinds were very influential for me. Performance Art became influential in the 1970s. I had been interested in dance since making music for many dancers including Anna Halprin in the 1960s. (PO)

Here in Chicago, the only stations that play instrumental music are the classical-music station and two low-signal-power college stations, one that plays dance music and one that plays absolutely anything from field recordings to noise punk. There really isn't a mainstream cultural channel that my work would fit into, although I can think of about twelve Internet-based podcasts or websites that are a near-perfect fit. And that's why the Internet is just so wonderful – you can discover all kinds of new music and network and interact with people with the same connoisseur-level taste in this kind of music that you wouldn't find in mainstream cultural channels. … I think gamelan is really interesting. It's heavily and sometimes complexly layered, with different parts coming in and out with variations or in another time signature. Some of it reminds me of earlier Autechre. (Q)

'The Twenty-First Century is a Better Place for Me.' This is the title of a paper I have had an idea for, although I am struggling to start the paper due to the enormity of the issues it keeps throwing up. In brief, the idea for the paper was to attempt to place my and other people's work within a cultural context. Being born in the 1960s, I have been fortunate to experience making music in more traditional ways with acoustic instruments such as the piano and double bass, as well as witnessing the incredible rise of the PC and being part of the digital era. Also, through teaching, I have seen the emergence of the first generation of purely digital musicians. Consequently, I am a polyglot musician: I speak many musical languages. I remember at university where I was studying music, there were those who could improvise and those who could not. Never the twain met. I suppose one of my attributes as a musician was that I could move across different musical terrains. It seemed completely natural. I had learnt some of the canon of Western classical music; I played in a jazz band and spent a good many years of my youth playing 'axe murdering' bass in a punk band. I also have experienced the dissemination boom of music. By this, I mean the opportunity to have on CD, for example, a vast range of music from around the globe. (JR)

What skills and attributes do you consider to be essential for you as a digital musician?

Several of the case study artists (AF, RG, TM, AT, MW) mention in their replies to this (and the next) question that they do not consider themselves to be 'digital musicians', but rather just musicians who work with digital technology:

> I don't consider myself a digital musician, but simply a musician that makes use of digital technology as part of what I do. I think all instruments afford certain ideas and work processes and it would be limiting to constrain oneself to one tool or technology. (TM)

> I'd argue that there isn't such a thing as a 'digital musician'. Digital is a meaningless semiotic consequence of the information age. The idea of musician will prevail for all time. (AF)

> A musician is a musician, digital or not. This being said, we need to move beyond the vocational skill set often associated with musical training. Today, knowing the physics of acoustics and the physiology of auditory perception is more important than knowing functional harmony. (AT)

Others (NC, CJ, JR, PO, SP, Q, SS) seem happy enough to accept the label:

> I love being a digital musician as digital technology gives me the tools to be an extremely creative and flexible composer. (SS)

This difference illustrates the points made in the Preface and throughout the book about the relative transience of the digital as a culturally and musically defining characteristic. The phrase 'digital musician' is merely a convenient 'shorthand' way of describing musicians who work with digital technology. Yet, as all the case study artists agree, there are skills and attributes that are peculiar to musicians who work with digital technologies.

Half of them listed programming skills, knowledge of acoustics and psychoacoustics, and computer knowledge as essential. A quarter suggested that knowledge of mathematics is very important, and DSP, synthesis, recording, production, archiving and patching skills were all highlighted as essential. On the human side, more than half the respondents agreed that *persistence and determination* are the most important attributes. An ability to conduct background research, to be flexible, to be open-minded, to have good networking skills, a sense of humour, an ability to collaborate, to have a good imagination, and other similar attributes were all singled out. Many of the replies also highlighted the importance of staying abreast of current developments while also being literate in past music.

> verbalized positively in the order of descending generality: humor, curiosity, persistence, luck, classical literacy, having readily access to electronic calculating machinery of recent make including libraries of open software for their operation, literacy in mathematics, the internals and black magic of aforementioned machinery. (OB)

> Some are in common with and critical to an acoustic musician: dedication/enthusiasm, networking, effort/practice, but some are exclusive, these are possibly more what you're asking for: computer programming ability in a number of languages (i.e., SuperCollider, C, MATLAB); instrument builder's/system designer's spirit – desire to tinker and explore potential (and the necessary patience to defer outcomes here, plus the necessary impatience not to spend the entire time designing); grasp of electronic musician's music theory: psychoacoustics, DSP, discrete math, representations/formalisms; ability to be operating system and platform/ software free; essentially to reach to ideas independent of particular implementations (helping with future proofing in this over anxious environment of upgrades – we should have a moratorium on progress for some years and take advantage of what we have right now!); live electronics/interfacing. (NC)

> A deep interest in synthesis, recording and production of sound. Some computer coding skills. Technological shamelessness. A high threshold for embarrassment from failure. (JE)

> The 'traditional' skills of listening and imagination are extremely important to me. I enjoy reading a score on a train (without the iPod accompaniment) and I find it

depressing when my students' ask me what I'm doing (and why!). Learning how to code has probably been the most liberating side of my work with technology. I detest being told what to do (by anyone/thing!). Being told what to do by software and hardware is unforgivable. Coding goes some way to alleviating that situation so I probably would describe programming as essential to the digital musician. … As my work explores acoustics a great deal, clearly having knowledge of the physics behind spatial movement of sound is essential too. (RG)

As with any musician, a basic love of music, an ability to be happy sitting alone for (sometimes long) periods of time, and an awareness of copyright; for the specifically digital musician, an interest in learning new musical softwares and other related digital skills. Beyond that, there are lots of useful skills, but probably none essential. (CJ)

Personally, I think knowledge of a programming language and sound physics is the most important. … For specific things like algorithmic composition, machine learning, signal analysis or other generative approaches I think a textual programming language suits better than graphical environments, but that's just my opinion/experience, and I acknowledge that people's minds work in different ways. (TM)

All kinds of skills, but the main one has been collaborating with other people, such as programmers and other musicians. … Another important skill is to jettison stereo and to work with the acoustic properties of the space you are in at the time. I'm no longer a soloist. Now I work with other people and aim for a wider audience. I would add that awareness and gentle perseverance are also essential skills! (KM)

My transition from forty years of analog music making began in 1991 with my first piece that was recorded digitally. This was about the time that digital recording became 16bit. Up until that time 8bit recording was not sufficient for use with my EIS as recorded delay was essential. I continued my transition when I joined the faculty at RPI in 2001. Since then I do my best to stay current with all the acceleration of changes in digital music technology. Ability to continue learning is essential. Ability to work with team members is essential. There is no way to know all that you need to know. (PO)

The ability to integrate ideas with technical skills. (RP)

Research and networking are important skills, and being relentless. Even the most knowledgeable digiticians get stuck and have to look stuff up so don't expect someone with more experience to have all the answers for you! Be a contributor of knowledge. Don't let technical problems get you down. Don't let computers intimidate you. Get comfortable with wiping your hard drive and re-installing everything from scratch. (SP)

File management and archiving is something I should be better at and really is a skill the digital musician needs. Over the years, I have created thousands of files that are now sprawled across many hard disks. I sometimes feel it is easier to create a new sound rather than try to retrieve a file I made, for example, five years ago. Also, understanding ins and outs and patching skills is essential. The binary world has no in between with regard to this. Being a digital musician is not any different for me from being a musician in general, where, for example, I would want to experiment, explore and find the 'edges' of the medium. (JR)

Technically: keeping up on current technologies, upgrades, plug-ins, processor speeds, available VSTs. Knowing how to optimize the performance of one's computer for digital audio, keeping an eye on the sort of peripherals and MIDI interfaces and whatnot that become available, and looking at tech news to think about the future of one's set-up as technology progresses.

Professionally: networking and sharing ideas with fellow digital musicians, having a local peer base, having an Internet peer base, being committed to the larger digital musician community and helping out others with talent (either by sharing knowledge or helping to connect musicians with labels or musicians with venues to perform in), not letting one's ego get in the way, keeping in touch with people in the press who've been supportive in the past, as well as labels or promotions crews that have booked me.

Mentally: commitment, goal orientation, foresight and planning ahead, just doing things that are musically fun (like DJing privately or in a low key setting and not being constrained by a genre, or entering remix contests for the fun of it), collaborating with other musicians, having another income stream so I don't have to care if my music is commercially viable, going to music events that aren't electronic just for a change of pace. (Q)

> In no particular order …

- creativity to work within 'constraints' of technology
- ability to use the technology creatively and push its boundaries
- flexibility
- patience(!)
- knowledge of music outside the digital domain – trying different compositional approaches, etc. (SS)

[W]e need to move beyond the vocational skill set often associated with musical training. Today, knowing the physics of acoustics and the physiology of auditory perception is more important than knowing functional harmony. (AT)

You need a degree of talent, a good ear. I'm not a talented musician in the traditional sense: I struggle to play keyboards properly, I can only read music at a snail's pace, I never had any formal training. The important thing is that I can conceptualize how I want something to sound, based on the timbres and melodic aspects – counterpoint, etc. I can hear a multitrack going on in my mind that I just have to get out. If I can't play some things I know people who can, or I can programme it.

Open-mindedness is very important. … What I would encourage digital musicians in particular to do is: take a step back, do a little thought and research about what you want to achieve before you start. … What digital musicians have to aim for is to escape the normal, pre-set paths that are offered to us at all times. All musicians, myself included, can go for the easy option, the lazy way, and it is always on offer today, particularly in computer composition. The most valuable advice I can offer people starting out on this path is: take a step back, look at what you are trying to achieve and do a bit of research. Make it hard for yourself. Limit your palette, even. Deliberately limiting yourself can enable more unique creations. (MW)

Do you have any other useful or relevant things to say about being a digital musician today?

Some of the case study artists had nothing more to add, others made quite lengthy remarks. Space does not permit these to be reproduced in full here (they may be viewed on the website), so a pithy selection will have to suffice:

> The avenues for truly experimental new music are highly centred on digital technology. However, a few of the debates and themes seem to me chimerical or unnecessary: there's nothing special about laptop music, cognitive skills have a lot in common with physical skills, and we shouldn't be too biased against either. (NC)

> It doesn't matter how complicated your Max or SuperCollider patch is if you have nothing to say musically. I have to confess (at the risk of never being employed in an institution focusing on digital technology again!) that I have little interest in technology per se. When the sound that is being delivered is purely a means of demonstrating the technology, we have a serious problem. (RG)

> The relative ease with which anyone can create electronic music today is a great thing; however, it sometimes obscures two important issues. First, that the majority of people in the world do not have the resources (financial or other) to become digital musicians (or digital artists of any description). Second, traditional music theory and skills can greatly help electronic musicians with their art. (CJ)

> The future is very exciting. We are in the early stages of virtual synth abilities. I do quite a bit of lecturing, and one warning flag I'd raise is that the standards in universities and colleges are not generally agreed. … We're all under more time and financial pressure than ever before, but I would still urge people to go off-piste from time to time, and even to start with a blank canvas, no presets. (MW)

> It is exciting to observe how the music industry is being transformed at the moment which creates lots of opportunities for 'digital' musicians, for example where the app is replacing the mp3. The interconnected locative mobile media devices give composers and musicians fantastic possibilities for interesting musical composition. (TM)

> Digital makes us appreciate analogue – not just for the specific sound qualities of certain historical instruments but for the qualities of analogue electronics as a medium of sound transmission. You can keep adding to analog, you can feel analog. Digital is not in the impossibility of acquiring these capabilities, but the digital musician must sensitize himself to this potential. (AT)

> I'm asking more from technology. I set up the rules and the ingredients, and something different must happen. That's why I'm making installations. Let's replace a few of these new gyms with huge multichannelled sound systems for people to come and spin around their favourite disco, opera or swing CDs. (KM)

It is no longer possible to be concerned only with music; we live in a global world where interdisciplinary approaches are critical to artistic expression. (RP)

Being a digital musician is not just about the practical application of technology but also a way of being or thinking. (JR)

The digital musician of today has to be ready for change! (PO)

Discussion Questions

- What music do you make?

- Why do you make music?

- Is any of your sound-based work not 'music', as such?

- Do you consider yourself a performer, a composer, a technologist, an engineer, some combination of these or, indeed, something else?

- What is the cultural context for your work? Are you influenced by music in other cultures? And the other arts?

- What skills and attributes do you consider to be essential for you as a digital musician?

Historical Listening List

The following is a long (but nowhere near long enough to cover everything) historical listening list, that adds up to an account of the evolution of electronic and electro-acoustic music in the twentieth century. It begins with tape composition, and digital music gradually enters the list as it begins to appear from the early 1950s onwards. Max Mathews wrote the first music programming language, MUSIC1, in 1957 at Bell Labs and created some of the earliest computer music compositions. Not surprisingly, this music emerged from the electronic and electro-acoustic music that had gone before. This listening list may therefore be regarded as the beginnings of a collection of essential historical recordings (however, note that it does omit the works that appear as recommended listenings elsewhere in this book).

The website that accompanies this book contains a playlist that includes all the music that is listed below.

Some useful questions to ask when listening are: What is the artist's intention? How well is it realized? What is the cultural context for the work? What are its compositional techniques? What is the musical language?

- Pierre Schaeffer (1948) 'Étude aux chemins de fer' from *Cinq études de bruits* on [CD] *OHM: The Early Gurus of Electronic Music: 1948–1980*, Ellipsis Arts, M1473O462000. This was the first time recorded sound was assembled into a musical composition. The sounds included steam engines, whistles and railway noises.
- Pierre Schaeffer and Pierre Henry (1950) *Symphonie pour un homme seul* on *Pierre Schaeffer: L'Oeuvre musicale* [CD] EMF, EM114. A twelve-movement musical account of a man's day using recorded sounds. This was performed live, and originally required real-time manipulation of many turntables and mixing desks.
- John Cage (1951) *Imaginary Landscape No. 4 for 12 radios* [CD] Hat Hut Records, hatArt 6179. Two performers are stationed at each radio, one for dialling the radio-stations, the second performer controlling amplitude and 'timbre'. Durations are written in conventional notation, using notes, placed on a five-line staff. The score gives notations for tuning (controlled by player 1) as well as volume and tone colour (controlled by player 2).
- Otto Luening (1952) *Low Speed* [CD] CRI, CD611. Luening and Ussachevsky worked in the Columbia-Princeton Electronic Music Center on tape composition. This piece explores slowed down flute sounds.
- Vladimir Ussachevsky (1952) *Sonic Contours* [CD] CRI, CD611. Ussachevsky worked with tape feedback, looping, and echo effects in this piece that combines piano and varispeed vocals.

- John Cage (1953) 'Williams Mix' on *OHM: The Early Gurus of Electronic Music: 1948–1980* [CD] Ellipsis Arts, M1473O462000. Tape fragments of various sounds are recombined in a random order (determined by coin tosses).
- Earle Brown (1953) *Octet I for Tape* [CD] New World Records, 80650. An early tape piece for eight loudspeakers surrounding an audience.
- Karlheinz Stockhausen (1954) *Studie II* [CD] Stockhausen Verlag, CD3. An early example of *Elektronische Musik* (electronic music) which used sine tones superimposed in groups of five.
- Hugh Le Caine (1955) *Dripsody* [CD] EMF, EM115. Created from the sound of a single water drop, and using splicing and speed control to make various rhythms and melodies.
- Karlheinz Stockhausen (1955–1956) 'Gesang der Jünglinge' on *Stockhausen: Elektronische Musik 1952–1960* [CD] Stockhausen-Verlag, CD3. This combines electronic sounds and a recording of a boy's voice. It is a serial 2 composition, but with strong connections drawn between the sound of the sine wave oscillators and the timbre of the boy's voice. It not only serializes durations, loudness, and thickness of texture, but also the spatialization.
- Louis and Bébé Barron (1956) *Forbidden Planet* [CD] Planet Records. This film was the first motion picture to feature an electronic music score.
- Lejaren Hiller and Leonard Isaacson (1957) *Iliac Suite*. The first piece of music composed by a computer.
- Edgard Varèse (1958) *Poéme Electronique* [CD] Decca, 460208. Composed for the Philips Pavilion of the 1958 World's Fair, a massive multi-media environment featuring projected images, film, and multi-channel sound. As the listeners walk through the space, the sound moves around them.
- Luciano Berio (1958) *Thema – Omaggio a Joyce* [CD] RCA Victor Red Seal, 09026-68302-2. All the sounds are derived from a recording of Cathy Berberian reciting a passage from James Joyce's *Ulysses*. This is a compendium of tape splicing techniques.
- Iannis Xenakis (1958) 'Concrète PH' on *Xenakis: Electronic Music*. Electronic Music Foundation [CD] EMF, CD003. A musique concrète piece made from the sound of burning charcoal.
- György Ligeti (1958) *Artikulation* [CD] Schotts Music Ltd., WER60161-50. A very short, but highly virtuosic tape composition, made from small electronic sounds that are combined to resemble utterances.
- Karlheinz Stockhausen (1959–1960) *Kontakte* [CD] Wergo, 6009. The 'contact' in the title is between the taped sounds and the acoustic sounds of piano and percussion. By adding the two together, a richer palette of sounds is discovered.
- Milton Babbitt (1960–61) *Ensembles for Synthesizer*. Created at the Columbia-Princeton Electronic Music Center and using one of the early synthesizers, the RCA Electronic Music Synthesizer, this piece explores the application of serial techniques to electronic music.
- Ornette Coleman (1961) *Free Jazz: A Collective Improvisation* [CD] Atlantic, 812273609-2. Two independent jazz quartets play opposite each other (one on each stereo channel), improvising on a limited selection of directions, without harmonic structure, driven by melodic and rhythmic concerns, and each musician contributing according to own style. Highly influential in subsequent jazz improvisational technique.

- Pierre Henry (1963) *Variations pour une Porte et un Soupir* (*Variations for a Door and a Sigh*) [CD] Harmonia Mundi, HMC 905200. This is a tour-de-force of tape splicing and editing techniques.
- Steve Reich (1965) 'Come Out' on *Steve Reich: Early Works, 1987* [CD] Elektra/ Nonesuch, 979169-2. An early piece using phasing: looped tape recordings of speech (the phrase 'come out to show them') gradually move out of synchronization. This process is then repeated and repeated until the multiple layerings remove the meaning of the words.
- The Righteous Brothers (1965) *You've Lost That Lovin' Feeling* [CD] Polydor, 847 248. An example of the celebrated 'wall of sound' studio treatment (rich vocals and orchestral accompaniment) characteristic of Phil Spector.
- The Beach Boys (1966) *Good Vibrations*, [CD] EMI, CDEMTVD51. Brian Wilson's production was highly advanced for its time, reflected in the fact that it took six months to record this single. It involves unusual instrumentation for a pop song, including an electro-theremin. The mix is mono, but all five parts are still clearly audible.
- The Beatles (1966) 'Tomorrow Never Knows' on *Revolver* [CD] Capitol/EMI, ST2576. Early psychedelia, heavily influenced by Indian music and Eastern philosophy. The Beatles' first experiments with tape loops.
- John Cage and Lejaren Hiller (1967–69) *HPSCHD* [CD] EMF, CD038. Applies computer-derived chance procedures to both composition and listening strategies. The music processes classical pieces for harpsichord using a FORTRAN program based on the *I Ching*, designed by Ed Kobrin.
- The Beatles (1968) 'Revolution #9' from the *White Album* [CD] Apple PCS 7067-8. According to John Lennon: 'It has the basic rhythm of the original 'Revolution' going on, with some twenty loops we put on, things from the archives of EMI. … There were about ten machines with people holding pencils on the loops … I fed them all in and mixed them live.'
- Frank Zappa (1968) *Frank Zappa and the Mothers of Invention: We're Only in It for the Money* [CD] Ryco, RCD40024. This album features radical audio editing and production techniques. The album was highly virtuosic and satirical of contemporary cultural fashions (flower-power and hippie-dom). There also seem to be some tongue-in-cheek references to 'serious' electronic music.
- Can (1969) 'Father Cannot Yell' on *Cannibalism* (released in 1980) [CD] Spoon, CD004. Can was a German rock group who had considerable influence on electronic and experimental music.
- Raymond Scott (1969) *The Pygmy Taxi Corporation* [CD] Basta Records. This is one of Scott's non-commercial compositions, written as a musical experiment with his Electronium.
- Alvin Lucier (1970) *I Am Sitting in a Room* [CD] Lovely Music, CD1013. The liner notes explain that 'several sentences of recorded speech are simultaneously played back into a room and re-recorded there many times. As the repetitive process continues, those sounds common to the original spoken statement and those implied by the structural dimensions of the room are reinforced. The others are gradually eliminated. The space acts as a filter; the speech is transformed into pure sound. All the recorded segments are spliced together in the order in which they were made and constitute the work.'

- Miles Davis (1970) *Bitches Brew* [CD] Columbia, C2K 65774. The Bitches Brew album was not only a landmark in the establishment of 'fusion' jazz, but also important in its pioneering use of studio technology, led by Teo Macero.
- Wendy Carlos (1972) *Timesteps* [CD] East Side Digital, ESD81362. This was composed for Stanley Kubrick's film *A Clockwork Orange* and used a vocoder to create 'synthesized speech'.
- Pink Floyd (1973) *Dark Side of the Moon* [CD] Harvest/Capitol, 3609. Classic concept album that sits between electronic music and blues rock. Employs many musique concrète techniques alongside double-tracking, flanging, panning and reverb effects.[1]
- Faust (1973, reissued 1993) *The Faust Tapes* [CD] Recommended, RERF2CD. Faust used the studio as a creative tool in the 1970s and spliced together improvised music, electronics, folk music, musique concrete, punk, psychedelia, and jazz.
- Kraftwerk (1974) *Autobahn* [CD] EMI, CDP7461532. Influential German electronic music group, particularly known for their 1970s work which has had a broad impact on popular music.
- Lou Reed (1975) *Metal Machine Music* [CD] BMG, ND90670. A celebrated album comprising layered guitar feedback, and nothing else.
- The Residents (1976) *The Third Reich and Roll* [CD] Torso, CD405. Long-standing American underground avant garde group, who consistently maintain their anonymity. Many of their works are cultural commentaries utilizing samples and media hi-jinks.
- Brian Eno (1978) *Ambient 1/Music for Airports* [CD] Virgin Records, EEGCD17. I. Influential English composer, producer, engineer, writer, and visual artist. He is known as the father of 'ambient' music. His production credits include U2 and Talking Heads.
- Gavin Bryars (1978) *The Sinking of the Titanic* [CD] EG Records, CDVE938. Uses a collection of 'found materials' on tape along with a live ensemble, plus sounds recorded underwater. The music consists of immensely slowed-down hymn tunes and other sonic materials.
- Iannis Xenakis (1978) *Mycenae-Alpha* [CD] Mode, 98/99. This was the first piece ever to be made with the UPIC computer system. Instead of a keyboard to perform the music, the UPIC's performance device is a mouse and/or a digital drawing board, which trace the composer's graphic score into the program. This then interprets the drawings as real time instructions for sound synthesis.
- David Behrman (1978) 'On the Other Ocean' on *OHM: The Early Gurus of Electronic Music: 1948–1980* [CD] Ellipsis Arts, M1473O462000. An improvisation on acoustic instruments with pitch-detection controlling a computer, which in turn controls two handmade synthesizers. This is an early example of an interactive work with live computer response to human performers.
- Iannis Xenakis (1977/8) *La Legende d'Eer* [CD] Mode, 148. A seven-channel electro-acoustic composition designed to be played as a multimedia piece with lasers in a specially constructed building called 'Le Diatope'. There are three sound sources: instrumental sounds, noises, and electronically generated sounds.
- Robert Ashley (1978/80) *Perfect Lives* [DVD] Lovely Music, DVD4917. A highly innovative cross-media 'television opera' in seven 30-minute episodes.
- Charles Dodge (1979) *Any Resemblance is Purely Coincidental* [CD] New Albion, 043.

Scored for piano and tape, the latter consisting of electronic sounds and a compu-ter-transformed rendering of Enrico Caruso's 1907 recording of the aria 'Vesti la giubba' from Leoncavallo's *I Pagliacci*.

- Einsturzende Neubaten (1980–1983) *Strategies against Architecture* [CD] Mute, STUMM14. Classic and shocking work from the pioneers of German 'industrial' music.
- King Tubby/Roots Radics (1981) *Dangerous Dub* [CD] Greensleeves, GREWCD229. King Tubby is a Jamaican sound engineer who has been highly influential in the development of Jamaican dub. This has heavy reverb and other effects overlaying a remixed reggae/ska track from which vocals and lead instruments are omitted.
- Glenn Branca (1981, reissued 2003) *The Ascension Acute* [CD] 9EIPG. Trademark layered electric guitars and a cacophony of riffs, beats and rhythms.
- Pierre Boulez (1981) *Répons* [CD] Deutsche Grammophon, 457605. A huge work for nine percussionists, orchestra and digital sound system.
- Grandmaster Flash (1981) *The Adventures of Grandmaster Flash on the Wheels of Steel* [CD] Sugar Hill Records, 310917. Grandmaster Flash is a New York DJ artist who was instrumental in the development of turntable technique during the 1970s to 1980s. This track uses samples from Queen, CHIC and Blondie, among others.
- Nicolas Collins (1982) *Little Spiders* [CD] Lovely Music, VR1701. A duet for two computers that respond to keystrokes to generate sounds 'characterized by an ambig-uous pitch center and shifting overtone structure'.[2]
- Laurie Anderson (1982) *Big Science* [CD] Warner, 2KNM. An important figure in the establishment of performance art, Anderson's stripped-down, ironic tone and techno-logically quirky delivery helped define the idea of the postmodern in the 1980s.
- David Behrman (1983–1986) *Leapday Night* [CD] Lovely Music, LCD1042. A series of three pieces exploiting machine listening techniques.
- Jean-Michel Jarre (1984) *Zoolok* [CD] Disques Dreyfus. Samples singing and speech in twenty-five different languages, combined with digital sounds, all created on the Fairlight CMI.
- The Art of Noise (1984) 'Beat Box (Diversion One)' on *The Best of The Art of Noise* [CD] China/Polydor, 837 367-2. An influential electronic music group formed by producer Trevor Horn, helping to define the potential of new digital sampling technology in dance and popular forms in the 1980s. The name of the group is, obviously, a reference to Luigi Russolo's essay of the same name.
- Kaija Saariaho (1984) *Verblendungen* [CD] Finlandia, FACD374. Successful balanc-ing of live orchestra and electro–acoustic music, using the Groupe de Recherches Musicale's digital toolset to process concrete sounds. The two elements traverse the pitch-noise continuum in opposite directions.
- Paul Lansky (1985) *Idle Chatter* [CD] Bridge, 9103. This is one of a family of pieces that explore vocal sounds, overdubbed, edited and processed. The music comprises an inflected babble of barely recognizable sounds.
- George Lewis (1985 onwards) *Voyager* [CD] Disk Union, R-3800029. 'Voyager (the [computer] program) analyzes aspects of an improviser's performance in real time, using that analysis to guide an automatic composing program that generates complex responses to the musician's playing. This implies a certain independence of action, and indeed, the program exhibits generative behaviour independent of the human performer. The system is not an instrument, and therefore cannot be controlled by a performer' (from the liner notes).

- Trevor Wishart (1986) 'Vox 5' on *Computer Music Currents, vol. 4, 1989* [CD] Wergo, 2024–50. An English composer who has contributed significantly to the development of computer music.
- New Order (1987) *Substance* [CD] Factory Records, FAC 200. English band known for its melding of electronic-dance and post-punk styles.
- Denis Smalley (1987) *Wind Chimes* [CD] Empreintes Digitales, IMED-9209-CD. The sound of wind chimes is processed and developed in astonishing detail.
- Morton Subotnick (1988) *And the Butterflies begin to Sing* [CD] New World Records. Scored for string quartet, bass, MIDI keybaord and computer.
- Christian Marclay (1988) *More Encores* [CD] Recommended, RERCM1. Turntablism that mixes music by Johann Strauss, John Zorn, John Cage, Serge Gainsbourg and Jane Birkin, Ferrante and Teicher, Louis Armstrong, Martin Denny, Maria Callas, Jimi Hendrix, and Frederic Chopin.
- John Zorn (1988) *Forbidden Fruit* [CD] Nonesuch, D100675. With Christian Marclay (turntables), Ohta Hiromi (voice) and the Kronos String Quartet. Zorn said: 'Composed of sixty sections in all, four sets of twelve variations each, and twelve themes, all squeezed into ten minutes, this is perhaps my most compact and fast-moving piece to date.'
- Diamanda Galás (1988) *You Must Be Certain of the Devil* [CD] Mute, STUMM46. 'Galás emerged within the post-modern performance art scene in the seventies ... protesting ... the treatment of victims of the Greek junta, attitudes towards victims of AIDS. Her pieces are constructed from the ululation of traditional Mediterranean keening ... whispers, shrieks, and moans'.[3] Galás uses an unusual microphone array and time-varying reverberation to enhance her extraordinary vocal range and the brooding intensity of the music.
- Pauline Oliveros (1990) *Crone Music* [CD] Lovely Music, LCD1903. 'As a musician I am interested in the sensual nature of sound, its power of release and change. In my performances throughout the world I try to transmit to the audience the way I am experiencing sound as I hear it and play in a style that I call deep listening. Deep listening is listening in every possible way to everything possible to hear no matter what you are doing. Such intense listening includes the sounds of daily life, of nature, of one's own thoughts as well as musical sounds. Deep listening is my life practice' – Oliveros (from the liner notes).
- Tim Perkis (1992) *Wax Lips* [CD] Tzadik, TZ 8050-3. An early example of networked music, performed by The Hub.
- Michael McNabb (1993) *Dreamsong* [CD] Wergo, RWER20202. Dreamsong was created with the MUS10 computer music language on a DEC KL-10 computer. McNabb programmed the computer to create smooth transformations between different sounds. For McNabb, these shifts were poetically like the shifting experiences of a dream.
- Francis Dhomont (1994/6) *Forêt Profonde* [CD] Empreintes Digitales, IMED9634. Dhomont is one of the leading exponents of 'acousmatic' music, or 'cinema for the ears'.
- Goldie (1995) *Timeless* [CD] FFRR, CD697-124073-2. The debut album by Goldie, and still one of the finest examples of drum and bass.
- Autechre (1995) *Tri Repetae* [CD] Warp Records, 38. Autechre (Rob Brown and Sean Booth) have been influential on the development of IDM (Intelligent Dance Music),

but their work does not fit easily into a single genre. They explore a variety of techno instruments and techniques and sometimes use modular software environments.

- Tupac Shakur (1996) *All Eyez on Me* [CD] Death Row/Koch, 63008. Probably the most influential rap album of the 1990s.
- John Oswald (1996) *69 Plunderphonics 96* [CD] Seeland, 515. 'If creativity is a field, copyright is the fence' (John Oswald).
- Tortoise (1996) *Millions Now Living Will Never Die* [CD] Thrill Jockey, THRILL025. An eclectic fusion of jazz, electronica and experimental rock (among other influences) from an American 'postrock' band.
- Amon Tobin (1997) *Bricolage* [CD] Ninja Tunes, zenCD29. Contains influences from drum and bass, hip-hop, blues, jazz and samba, all digitally processed to create a sense of the bricolage suggested by the title.
- The Prodigy (1997) *The Fat of the Land* [CD] XL Recordings, XLCDID 121. Controversial British 'Big Beat' band.
- Aphex Twin (1997) 'Bucephalus Bouncing Ball' on *Come to Daddy* [CD] Warp Records, 31001. Richard James, aka Aphex Twin, is an innovator in contemporary electronic ambient, drum and bass, and related genres.
- Steve Reich (1998) *Different Trains* [CD] Signum Records, SIGCD066. Combines recorded speech with string quartet.
- Coldcut (1998) 'Timber' on *Hexstatic* [CD] Ninja Tunes, ZencdS65A. 'In Timber all sound components are linked to their video sources. Whole rhythms have been painstakingly edited out of individual beats and video frames.'[4]
- Farmer's Manual (1998) *Explorers We* [CD] Or, SQUISH04. Described as 'a sinewave massacre', this is a 60-minute long, continuous track of electronic sound manipulations by the band of which case study Oswald Berthold is a member. Index points have been placed at 60-second intervals, making this very suitable for random play, looping and home-DJing.
- Ryoji Ikeda (1998) *0°C* [CD] Touch, TO:30. Classic early microsound album.
- Scanner (1999) *Lauwarm Instrumentals* [CD] Sulphur, SULCD002. Exploits many vocal and almost-vocal samples to create a dark and carefully orchestrated album of great intensity.
- Pan Sonic (1999) 'Maa' on *Album A* [CD] Blast First, BFFP132. Pan Sonic is a Finnish electronic music duo: Mika Vainio and Ilpo Väisänen.
- Various Artists (2000) *OH: The Early Gurus of Electronic Music: 1948–1980* [CD] Ellipsis Arts M1473 O46 2000. A very useful compilation album of the history of electronic music.
- Sonic Youth (1999) *Goodbye 20th Century* [CD] SYR4. A rock and roll band perform experimental music by John Cage, Cornelius Cardew, Pauline Oliveros, Yoko Ono, Christian Wolff and others.
- Kim Cascone (2000) *1parasitefordeleuze* [CD] anechoic media, a001. The title explicitly references *Milles Plateaux* by Giles Deleuze and Félix Guattari.
- Jonty Harrison (2000) *Evidence Matérielle* [CD] empreintes DIGITALes, IMED0052. Compilation of acousmatic works which sometimes look at the structure of sound (assessing sound for what it is), and sometimes look at the story behind the sound (assessing it for what it tells). Two ways to look at sound, two different ways to listen.
- Steve Roden (2000) *Four Possible Landscapes* [CD] Trente Oiseaux, TOC00. Blends concrete and electronic sounds to create highly minimal aural landscapes.

- AMM (2001) *Fine* [CD] Matchless Recordings, MRCD46. A highly influential free-improvisation group. They are said to never discuss the content of a performance ahead of time.

- Squarepusher (2001) *Go Plastic* [CD] Warp, CD85. 'The modern musician is subject to a barrage of persuasion from manufacturers of music technology. The general implication is that buying new tools leads to being able to make new and exciting music. While it is true that certain degrees of freedom are added by new equipment, it is not the case that this entails wholesale musical innovation. What seems more likely is that new clichés are generated by users unanalytically being forced into certain actions by the architecture of the machine. For me it is parallel, if not synonymous with a dogmatic consumer mentality that seems to hold that our lives are always improved by possessions' (Tom Jenkinson, aka Squarepusher).[5]

- Negativland (2001) *These Guys Are from England and Who Gives a Shit* [CD] Seeland (or rather Seelard), 0021. Controversial album that includes a track parodying U2 that orginally landed Negativland in court on Intellectual Property violation charges. In the end, U2 seem to have colluded, or at least sanctioned, the record, but the story is complicated.

- Matthew Adkins (2002) *Fragmented Visions* [CD] MPS Music and Video, MPSCD015. 'Walk into the games arcade of the future and you walk into a world of liquid neon: a world of high stakes, high energy and high risk' (from the liner notes).

- Missy Elliot (2002) 'Work It' on *Under Construction* [CD] Goldmind/Elektra, 7559-62875-2. Highly successful American singer, songwriter, and hip-hop artist, who also uses some sophisticated digital techniques.

- DJ Spooky (2002) *Optometry* [CD] Thirsty Ear, THI57121.2. A virtuoso and seamless mix of live and sampled materials in this landmark hybrid of free jazz and dub.

- Tetsu Inoue and Carl Stone (2002) *pict.soul* [CD] Cycling '74, c74-005. 'pict.soul documents the first meeting between these two giants in the experimental, ambient, and post-ambient world. … As is always the case with Inoue and Stone, their source materials remain mysterious, identifiable for fleeting instants. The precise nature of the collaborations for each of the ten pieces on *pict.soul* is equally mysterious.'[6]

- Phil Jeck (2003) *Vinyl Coda I–III* [CD] Intermedium, INTER002. A completely non-digital piece of turntablism that, through its deconstruction and editing of old recordings, manages to convey much about digital cut-and-paste culture.

- Kaffe Matthews (2003) *Eb+flo* [CD] Annette Works, AWCD0005-6. Despite the title, the album (by one of the case study artists) is mostly made of static electronic soundscapes, featuring, amongst many other instruments, the theremin.

- Björk (2004) *Medúlla* [CD] Atlantic Records, One Little Indian 6294. An album made entirely from digitally manipulated vocal sounds, including the throat-singer Tagaq, hip-hop beatboxer Rahzel, Japanese beatboxer Dokaka, avant-rocker Mike Patton, Soft Machine drummer/singer Robert Wyatt, and various choirs.

- Gilles Gobeil (2005) *Trilogie d'ondes* [CD] empreintes DIGITALes, IMED0756. Includes works spanning three decades featuring the *ondes martenot*.

- Pete Stollery (2006) *Un son peut en cacher un autre* [CD] empreintes DIGITALes, IMED0678. Plays with the ambiguities of listening, as one sound opens to reveal another inside.

Notes

1 Creative Identity

1 The word 'electro-acoustic' comes from engineering, where it is defined as 'an adjective describing any process involving the transfer of a signal from acoustic to electrical form, or vice versa'. B. Truax (ed.) *Handbook for Acoustic Ecology*, 1999. Online. Available HTTP: http://www.sfu. ca/sonic-studio/handbook/Electro-Acoustic.html> (accessed 7 October 2011).

2 'Radiophonic' refers to the experimental use of sound in radio.

3 The term 'nobrow' was coined by John Seabrook in his book of that title, published in 2000, and more recently used by Peter Swirski in his *From Lowbrow to Nobrow* (2005).

4 W. Benjamin, 'The Work of Art in the Age of Mechanical Reproduction', 1936. Reprinted in W. Benjamin, trans. H. Zohn, *Illuminations*, London: Jonathan Cape, 1970, pp. 219–253.

5 A. Casella, 'Matter and Timbre: Tone-Problems of Today', *Musical Quarterly*, 10, 1924, 159–171.

6 F. Busoni 'Sketch of a New Aesthetic of Music', 1911. Reprinted in *Three Classics in the Aesthetic of Music*, New York: Dover Editions, 1962, pp. 89–95.

7 L. Russolo, *The Art of Noises*, New York: Pendragon Press, 1986, pp. 27–28.

8 E. Varèse, *The Liberation of Sound*, 1936. Reprinted in E. Schwartz and B. Childs, *Contemporary Composers on Contemporary Music*, New York: Da Capo Press, 1998, pp. 195–208.

9 '*Musique concrète*', or concrete music, is a somewhat misunderstood term. Traditional classical music is 'abstract', in the sense that it begins as notations on paper, which are then translated into sounds by performers. 'Concrete' music takes the opposite approach by beginning with actual sounds and abstracting a musical composition from them. By extension, the term *musique concrète* has become a commonly used shorthand for music made from 'real-world' sounds rather than musical notes.

10 J. Cage, *Silence*, London: Marion Boyars, 1971, pp. 3–6.

11 Described as: '20-minute solos for one to 7 amplified harpsichords and tapes for one to 52 amplified monaural machines to be used in whole or in part in any combination with or without interruptions, etc., to make an indeterminate concert of any agreed-upon length having 2 to 59 channels with loud-speakers around the audience.' J. Rivest 'In Advance of the Avant Garde: John Cage at the University of Illinois, 1952–69', New York: Electronic Music Foundation, 1999.

12 A. Culver, *John Cage Computer Programs*, 2007. Online. Available HTPP: http://www.anarchicharmony.org (accessed 7 October 2011).

13 R. Taylor, L. Menabrea and A. Lovelace, 'Sketch of the Analytical Engine', *Scientific Memoirs No.3*, London: Taylor, 1842, pp. 666–731.

14 Source: United Nations Development Programme. Cited in N. Gronewald, 'One Quarter of World's Population Lacks Electricity', *Scientific American*, 2009. Online. Available HTTP: http://www.scientificamerican.com (accessed 20 September 2011).

15 The picture was created by NASA from data gathered by the Defense Meteorological Satellite Program.

16 Source: World Internet Usage Statistics. Online. Available HTTP: http://www.internetworldstats.com/ (accessed 20 September 2011).

17 US Census Bureau, International Programs Center, Online. Available HTTP: http://www.census.gov/ipc/www/ (accessed 9 September 2005).

18 *The Edge*. Online. Available HTTP: http://www.edge.org/ (accessed 12 February 2006).

2 Aural Awareness

1 This is a logical consequence for Western music of the colouristic discoveries made in the late nineteenth century by Claude Debussy and others.

2 The translations of Schaeffer's text are all taken from Chion, M., trans. Dack, J. and North, C. *Guide des Objets Sonores: Pierre Schaeffer et la recherche musicale*, Paris: Buchet/Chastel. 1982.

3 Ibid.

4 The French word for this is 'époché', a term borrowed from the philosopher and phenomenologist Husserl, meaning: 'a deconditioning of habitual listening patterns, to return to the original experience of perception, enabling us to grasp the sound object at its own level which takes it as the vehicle of a meaning to be understood or a cause to be identified.' Source: *EARS: The Electroacoustic Resource Site*. Online. Available HTTP: http://www.ears.dmu.ac.uk (accessed 7 October 2011).

5 Ibid., p. 26.

6 D. Smalley, 'Spectromorphology: Explaining Sound-shapes', *Organized Sound*, 2:2, 1997, 107–126.

7 J. Cage, *A Year from Monday*, Middletown, CT: Wesleyan University Press, 1967.

8 B. Truax, *Acoustic Communication*, Westport, CT: Ablex, 2001, p. 15.

9 Ibid., p. 22.

10 Ibid., p. 23.

11 Ibid. p. 24.

12 P. Oliveros, *Software for People: Collected Writings 1963–80*, Baltimore, MD: Smith Publications, 1984.

13 B. Eno, 'Ambient Music', in *A Year with Swollen Appendices*, London: Faber & Faber, 1996.

14 Truax, B. ed. (1999) *Handbook for Acoustic Ecology*, Vancouver: Cambridge St. Publishing. Available HTTP: http://www.sfu.ca/sonic-studio/handbook/ (accessed 20 April 2012).

15 H. Westerkamp, 'Soundwalking', *Sound Heritage* III: 4. 1974, rev. 2001.

16 B. Truax, *Soundscape Composition*, 2007. Online. Available HTTP: http://www.sfu.ca/~truax/scomp.html (accessed 7 October 2011).

17 B. Truax, 'Genres and Techniques of Soundscape Composition as developed at Simon Fraser University', *Organized Sound* 7:1. 2002, 5–14.

18 Masking is a perceptual phenomenon in which one sound apparently masks another. There are several ways in which it can occur. If a single tone pitched at 1,000 Hz is played simultaneously with one of 1,100 Hz, but with a slight difference in volume level between the two, the quieter wave will be inaudible. Also, humans cannot hear a quieter sound against a louder sound if there is up to a 5 millisecond delay between the two. Where two similar sounds are played at similar volume levels, the relationship becomes more dynamic between the masker and the masked.

19 E. Glennie, *Evelyn's Hearing*, 2005. Online. Available HTTP: http://www.evelyn.co.uk/hearing.htm (accessed 8 June 2007, quoted with permission).

20 Stelarc (1999) *Ear on arm*. Avialble HTTP: http://www.stelarc.org/?catID=20242 (accessed 20 April 2012). Warning – site includes surgical images.

21 Frequency, or the number of cycles or periods of a sound wave per unit of time (normally seconds), is measured in hertz (Hz) and kilohertz (kHz) (1 kHz = 1,000 Hz). A fundamental frequency of 4 kHz is high – above the natural range of the female voice, for example.

22 In particular, those of Georg von Békésy (1899–1972), who won the Nobel Prize for his discovery that sound travels along the basilar membrane in waves. He showed how these waves peak at different places on the membrane, and he discovered that the location of the nerve receptors and the number of receptors involved are the most important factors in determining pitch and loudness. This has now become known as 'Place Theory'.

23 There are many complex overlaps in neuroscience between *cognitive psychology* (which studies cognition, the mental processes that are presumed to underlie behaviour), *cognition* (information processing, but also extending to knowledge in general), and *biological psychology* (the study of the organic basis of mental processes).

24 'Positron Emission Tomography, a type of scan that measures changes in blood flow associated with brain function by detecting positrons, positively charged particles emitted by radioactively labelled substances that have been injected into the body.' Source: Howard Hughes Medical Institute.

25 'Functional Magnetic Resonance Imaging, a new method of scanning the brain's activity that needs no radioactive materials and produces images at a higher resolution than PET. It is based on differences in the magnetic resonance of certain atomic nuclei in areas of neuronal activity.' Source: Howard Hughes Medical Institute.

26 It is interesting to compare images of neural networks with maps of the Internet, such as those produced by the Opte Project. While the Internet was not built to a model of a neural network, it is

hard to resist drawing a parallel between the synaptic firings and communications traffic, the neurons and the individual processors connected by the data cables.

27 'Neural network music composition by prediction: Exploring the benefits of psychophysical constraints and multiscale processing' http://www.cs.colorado.edu/~mozer/papers/music.html.

28 See http://www.brandmaier.de/alice/.

29 For a full account, see T. Myatt, 'Strategies for Interaction in *Construction 3*', *Organized Sound*, 7:2, 2002, 157–169.

3   Exploring Sound

1 The British Broadcasting Corporation's Radiophonic Workshop was set up in 1958 to provide soundtracks, sound effects and music for BBC broadcasts. Early projects included Samuel Beckett's play *All that Fall* and 'radiophonic poems', and many more radio and television programmes. The workshop was renowned for its experimentation with unlikely sound objects and new technologies.

2 *Doctor Who* is a popular UK television series featuring a time-travelling central character and numerous companions and enemies, including the famous Daleks. The series began in 1963, and was recently revived after a fifteen-year gap (at least on television) to great acclaim in the UK.

3 Howard, D. and Angus, J., *Acoustics and Psychoacoustics*, Oxford: Focal Press, 2001, p. 333.

4 The pascal (symbol Pa) is the SI unit of pressure, and is equivalent to 1 newton per square metre. It is named after Blaise Pascal (1623–1662), the French mathematician, physicist and philosopher.

5 Phase is the fraction of the time required to complete a full cycle that a point completes after last passing through an arbitrary reference position.

6 Named after Heinrich Rudolf Hertz (1857–1894), a German physicist.

7 C. Roads, *Microsound*, Cambridge, MA: MIT Press, 2001, pp. 3–4.

8 Ibid., p. 55.

9 This experiment has since been redone many times, and various standard equal-loudness curves have resulted.

10 One Watt is 1 joule of energy per second, that is, power.

11 Interview with Oskari Mertalo, 1991.

12 P. Hegarty, *Noise Music: A History*, New York: Continuum, 2007, p. ix.

4   Listening to Music

1 Online. Available HTTP: http://www.spacedog.biz/infrasonic/infrasonicindex.htm (accessed 7 August 2007).

2 The *Doppler* effect is created when the sound source itself is in motion. A sound source moving quickly towards you will seem to *rise* in pitch, whereas a sound source moving quickly away from you will seem to *fall* in pitch (hear a passing emergency vehicle siren to recognize this effect). The amount of frequency bending depends on the ratio of the speed of sound to the speed at which the object is travelling.

3 Difference tone is the result of subtracting the value of the lower of two frequencies from the higher. This result is normally a smaller number than the highest original frequency and is, consequently, a lower sound. The extent to which such difference tones are audible will greatly depend on the purity of the original pitches, the nature of space in which they are being produced, and the aural awareness of the listener.

4 D. Deutsch (ed.), *The Psychology of Music*, 2nd edition, San Diego: Academic Press, 1999.

5 H. Brün, *When Music Resists Meaning*, Middletown, CT: Wesleyan University Press, 2004, p. 58.

6 D. Bohm, *The Quantum Theory*, New York: Dover, 1951.

7 L. Landy, *Understanding the Art of Sound Organization*, Cambridge, MA: The MIT Press, 2007, p. 43.

8 Ibid., p. 29.

9 G. M. de S. A. Ferreira, 'Perceptual Approaches to the Analysis of J. C. Risset's *Sud*: Sound, Structure and Symbol', *Organized Sound* 2:2, 1997, 97–106.

5   Organizing Sound

1 For an exploration of the difficulties of translation and making definitions, see Leigh Landy's review of H. de la Motte-Haber, *Klangkunst: Tönende Objekte und kligende Räume. Volume 12. Handbuch der*

Musik im 20. Jahrhundert, 1999, Laaber: LaaberVerlag, and the CD-ROM *Klangkunst in Deutschland, Organized Sound*, 5:3, 2000, 191–194.

2 Sound-art here owes a great deal to Marcel Duchamp, whose invention of the 'readymade', a found or bought object that was then exhibited in an art gallery, first defined the artistic potential of such recontextualization.

3 Jem Finer, interviewed by Steven Poole in *The Guardian*, September 2001.

4 W. Murch, 'Dense Clarity – Clear Density', The Transom Review, 5/1, 2005.

5 D. Campbell and C. Greated, *The Musicians Guide to Acoustics*, London: Dent, 1987, pp. 542–545.

6 Sabine's formula: T = 0.16 x (V / A), where T = reverberation time, V = volume of the room in cubic metres and A^r= total absorption (absorben^{r}cy × area).

7 Pauline Oliveros, 16 August 2011. E-mail to A. Hugill.

8 Synthia Payne, 16 August 2011. E-mail to A. Hugill.

9 A. Tanaka and K. Toeplitz (1998) *Global String*. Online. Available HTTP: http://www.sensorband.com/atau/globalstring/globalstring.pdf (accessed 18 August 2007).

10 In 1931, Alan Blumlein patented a method of recreating the phase difference between human ears using amplitude, which he called 'binaural audio'. This was the beginning of stereophonic sound.

11 Christian Huygens (1629–1695) was a Dutch physicist.

12 R. Normandeau (2001) *Clair de Terre*. Empreintes digitales IMED 0157 (liner notes).

13 The traditional musical terms for these are *monophony* and *polyphony* or *counterpoint*.

14 Source: The Electroacoustic Resource Site.

15 D. Smalley, 'Spectro-Morphology and Structuring Processes', in S. Emmerson, (ed.) *The Language of Electroacoustic Music*, London: Macmillan, 1986, pp. 61–93.

16 D. Smalley (1992) *Valley Flow*. Concert programme, University of East Anglia.

6   Digitizing Sound

1 Named after the mathematician Jean-Baptiste Joseph Fourier (1768–1830) who first elaborated the theoretical principles.

2 An algorithm is a set of instructions for accomplishing a task which, given an initial state, will produce a corresponding and recognizable end state. A recipe is a typical algorithm. Algorithms are used widely in computer processes.

3 These envelopes will not correct all of the errors that typically arise in such complex calculations, so overlap is sometimes used to increase the overall accuracy.

4 Werner Heisenberg (1901–1976) laid the foundations of quantum mechanics in the 1920s.

5 *Phase* is an acoustic phenomenon. When two or more waves (for example, from independent microphones) of the same frequency meet, their amplitudes combine, adding to each other. If the peaks and troughs of the wave forms line up, they are said to be 'in phase'. In this situation, each peak adds to the peak on the other wave form, and each trough adds to the other troughs, resulting in a wave form which is twice the amplitude of the original wave form. If the peaks of one wave form match the troughs of another wave form, the peaks and the troughs will cancel each other out, resulting in no wave form at all. Such wave forms are said to be 180 degrees 'out of phase'. This is rare, however, and in most cases, the waves are out of phase by a different amount. This results in a more complicated wave form than either of the original waves, as the amplitudes at each point along the wave form are added together.

6 There are a number of examples of colour spectrograms at the book website.

7 For example, the acoustic phenomenon that a rhythmically repeated impulse becomes continuous pitch when the rate increases beyond the point at which a human ear can differentiate the individual impulses. Herbert Eimert was the first to synthesize this, and it became an important aspect of Karlheinz Stockhausen's music in the 1950s.

8 Readers are referred to U. Zölzer, *DAFX: Digital Audio Effects*, Chichester: Wiley, 2002.

9 'The *envelope* of a sound is the profile of the evolution of its intensity and/or spectrum during its duration'. EARS: The Electroacoustic Resource Site http://www.ears.dmu.ac.uk.

10 *Phase cancellation* occurs when two sound waves that are out of phase with each other are added together, resulting in a wave that has less overall amplitude than either of the original waves.

11 There are many other types of digital filter: the Butterworth filter is a band-pass filter designed to have as flat a frequency response as possible; the Bessel, the Cauer, and the Chebyshev filters all take slightly different approaches to the minimizing of error in the passband and stopband of a band-pass filter.

12   EARS: The Electroacoustic Resource Site http://www.ears.dmu.ac.uk.
13   Wishart specifically mentions the transformations of 'lis' (from the word 'listen') into birdsong, 'rea' (from the word 'reason') to animal sounds, and 'reasonabl' into water. He also describes ways of manipulating sound using *wavesets*, which are sound-packets grouped together by zero-crossings of the wave form (i.e., where the amplitude is zero). This way of dividing up sound enables a number of DSP processes such as waveset inversion, omission, reversal, shaking, shuffling, substitution, averaging, harmonic distortion and 'power-distortion', in which the amplitude of each sample of the sound is raised mathematically by a 'power', such as squared, cubed and so on. See his 1994 book *Audible Design* and the essay *Computer Sound Transformation*, both available from his website: http://www.trevorwishart.co.uk/.

7   Creating Music

1   This literal interpretation of the word is even more explicit in post-production of visual effects and cinema, where 'compositing' (rather than composition) refers to the combination of images from various sources. 'Composition' is not quite the same as 'compositing' but is a conceptual neighbour, sharing some similar characteristics.
2   Based in part on an e-mail exchange with Bret Battey (bbattey@dmu.ac.uk) 21 May 2005. *RE: what is music for?* E-mail to A. Hugill (ahu@dmu.ac.uk).
3   I. Stravinsky, *Poetics of Music*, Cambridge, MA: Harvard University Press, 1939.
4   Weale, R. (2005) 'Intention/Reception in Electroacoustic Music'. Unpublished PhD thesis, De Montfort University, Leicester.
5   In 1961, Mel Rhodes conducted research into creativity that identified its three main aspects. The first he called 'person', which refers to the skills, traits, motivation and abilities that make someone creative. The second was 'environment': the individual's physical and psychological surroundings that either enable or undermine creative thought. Third, he identified 'process', or the mental activities an individual (or a group) goes through to achieve a creative result. These three need to be in the right balance if a good outcome is to be achieved. The products of these (a piece of music, in this case) are merely the tips of a large iceberg. They are the evidence that creativity is present.
6   Brown, E. quoted in R. Kostelanetz and J. Darby, *Classic Essays on Twentieth Century Music*, New York: Schirmer, 1996, p. 202.
7   J. Zorn, *Arcana: Musicians on Music*, New York: Granary Books, 2002.
8   A. Schoenberg, *Fundamentals of Musical Composition*, London, Faber & Faber, 1967. First published in 1948, this book, although it discusses exclusively classical music, nevertheless contains some extremely useful ideas for anyone embarking on composition.
9   'Montage' is a term derived from cinema, in which rapid editing, special effects, sound and music combine to present compressed narrative information.
10   Johann Wolfgang von Goethe (1749–1832) was a German writer, scientist and painter, and the author of *Faust* and *A Theory of Colours*.
11   D. Smalley, 'Spectro-morphology and Structuring Processes' in S. Emmerson (ed.) *The Language of Electroacoustic Music*, London: Macmillan, 1986, p. 71.
12   Xenakis formed the CEMAMu (Centre d'Études de Mathématiques et Automatiques Musicales/ Centre for Studies in Mathematics and Automated Music) in Paris in 1972. He then developed UPIC (Unité Polyagogique Informatique du CEMAMu) in 1977.
13   N. Negroponte, *Being Digital*, New York: First Vintage Books, 1996.
14   Traub, P. (1999) *Bits & Pieces*. Online. Available HTTP: http://rhizome.org/ (accessed 17 March 2012).
15   J. Richards, *New Modality: Sonic Magnification*, paper given at the 'Music without Walls? Music without Instruments?' conference, De Montfort University, Leicester, 2001.

8   Instruments and Media

1   T. Magnusson and M. Hurtado, 'The Acoustic, the Digital and the Body: A Survey of Musical Instruments', *Proceedings of the NIME Conference, New York University, NY, USA.* 2007, pp. 94–99.
2   Ibid.
3   For detailed accounts of the physiological effects and health benefits of music, see D. J. Schneck and

D. S. Berger, *The Music Effect: Music Physiology and Clinical Applications*, Philadelphia, PA: Jessica Kingsley Publishers, 2006; and D. Aldridge, *Music Therapy Research and Practice in Medicine: From Out of the Silence*, Philadelphia, PA: Jessica Kingsley Publishers, 1996.

4 http://www.steim.org/steim/info.html.

5 NIME is also the name of a leading annual conference on the subject.

6 N. Collins, (2004) *Hardware Hacking*, p. 4. Online. Available HTTP: http://*www.nicolascollins.com/texts/originalhackingmanual.pdf* (accessed 18 July 2011).

7 A. Divers (2009) *Interview with Rheed Ghazala*. Online. Available HTTP: http://www.anti-theory.com/texts/ (accessed 20 July 2011).

8 J. Richards, 'Getting the Hands Dirty', *Leonardo Music Journal*, 18, 2008, 25–31.

9 R. Packer and K. Jordan, *Multimedia: From Wagner to Virtual Reality*, New York: Norton, 2003.

10 R. Wagner, *The Artwork of the Future*, 1849.

11 G. Paine (1998) *MAP1* (notes) Online. Available HTTP: http://www.activatedspace.com (accessed 2 September 2007).

12 C. Yavelow (1997) *The Music is the Message*. Installation at The New Metropolis Centre for Science and Technology in Amsterdam, The Netherlands.

13 S. Smith, 13 September 2011. E-mail to A. Hugill.

14 S. Emmerson, *Living Electronic Music*, Aldershot: Ashgate, 2007, p. 92.

15 Ibid., p. 103.

9 Performing and Musicianship

1 M. Chanan, *Musica Practica: The Social Practice of Western Music from Gregorian Chant to Postmodernism*, London: Verso, 1994, p. 23.

2 S. Payne, 5 November 2011. E-mail to A. Hugill.

3 Á. Barbosa, 'Displaced Soundscapes: A Survey of Network Systems for Music and Sonic Art Creation', *Leonardo Music Journal*, 13, 2003, 53–59.

4 Developed by Phil Burk and others, it is distributed through Burk's company, Soft-Synth.

5 http://www.electrotap.com/jade.

6 S. Wyatt et al, *Investigative Studies on Sound Diffuson/Projection at the University of Illinois: A Report on an Explorative Collaboration*, University of Illinois, 2005.

7 D. Bailey, *Improvisation: Its Nature and Practice in Music*, New York: Da Capo Press, 1993.

8 For example, Cornelius Cardew's *The Tiger's Mind*.

9 N. Collins, 'Live Coding Practice', *Proceedings of the NIME Conference*, New York University, New York, 2007, pp. 112–117.

10 Ibid.

11 P. R. Cook and G. Wang, 'On-the-Fly Programming: Using Code as an Expressive Musical Instrument', *Proceedings of the 2004 International Conference on New Interfaces for Musical Expression (NIME-04)*, Hamamatsu, Japan, 2004, pp. 138–143.

12 See http://deprogramming.us/perfs.

13 See http://www.pawfal.org/index.php?page=BetaBlocker.

14 TOPLAP, the (Temporary/Transnational/Terrestrial/Transdimensional) Organization for the (Promotion/Proliferation/Permanence/Purity) of Live (Algorithm/Audio/Art/ Artistic) Programming, may be found at http://www.toplap.org.

15 Ibid.

16 R. Rowe, *Machine Musicianship*, Cambridge, MA: MIT Press, 2001, p. 1.

17 N. Collins, *Introduction to Computer Music*, Chichester: Wiley, 2010.

18 '[R]egardless of the style of music performed, creativity is a fundamental part of musical skill development, as musicians constantly work towards an ideal sound which itself is constantly being refined.' S. Amitani, E. Edmonds and A. Johnston, 'Amplifying Reflective Thinking in Musical Performance', paper given at the Creativity and Cognition Conference, 2005, University of London: Goldsmiths College.

19 D. Schön, *The Reflective Practitioner*, London: Temple Smith, 1983, p. 68.

20 Ibid.

21 C. Small, *Musicking*, Middletown, CT: Wesleyan University Press, 1998, p. 5.

22 S. Thomas, 'Transliteracy – Reading in the Digital Age', *Higher Education Academy, English Subject Centre Newsletter*, November 2005. 'Transliteracies' were first discussed by Professor Alan Liu in the Department of English at the University of California Santa Barbara and applied exclusively to

the written word. 'Transliteracy', as defined by Professor Sue Thomas of De Montfort University, Leicester, extends that concept to new media.

10   Cultural Context

1   Chanan, M. (1994) *Musica Practica: The Social Practice of Western Music from Gregorian Chant to Postmodernism*, London: Verso. Prologue.
2   Available at the following websites: Ubuweb; Music Mavericks; British Music Information Centre; eBay.
3   L. Manovich, *The Language of New Media*, Cambridge, MA: MIT Press. 2001, pp. 27–45.
4   Some writers, notably Kim Cascone, have labelled this tendency 'post-digital'. K. Cascone, 'The Aesthetics of Failure: "Post-Digital" Tendencies in Contemporary Computer Music', *Computer Music Journal*, 24:4, 2002, 12–18.
5   An ethnomusicologist studies the music of a given culture with a view to understanding its ethnicity first and foremost.
6   Timar, A. (2006) 'What is Gamelan?', Deep Down Productions. Online. Available HTTP: http://www.deepdownproductions.com/.
7   See http://www.gatesstreet.com/Heavy_Metal_512.mov.
8   A. Kapur et al, 'GigaPop Ritual', *Proceedings of the Conference on New Instruments for Musical Expression*, 2003.
9   B. Battey, 'Bézier Spline Modeling of Pitch-continuous Melodic Expression and Ornamentation', *Computer Music Journal*, 28:4, 2003, 25-39.
10   Bret Battey, interviewed by the author, 2006.
11   Steve Reich, quoted in W. Duckworth, *Talking Music*, New York: Schirmer, 1995.
12   L. Ligeti, 'Beta Foley: Experiments with Tradition and Technology in West Africa', *Leonardo Music Journal*, 10, 2000, 41–47.
13   W. Carlos, 'A Guided Tour of *Beauty in the Beast*', *Keyboard Magazine*, 3, November 1986.
14   There is a fascinating sonographic version of this piece at http://www.ina.fr/fresques/artsonores (in French) (accessed 18 September 2011).

11   Critical Engagement

1   Stravinsky composed only one film score, for *The Commandos Strike at Dawn*, which was rejected by the studio. He did have several other offers, but none of them came to anything. Schoenberg was asked by Irving Thalberg to write the music for *The Good Earth*, but this project also fell through when the composer demanded final editing rights. In the end, Schoenberg only composed the soundtrack to an imaginary film: *Music to Accompany a Film Scene*.
2   R. Barthes, 'The Death of the Author', *Image, Music, Text*, London: Fontana, 1977, p. 146.
3   G. Genette, *Structuralism and Literary Criticism*, New Delhi: Bahri, 1989, p. 67 fn.
4   J. Attali, *Noise: The Political Economy of Music*, Minneapolis: University of Minnesota Press, 1985.
5   Ibid., p. 10.
6   Ibid., pp. 8–9.
7   P. Tagg, (1999) *Introductory Notes to the Semiotics of Music*. Online. Available HTTP: http://www.tagg.org/xpdfs/semiotug.pdf (accessed 7 October 2011).
8   J-J. Nattiez, *Music and Discourse: Towards a Semiology of Music*, Princeton: Princeton University Press, 1990, p. 101.
9   S. McClary, 'Constructions of Subjectivity in Schubert's Music', *Queering the Pitch: The New Gay and Lesbian Musicology*, New York: Routledge, 1994, pp. 205–233.
10   J. Dewey, *Art as Experience*, New York: Perigee, 1934, p. 220.
11   W.K. Wimsatt and Monroe Beardsley, 'The Affective Fallacy', *Sewanee Review*, 57:1 1949, 31–55.
12   M. Boden (ed.), *Dimensions of Creativity*, Cambridge, MA: The MIT Press, 1994, p. 161.
13   J.-F. Lyotard, *The Postmodern Condition*, Minneapolis: Minnesota University Press, 1979, p. 77.
14   J. Schmidhuber, 'Low-Complexity Art', *Leonardo*, 30:2, 1997, 97–103, p. 2.
15   R. Ascott, 'Behaviourist Art and the Cybernetic Vision', *Cybernetica: Journal of the International Association for Cybernetics* (Namur), 1964, p. 129.
16   Ibid., p. 97.
17   H. W. Franke, 'A Cybernetic Approach to Aesthetics', *Leonardo* 10, 1977, 203–206.

12   Understanding Digital Music

1   C. Small, *Music, Society, Education*, Middletown, CT: Wesleyan University Press, 1977, p. 47.
2   Fractals are geometrically self-similar objects at all levels of magnification, such as the famous Mandelbrot set, or a fern.
3   An L-system or Lindenmayer system is a formal grammar (a set of rules and symbols) often used to model the growth processes of plant development, although able to model the morphology of a variety of organisms.
4   In fact, it is not necessary to use a computer to make an algorithm, and 'algorithmic music' may be found in the medieval period and earlier. In this context, however, the meaning is restricted to the digital domain.
5   See http://www.plunderphonics.com/.
6   This is one of many such charts that circulate around the Internet. This one came from Wikipedia, but a general search on 'electronic dance music' will produce more extensive examples listing hundreds of genres and sub-genres.
7   F. Lerdahl and R. Jackendoff, *A Generative Theory of Tonal Music*, Cambridge, MA: MIT Press, 1999.
8   J. Blacking, *How Musical is Man?* Washington: University of Washington Press (reprint edition), 1973.
9   S. Emmerson, 'Relation of Language to Materials', *The Language of Electroacoustic Music*, London: Macmillan, 1986, p. 24.
10   F. Delalande, 'Music Analysis and Reception Behaviours: *Sommeil* by Pierre Henry', *Journal of New Music Research*, 27:1-2, 1998, 13–66.

13   The Digital World

1   A. Hugill, interview with Dimitris Moraitis, 2005.
2   A. Hugill, interview with Ronald Herrema, 2005.
3   J. Cage, *Silence*, London: Marion Boyars, 1968, p. 109.
4   See http://www.collectionscanada.ca/glenngould/index-e.html.
5   M. Paddison, 'Frank Zappa' in S. Sadie and J. Tyrrell (eds) *The New Grove Dictionary of Music and Musicians*, London: Macmillan, 2000; and B. Watson, *Frank Zappa: The Negative Dialectics of Poodle Play*, London: Quartet, 1995.
6   *Son et lumière* is a form of night-time entertainment usually presented outdoors at a site of historical interest, which combines lighting, image and sound in a spectacular show. *Cirque de soleil* is a modern circus franchise that does not use animals and features colourful costumes, extraordinary design and specially created music and light, along with the acrobatics.
7   S. Faulder, *Moral Rights*. Online. Available HTTP: http://www.iamusic.com/articles/copyright.html (accessed 20 September 2011).
8   See http://creativecommons.org/licenses/.
9   A. Harrower, 'Copyright Issues in Internet Music', *Contemporary Music Review*, 24:5, 2005, 1–6.
10   The Foley artist on a film crew is the person who creates and records many of the sound effects. This is a highly specialized job. The name comes from Jack Foley (1891–1967), one of the first, who helped to introduce sound effects into the movies.
11   A. Fusiarski (2009) *Exploring the Digital Music Distribution 'Jungle'*. Online. Available HTTP: http://buzzsonic.com/ (accessed 15 September 2011).
12   A. Dubber, A. (2011) *The Economics of Free*. Online. Available HTTP: http://www.soundandmusic.org/ (accessed 15 September 2011).
13   Adkins, M. (2005) 'The Changing Skillset of the Contemporary Musician', paper given at the *National Association of Music in Higher Education* Conference, University of Southampton.

Appendix

1   A. Mabbett, *The Complete Guide to the Music of Pink Floyd*, London: Omnibus Press, 1995.
2   N. Collins (2009) *Before Apple There Was Kim – the Microcomputer, Music and Me*. Online. Available HTTP: http://www.nicolascollins.com/essays.htm (accessed 18 September 2011).
3   S. McClary, *Feminine Endings: Music, Gender and Sexuality*, Minnesota: University of Minnesota Press, 1991. p. 110.

4   Coldcut (1998) *Timber*. Hexstatic ZencdS65A. Online. Available HTTP: http://www.ninjatune. net/ninja/release.php?id=90 (accessed 26 August 2007).

5   *Squarepusher* (2004) 'Philosophy'. Available HTTP: http://www.squarepusher.net (accessed 28 August 2007).

6   From the Cycling '74 website.

Index